MEDIEVAL AFFECT, FEELING, AND EMOTION

Representations of feeling in medieval literature are varied and complex. This new collection of essays demonstrates that the history of emotions and affect theory are similarly insufficient for investigating the intersection of body and mind that late Middle English literatures evoke. While medieval studies has generated a rich scholarly literature on "affective piety," this collection charts an intersectional new investigation of affects, feelings, and emotions in non-religious contexts. From Geoffrey Chaucer to Gavin Douglas, and from practices of witnessing to the adoration of objects: essays in this volume analyze the coexistence of emotion and affect in late medieval representations of feeling.

GLENN D. BURGER is Professor of English and Medieval Studies at Queens College and The Graduate Center, CUNY, and Dean of Graduate Studies at Queens College. He has edited Hetoum's *A Lytell Cronycle* (1988) and *Queering the Middle Ages* (2000; with Steven Kruger). He is author of *Chaucer's Queer Nation* (2003) and *Conduct Becoming: Good Wives and Husbands in the Later Middle Ages* (2017).

HOLLY A. CROCKER is Professor of English at the University of South Carolina. She is author of *The Matter of Virtue: Women's Ethical Action from Chaucer to Shakespeare* (2019) and *Chaucer's Visions of Manhood* (2007), editor of *Comic Provocations: Exposing the Corpus of Old French Fabliaux* (2006), and co-editor of *Medieval Literature: Criticism and Debates* (2014; with D. Vance Smith).

CAMBRIDGE STUDIES IN MEDIEVAL LITERATURE

General Editor
Alastair Minnis, *Yale University*

Editorial Board
Zygmunt G. Baránski, *University of Cambridge*
Christopher C. Baswell, *Barnard College and Columbia University*
Mary Carruthers, *New York University*
Rita Copeland, *University of Pennsylvania*
Roberta Frank, *Yale University*
Jocelyn Wogan-Browne, *Fordham University*

This series of critical books seeks to cover the whole area of literature written in the major medieval languages – the main European vernaculars, and medieval Latin and Greek – during the period c. 1100–1500. Its chief aim is to publish and stimulate fresh scholarship and criticism on medieval literature, special emphasis being placed on understanding major works of poetry, prose, and drama in relation to the contemporary culture and learning which fostered them.

Recent titles in the series
Tim William Machan (ed.) *Imagining Medieval English: Language Structures and Theories, 500–1500*
Eric Weiskott *English Alliterative Verse: Poetic Tradition and Literary History*
Sarah Elliott Novacich *Shaping the Archive in Late Medieval England: History, Poetry, and Performance*
Geoffrey Russom *The Evolution of Verse Structure in Old and Middle English Poetry: From the Earliest Alliterative Poems to Iambic Pentameter*
Ian Cornelius *Reconstructing Alliterative Verse: The Pursuit of a Medieval Meter*
Sara Harris *The Linguistic Past in Twelfth-Century Britain*
Erik Kwakkel and Rodney Thomson (eds.) *The European Book in the Twelfth Century*
Irina Dumitrescu *The Experience of Education in Anglo-Saxon Literature*
Jonas Wellendorf *Gods and Humans in Medieval Scandinavia: Retying the Bonds*
Thomas A. Prendergast and Jessica Rosenfeld (eds.) *Chaucer and the Subversion of Form*
Katie L. Walter *Middle English Mouths*
Lawrence Warner *Chaucer's Scribes*
Glenn D. Burger and Holly A. Crocker (eds.) *Medieval Affect, Feeling, and Emotion*

A complete list of titles in the series can be found at the end of the volume.

MEDIEVAL AFFECT, FEELING, AND EMOTION

EDITED BY

GLENN D. BURGER
Queens College and The Graduate Center, CUNY

and

HOLLY A. CROCKER
University of South Carolina

CAMBRIDGE
UNIVERSITY PRESS

University Printing House, Cambridge CB2 8BS, United Kingdom

One Liberty Plaza, 20th Floor, New York, NY 10006, USA

477 Williamstown Road, Port Melbourne, VIC 3207, Australia

314-321, 3rd Floor, Plot 3, Splendor Forum, Jasola District Centre, New Delhi - 110025, India

79 Anson Road, #06-04/06, Singapore 079906

Cambridge University Press is part of the University of Cambridge.

It furthers the University's mission by disseminating knowledge in the pursuit of education, learning and research at the highest international levels of excellence.

www.cambridge.org
Information on this title: www.cambridge.org/9781108458887
DOI: 10.1017/9781108672474

© Cambridge University Press 2019

This publication is in copyright. Subject to statutory exception and to the provisions of relevant collective licensing agreements, no reproduction of any part may take place without the written permission of Cambridge University Press.

First published 2019
First paperback edition 2021

A catalogue record for this publication is available from the British Library

ISBN 978-1-108-47196-1 Hardback
ISBN 978-1-108-45888-7 Paperback

Cambridge University Press has no responsibility for the persistence or accuracy of URLs for external or third-party internet websites referred to in this publication, and does not guarantee that any content on such websites is, or will remain, accurate or appropriate.

Contents

List of Illustrations		*page* vii
List of Contributors		viii
	Introduction *Glenn D. Burger and Holly A. Crocker*	1
1	Weeping Like a Beaten Child: Figurative Language and the Emotions in Chaucer and Malory *Stephanie Trigg*	25
2	Imagining Jewish Affect in the *Siege of Jerusalem* *Patricia DeMarco*	47
3	Engendering Affect in Hoccleve's *Series* *Holly A. Crocker*	70
4	Becoming One Flesh, Inhabiting Two Genders: Ugly Feelings and Blocked Emotion in the *Wife of Bath's Prologue and Tale* *Glenn D. Burger*	90
5	Accounting for Affect in the *Reeve's Tale* *Brantley L. Bryant*	118
6	Affect Machines *Sarah Salih*	139
7	Witnessing and Legal Affect in the York Trial Plays *Emma Lipton*	158

8 Affecting Forms: Theorizing with the *Palis of Honoure* 181
   Anke Bernau

   Afterword: Three Letters 203
   Anthony Bale

Bibliography 218
Index 239

Illustrations

1 Worship of Baal-Peor. Paris: Bibliothèque nationale de France, ms lat 9471, f. 235. *page* 143
2 Anniversary of Hector's Funeral. Glasgow: Burrell Collection 149
3 Phallic procession badge. Collection Van Beuningen Family. 152
4 St Swithun Wells. London: St Etheldreda's Church, Ely Place 154

Contributors

ANTHONY BALE is Professor of Medieval Studies at Birkbeck, University of London. He is author of *The Jew in the Medieval Book: English Antisemitisms, 1350–1500* (2006) and *Feeling Persecuted: Christians, Jews and Images of Violence in the Middle Ages* (2010). He is editor of *St Edmund King and Martyr: Changing Images of a Medieval Saint* (2009), translator of John Mandeville, *The Book of Marvels and Travels* (2012) and *The Book of Margery Kempe* (2015), and co-editor of *John Lydgate's "Lives of Ss Edmund & Fremund" and the "Extra Miracles of St Edmund," Edited from British Library MS Harley 2278 and Bodleian Library MS Ashmole 46* (2009; with A. S. G. Edwards).

ANKE BERNAU is Senior Lecturer in Medieval Literature and Culture at the University of Manchester. She studies vernacular poetics and the political imagination, as well as sanctity, virginity, and abstinence in medieval and modern cultures. She is author of *Virgins: A Cultural History* (2007), and co-editor of *Sanctity as Literature in Late Medieval Britain* (2015; with Eva von Contzen), *Medieval Film* (2009; with Bettina Bildhauer), and *Medieval Virginities* (2003; with Ruth Evans and Sarah Salih). She is currently completing a book studying how vernacular, literary treatments of memory, imagination, and curiosity are used to explore and articulate changing ideas concerning poetics (especially in the fifteenth and sixteenth centuries). She is co-editor of *Exemplaria*.

BRANTLEY L. BRYANT is Professor of English at Sonoma State University. His research interests include later medieval literature, Geoffrey Chaucer and his contemporaries, intersections of medieval literature and popular culture, and recent developments in "posthuman" approaches to literature. He is author of *Geoffrey Chaucer Hath A Blog* (2010) and his articles have appeared in the *Chaucer Review*, *Studies in Medieval and Renaissance History*, and a number of edited collections.

His current long-term project is a book on representations of water in late medieval literature.

GLENN D. BURGER is Professor of English and Medieval Studies at Queens College and The Graduate Center, CUNY, and Dean of Graduate Studies at Queens College. He has edited Hetoum's *A Lytell Cronycle* (1988) and *Queering the Middle Ages* (2000; with Steven Kruger). He is author of *Chaucer's Queer Nation* (2003) and *Conduct Becoming: Good Wives and Husbands in the Later Middle Ages* (2017), as well as numerous articles on issues of gender and sexuality, affect, and conduct in medieval textual culture.

HOLLY A. CROCKER is Professor of English at the University of South Carolina. She is author of *The Matter of Virtue: Women's Ethical Action from Chaucer to Shakespeare* (2019), *Chaucer's Visions of Manhood* (2007), editor of *Comic Provocations: Exposing the Corpus of Old French Fabliaux* (2006), and co-editor of *Medieval Literature: Criticism and Debate* (2014; with D. Vance Smith), as well as articles on affect and premodern literature in *Studies in the Age of Chaucer, Exemplaria*, and *New Medieval Literatures*.

PATRICIA DEMARCO is Professor of English at Ohio Wesleyan University. She is a specialist in late medieval literature in England and France, with particular interests in the romance tradition and the poetry of the Ricardian court. Her current book in progress is a comprehensive study of literary depictions of war (private, public, holy) and the changing place of vengeance in the identity of the "chivalric classes." Her articles have appeared in *Speculum* and *Studies in the Age of Chaucer*, as well as numerous edited collections.

EMMA LIPTON is Associate Professor of English at the University of Missouri. She is author of *Affections of the Mind: The Politics of Sacramental Marriage in Late Medieval English Literature* (2007). Her articles have appeared in *Chaucer Review, Journal of English and Germanic Philology*, and *Studies in the Age of Chaucer*, as well as numerous edited collections. Her current book project, *Culture of Witnessing: Law and the York Plays*, investigates the relationship between legal and dramatic ideas of witnessing in the York plays.

SARAH SALIH is Senior Lecturer in English at King's College London. She is author of *Versions of Virginity in Late Medieval England* (2001), editor of *A Companion to Middle English Hagiography* (2006), and co-editor of

Medieval Virginities (2003; with Ruth Evans and Anke Bernau) and *Julian of Norwich's Legacy: Medieval Mysticism and Post-Medieval Reception* (2009; with Denise Baker). She edited *Studies in the Age of Chaucer* (2014–18).

STEPHANIE TRIGG is Professor in the School of Culture and Communication at the University of Melbourne. She is author of *Congenial Souls: Reading Chaucer from Medieval to Postmodern* (2002) and *Shame and Honor: A Vulgar History of the Order of the Garter* (2012). Her articles on emotion in medieval literature have appeared in the *Yearbook of Langland Studies, postmedieval,* and *SPELL: Swiss Papers in English Language and Literature.* In 2014 she edited a special issue on "Premodern Emotions" for *Exemplaria.* She is Chief Investigator at the Australian Research Council Centre of Excellence for the History of the Emotions.

Introduction

Glenn D. Burger and Holly A. Crocker

Chaucer's *Book of the Duchess* concludes with an unusually terse exchange between the Black Knight and dreamer:

> "She ys ded!" "Nay!" "Yis, be my trouthe!"
> "Is that youre los? Be God, hyt ys routhe!"[1]

The Knight's simple statement of loss contrasts starkly with his earlier elaborately rhetorical descriptions of his love for White. In them the Knight outlined the path to *fin'amor* as a carefully staged teleological movement from initially painful feelings of love, to lessons from his lady in how to structure that experience, and finally to the fulfillment he felt when White eventually showed him true *pite*. The awkward rawness of this last exchange between dreamer and Knight, however, pulls the poem up short. That the episode communicates a palpably intense, yet nearly inexpressible connection between Knight and dreamer is clear. But at the conclusion of this truncated exchange, when "al was doon, / For that tyme, the hert-huntyng" (1312–13), something remains unsaid between them. Unarticulated feelings are left hanging as "this kyng / Gan homwarde for to ryde" (1314–15) and the dreamer wakes up.

How, exactly, should we understand the significance of the emotional connection here – at once physical and spiritual, involving both mind and body? Contemporary affect theories offer one set of critical vocabularies and methodological frameworks with which to consider the pre-social, pre-linguistic intensities of feeling circulating between the Knight and dreamer, and to suggest how such feeling might provide forms of embodied cognition capable of linking individuals with the social in new ways. Historians of emotion offer an alternative model that focuses instead on the recovery of emotion as a social artifact capable of change and re-articulation across different social situations and historical periods. But neither approach, on its own, would appear to capture fully the play of affect, feeling, and emotion that Chaucer's poem presents here. For the something left unsaid foregrounded at the conclusion of the *Book of the Duchess* incites a kind of embodied cognition on the part of the dreamer and his audience that exceeds the methodologies and critical vocabularies developed by contemporary affect theorists and scholars of the history of emotions.[2] The Black Knight's self-identification as one overcome with loss clearly corresponds at crucial points to an account of elite masculinity scripted by medieval narratives of *fin'amor*. In other words, his identity as a courtly lover becomes legible according to what history of emotions scholars might see as scripted norms of feeling for a community-produced identity. Yet, when the Black Knight repeatedly shows himself unable to express his loss, he does more than conform to an "emotional script" that is expected for courtly lovers; he also shows the ways that affective intensity takes on a power of its own, one that exhausts the Knight's rational and somatic resources. We witness him overcome by feeling *tout court*, in a way that resonates with contemporary accounts of affective intensities felt on the body and before socialization. And when the dreamer takes up the Knight's tale, his account challenges distinctions of inside and outside that usually distinguish subject and object. We are left asking: Whose story is this, and whose feelings are involved?

This brief example from the *Book of the Duchess* underscores how premodern writings theorize affect and emotion in ways that show their inherent intersectionality. In thinking through this intersection of affect, feeling, and emotion more generally in late medieval literatures, the essays in this volume chart a relationship between ideas that have often been treated as separate, even adversarial. In doing so, they suggest that medieval writings offer a unique opportunity to reassess the importance of feelings – their physical and rational elements – because medievals did not think about affects or emotions in the same ways that we do. As medievalists acknowledge in different ways, the word "emotion" did not enter English until the early modern period. Equally, affect's Latin history gives the concept of *affectus* a distinctly rhetorical or religio-philosophical cast often at odds with the use of affect in contemporary theory. Historicizing premodern affect, feeling, and emotion, then, requires creating a certain degree of conceptual space between modern theories of affect and emotion where they might better do justice to the specificities of medieval representations of the cognitive and corporeal experiences that feelings involve. The essays in this volume thus foreground the necessary intersectionality of contemporary affect studies, histories of emotion, and medievalist historicization.[3]

In the remainder of this introduction we explore how an intersectional premodern affect/emotion studies seeks first, to historicize affect, and thus to speak to what Patricia Clough has called the "affective turn" in contemporary literary and cultural studies; and second, to challenge an assumption that the history of emotions should function as the privileged method of investigation for feeling before the modern period. This requires us to outline the most salient features of contemporary affect studies, as well as key differences between modern and medieval understandings. We then consider the benefits that the history of emotions offers to studies of premodern sources, as well as limitations or "gaps" that might be overlooked by this methodology. Most importantly, we ultimately outline a new, intersectional approach to what medievals called affects and what moderns call emotions, paying particular attention to how this alternative methodology is taken up in the essays of this volume.

Paying attention to the intersections of affect and emotion in the premodern period first requires us to confront several lacunae in modern affect theory: Can the body's unprocessed feelings be represented? How do affects create communities? What would it mean to admit that different affects have particular histories? For example, Fiona Somerset's recent argument – contending that Lollard writers "taught their audiences how to feel" – attests to affect's ability to traverse inside and outside, the spiritual and social, in ways that modern theorists have yet to recognize or contemplate.[4] If affect theory often seems closed off to historicist study, perhaps this is because it has too easily allowed itself to be confined to a consideration of modernity's shaping questions. In arguing for the recovery of specific premodern affects, this volume offers a "medieval turn" in affect studies in order to challenge this history of implicit "presentism" in affect theory.

As Michael Hardt has noted, the recent "affective turn" in the humanities and social sciences, self-consciously distinguishing itself from an earlier linguistic turn in much postmodern theory of the 1980s and 90s, has two precursors: "the focus on the body, which has been most extensively advanced in feminist theory, and the exploration of emotions, conducted predominantly in queer theory."[5] As Hardt and others have observed, crucial to this rethinking of the mind's power to think as parallel to the body's power to act is a non-Cartesian philosophical tradition inspired by the work of Baruch Spinoza and developed most innovatively in terms of affect by Gilles Deleuze. A related line of queer inquiry, pioneered in the work of Eve Sedgwick, arises out of psychoanalytic models of affects developed by Sigmund Freud and Silvan Tomkins.[6] As even this brief synopsis makes clear, the affective turn is really a complex assemblage of turns.[7] And affect theory is still unfolding, of course, with powerful articulations by Rosi Braidotti, Lauren Berlant, Sara Ahmed, and Teresa Brennan, among others.[8] These thinkers, like those we discuss in more detail, challenge the intentionalist, ableist model of modern subjectivity, and yet, we would also note, in their calls to rethink the workings of politics, language, identity, and even proximity, they share with medieval writers a fundamental disinterest in privileging the self-cultivating individual as the prime mover in shared forms of life. Contemporary affect theory has much to offer medievalists, and we cannot do justice, we should say from the outset, to the dynamic, changing shape of this field. For our purposes, we would like to highlight *two* areas where the contemporary affective turn is generative for a new historicization of premodern affect.

Not surprisingly, one early (and continuing) critical question raised by affect studies has been exactly how (or if) affect can be clearly distinguished from emotion. Brian Massumi and Patricia Clough have articulated most strongly the need to clearly distinguish between affect and emotion. Massumi, for example, argues that emotion is "a subjective content, the sociolinguistic fixing of the quality of an experience which is from that point onward defined as personal," while affect is feeling or "intensity" disconnected from "meaningful sequencing, from narration."[9] Yet as Clough acknowledges, affect cannot simply be thought of as "presocial" and emotion as "social." Quoting Massumi, Clough stresses the *in-between-ness* of affect:

> There is a reflux back from conscious experience to affect, which is registered, however, as affect, such that "past action and contexts are conserved and repeated, autonomically reactivated but not accomplished; begun but not completed." Affect constitutes a nonlinear complexity out of which the narration of conscious states such as emotion are subtracted, but always with "a never-to-be-conscious autonomic remainder."[10]

And many of the most influential critics and theorists of affect in contemporary literary and cultural studies have found it useful to resist too fixed a distinction between affect and emotion. Sianne Ngai, for example, argues that the difference between affect and emotion is:

> a modal difference of intensity or degree, rather than a formal difference of quality or kind. My assumption is that affects are *less* formed and structured than emotions, but not lacking form or structure altogether; *less* "sociolinguistically fixed," but by no means code-free or meaningless; *less* "organized in response to our interpretations of situations," but by no means entirely devoid of organization or diagnostic powers ... What the switch from formal to modal difference enables is an analysis of the *transitions* from one pole to the other: the passages whereby affects acquire the semantic

density and narrative complexity of emotions, and emotions conversely denature into affects."

Ngai's suggestion that the difference between affect and emotion might be a modal difference of intensity or degree rather than a formal difference of quality or kind is particularly useful in underscoring the particular contributions that medieval literary contexts might provide for the study of medieval affect.[12] To return to the example from the *Book of the Duchess*, above, how do the dreamer's questions trace the transition from affect to emotion, and how do they produce new intensities that potentially overwhelm the dialogue between Knight and dreamer?

Contemporary affect studies have also challenged the primacy of the bounded human body as a model for theorizing affect, feeling, and emotion. Sara Ahmed, for example, has focused attention on the role that objects can play in providing affective connections between individuals and social groupings. "Affect," she notes, "is what sticks, or what sustains or preserves the connection between ideas, values, and objects." As such, certain objects may accumulate positive affective value as they are passed around, become "sticky," in her words, and thereby circulate as social goods.[13] And Patricia Clough has argued that affect must be theorized not only in terms of the human body but "in relation to the technologies that are allowing us both to 'see' affect and to produce affective bodily capacities beyond the body's organic-physiological constraints ... The affective turn, therefore, expresses a new configuration of bodies, technology, and matter instigating a shift in thought in critical theory."[14] These would seem important areas of overlap for both contemporary and medieval affect studies.

Despite these promising points of contact, the affective turn in literary and cultural studies has until recently been a largely presentist one, preoccupied with modernity and postmodernity, and thus standing outside the project of historicizing as most medievalists would understand it. Heather Love's *Feeling Backward: Loss and the Politics of Queer History*, for example, despite its many strengths, limits what can be understood as constituting queer history by grouping together "a handful of late nineteenth- and early twentieth-century authors under the rubric of backward modernism."[15] Yet the emphasis in contemporary affect theory on the material, embodied context for feeling suggests the usefulness of literary textual culture in excavating affect's past and providing alternative modes of historicization, or at least new ways of seeing embodied forms of agency that bring the individual and the social into contact in innovative and mobile ways. To return to our example of the *Book of the Duchess*, White as a character in the Knight's *fin'amor* narratives can take him outside history into a modality of feeling where love's service is perceived as endlessly repeatable and applicable to lovers of any age or situation. Or, it can take him back into history felt in its harshly material specificities – White as dead and gone, and the significance of this experience limited to the poem's status as an occasional poem addressed to John of Gaunt in memory of his dead wife. Seeing the Knight's history in this way, though, requires two other elements that are largely absent from modern affect theory: it requires us to consider bodily intensity as the effect of a creative (not simply diagnostic) process, and it urges us to regard non-intentional experiences as sites where social inscriptions (including what we think of as emotions) take hold. The play of affect, feeling, and emotion that is constituted by the dialogue framing the Black Knight's monologues, and kept open by the poem's unresolved ending, keeps Chaucer's narrative productively in between "history" (a narrow pinning down of who means what) and abstraction (reinforcing some "timeless" truth about love). In the process audiences may come to understand just how a lover is constituted as an identity by *fin'amor* service and with that the continued use value of *fin'amor* and the aristocratic definitions of nobility it undergirds. We thus become aware of the "Englishness" of this dialogue, as well as a certain useful, revivifying (and potentially disturbing) uncertainty about just what that signifies: Is *fin'amor* here shown to be irremediably "foreign," "dead," untranslatable? As our reading of the *Book of the Duchess* hopefully demonstrates, affect and emotion are contemporaneous, since the Black Knight experiences an irruption of bodily intensity even as he endeavors to organize his account according to the recognizable contours of *fin'amor*.

Those recognizable contours, we would like to emphasize, should be credited to those adapting a "history of emotions" approach to medieval texts and societies. The appeal of this methodology, as several authors in this collection attest, lies in its ability to study the social conventions that make feelings historically legible. Medieval studies of emotion began with legal historians such as Stephen D. White, Paul Hyams, and Daniel Lord Smail, who in the 1980s and 90s took on such topics as affect and honor, anger and lordship, rancor and hatred in legal discourse.[16] But arguably it is the paradigmatic work of Barbara H. Rosenwein that has had the strongest and widest influence inside and outside medieval studies.[17] In her important 2006 book, *Emotional Communities in the Early Middle Ages*, Rosenwein draws on the work of early modern historian William Reddy and his articulation of a theory of emotives, that is, "first-person, present tense emotion claims" that, like performatives, have the potential to do things to the world.[18] Reddy uses the concept of an emotive to analyze how groups can be bound together to form emotional "regimes" tied to state formation and hegemony (or its opposite). Rosenwein argues instead for the value of studying looser, more varied groupings in the Middle Ages, which she terms "emotional communities."[19] By resisting the "grand narrative" that characterized medieval feelings as primitive, even childish, Rosenwein's work has invited medievalists to investigate the historical specificity of emotions as deliberate cultural constructions.[20]

Scholars studying medieval emotions as historical productions are attentive to issues of representation, circulation, and dissemination. For instance, in her 2009 essay, "Feeling," Sarah McNamer calls for "a more imaginative, large-scale experiment with the literal: with conceiving of a wide array of Middle English texts as literal scripts that vigorously enlist *literariness* as a means of generating feelings and putting them into play in history."[21] And in her 2010 book, *Affective Meditation and the Invention of Medieval Compassion*, McNamer examines a series of literary texts promoting affective meditation on the Passion. Arguing that such texts function quite literally as intimate "scripts for the performance of feeling" and "often explicitly aspire to performative efficacy," McNamer claims that the study of them "contributes to a body of empirical work that is building a case for a performative model of affect as the default mode for this period."[22] As with Rosenwein's work, McNamer's discussion of compassion as an emotion "invented" by medieval culture takes up its long history, spanning the period from 1050 to 1550. McNamer also explores the particular usefulness of this emotion in developing "emotional communities" of women (as well as the particularly gendered performative reading practices its intimate scripts made possible). As the essays in this volume affirm, there is much to recommend this approach; it has added significantly, and continues to add, to our understanding of the importance of medieval emotional practices. Perhaps most fundamentally, recognizing that emotions have histories allows us to begin to understand how emotions are not biological, coming from inside, as early modern theories of the passions or some modern biological theories might suggest, but historically contingent, arising out of a set of particular cultural and linguistic practices. As these essays suggest, we should not assume that medieval emotions, even if they share the same names as modern emotions, are describing the same experience or having the same effects in the world.[23]

Historicizing medieval emotions can also help us understand how performing emotion can produce embodied forms of agency that link the individual and the social in ways that function alongside, but also in excess of, institutional and state formations. They can show us where affects happen, and how affects might arise from certain emotional scripts, or within particular emotional experiences. Rosenwein's concept of an "emotional community," to that end, allows for a nuanced understanding of the kinds of shared practices that define and enable gendered identity *in-between* feeling and intellectual assent. Also, as McNamer argues, the performative nature of how emotion is established, felt, and put into action allows us to approach medieval emotion outside the modern authentic/inauthentic binary. If affective attachments are constructed, then such associations must be performed for them to become culturally intelligible. Historians of emotion who study the Middle Ages, we suggest, are already attuned to the intersection of emotion with other states of feeling, namely affect.

Indeed, the intersection of emotion and affect, we believe, has long been present in medievalist scholarship. Almost from the beginning, work on medieval "affective piety" has stressed a complex interplay of affect, feeling, and emotion. In Southern's fascination with Anselm's articulation of a Christianity of love and gentleness rather than one of revenge and authority, there resides an acknowledgment of the ways in which bodily intensities get taken up by and taken into what Rosenwein would later call "emotional communities."[24] Similarly, swooning at the sight of a beloved – either in religious or erotic devotion – is a crucial part of identity cultivation for distinctly different groups in the Middle Ages. Being overcome, in other words, can become part of what McNamer later calls an "intimate script" for the performance of emotion. Caroline Walker Bynum's work on holy women, like that of other feminist scholars of religion, bases the cultivation of an emotional experience of piety on somatic experiences traditionally associated with the feminine, ones that often, if not frequently, take on an independent intensity that overruns, or re-scripts, conventional religious experience.[25] By engaging the scholarly tradition on "affective piety," we hope to emphasize the centrality of medieval writings to what we are arguing is the interdependence of affect, feeling, and emotion.

We do so mainly to acknowledge the complexity of medieval thinking about different forms of feeling. For medieval philosophers, the affects were movements of the intellectual soul, which formed part of the governing apparatus of medieval moral psychology. Affects, like motions of the sensitive soul (akin to the emotions), could be shaped by a program of moral training captured by the *habitus*.²⁶ As work by medievalists including Bruce Holsinger and Katharine Breen has established, *habitus* is a concept widely used in contemporary theory to indicate the background cultural conditions that structure subjectivity, but it is a concept that is deeply indebted to medieval thinkers.²⁷ Despite her more contemporary usage, Monique Scheer challenges us as medievalists to consider the importance of habituation and social context in understanding emotional practices in history.²⁸ If emotion does not already exist "inside" the individual, but is formed through individual embodied action within a *habitus*, or set of cultural, social, and linguistic practices already naturalized within the context of the individual emotional actant, then it is the repeated performance of emotion by individual actants that makes the emotion "real" and establishes the "authenticity" of the emotional experience. Unlike modern conceptions, which regard the *habitus* with a degree of suspicion, essays in this volume explore how medieval understandings of the *habitus* link affect and emotion in the production of socially legible, sometimes creative, subjectivities. These essays largely do so in secular contexts, suggesting, unlike scholars of affective piety, that the production of a *habitus* in which affect and emotion intersect is foundational to understanding all domains of medieval subjectivity.

Historicizing feeling gives us new insight into both the supposedly pro forma nature of much didactic literature and orthodox practice and the staged performance of so much other medieval emotion (for example, the anger followed by mercy shown by medieval rulers). But the essays in this collection also suggest that something has been left out in this approach to medieval affect, feeling, and emotion. "History" in such "history of emotion" models is framed largely in diachronic terms that privilege a sequenced account of the external, socially recognizable forms of feeling. Even McNamer's work results in a longitudinal history of one socialized form of medieval emotion. There is also a tendency in such studies to treat literary texts simply as archival data equivalent to the material used by historians of emotion. How feelings are put into play in history remains primarily concerned with the recoverable, objective social forms of feeling as they are expressed textually over time. The particular material contexts for individual performances of emotion, as well as the various literary representations of the play of affect, feeling, and emotion, are at stake across the different chapters in this collection.

An attention to the intersection of affect's "bodily feelings" with the "conscious states" of emotion allows authors in the present anthology to treat feelings with more feeling.[29] This is not a gesture of "lumping together," but rather represents a fine parsing of how affect works in tandem with, and sometimes in excess of, socially recognizable emotions. Specific moments in the *Book of the Duchess*, when the Black Knight swoons, or when he ends his tale as a response to overwhelming loss, are outbreaks of intense feeling that cannot adequately be rendered using the expressivist, intentionalist idiom of emotion. It is not that medievalists are unaware of these irruptions. Medieval melancholia has merited careful and detailed study, and inexpressibility is marked by its own *topos* in formal analysis of medieval writings. And as Corinne Saunders has persuasively demonstrated, mind, body, and affect are understood as inextricably linked in medieval medical theory, psychology, philosophy, and theology, in ways that often parallel current theories of embodiment advanced by modern philosophers and cognitive neuroscientists. Saunders has also argued that the nexus of mind, body, and affect is "crucial too for secular writing, and to any analysis of reading imaginative fiction," examining in particular how "across Chaucer's romance writings, mind, body, and affect are inscribed in complex ways that link thinking, feeling, imagining, and remembering: the acts intrinsic to the process of reading."[30] As recent work by Michelle Karnes and D. Vance Smith attests, tracing the presence of cognitive sophistication in what was long characterized as a bodily, feminized, and non-clerical practice of religious intensity has been a major concern in this area of medieval studies.[31]

This is because, to return to Chaucer's *Book of the Duchess*, medieval writings include what we would think of as affects *and* emotions. When the dreamer stumbles upon him, he finds the Knight only able to complain to himself. And while his malady has clear and strong physical effects, it remains largely unprocessed before he enters into dialogue with the dreamer. His recitation, "Withoute noote, withoute song" (472), does not bear the marks of emotion, which organize the intensity of feeling into recognizable, communicable iterations of experience. The Knight's identity is consolidated by such amorphous feeling, however, since other elite lovers are similarly undone.[32] We might say that falling apart in response to desire operates as an "intimate script" that works to make the intensity of a certain kind of bodily experience culturally legible. It does not achieve the status of emotion in this case, however, as the dreamer's response to the Knight's condition subsequently makes clear.

Through his expressions of concern, the dreamer in Chaucer's poem recognizes that the Knight cannot stay in this condition; when he offers to help and "Amende" the Knight's "gret sorowe" (551, 547), he suggests that affect is an intensity that the Knight must manage. The Knight must be brought to a state of articulate feeling where he can process his affective experience so that it might be recognized as a story of love. The Knight's account of his education in love at the hands of his lady White as something that moves him from being a *tabula rasa* to a fully formed noble lover can be read as the growing ability to articulate a set of emotives that bind him with White (and the other members of their circle) into a kind of emotional community. Furthermore, the lyric poem he utters, and then the personal narrative that he builds around it as explanation, together could provide the kind of "intimate script" for the performance of feeling that McNamer studies. As the Knight describes it, the kind of pity that White showed him provided a form of emotional display capable of embodying and encoding a set of social practices, broadly defined as *fin'amor*. Such love practice, it is implied, should thus bind together lover and lady, text and reader, in mutually constitutive patterns of self-identification that together would define and ground what it means to be noble in the world.

But the Knight's narrative persuades only if we approach him and White *as if* they are historical and exactly that which they say they are. Certainly, there is a history of *fin'amor* emotion that we see the Black Knight attempting to embody. In McNamer's words, if the Knight's song and narrative are a text, we can see how it "seeks to produce emotion through careful attention to its affective stylistics."[33] But this works as *fin'amor* emotion only if we allow ourselves to remain bounded by the contours of the Knight's monologues. The dialogue *between* dreamer and Knight draws us up short by creating an altogether different register of affective stylistics. These depict the gaps and disjunctures within the construction of *fin'amor*'s structures of feeling (as described by the Knight). The *pite* that the dreamer shows to the Black Knight in drawing him out of his melancholic funk, while in certain ways mirroring the pity of White to the young Knight, is also dramatically different. It elicits not emotion – in the sense of fully formed, socially legible feeling, one that will successfully identify the feeling subject in the world – but something that "feels" in between the individually felt and the social, personally felt in a way that impedes rather than facilitates communication, where cognition, if possible at all, occurs in embodied, sub-linguistic forms. Attention to affect does not seamlessly yield to a consideration of emotion's historical construction; rather, affect and emotion are held in tension by a historical articulation that also involves the poem's audience.

The essays in *Medieval Affect, Feeling, and Emotion* suggest that both the history of emotions and contemporary affect theory are insufficient for dealing with the complexity and nuance of medieval renderings, and instead begin to chart the intersection of affect, feeling, and emotion. These essays argue that we need to explore further the historicizing effects of thinking about affect and emotion synchronically. And a feature of this collection is its decision to focus within the "regional" and "local" effects of late Middle English literature – whether that be Brantley L. Bryant's discussion of the affective economies of the late medieval English manorial system, Emma Lipton's argument for the creation of a "legal affect" in the York trial plays, or Holly A. Crocker's consideration of the affect management consolidating workaday urban masculinity in Hoccleve's *Series*. One result is a crucial "secularization" of medieval affect and emotion. The focus on affective piety in so much medieval "history of emotion," while understandable, given the immediacy of affective piety as a textual and social force in the later Middle Ages, and immensely productive (in, for example, a book such as McNamer's), has tended to narrow what we expect the focus of medieval studies of affect and emotion to be.[34] As a result, we have only begun to tap the rich offerings of medieval representations. In their different ways, essays by Emma Lipton, Sarah Salih, and Patricia DeMarco highlight the complex interrelationships affect forges between the secular and religious in late medieval English literary expression – whether the turn to contemporary forms of witnessing rather than the confessional manual's emphasis on envy in understanding the condemnation of Christ in the York trial plays, Lydgate's depiction of Hector's dead body as a relic and affect machine, or the role of Jewish affect in the *Siege of Jerusalem* as contrast to a properly masculine and aristocratic manifestation of feeling. Another result is a focus on medieval primary texts themselves and a holding at bay of the charting of emotions as if they have a history. The essays in this collection demonstrate that there is great value in letting the medieval literary and cultural sources lead the way for medievalists' discussions (in other words, letting the focus be on the medieval primary texts rather than on a study of shame, envy, weeping, and so on). The formal contours of affect – the ways that it might be patterned, flattened, or extended – will give us a more historically nuanced understanding of the ways that certain feelings have been ensconced as "canonical," normative, or even ethical emotions.[35]

Chapter Summaries

The chapters that follow resist a progressive account of affect, feeling, or emotion. But they are organized to highlight different junctures of history, embodiment, form, and identity within a delimited temporal and geographic sphere, and in a way that, we hope, provides a survey of what an intersectional approach to emotion and affect can offer in the current moment. Thus, we begin, in Chapters 1 and 2, with essays that connect to more "traditional" objects of study – the social construction of emotions through the use of key emotion words and the realm of affective piety. But each of these essays takes the expected in new directions – considering the role of literary form and genre in the case of Stephanie Trigg's essay, and the uses of religious affect to construct powerful secular identity positions in the case of Patricia DeMarco's. Chapters 3 and 4 continue this turn to the specifically secular contexts for medieval affect, as well as the importance of affect management in creating new modes of enabling gendered presences in late medieval society. Both Holly A. Crocker and Glenn D. Burger, in different ways, engage medieval texts with contemporary affect theory as a way to think differently about the project of historicizing premodern affect, feeling, and emotion. In Chapter 5, Brantley L. Bryant challenges us to consider the role of affect management in the late medieval economic order, beginning where most medievalists would not see affect and taking it back to questions of literary representation and emergent social self-identification. Similarly, in Chapters 6 and 7 Sarah Salih and Emma Lipton return us to "feeling religious" in the period, but in a way that goes outside traditional affective piety to consider the communal aspects of religious feeling. In Chapter 8, Anke Bernau shifts our thinking about affect to a wider consideration of form and affect in a late medieval philosophical dream vision. And finally, Anthony Bale's "Afterword: Three Letters" issues a reminder that medieval affects, feelings, and emotions coalesce within and through different contexts – cultural, personal, and ultimately historical – as he shows with his brief meditation on premodern letters.

Chapter 1: In "Weeping Like a Beaten Child: Figurative Language and the Emotions in Chaucer and Malory," Stephanie Trigg affirms the rich potential of literary texts for a history of the emotions. Although the figurative density of medieval narratives presents interpretive challenges, Trigg provides a contrasting account of Lancelot's and Absolon's tears that shows the importance of literary production in our thinking about the social histories of feeling. Tracing Chaucer's and Malory's contrasting uses of the simile, *wept like a beaten child* – the first describing Absolon's emotional state after kissing Alison's behind in Chaucer's *Miller's Tale*, and the second, the difference between the reaction of Arthur's court and of Lancelot after the healing of Sir Urry in Malory's *Morte d'Arthure*, Trigg examines how this motif can give us a sense of how certain emotions can be recognized in their social contexts. She argues that the use of figurative expressions such as similes, proverbs, and metaphors in medieval literary texts, while unable to offer a direct identification of emotions, nonetheless can show us what emotions look and feel like in very precise and nuanced narrative and social contexts. Their use across different situations can give us a range of contexts for thinking about how medieval people coded and decoded emotion, translating emotional behavior from one context to another. She demonstrates how such similes appeal, as proverbs do, to a conventional or shared understanding that is often emotional or affective, akin to what Reddy terms "emotives." The whole point of a proverbial simile is to explain emotional behavior by rendering it recognizable and familiar. At the same time, Trigg's account of how this simile is handled by Chaucer and Malory also exposes the "literariness" of their use to develop the characters of Absolon and Lancelot and mark a transition in the psychological narrative of their character. While Malory's is celebrated for its pathos, and Chaucer's is overlooked for its absurdity, other examples of weeping, taken alongside discussions of tears and considerations of gender, provide historical evidence that medieval artists and audiences thought of emotions in relation to particular, and particularly constructed, literary motifs. Trigg's complex account of the emotional valence of what appears on the surface to be a straightforward simile compellingly demonstrates how emotions vary across cultural and temporal boundaries.

Chapter 2: In "Imagining Jewish Affect in the *Siege of Jerusalem*," Patricia DeMarco notes the "remarkably detailed portraits of Jewish suffering and affective response" depicted in the fourteenth-century alliterative poem, the *Siege of Jerusalem*, notably in the crucifixion of the Jewish leader, Caiaphas, alongside his two clerks. In contrast to Christ's suffering on the cross, however, Jewish suffering provokes an ambivalent affective response. Using medieval faculty psychology, DeMarco argues that in the poem Jews are incapable of governing their sense appetites and overwhelmed by the distress they feel as beholders of suffering. Christians, on the other hand, are distinguished by the ability to contain the passions of the sensitive soul and to cultivate the irascible emotions, such as anger. At the same time, they also feel pity, which threatens the performance of religious difference and undermines Christians' claims to superiority. Anger is thus a more manly response than pity for Christian protaganists in the poem. DeMarco argues that the *Siege of Jerusalem* therefore suggests that normative aristocratic masculinity entails both the vigilant regulation of sorrowful compassionate feelings and the continual cultivation of anger at the indignities suffered by Christ.

Chapter 3: In "Engendering Affect in Hoccleve's *Series*," Holly A. Crocker focuses on the affective somatic states that together "galvanize" the "engendered assemblage" that constitutes the "workaday masculinity of Hoccleve's clerkly persona" in the *Series*. While most of these affects do not qualify as emotions, they do connect inward conditions and outward presentations, and thus play a crucial role in consolidating difficult identities. In medieval affect theory, Crocker argues, affects make up part of the soul. When the soul is well ordered, its sensitive (feminine) part, which includes the affects, is governed by its rational (masculine) part. Masculinity, she notes, is therefore as ethical as it is social. In Hoccleve's *Series* managing affect becomes an aesthetic endeavor that ultimately provides Thomas with a socially restored masculinity. Thus, for Crocker, it is especially important to move outside the self-revelations and confessional exchanges of *My Compleinte* and the *Dialog with a Friend*, sections privileged by many "autobiographical" critics of the poem, and attend as well to the later, non-autobiographical sections of the poem. These sections, which include genres such as romance and manuals for dying, represent the ways in which individual selfhood is subsumed by universalizing conventions and demonstrate the role of affect in the creation of a socially intelligible masculinity in late medieval London. Thus, while Thomas' middling subject position may have little in common with the elite status of someone such as Duke Humphrey, both men "share an investment in displaying visible control over the affective states that define their masculinities in specific social contexts."

Chapter 4: In "Becoming One Flesh, Inhabiting Two Genders: Ugly Feelings and Blocked Emotion in the *Wife of Bath's Prologue and Tale*," Glenn D. Burger explores the complex interplay of affect and emotion in Prologue and Tale in order to understand how they intervene in a broader discussion of female conduct, marital affection, and social innovation taking place in the later Middle Ages. Comparing and contrasting Chaucer's text with *Le Ménagier de Paris* (*The Good Wife's Guide*), he argues that the Wife's autobiographical Prologue functions as a kind of anti-conduct book, her life story similar to the exemplary stories of bad women found in contemporary conduct texts. At the same time, the Wife's audience remains caught up in the affective intensity of her negative emotions. As a result, throughout the Prologue, and especially in her account of the final domestic quarrel she has with Jankyn, her fifth husband, the Wife forces us to experience the married estate in more complexly material terms, not simply as an already socialized emotion, the "wo that is in mariage," but as what Sianne Ngai calls "ugly feelings" or blocked emotions that result in "ambivalent situations of suspended agency."[36] The *Wife's Tale* in turn presents a mirror image to the stabilizing reconfiguration of masculine and feminine articulated in a conduct text such as the *Ménagier*. If the latter text reconfigures gender as a way of authorizing emergent subject positions, the *Wife's Tale*, especially the final bedroom debate between rapist knight and loathly hag, pushes the kind of social innovation imagined in such conduct texts to its logical limits in challenging, even utopian ways. As a result, to an extent not taken up in contemporary conduct literature for women, we are encouraged to explore from below the anxieties raised by bourgeois and gentry attempts to develop new ethical subject positions based on heterosexual desire and married relations.

Chapter 5: In "Accounting for Affect in the *Reeve's Tale*," Brantley L. Bryant details how the rigorous account-keeping and surveillance that drove manorial agriculture made the late medieval manor a site for the textual exploration of affective intensity. Bryant argues that the Reeve recasts the customarily freewheeling genre of fabliau according to the interests of a supervisory manorial official. Drawing on medieval treatises on estate management and accounting such as *The Husbandry* and *Walter of Henley*, which demonstrate a pervasive connection between affect management and the tallying of accounts for which reeves were responsible, Bryant considers how manorial accounting both registers and manages bodily intensities, and in particular how dread infuses the culture of surveillance that pervades the manorial workplace of Chaucer's Reeve. Bryant thus returns us to the *irous* disposition of Chaucer's Reeve in new ways, as he shows how, by thinking of things, goods, and persons as monetized items that need to be accounted for, the characters in this tale affirm the circulation of negative affect as part of a manorial economy. He argues that the late medieval manorial system thus provides an example of what Sara Ahmed has called an "affective economy," a situation in which "affect does not reside positively in the sign or commodity but is produced as an effect of its circulation."[37] Bryant's analysis provides us with an important new way of understanding how the Reeve's professional preoccupations inform his tale and how labor and formal concerns intersect in his tale. As such, the essay argues for Chaucer's deep engagement with the felt realities of this kind of labor.

Chapter 6: In "Affect Machines," Sarah Salih argues that medieval Christians found pagans good to think with because they enabled a sociological analysis of religions as human cultural formations. In particular she maintains that examining pagans in the wake of the late fourteenth-century image crisis yields greater insight into the workings of late medieval devotion as a practice that depended upon the activation of the power of beloved objects within an affective network. Idolators, Salih argues, were useful for considering how affect could be poured into and generated by material things. What makes idols so frightening is their power to "stick" to viewers in ways that reduce onlookers' capacities. Christian affective devotion crystallized such concerns, for both orthodox writers and Wycliffite heretics, as image debates during this period sought to regulate the intensity of this affective encounter between worshippers, religious images, and devotional objects. A wide survey of thinking about images, affect, and their interaction thus grounds Salih's detailed discussion of Hector's tomb in Lydgate's *Troy Book*. As she argues, the elaborate apparatus that sustains Hector's dead body is an "affect machine" that does not produce idolatry. While his animated corpse is not living, it is also not merely a dead thing that corrupts the affections of its viewers. In Salih's analysis, "Hector's preserved body shows how a relic is imagined: as a thing that orchestrates a circuit of affect whilst itself remaining constant and self-identical, immune to change and decay." Salih's approach provides a fresh look at the social dynamics of affect in late medieval religious practice, and also acknowledges that affect is not just an interior or innate capacity that spontaneously overflows in devotional contexts. With a concluding consideration of how medieval affect machines continue to elicit responses from modern viewers, Salih's essay affirms that medieval artists understood the presence and potential of affect, perhaps better than we do today.

Chapter 7: In "Witnessing and Legal Affect in the York Trial Plays," Emma Lipton notes that there has been a tendency among critics to privilege medieval models of inward devotion as the way to understand the emotional involvement that the York plays produce with their audience. Lipton draws on the work of contemporary affect theorists Sara Ahmed and Sianne Ngai to argue instead for a model of "legal affect" posed between the social and the individual. The plays, she maintains, employ medieval legal theories of witnessing "to explore the relationship between individual perception and the collective experience of emotion." In the York cycle, Lipton notes, the Passion is often depicted in legal terms and specifically linked to the problem of witnessing and false speech. Nor do the York plays reproduce the conventional emphasis in confessional manuals on envy as the main motive for the condemnation of Christ. Instead they engage contemporary concepts of witnessing in order to develop a civic model of affect. The York plays thus explore the relationship between individual perception and the collective experience of emotion and focus on the audience's collective act of beholding in the urban neighborhood. Discussing how the plays produce a legal affect that is poised between the social and the individual, Lipton demonstrates how these plays create not "a private drama of the heart" but a public affective experience.

Chapter 8: Gavin Douglas' predilection for lists in the *Palis of Honoure* has long been taken as a sign of the narrator's simplicity, especially of his inability to manage the affects appropriate to poetry. Anke Bernau, in "Affecting Forms: Theorizing with the *Palis of Honoure*," draws on Charles Altieri, and his focus in *The Particulars of Rapture* on affect as something that is resistant to reason's authority, in order to rethink how the authoritative catalogue and the emotionally troubled narrator have been read critically in Douglas' dream vision. Rather than seeing Douglas' penchant for lists in the *Palis of Honoure* as an aesthetic or emotional fault, Bernau argues that Douglas uses them to set an affective pace for his poem, one that reflects and transforms the dreamer's condition through his fantastic encounters. Through lists, Bernau demonstrates, the dreamer learns what poetry might be able to do to its readers' feelings. The dreamer is thus able to coalesce the non-linguistic, pre-social, embodied intensities that are in excess of received accounts of poetic experience. This reading of the ways that certain formal expectations condition affect is important not just for its reappraisal of Douglas' dreamer. Bernau's analysis also affirms that we are emotionally conditioned by poetry itself, to the extent that the formal characteristics of poetry help readers process affects into socially recognizable feelings, or emotions. The poem's claim that poetry is a joyous discipline thus emerges as a dynamic event rather than a secure designation as the negatively affected dreamer is placed in relation to that ideal.

Notes

1. Geoffrey Chaucer, *The Book of the Duchess*, in *The Riverside Chaucer*, ed. Larry D. Benson, 3rd edn (Boston, MA: Houghton Mifflin Co., 1987), ll. 1309–10. All future references will be to this edition; line numbers will be given parenthetically in the text.

2. Cf. Corrine Saunders, "Affective Reading: Chaucer, Women, and Romance," *Chaucer Review* 51,1 (2016): 11–14, for her recent discussion of Chaucer's exploration of the physiology of reading in the *Book of the Duchess*. In the inset story of Alcyone, "Extremes of emotion are offset by affective failures of sensibility. This balance also characterizes the narrator's dream. In his depiction of the Man in Black, Chaucer explores the complex connections between mind, body, and affect that characterize extreme grief, while the narrator's response reiterates the affective failure of understanding. The Dreamer stands in for the reader, feeling and seeing the affective power of a grief that is written on the body as the spirits withdraw" (18). Where Saunders sees a continuum between affect and emotion, we would emphasize a certain productive tension.
3. Here we would distinguish the question of terminology and the historicizing aims of this collection from that articulated by the editor of another recent collection of essays. In her introduction to a 2014 *Exemplaria* special issue on "Premodern Emotions," Stephanie Trigg notes: "Each of these five key terms – feeling, passion, emotion, sentiment and affect – has been the dominant one in English writing at different times; and they have also trailed different ideological, physical, humoral, ethical, and hermeneutic associations. If we kept these historical and cultural variations in mind, any one of these terms might potentially serve as an umbrella term for all these others. 'Affect' may indeed be able to press the strongest claim here ... Understood in the most general way, the scope of 'affect' is widest. Nevertheless, for studies that are more longitudinal or historical in orientation, the phrase 'the history of emotions' suggests a complex and productively layered sense of inquiry into historical change, historical emotions, and the history of the term and concept of the 'emotions' themselves. As a discipline, or as an institutional frame, the history of emotions allows fruitful and intriguing connections to be made between the present and the past, as well as encouraging dialogue and interchange across the network of terms such as feelings, passions, emotions, and affects" ("Introduction: Emotional Histories – Beyond the Personalization of the Past and the Abstractions of Affect Theory," *Exemplaria* 26,1 (2014): 7–8). So too, we suggest, simply turning to "feeling" as the appropriate, unanachronistic premodern term is insufficient for the complex interplay we are charting in this collection. Sarah McNamer, for example, in "Feeling," in *Middle English: Oxford Twenty-First Century Approaches to Literature*, ed. Paul Strohm (Oxford: Oxford University Press, 2009), 241–57, has suggested this intermediate term might offer a way to capture the workings of emotion *and* affect in medieval texts. Yet as her subsequent work demonstrates, "feeling" alone remains limited for thinking about how bodies get associated (or "stuck together," to use terms from affect theory), or how emotions might shake free from the normative scripts they are cultivated to support. See McNamer, "The Literariness of Literature and the History of Emotion," *PMLA* 130,5 (2015): 1433–42.
4. Fiona Somerset, *Feeling Like Saints: Lollard Writings After Wyclif* (Ithaca, NY: Cornell University Press, 2014), 183.

5. Michael Hardt, "Foreword: What Affects Are Good For," in *The Affective Turn: Theorizing the Social*, ed. Patricia Ticineto Clough and Jean Halley (Durham, NC: Duke University Press, 2007), ix. As examples of feminist theorists focusing on the body, Hardt cites Judith Butler, *Bodies That Matter: On the Discursive Limits of "Sex"* (New York: Routledge, 1993) and Elizabeth Grosz, *Volatile Bodies: Toward a Corporeal Feminism* (Bloomington, IN: Indiana University Press, 1994); for queer theory's exploration of emotions, he cites Eve Kosofsky Sedgwick and Adam Frank, eds., *Shame and Its Sisters: A Silvan Tomkins Reader* (Durham, NC: Duke University Press, 1995).
6. Melissa Gregg and Gregory J. Seigworth, in "An Inventory of Shimmers," in *The Affect Theory Reader*, ed. Gregg and Seigworth (Durham, NC: Duke University Press, 2010), outline a similar bifurcated trajectory for the beginning of contemporary affect studies, situating it at a watershed moment in 1995, with the publication of two essays – one by Eve Sedgwick and Adam Frank ("Shame in the Cybernetic Fold") and the other by Brian Massumi ("The Autonomy of Affect") – that gave "substantial shape to the two dominant vectors of affect study in the humanities: Silvan Tomkins' psychobiology of differential affects ... and Gilles Deleuze's Spinozist ethology of bodily capacities." They go on to note that:

> With Tomkins, affect follows a quasi-Darwinian 'innate-ist' bent toward matters of evolutionary hardwiring. But these wires are by no means fully insulated nor do they terminate with the brain or flesh; instead they spark and fray just enough to transduce those influences borne along by the ambient irradiation of social relations. Meanwhile, Deleuze's Spinozan route locates affect in the midst of things and relations (in immanence) and, then, in the complex assemblages that come to compose bodies and worlds simultaneously. There is, then, a certain sense of reverse flow between these lines of inquiry – a certain inside-out/outside-in difference in directionality: affect as the prime 'interest' motivator that comes to put the drive in bodily drives (Tomkins); affect as an entire, vital, and modulating field of myriad becomings across human and nonhuman (Deleuze). While there is no pretending that these two vectors of affect theory could ever be easily or fully reconciled, they can be made to interpenetrate at particular points and to resonate. (5–6)

7. Gregg and Seigworth, for example, after noting the two major vectors of affect theory represented by Spinoza/Deleuze versus Freud/Tomkins, Massumi versus Sedgwick, add that "there are far more than just two angles onto affect's theorization. For now (and only for now) we can tentatively lay out, as a set of necessarily brief and blurry snapshots, *eight* of the main orientations that undulate and sometimes overlap in their approaches to affect" ("An Inventory of Shimmers," 6; our emphasis).

8. See, for example, Rosi Braidotti, *Nomadic Subjects: Embodiment and Sexual Difference in Contemporary Feminist Theory* (New York: Columbia University Press, 1983; 2011) and *Nomadic Theory: The Portable Rosi Braidotti* (New York: Columbia University Press, 2011); Lauren Berlant, *The Female Complaint: The Unfinished Business of Sentimentality in American Culture* (Durham, NC: Duke University Press, 2008) and *Cruel Optimism* (Durham, NC: Duke University Press, 2011); Sara Ahmed, *The Cultural Politics of Emotion* (New York: Routledge, 2004), *Queer Phenomenology: Orientations, Objects, Others* (Durham, NC: Duke University Press, 2006), and *The Promise of Happiness* (Durham, NC: Duke University Press, 2010); and Teresa Brennan, *The Transmission of Affect* (Ithaca, NY: Cornell University Press, 2004). For a useful introduction to affect theory, see the essays in Gregg and Seigworth, eds., *The Affect Theory Reader*.
9. Brian Massumi, *Parables for the Virtual: Movement, Affect, Sensation* (Durham, NC: Duke University Press, 2002), 28.
10. Patricia Ticineto Clough, "Introduction," in *The Affective Turn: Theorizing the Social*, ed. Clough and Jean Halley (Durham, NC: Duke University Press, 2007), 2; quoted in Massumi, *Parables for the Virtual*, 30, 25. See also Gregg and Seigworth's definition of affect in "An Inventory of Shimmers": "How to begin when, after all, there is no pure or somehow originary state for affect: Affect arises in the midst of *in-between-ness*: in the capacities to act and be acted upon. Affect is an impingement or extrusion of a momentary or sometimes more sustained state of relation *as well as* the passage (and the duration of passage) of forces or intensities. That is, affect is found in those intensities that pass body to body (human, nonhuman, part-body, and otherwise), in those resonances that circulate about, between, and sometimes stick to bodies and worlds, *and* in the very passages or variations between these intensities and resonances themselves" (1).
11. Sianne Ngai, *Ugly Feelings* (Cambridge, MA: Harvard University Press, 2005), 27. See also, Sianne Ngai, *Our Aesthetic Categories: Zany, Cute, Interesting* (Cambridge, MA: Harvard University Press, 2015), 1–13, as well as Ahmed, *Cultural Politics of Emotion*, esp. "Introduction," 1–19, and Berlant, "Cruel Optimism," 93–117.
12. Thus Brantley L. Bryant's focus in his essay in this volume on the circulation of negative affect in the *Reeve's Tale* allows us to attend more precisely to the consequences of the Reeve's *irous* nature *not* being able to settle as emotion, and what that tells us about the culture of surveillance that pervades the manorial workplace in this period. Similarly, it is this circulation of feeling in between affect and emotion that allows for the kind of productive affect management discussed by Glenn D. Burger, Holly A. Crocker, and Patricia DeMarco in their essays in this volume.
13. Sara Ahmed, "Happy Objects," in *The Affect Theory Reader*, ed. Gregg and Seigworth, 29.
14. Clough, "Introduction," 2.

15. Heather Love, *Feeling Backward: Loss and the Politics of Queer History* (Cambridge, MA: Harvard University Press, 2007).
16. See the essays collected in Barbara H. Rosenwein, ed., *Anger's Past: The Social Uses of an Emotion in the Middle Ages* (Ithaca, NY: Cornell University Press, 1998). See also Daniel Lord Smail, "Hatred as a Social Institution in Late-Medieval Society," *Speculum* 76 (2001): 90–126.
17. Barbara H. Rosenwein, *Emotional Communities in the Early Middle Ages* (Ithaca, NY: Cornell University Press, 2006); Jan Plamper, William Reddy, Barbara Rosenwein, and Peter Stearns, "The History of Emotions: An Interview with William Reddy, Barbara Rosenwein, and Peter Stearns," *History and Theory*, 49,2 (May 2010): 237–65; and Barbara H. Rosenwein, *Generations of Feeling: A History of Emotions, 600–1700* (Cambridge: Cambridge University Press, 2016).
18. William M. Reddy, *The Navigation of Feeling: A Framework for the History of Emotions* (Cambridge: Cambridge University Press, 2001): "[Emotives are] similar to performatives (and different from constatives) in that emotives do things to the world. Emotives are themselves instruments for directly changing, building, hiding, intensifying emotions, instruments that may be more or less successful" (104–5).
19. "An emotional community is a group in which people have a common stake, interests, values, and goals. Thus it is often a social community. But it is also possibly a 'textual community' created and reinforced by ideologies, teachings, and common presuppositions ... Thus emotional communities are in some ways what Foucault called a common 'discourse': shared vocabularies and ways of thinking that have a controlling function, a disciplining function. Emotional communities are similar as well to Bourdieu's notion of 'habitus': internalized norms that determine how we think and act and that may be different in different groups ... I use the term 'communities' in order to stress the social and relational nature of emotions; to allow room for Reddy's very useful notion of 'emotives,' which change the discourse and the habitus by their very existence; and to emphasize some people's adaptability to different sorts of emotional conventions as they move from one group to another" (Rosenwein, *Emotional Communities*, 24–5).
20. This work continues in Rosenwein's most recent book-length study of the history of emotion, *Generations of Feeling*, which alternates short chapters on theories of emotions with longer chapters that explore two or more existing emotional communities, ranging from Alcuin to Hobbes. Focusing on England and France, her survey attempts both to counter an over-emphasis in current historical studies on the state and the political uses of emotion and to cross the medieval/early modern divide. Her chapter 6, "Theatricality and Sobriety" (169–226), overlaps most closely with the temporal range of this collection, examining fifteenth-century Burgundian chroniclers, the Paston letters, and the *Book of Margery Kempe*.
21. McNamer, "Feeling," 246.

22. Sara McNamer, *Affective Meditation and the Invention of Medieval Compassion* (Philadelphia, PA: University of Pennsylvania Press, 2010), 12–13.
23. Heeding this lesson, Stephanie Trigg, in her chapter in this volume, roots her analysis of two representations of medieval men weeping within the cultural and linguistic formations of medieval romance. And, as different authors argue, the Middle Ages may also have its own moments of innovation in terms of emotion, establishing (as with compassion) the foundation for modern understandings and practices. Emma Lipton's analysis in this volume of fifteenth-century cycle drama, in this vein shows how emotions become collective for their audiences in light of specific legal practices of witnessing.
24. See Richard W. Southern, *The Making of the Middle Ages* (New Haven, CT: Yale University Press, 1953), 220–65. For a helpful survey of this trajectory in medieval studies, see the Wikipedia entry, written principally by Mary Agnes Edsall, on "Affective Piety" (accessed January 25, 2017).
25. Thus Caroline Walker Bynum argues, in *Holy Feast and Holy Fast: The Religious Significance of Food to Medieval Women* (Berkeley, CA: University of California Press, 1987), "that medieval efforts to discipline and manipulate the body should be interpreted more as elaborate changes rung upon the possibilities provided by fleshliness than as flights from physicality. I also demonstrate the extent to which religious women derived their basic symbols from such ordinary biological and social experiences as giving birth, lactating, suffering, and preparing and distributing food" (6).
26. For an overview of medieval moral psychology, particularly as the *habitus* might be trained, see Robert Pasnau, *Thomas Aquinas on Human Nature: A Philosophical Study of Summa Theologiae 1a 75–89* (Cambridge: Cambridge University Press, 2002), 243–8; Robert Miner, *Thomas Aquinas on the Passions: A Study of "Summa Theologiae" 1a2ae 22–48* (Cambridge: Cambridge University Press, 2009), 13–28; and John Dryden, "Passions, Affections, and Emotions: Methodological Difficulties in Reconstructing Aquinas's Philosophical Psychology," *Literature Compass* 13,6 (2016): 343–50.
27. See Bruce Holsinger, *The Premodern Condition: Medievalism and the Making of Theory* (Chicago, IL: University of Chicago Press, 2005), and Katharine Breen, *Imagining an English Reading Public, 1150–1400* (Cambridge: Cambridge University Press, 2010).
28. Monique Scheer, "Are Emotions a Kind of Practice (And Is That What Makes Them Have a History)? A Bourdieuian Approach to Understanding Emotion," *History and Theory* 51,2 (2012): 193–220.
29. Fredric Jameson, *The Antinomies of Realism* (London: Verso, 2013), distinguishes between an attention to affect, which he articulates as "bodily feelings," and the "conscious states of emotions" (32). Jameson credits this characterization of affect to Rei Terada, *Feeling in Theory: Emotion after the "Death of the Subject"* (Cambridge, MA: Harvard University Press, 2001), 82.
30. Saunders, "Affective Reading," 29. See also, Corinne Saunders, "Mind, Body and Affect in Medieval English Arthurian Romance," in *Emotions in Medieval*

Arthurian Literature: Body, Mind, *Voice*, ed. Frank Brandsma, Carolyne Larrington, and Saunders (Cambridge: D. S. Brewer, 2015), 31–46.
31. See Michelle Karnes, *Imagination, Meditation, and Cognition in the Middle Ages* (Chicago, IL: University of Chicago Press, 2011), 15–18; 114–20; and D. Vance Smith, "The Application of Thought to Medieval Studies: The Twenty-First Century," *Exemplaria* 22,1 (2010): 85–94.
32. As Simon Meecham-Jones details in "'He In Salte Teres Dreynte': Understanding Troilus's Tears," in *Emotions and War: Medieval to Romantic Literature*, ed. Stephanie Downes, Andrew Lynch, and Katrina O'Loughlin (New York: Palgrave Macmillan, 2015), modern readers remain disturbed by the hero's weeping in *Troilus and Criseyde*.
33. McNamer, "Feeling," 247.
34. See Somerset, *Feeling Like Saints*, especially chapters 3 and 4, for a powerful and provocative analysis that troubles longstanding scholarly assumptions about differences between mainstream and Lollard expressions of pious feeling.
35. For a fuller statement of this relationship, and our particular responses to the development of affect theory and the history of emotions in medieval studies, see Glenn D. Burger, *Conduct Becoming: Good Wives and Husbands in the Later Middle Ages* (Philadelphia, PA: University of Pennsylvania Press, 2017), 173–90, 194–7, and Holly A. Crocker, "Medieval Affects Now," *Exemplaria* 29,1 (2017): 82–98.
36. Ngai, *Ugly Feelings*, 1.
37. Sara Ahmed, *The Cultural Politics of Emotion* (New York: Routledge, 2004), 45.

CHAPTER 1

Weeping Like a Beaten Child: Figurative Language and the Emotions in Chaucer and Malory

Stephanie Trigg

Weeping like a child. Crying like a baby. Weeping like a baby. Crying like a child. What do we see, hear, and feel, as we read and think about these four comparisons? What is the difference between weeping and crying? Between the tears or cries of a baby and a child? The force of figurative comparisons such as these depends on established social norms and expectations. When a speaker, writer, or lyricist describes an adult's tears in this way, they appeal to a shared understanding that babies or children weep and cry in a distinctive manner that is not normally shared by adults. Such comparisons are far from stable, however. Each of my four examples carries slightly different semantic and cultural associations, while the comparison also signifies different things when used of a younger or older man or woman. When we try to attend to these associations across a gap of centuries, the difficulties are compounded. Figurative expressions describing emotional states and affects can be a promising resource for the history of affects and emotions in the reading and reception of medieval literature. Their use across a range of genres, translations, and adaptations can give us a range of contexts for thinking about the ways medieval people coded and decoded emotions and translated emotional behavior from one context to another. They may also be able to help us track historical changes in those feelings and their expression. The complexity of figurative language, however, certainly represents a challenge for those who might approach the history of emotions by asking only, "How did people feel in the Middle Ages?"

Scholars in literary studies typically answer such questions by answering – quite properly – "It's complicated!" The indirection and ambiguity of many literary texts, their heightened emotional range, and the elaborate architecture of figurative expression constitute a rich archive for the history of feeling, but not one that is always easy to interpret. Literary texts explore emotion in a range of imagined contexts and across a wide range of feeling. They allow writers and readers to experiment safely, or vicariously, with extreme or borderline emotional situations, affects, and feelings. Crucially, they also work mimetically by playing out emotions in mythical, historical, and fictional contexts, modeling the diverse ways humans imagine the feelings – rightly or wrongly – of those in other cultural or temporal contexts. The subtle and allusive texts of literary traditions can seem troublingly imprecise sources for the history of emotions. Indeed, they are sometimes marginalized by those historians who treat literary texts with suspicion as productions only of an educated, literate minority. And within literary studies itself, the disciplinary impulse to celebrate hermeneutic and interpretative undecideability sometimes constrains literature's contribution to the history of emotion and affect. Literature's witness, then, is complex and ambiguous; historically and culturally layered. The challenge of untangling that witness and putting literary texts closer to the center of the history of emotions – as that field is currently configured, with its principal methodologies being principally historiographic – is formidable. Nevertheless, the use and history of particular motifs and expressions can be an important source for the mutable history of emotions and emotional expression. Figurative expressions such as similes, proverbs, and metaphors may not offer us the direct or unambiguous identification of emotions, but they can be read as powerful attempts to tell and show us what emotions look and feel like, in very particular narrative and social contexts.

This essay takes as its starting point two similar comparisons made by Chaucer and Malory between weeping men and weeping, beaten children. It will then consider a range of satellite examples – weeping in other languages, weeping children who may or may not have been beaten, a man who *might* be about to be beaten, lectures about weeping – to develop the semantic and semiotic fields that surround my two key examples. Chaucer and Malory use this simile only once each, so it is hardly very common, yet the phrase has suggestive associations with other familiar expressions such as "weeping like a child," or other proverbial expressions about weeping or being beaten. This phrase then simultaneously draws attention to authorial exceptionality and its capacity to vary the tone of high poetic register while also testifying to normative or proverbial medieval ideas about both childish *and* adult weeping. These are ideas about the emotions, about gender, and about the ideology of discipline, nurture, and maturity; and also the difference between children and men. There is a further degree of difficulty in this enterprise, in that the phrase "to weep like a child" and its cognate "to cry like a baby" are still familiar in modern English, especially in the lyrics of popular songs. This familiarity makes it a little harder to judge the effect of this phrase, and to disentangle its resonance in medieval literature. My two examples are quite focused, in that they both describe an adult male as weeping like a child who has been beaten, though this in turn introduces the problematic ideas of punishment and agency. Moreover, my two texts strain against each other, since their generic affiliations and tonal registers are so different. They do not easily shed light on each other. Their reception history tells its own story, too. One is a famous, much analyzed example; the other has taken some medievalists by surprise when I have drawn this comparison in oral presentations of this material.

In the more celebrated example, Malory's Lancelot has reluctantly agreed to try and heal the wounds of Sir Urry, a feat that no other knight or king has been able to accomplish. He successfully does so, and is affirmed as the "best knight of the world":

> Than kynge Arthur and all the kynges and knyghtes kneled downe and gave thankynges and lovynge unto God and unto Hys Blyssed Modir. And evir sir Launcelote wepte, as he had been a chylde that had bene beatyn![1]

In Chaucer's *Miller's Tale*, Absolon has kissed Alisoun's "thyng al rough and long yhered" and reels in shock:

> His hoote love was coold and al yqueynt;
> For fro that tyme that he hadde kist hir ers,
> Of paramours he sette nat a kers,
> For he was heeled of his maladie.
> Ful ofte paramours he gan deffie,
> And weep as dooth a child that is ybete.[2]

Although the simile in these two examples is structured in almost identical terms, using the same noun ("child") and two verbs ("wepen" and "beaten"), the emotional contexts are of a very different order, while the two characters could hardly be more dissimilar. Absolon is introduced as a comical childish character, in love with the idea of love, a boyish man who is brought to weeping in shame and humiliation at being tricked, and in shock at his discoveries about female anatomy. His courtly aspirations are reduced quite literally to the taste of excrement in his mouth, after he has kissed Alison's arse "ful savoury." Absolon's weeping is laughable. By contrast, in Malory's tale of miraculous healing and divine intervention into the world of the courtly tournament, Lancelot is his most complex tragic hero, carrying the contradictory weight of his dual role as best knight of the king and most faithful lover of the queen on his shoulders. The emotions that underlie his weeping – guilt, relief, pity, or devotion –

are unclear (we will return to this question shortly) but Lancelot's tears are far from laughable. They are contrasted clearly with the Arthurian court's jubilation and shared prayers, in a moment that recalls the cultural, emotional, and spiritual disjuncture between Gawain's humiliation and the court's laughter and rejoicing in his triumphal return in the closing moments of *Sir Gawain and the Green Knight*. This is the disparity between a private, inner self and a public, communal, or social one.[3]

Both comparisons with the weeping child, Chaucer's and Malory's, appear at narrative turning points. Absolon's amorous obsessions and their dramatic collapse set in train the crucial turning point in the fabliau plot, and the final scene in which laughter of "the folk" drowns out the carpenter's unheard protestations, while Malory's text will now begin to wind towards its tragic conclusion: the episode closes with an ominous description of the close watch Sir Aggravayne is keeping on Lancelot and Guenevere. This tragic plot will ultimately conclude with another moment of emotional disjunction between individual and community. As his supporters mourn and weep for Lancelot's imminent death, the Bishop "fyl upon a gret laughter" as he sleeps and dreams of Lancelot being received into heaven. When he wakes, he and his company find Lancelot dead. The knight "laye as he had smyled, and the swettest savour about hym that ever they felte. Than was there wepynge and wryngyng of handes, and the grettest dole they made that ever made men" (3.1258).[4] In this case the weeping is collective and worldly, in contrast to Lancelot's spiritual smiling.

Absolon and Lancelot are both on the margins. Absolon has been brutally excluded from the feast of love in Alison's bedroom and Lancelot has escaped public shame by the grace of God. The contrast between comic fabliau plot and spiritual tragic romance could hardly be greater, but when our two men weep, the same phrase is used in both instances. The *Middle English Dictionary* lists both the *Miller's Tale* and the Malory example under *wepen* (j) "in proverbs, prov[erbial] expressions, and conventional comparisons."[5] Whiting, similarly, lists "to weep like a Child" as a proverb, number C223, though only these two instances are included there.[6] But we need to do more, of course, than simply identify the proverbial affiliations of emotional expressions.

In order to build up a thicker, more detailed picture of the late medieval resonance of this comparison, I will turn first to consider the history of similar proverbs and expressions in other medieval texts, including a contested example from *Piers Plowman*, and what may be an influential precedent from Dante's *La Vita Nuova*. Other texts that do not employ this simile directly nevertheless offer powerful and suggestive contexts for reading. Chaucer's Criseyde chastises Troilus' childish jealousy, saying to her lover that he is worthy to be beaten, while in Boccaccio's *Decameron*, Ghismonda offers an authoritative disquisition on the shameful nature of her father's childish tears. I will also consider some later instances of invocations of both the beaten child as well as later commentaries on and translations of the texts by Boccaccio and Malory. The passage of this comparison from the medieval through to the early modern period is far from smooth, suggesting a degree of uneasiness with the simile in later contexts.

Proverbial literature in the medieval period, along with the genre of political or ethical advice and the literature of nurture and training, has been the object of considerable study in recent years, but little attention has been paid to the relationship between emotions and proverbs, or the affective charge of proverbial expressions in medieval literature. An important exception is an essay by Christopher Cannon, who compares the pleasures of recognizing proverbs to the pleasures of recognizing familiar motifs and stories in medieval literature. Cannon aims to "reclaim ... a whole aesthetic, a system of value and modes of enjoyment in which both the work of the proverb and the charm of the play or poem were thought to lie, not in rarity or originality, but in exactly the affection familiarity can breed – in the acts of *recognition* that are produced by the repetition of well-known truths."[7] Cannon sees the wisdom offered by proverbs as a "uniquely *friendly* sort of knowledge," because of its sheer expansiveness. This is the pleasure that literature "borrows" from the proverb. Cannon suggests we redescribe medieval wisdom literature's key attributes of availability and familiarity as "a passionate commitment to *unoriginality*."[8] In relation to the history of emotion, however, in contrast to poems and stories that aim to dramatize individual or collective feeling, the anonymous voice of many proverbs seems to speak *without* emotion, or from a secondary position that comments *on* emotion or feeling, to use the medieval word. Proverbs can be read as snapshots into dominant structures of ethical or emotional wisdom, although as many commentators observe, they can hardly be said to express a consistent worldview. Instead, their "wisdom" is deeply contextual, just as there often seems to be a proverb for every occasion. Formal proverbs ("a stitch in time saves nine"; "slow and steady wins the race") tend to be applied *after* the event, or applied in such a way that seems to provide interpretative closure on events. Chaucer uses a proverb in this way in the *Miller's Tale*, for example, when he wants to explain that Nicholas, living in closer proximity to Alison, has the advantage over Absolon:

> Ful sooth is this proverbe, it is no lye,
> Men seyn right thus: "Alwey the nye slye
> Maketh the ferre leeve to be looth."
> For though that Absolon be wood or wrooth,
> By cause that he fer was from hire sight,
> This nye Nicholas stood in his light.   (I.3391–6)

The proverb sums up the situation; but also generates its own explanatory gloss to form a neat hermeneutic circle. The truth of the proverb and the accuracy of its citation are emphatically affirmed; the proverb is given; and then three further lines develop a detailed contextual gloss. The proverb, here, is hardly an instrument of concision; on the contrary, it is lovingly expanded. The structural economy of its neat rhyme and its conceptual opposition is supplemented by a literal explanation by naming the two characters and affirming that Nicholas is both "nye," and by implication, also "slye." If a narrative context seems to call forth a proverb, a proverb can also generate more narrative detail.

Cannon makes the related point that in spite of their apparent economy, proverbs rarely deliver their wisdom in time: instead, the proverbs at the end of the *Nun's Priest's Tale*, for example, serve to "ameliorate a disaster's aftermath," as "the 'medicine' that could make whoever cited it feel better" (412).

Framed in the present tense and customarily applied to particular circumstances, proverbs seem to contain a kind of doubled temporality. The immediacy of their applicability – their function as *le mot juste* – draws attention to that particular moment in narrative time, although their underlying assumptions also take for granted that emotional and ethical structures and responses are historically stable. This has implications both for the history of emotions and the reception of medieval literary texts.

While Cannon develops the second-order comparisons between literature and proverbs, and the affective pleasures of appealing to what is familiar, my interests are narrower. I am concerned less with formal proverbs, and rather with formulaic or conventional expressions that evoke a normative ethos or shared understanding of emotional or affective response without necessarily conjuring up the genre of anonymous *sententiae*.

The figure of "weeping like a child" appeals as proverbs do to conventional or shared understanding that is often emotional or affective, though in different narrative contexts, those appeals are historically, socially, and culturally variable. We might compare proverbs and figurative expressions like the weeping child to the emotional expressions William Reddy names as "emotional utterances" or "emotives."[9] In Reddy's definition, an emotive is a speech-act that is neither constative nor performative: "an emotional expression is an attempt to call up the emotion that is expressed; it is an attempt to feel what one says one feels."[10]

Reddy is talking about first-person, present-tense emotion claims – "I think I'm in love with you"; "I'm so sorry" – that don't just describe emotions and don't straightforwardly perform them either, but that *do* have an effect on social discourse and on the way we shape and make meaning. As Reddy says, "emotives are similar to performatives (and differ from constatives) in that emotives do things to the world. Emotives are themselves instruments for directly changing, building, hiding, intensifying emotions, instruments that may be more or less successful."[11]

Reddy's emphasis on the productive gaps and slippages in our attempts to say what we feel allows us to consider the broader role that indirect or figurative language may play in the expression and production of emotion, and to recognize that the study of emotions in history involves more than simply naming or categorizing emotions, passions, or sins in medieval English literature as static, constant, and knowable states.

Reddy's work sits behind Sarah McNamer's suggestion that Middle English texts "vigorously enlist *literariness* as a means of generating feelings and putting them into play in history."[12] Literary texts depend fruitfully on ambiguity, displacement, and suggestion, rather than the analytic dissection of feeling or the taxonomic naming of emotions. Conversely, the structures and constraints of poetic form both limit and enable these attempts to feel, say, and feel in sequence. The anonymous character of conventional expressions may be read as an attempt to disguise this uncertainty: there is often a productive tension between a proverb's tendency to closure, and a poem's flirtatious resistance to such certainty.

In my two central examples, one expression of emotional behavior (a weeping man) is compared with another (a child weeping after being beaten). This simile attempts to tie exceptional narrative cases to ordinary, everyday situations. The whole point of the proverbial simile is to *explain* emotional behavior by rendering it recognizable and familiar, though in both cases the narrative context makes it clear that this behavior is exceptional: a provocation to laughter in the case of Absolon; and to pity, in the case of Lancelot. These texts thus offer an instructive interplay between what is "ordinary" or everyday, and what is deemed worthy of emotional or affective narrative representation. While the proverbial expression does not function like an "emotive" in any direct sense, it similarly draws attention to the active role of language in shaping both feeling, and the representation of feeling.

The textual and reception history of medieval literature adds a further layer of complexity that is instructive for the history of feeling and emotion. One of the most problematic and indicative examples of proverbial uncertainty – using another simile structured around a weeping child – comes from *Piers Plowman*.[13] Langland's Holy Church addresses the dreamer, Will, admonishing him that faithful and honest deeds need to be matched by *caritas*:

> For though ye be trewe of youre tonge and treweliche wynne,
> And as chaste as a child that in chirche wepeth,
> But if ye love leelly and lene the povere
> Of swich good as God sent goodliche parteth,
> Ye ne have na moore merite in Masse ne in houres
> Than Malkyn of hire maydenhede, that no man desireth.   (B.1.179–84)

Formally, Langland's example is of a slightly different order than the examples from Chaucer and Malory, as the comparison is not in the manner of weeping (and nor has this child been beaten), but between the chastity of the virtuous adult and that of the "chaste" child. The expression is all the more striking in Langland's poem as an episode in emotional history, however, in that it disappears in the C-revision, whether through Langland's uncertainty about its effect, or his distrust of figurative language, or perhaps even the distracting tug of this emotional expression. The modern commentary tradition disagrees on the nature of the child's crying here. Is this a baby crying in pain or hunger, or a pious older child who weeps in sympathy with Christ's sorrow, or in shame for his or her own sins and misdemeanors? Indeed, for all the affective charge of the image of the weeping child, it is worth noting that all three examples (from Chaucer, Malory, and Langland) tell us virtually nothing about the nature of this weeping or how old the putative child might be, or in the case of the beaten child, whether his (or her) tears are accompanied by yells of pain *during* the beating, or are muffled sobs of self-pity in the recovery *after* the beating.[14]

This example from *Piers Plowman* reminds us to acknowledge the physical and material instability – the textual *mouvance* – of medieval texts, and the factors that reproduce and shape our modern editions. Where there is such fluid variability of versions, such a process of making and unmaking, emotional responses inevitably play a role in our judgments about authorial and scribal composition and revision, in the multitude of competing readings. In contrast, proverbs tend to be collected out of context, presented and indexed in very different conceptual taxonomies, where differences and variations in phrasing are subordinated to dominant forms.

Editorial and critical interventions also play a crucial shaping role in our understanding of proverbial expressions in literary texts. Tellingly, Eugène Vinaver inserted an exclamation mark after the comparison of Lancelot weeping like a beaten child in his magisterial and influential three-volume edition in 1947.[15] This may well reflect the surprise of the post-war scholar at what may have seemed like a particularly dramatic form of masculine emotional display. It certainly helps create a sense of readerly astonishment. Of course, no such mark appears in either the Winchester manuscript or Caxton's edition. Other editors do not add the exclamation mark, but Vinaver's punctuation has undoubtedly influenced thousands of readers in the many editions and selections based on his edition to find Lancelot's tears exceptional and to make this moment memorable and the subject of critical commentary in a way that Absolon's tears are not. When comparisons *are* drawn between the two texts, the simile is described as "proverbial," but there is an interesting slippage in both the *MED* and Whiting, for example, between the form of the proverb and the idea of a "proverbial expression." In the case of "weeping like a child who has been beaten," the form is strictly that of a simile, not a proverb. These two examples, moreover, are the only ones listed in both collections: a very small hermeneutic circle of just two examples. As far as I am aware, no one has suggested that Malory was borrowing from Chaucer; it is easier to suggest they draw equally on a proverbial association or expression in English or from literary sources in other languages.

The simile works by abstracting a comparison from one situation to another, drawing a parallel between two disparate figures: the grown man and the beaten child. Significantly, too, it trails some strong associations with a number of formal proverbs, especially those that feature children; and this may sit behind its association with the proverb genre. A well-attested proverb is categorized in Whiting's collection as "Better is a Child unborn than unbeaten."[16] Some of the recorded variants have "untaught" or "unchastised" instead of "unbeaten," but there is a consistent pattern that normalizes the chastised or beaten child who is thus brought under patriarchal discipline that is culturally sanctioned. It is a sentiment attested in Proverbs 13:24: *Qui parcit virgae, odit filium suum; qui autem diligit illum, instanter erudit*, and appearing in *Piers Plowman* in the form "Who so spareth the sprynge, spilleth his children" (B V 41). (Incidentally, given changing modern attitudes to corporal punishment, this example draws attention to the risks of interpreting proverbs as timelessly appropriate or appealing to universal or timeless human emotions.)

Another proverb is less well attested, but similarly affirms the natural affinity between children and tears: "Better a young Child weep than an old man."[17] In these examples we witness the normative function of proverbs: their direct or indirect statements about ideal and proper behavior that also perform important work in the construction of gender.

This generalizing function of proverbs and the expressions and similes that draw on them is problematic for the history of tears and weeping. Some of these assumptions, that tears belong to children (and women) but not to adult males, are demonstrably historically variable. The history of men's tears is especially marked by vicissitudes and changes in social and cultural sensibility, changes that are potentially problematic in the reading of medieval literature, as many students encountering Troilus' helpless and lovelorn tears for the first time, as he flings himself on to his bed, will attest.[18]

Troilus' tears, and the comparison of a grown man with a beaten, weeping child have an important precedent in Dante's *La Vita Nuova*, whose lover similarly retreats from the crowd after seeing Beatrice, and finds a lonely place in which to weep:

> E poi che alquanto mi fue sollenato questo lagrimare, misimi ne la mia camera, la ov'io potea lamentarmi sanza essere udito; e quivi, chiamando misericordia a la donna de la cortesia, e dicendo
> "Amore, aiuta lo tuo fedele", m'addormentai come un pargoletto battuto lagrimando.[19]

> And after that weeping of mine had calmed down a little, I shut myself in my room, where I could lament without being heard: and there, calling for mercy from the lady of courtesy and saying, "Love, aid your devotee," I fell asleep in tears like a little boy who had been beaten.[20] (XII)

The lover weeps in grief, but he is beaten in every sense, forced into seclusion and reduced to begging and tears, infantilized, weeping and falling asleep. The agent of this subjection is the beloved woman.

Such agency, I argue, is far from incidental to the force of this proverbial simile or comparison. As we probe deeper into the narrative uses of this simile in medieval literature, we will find that sexualized female authority often sits behind its usage.

There is another suggestive context for the comparison of the lover with the beaten child in Chaucer's *Troilus and Criseyde*. After Pandarus has made Troilus concoct a story about being jealous of Horaste, to force the midnight encounter between the lovers, Criseyde chastises his childish folly:

> "... Swiche argumentes ne ben naught worth a beene.
> Wol ye the childissh jalous contrefete?
> Now were it worthi that ye were ybete." (II.1167–9)

This encounter delicately evokes a more experienced Criseyde threatening to discipline the childishly jealous Troilus (as she thinks him). This adds an awkward dimension to the uneven and changing relationships of courtly intimacy between medieval lovers, in which beloved women can exercise a form of sovereignty that infantilizes the lover. We note, too, the customary association of children being beaten as a good thing ("Now were it worthi"), though twelve lines later Criseyde is asking his forgiveness "that I have don yow smerte" (III.1182), a gesture that surprises Troilus and gives him the confidence to take her in his arms. Troilus does not weep in this passage but the idea of the youthful or childish lover weeping and/or being beaten, where the agency of that beating is the sexualized woman, may also sit behind Absolon's lover's folly, though as we will see shortly, the comparison is not straightforward.

It is not only lovers who weep in medieval literature, of course; and medieval weeping does not always infantilize, or feminize, the weeper. In the *Chanson de Roland*, when Charlemagne hears of the death of Roland, he falls to the ground in a faint: twenty thousand faint with him; and at another point, one hundred thousand knights weep. Such moments put tremendous pressure on any straightforward appeals to the continuity of emotion and its expression across time, or the realism of fictional representation of emotion. As Dorothy L. Sayers commented in the introduction to her translation of the poem in 1957, people express emotions differently in the modern era: "The idea that a strong man should react to great personal and national calamities by a slight compression of the lips and by silently throwing his cigarette into the fireplace is of very recent origin."[21] From the perspective of the twenty-first century, her example proves the point twice over, since it is itself now so dated. Indeed, it comes from an era much closer to the time when Vinaver inserted that exclamation point after Lancelot's weeping.

We may now return to my two chief examples, from Chaucer and Malory, with a sense of the complexity of this image and its cultural, rhetorical, and affective resonance. While proverbial forms – proverbs, similes, metaphors, and sayings – seem to normalize behavior, to reduce differences to types, nevertheless Chaucer and Malory both use this simile in what I can only describe as "literary" ways to develop the characters of Absolon and Lancelot; indeed, both mark a transition in the psychological narrative of each character. Even though the plot trajectories are startlingly different, in each case the dramatic simile of the child suggests they weep in part through loss of innocence, whether that loss is immediate (in Absolon's case) or of long standing (in Lancelot's). That is, neither man is any longer a child, even though he weeps like one. The simile works, then, almost counter-intuitively.

Absolon's case is particularly dramatic, as the story stages a traumatic transition from his childish love-longing, and his "jolyf," gay, and "myrie" demeanor. From the beginning, the parish clerk is portrayed as somewhat childish: a bit like Da Ponte's Cherubino in Mozart's *The Marriage of Figaro*, in love with love, with "swich a love-longynge" in his heart. (Absolon is also dressed like the young Squire of the General Prologue, in tight-fitting clothes.) Chaucer uses the word *joly*, or *jolyf*, four times in his initial description, as well as words like *gay*. Absolon's generalized *love-longynge* makes him woeful, but he is again consistently described as *merry* in his love-making: "A *myrie* child he was, so God me save." And he is often described as *at play*. When he returns from Oseneye and finds John the carpenter is missing, he is "joly and light" (3671), and again "joly" at line 3688 and "gay" in the following line.

All this childlike playfulness disappears after the fateful kiss, when he "gooth forth a sory pas" (3741). His merriment turns to anger and immediately "his hoote love was coold and al yqueynt" (3754). Chaucer is using the humoral language of passions, here, as well, perhaps, as the embedded pun on Alison's genitals. There is another important social transformation, too. Instead of his great courtesy to all women (at church, he will not accept any offerings from them "for curteisie"), he becomes socially dysfunctional; and can hardly speak to the smith: he "ne roghte nat a bene / Of al his pley; no word agayn he yaf" (3772–3).

Absolon's weeping, then, comes at a dramatic moment of turnaround, as he has been reduced from carefree joy and play to sudden humiliation. For Thomas Ross, indeed, "This infantile reaction is Absolon's low point."[22] Earlier, using a self-infantilizing emotive, he describes his own love-longing for Alisoun: "I moorne as dooth a lamb after the tete" (3704). All this language disappears after the fateful kiss; his general courtliness to women is replaced by silent, surly anger. In addition to the great confusion about body parts and orifices,[23] and the dashing of his romantic expectations, this also seems the moment when Absolon suddenly grows up. No longer can he represent himself to himself as a child but must now recognize that there is a world of adult sexuality and intercourse from which he is excluded, not as a child but as an unsuccessful rival: he knows John the carpenter is away and it is quite clear that there is someone else in the bedroom with Alison.

In his angry revenge, Absolon's shift into adult sexuality will take the form of a violent anal rape when he approaches the window a second time with his burning hot poker. His trauma is undeniable. Where previously he had had an itchy mouth and interpreted that as a proverbial sign of the kissing to come, now he fulfills his own prophecy as he takes to his own lips in iambic fury:

> Who rubbeth now, who frotheth now his lippes
> With dust, with sond, with straw, with clooth, with chippes.
> ... (3747–8)
>
> His hoote love was coold and al yqueynt;
> For fro that tyme that he hadde kist hir ers,
> Of paramours he sette nat a kers,
> For he was heeled of his maladie.
> Ful ofte paramours he gan deffie,
> And weep as dooth a child that is ybete. (3754–9)

When we set this against the passage from *Troilus and Criseyde*, in which Criseyde threatens to beat Troilus like a child, it is hard not to hear in Absolon's tears the suggestion of a female agent. After all, if a child has been beaten it has been beaten by someone. In this case, it looks as if *paramours* in general, the entire female sex, with its confusing orifices and duplicitous behavior, has done the metaphorical beating. Absolon then seeks out his own rod – the "hot cultour" – with which he takes his revenge. As in the example from *Troilus*, there is an uncomfortable, barely concealed suggestion that maternal authority and the female beloved's sovereignty are structured in similar ways: both are able to "beat" the childish lover. I will return to this point shortly.

In contrast, Lancelot is not associated at all with childhood. He embodies the ideal qualities of chivalric knighthood, and is the leading knight of Arthur's Round Table, but will also be the agent of its collapse. The *Tale of Sir Urry* draws attention to his position. Conscious of his failure in the Grail quest – the new spiritual order and revisionary chivalric hierarchy – as a result of his continued love affair with the queen, Lancelot is reluctant to put himself forward to attempt to heal the wounded knight, fearing pride, perhaps, or indeed, the possibility of humiliation. He is not at court when Sir Urry first arrives, and it is as if Arthur actually summons him into existence: "'Mercy Jesu!' seyde kynge Arthur, 'where ys sir Launcelot du Lake, that he ys nat here at thys tyme?'" Whereupon, "as they stood and spake of many thyngis," Lancelot is seen riding towards them (1150–1).

Arthur tells Lancelot he must try where all have failed. Lancelot demurs, but Arthur insists. "'Ye shall nat chose,' seyde kynge Arthur, 'for I commaunde you to do as we all have done.'" Still, Lancelot asks to be excused, but Arthur insists he make the attempt "to beare us felyshyp, insomuche as ye be a felow of the Rounde Table" (1151). The structure of authority here is irresistible, and Lancelot kneels beside the wounded knight.

It is curious that Lancelot's body language and gesture should now resemble those of Absolon. We recall that the architecture of the carpenter's house and its low window onto the street is described in detail: to solicit Alison's kiss, Absolon must stand *under* the window, and then kneel down in order to receive it,

> This Absolon doun sette hym on his knees
> And seyde, "I am a lord at alle degrees;
> For after this I hope ther cometh moore..." (3723–5)

The idea of this childish dancing and singing clerk seeing himself as a lord is an important part of the humiliation that will follow – from a grown-up lord he will be reduced to a crying child – but he is physically positioned on his knees, just before commencing his weeping.

So too is Lancelot on his knees, kneeling down to search the wounds of Sir Urry. A golden cushion has been placed by the side of the litter, and first King Arthur, and then the other knights, and finally Lancelot have knelt down to "serche" the wounds. Of course he kneels on the same cushion as the others, and he kneels in fellowship with them, but he kneels at Arthur's command, in the position of subjection. As Lancelot kneels, he prays he may heal Urry's wounds through the power of the Trinity, beseeching God to save his reputation, that "my symple worshyp and honesté be saved" (1152).

The wounds heal miraculously, and all kneel with Lancelot and give thanks and praise to God. But where the others kneel in joy and devotion, "ever sir Lancelote wepte, as he had bene a chylde that had bene beatyn" (1152). The episode, then, is not one of social integration. Arthur calls Urry to joust with them and they joust to win a diamond, "but there justed none of the daungerous knyghtes" (1153). The episode ends with the falling in love and the eventual wedding of Urry with Lavayn's sister, Fyleloly, but we hear no more of Lancelot that day.

The scene is not fully resolved, and has been read differently in the medievalist tradition. T. H. White's Lancelot, in *The Ill-Made Knight* (first published in 1940) contemplates hanging himself in the stables rather than facing the public humiliation of failure. White asks us to imagine his feelings. "The people outside are waiting for you to do this miracle because you have traded on their belief that your heart was pure – and now, with treachery and adultery and murder wringing the heart like a cloth, you are to go out into the sunlight for the test of honour."[24] In contrast, in the film *Camelot* (1967, directed by Joshua Logan), it is Lancelot who wounds Sir Dinadan, one of the queen's three champions, whom she hopes will defeat the proud newcomer. Lancelot begs the knight to live, "Please, please live, live, live, please, I beg you. Live, live, live, live." As the knight begins to breathe, Lancelot and Guenevere gaze at each other, both their faces tear-stained. It is clear that this is the moment their enmity turns to love. The scene is thus heavily secularized, without the Grail background or any Christian prayer. As in Malory, though, it reveals Lancelot's social isolation. As the court moves off, he remains kneeling, overcome, as if now anticipating the trauma this revelation of love will set in train. Through the encounter with Guenevere, Lancelot is already fallen and flawed. He has already been "beaten" by the queen long ago.

Earl Anderson describes the scene in Malory as a *tableau*, like a Freudian "primal scene" that is re-processed and re-interpreted over and over again, in an attempt to resolve an unresolvable trauma.[25] Anderson offers a powerful psychoanalytic reading of Malory's comparison of Lancelot with the beaten child, making a suggestive comparison with Absolon, too. Anderson emphasizes the psychological (Oedipal) law of the father (Arthur) as the authority figure here. He sets aside critical attempts to isolate and explain the emotion that might be signified by Lancelot's tears; and instead follows a Lacanian line of inquiry to argue that his weeping is best seen rather not as a representation to be decoded but "a *signifier* which has no explicable 'meaning' but which points to another signifier in a (potentially open-ended) chain of signifiers that are motivated by (inaccessible) knowledge in the Unconscious."[26] For Anderson, Lancelot's weeping signifies the weeping of the child being beaten, which signifies the image of Sir Urry being beaten in the original tournament, which signifies a masochistic sexual fantasy around the authority of King Arthur, and so forth.

Anderson also cites Freud's frequent records of patients who would say "a child is being beaten," "*ein Kind wird geschlagen*," as a way of displacing their unconscious fantasy of being beaten by their father (or being sexually penetrated by the father). Anderson invokes the *Miller's Tale* here as evidence, in the transition of Absolon from beaten child to sadomasochist subject, as he "achieves the sodomitic deflowering and rape of 'hende Nicholas.'"[27] At the same time, while I acknowledge the force of Anderson's reading, the historical – and proverbial – context of beaten children returns us to the role of women in medieval literature as agents of authority and discipline, and indeed, as adjudicators of male weeping.

The simile about the beaten child is often interpreted in the context of the medieval schoolroom, but the example of Criseyde reminds us that a mother can also be a disciplinary figure. The context might equally be female, domestic, and maternal: a child before he goes to school (or possibly even a girl child). Philip Sidney plays on this idea of female authority in *Astrophil and Stella*, in which Astrophil writes of himself, or of Love, as schoolboys under the "rod" of Stella, or of a mother (Sonnet 73).[28] Perhaps most tellingly, though, the authoritative figure who beats the poet in the opening sonnet is allegorized and feminized as "step-dame study." Such an image naturalizes the idea of the woman with power to enforce discipline. Certainly, Langland's female Studye does not want for authority, either over her husband Wit or the dreamer himself (B.X.). Lynn Enterline has also explored the "erotic wit associated with school flogging" in early modern writing, and "the considerable emotional and libidinal complexity of grammar school training."[29] Medieval narrative texts seem similarly conscious of the erotic resonances of this simile, and its dramatic force in describing an adult male.

It is true that women in the Middle Ages are most closely associated with weeping, either through their humoral inability to control it, or through their untrustworthy capacity to produce tears at will. These are standard features of anti-feminist discourse, from Theophrastus through to *Le Roman de la Rose*, as the Wife of Bath is aware:

> Deceite, weping, spynnyng God hath yive
> To wommen kyndely, whil that they may lyve.   (III.401–2)

Many other medieval texts firmly encode involuntary male weeping as feminized. In the alliterative *Morte Arthure*, for example, Sir Ewain and other lords are briskly dismissive of Arthur's tears over the death of Sir Gawain. Arthur has covered the dead body with kisses until his own face is as bloody as if he had been hunting, but his lords speak with one voice:

> "Blinn," says these bold men, "thou blunders thyselven!
> This is bootless bale, for better bes it never!
> It is no worship, iwis, to wring thine handes;
> To weep als a woman it is no wit holden!

> Be knightly of countenaunce, als a king sholde,
> And leve such clamour, for Cristes love of heven!"³⁰

This is the most common judgment of men's tears in the medieval period: that it renders them womanish and weak. The critique is made most forcefully and most damningly by a female character in Boccaccio's *Decameron*, my final medieval example. Fiammetta narrates the first novella of the fourth day, about Tancredi and his daughter Ghismonda, a young widow whom her father refuses to provide with a second husband. Ghismonda carefully chooses a lover for his excellent personal qualities, but her father spies on them, hiding under a blanket while they make love in her chamber. Tancredi takes the young man prisoner and then confronts his daughter. Having berated her for her sin, and expressed his conflicted emotions, torn between his great love for her and his indignation ("*sdegno*") "he bowed his head and cried like a child who's been well spanked," *come farebbe un fanciul ben battuto.*³¹

But Ghismonda is scornful. In a passionate defense of her rational choice, and the virtues of her lover (in spite of his poverty and low position), she defies her father, and in effect dares him to mete out the same punishment to his daughter as he will to her lover:

> "Or via, va con le femine a spander le lagrime, e incrudulendo, con un medesimo colpo, se cosí ti par che meritato abbiamo, uccidi."

> "Now go, shed your tears with women, and if you must be cruel, if you feel we deserve death, then kill both of us with one blow!"³²

Tancredi rises to this challenge and sends his daughter the heart of her lover in a gold cup. Ghismonda pours poison over it and weeps copious tears as she prepares with great eloquence and composure to die. Unlike her father's tears of indecision, these are presented as a wonderful flow of tears without any unbecoming female noise (*senza fare alcun feminil romore*).

As she is dying, her father comes to her once more and begins to weep again, *dolorosamente*. Ghismonda rebukes him again for weeping at the fulfillment of his own plan:

> "Tancredi, serbati coteste lagrime a meno disiderata fortuna che questa, né a me le dare, che non le disidero. Chi vide mai alcuno altro che te, piagnere di quello che egli ha voluto?"

> "Tancredi, save those tears for a less fortunate fate than this, and do not shed them on my account, for I do not want them. Who ever heard of someone weeping over what he himself wished for?"³³

Fiammetta is very precise about these tears, and codes them authoritatively as either improper, when Tancredi weeps at the consequences of his own actions, or proper, when they accompany true and genuine mourning for a lost love. There is nothing casual about Fiammetta's comparison of the father's tears with those of a beaten child, or Ghismonda's dismissal of those tears as womanly.

As we saw above, the comparison of a grown man with a weeping child does not appear in Middle English before Chaucer's *Miller's Tale*: it is possible he drew this from the examples of Dante or Boccaccio, and that the proverbial associations also extend into the Italian tradition. Interestingly, Boccaccio's careful hierarchy of attitudes to male and female tears is all but obscured in the several English translations which draw variously on the French and Latin versions of the *Decameron*. In one Middle English version the father weeps like "a yong infaunt sore scorgyd or bete" (597),[34] but the daughter does not condemn his weeping. In another translation, Gilbert Banester omits the father's weeping like a beaten child when he first confronts his daughter, but displaces and modifies the simile when the father comes to visit his dying daughter: "Wepyng as a child and wrang hys handys fast" (524).[35]

Later, when Dryden comes to translate the story, in the first encounter he contrasts the father's weeping with the daughter's strength. Ghismonda says "Away, with Women weep, and leave me here, / Fix'd, like a Man to die, without a tear."[36] However, she then weeps herself, though in a controlled and unfeminine way, in a becoming silence that echoes Boccaccio's understanding that women's tears are best when they are unfeminine, "free from female noise":

> She said: Her brim-full Eyes, that ready stood,
> And only wanted Will to weep a Flood,
> Releas'd their watry Store, and pour'd amain,
> Like Clouds low hung, a sober Show'r of Rain;
> Mute solemn Sorrow, free from Female Noise,
> Such as the Majesty of Grief destroys.[37]

From this quick survey of the story's history and later versions, it is clear that the representation of tears and weeping in medieval literature is part of a complex network of proverbial feeling, translation, genre instability and gender anxiety, across the medieval period and beyond. It should occasion no surprise that medieval literary texts and their reception disclose a range of responses and feelings about men who cry. This is only partly a function of the changing history of men's tears: there do not seem to be vast differences between medieval and early modern weeping. It is rather that medieval tears themselves can be coded in such a variety of ways, from penitence and the traditions of affective meditation, to large-scale public grief, or the tears of shame and humiliation (though in very different contexts) wept by Absolon and Lancelot. And, as the example of Ghismonda's scathing criticism of her father in the *Decameron* makes powerfully clear, masculine tears that are perceived as childish run the risk of ridicule and condemnation, and such condemnation may well come from women, or at least, from female characters.

This broader context and the sexual politics of this critique are not evident from an analysis of the proverbial tradition alone. The characteristic speaking voice of the proverb is neither personal nor emotional. It is only when those proverbs and proverbial similes are put to work in the highly emotional contexts we have been considering that we can start to analyze the emotional work they perform in medieval literature and begin to unpack the instability of a form that is often collected and presented as if it carries its own authority.

As we have seen, the image of crying like a child becomes somewhat unstable in the textual tradition, whether in the process of authorial revision (the case of Langland) or that of translation (in the English reception of Boccaccio), or later editorial practice (in Vinaver's exclamation mark). Even when it appears relatively stable, in my examples from Chaucer and Malory, its use in such divergent genres to explain such radically different emotional behavior means that neither text can function as a straightforward guide to the other, any more than the explanation of an expression as "proverbial" can fully account for its meaning in the literary text.

Moreover, in our survey of related images of adult men weeping like beaten children, we have been led at every turn to think about the relationship between men and women, whether they are figured as mothers, lovers, daughters, or teachers, leaving us to speculate about the implicit structures of female authority (whether that may be maternal or sexual) that the texts do not, or cannot foreground.

Proverbial or familiar expressions like *weeping like a child*, then, cannot be read as simple declarative or constative witnesses to the history of emotion and its lexicon: they need to be read both contextually and historically. Just as direct expressions of named emotions *do* things in the world, as William Reddy says, so too do emotional gestures like weeping, and so too do literary texts.

Notes

1. Sir Thomas Malory, *The Works*, ed. Eugène Vinaver and P. J. C. Field, 3 vols. (Oxford: Oxford University Press, 1990), vol. 3, 1152. Further in-text citations will be from this edition.
2. Geoffrey Chaucer, *The Miller's Tale*, in *The Riverside Chaucer*, ed. Larry D. Benson, 3rd edn (Boston, MA: Houghton Mifflin Co., 1987), I.3754–9.
3. Andrew Lynch comments in *Malory's Book of Arms: The Narrative of Combat in "Le Morte Darthur"* (Cambridge: D. S. Brewer, 1997): "It offers an instance of a potential split in Malorian identity between a knight's self-consciousness and the objective proof of his worship in the eyes of others" (6).
4. My thanks to Tony Edwards for helping me see this pattern.
5. Robert E. Lewis et al., eds., *Middle English Dictionary* (Ann Arbor, MI: University of Michigan Press, 2001), 1a (j). Hereafter cited as *MED*.
6. See Bartlett Jere Whiting with Helen Wescott Whiting, *Proverbs, Sentences, and Proverbial Phrases from English Writings Mainly before 1500* (Cambridge, MA: Harvard University Press, 1968), 83.
7. Christopher Cannon, "Proverbs and the Wisdom of Literature: *The Proverbs of Alfred* and Chaucer's *Tale of Melibee*," *Textual Practice* 24,3 (2010), 408.
8. Ibid., 425, 426. Cannon also tracks the emotional responses both to selected proverbs and the particular deployment of them in social and narrative contexts. He draws attention to the fact that in Chaucer's *Melibee*, for example, "*fewer* proverbs are actually more helpful in turning Melibee away from error than *many* proverbs ... As always, but here with an emphasis constituted by almost the whole of this narrative, proverbial wisdom is shown to be effectively useless" (423). For Cannon, then, the "consequences" of proverbial expressions are best seen as "emotional rather than cognitive" (424).
9. William M. Reddy, *The Navigation of Feeling: A Framework for the History of Emotions* (Cambridge: Cambridge University Press, 2001), 105–9.
10. Jan Plamper, William Reddy, Barbara Rosenwein, and Peter Stearns, "The History of Emotions: An Interview with William Reddy, Barbara Rosenwein, and Peter Stearns," *History and Theory* 49,2 (May 2010), 240. See also Reddy, *Navigation of Feeling*, 105.
11. Reddy, *Navigation of Feeling*, 105.
12. Sarah McNamer, "Feeling," in *Middle English: Oxford Twenty-First Century Approaches to Literature*, ed. Paul Strohm (Oxford: Oxford University Press, 2009), 246.
13. *William Langland's the Vision of Piers Plowman: A Critical Edition of the B-Text Based on Trinity College Cambridge MS, B.15.17*, ed. A. V. C. Schmidt (London: Everyman, 1995). All further in-text citations in parentheses will be from this edition.
14. For a fuller discussion of this passage, see my essay, "Langland's Tears: Poetry, Emotion, and Mouvance," *Yearbook of Langland Studies* 26 (2012): 27–48.
15. Malory, *Works*, ed. Vinaver and Field, vol. 3, 1152.
16. Whiting and Whiting, *Proverbs, Sentences, and Proverbial Phrases*, 81 (C200).

17. Ibid., 81 (C199).
18. Mary Carruthers, "On Affliction and Reading, Weeping and Argument: Chaucer's Lachrymose Troilus in Context," *Representations* 93,1 (2006): 1–21 (11–12).
19. Dante Alighieri, *The New Life/La Vita Nuova*, ed. and trans. Stanley Appelbaum (Mineola, NY: Dover, 2006), 19.
20. Ibid., 18.
21. *The Song of Roland*, ed. Dorothy L. Sayers (Harmondsworth: Penguin, 1957), 15.
22. Thomas W. Ross in Geoffrey Chaucer, *The Miller's Tale: A Variorum Edition of the Works of Geoffrey Chaucer*, Vol. 2: *The Canterbury Tales*, Part 2, ed. Ross (Norman, OK: University of Oklahoma Press, 1983), 232.
23. Louise Bishop, "'Of Goddes pryvetee nor of his wyf,': Confusion of Orifices in Chaucer's Miller's Tale," *Texas Studies in Language and Literature* 44,3 (2002): 231–46.
24. T. H. White, *The Once and Future King* (1958; London: Harper Collins, 1996), 554–5. *The Ill-Made Knight* novel was first collected with the others in this series under the generic title in 1958. In a review of the novel, Olive B. White writes of Lancelot, "His is the human dignity and agony of self-knowledge. The violence of our day is recapturing one honesty at least for literature: as in Homer and Virgil, Dante and Shakespeare, a strong man may weep and be the more honorable and manly for his tears." "The Ill-Made Knight," *Commonweal* 33,9 (December 20, 1940), 235.
25. Earl R. Anderson, "'Ein Kind wird geschlagen': The Meaning of Malory's Tale of the Healing of Sir Urry," *Literature and Psychology* 49,3 (2003): 45–74.
26. Ibid., 46.
27. Ibid., 53.
28. Sir Philip Sidney, *The Major Works*, ed. Catherine Duncan-Jones (Oxford: Oxford University Press, 2009), 153.
29. Lynn Enterline, *Shakespeare's Schoolroom: Rhetoric, Discipline, Emotion* (Philadelphia, PA: University of Pennsylvania Press, 2012), 50, 60.
30. Larry D. Benson, ed., *King Arthur's Death: The Middle English Stanzaic Morte Arthur and Alliterative Morte Arthure* (Kalamazoo, MI: TEAMS Medieval Institute Publications, 1994), ll. 3975–80.
31. Giovanni Boccaccio and Vittore Branca (1900), *Tutte le Opere*, Classici Mondadori, Vol. 4 (Milan: Mondadori, 1964–1992), 362.
32. Giovanni Boccaccio, *The Decameron*, trans. Mark Musa and Peter E. Bondanella (New York: Norton, 1982), 256.
33. Ibid., 258.
34. Giovanni Boccaccio, *Early English Versions of the Tales of Guiscardo and Ghismonda and Titus and Gisippus from the Decameron*, ed. Herbert G. Wright, EETS o.s. 205 (London: Oxford University Press, 1937), 72. This version is preserved in MS R.3.19 at Trinity College, Cambridge, and is very similar to the *Statelie Tragedy of Guistard and Sismon* printed in 1597.

35. Banester, in Boccaccio, *Early English Versions*, ed. Wright, 33. This version is preserved in two manuscripts: BL Addit. 12524 and Bodl. Rawlinson C. 86.
36. John Dryden, "Sigismonda and Guiscardo," in *The Poems*, Vol. 4, ed. James Kinsley (Oxford: Clarendon Press, 1958), ll. 578–9.
37. Ibid., ll. 681–6.

CHAPTER 2

Imagining Jewish Affect in the Siege of Jerusalem
Patricia DeMarco

Written in the last quarter of the fourteenth century, the alliterative poem the *Siege of Jerusalem* tells the story of the conquest of Jerusalem in AD 70 by the Roman leader Waspasian and his son, Titus, who seek, as newly converted Christians, to avenge Christ's death by conquering Jerusalem, destroying the temple, and expelling the Jews from the city. In the Prologue to the *Siege of Jerusalem*, the poet describes the violence done to Christ during the events known collectively as the "Passion":

> A pyler pyght was doun upon the playn erthe,
> His body bonden thereto, and beten with scourgis.
> Whyppes of quyrboyle by-wente His white sides
> Til He al on rede blode ran, as rayn in the strete.

> ***

> Suth stoked Hym on a stole with styf mannes hondis,
> Blyndfelled Hym as a be and boffetis Hym raghte:
> "Gif thou be prophete of pris, prophecie!" they sayde,
> "Whiche berne here aboute bolled Thee laste?"

> ***

> A thrange thornen croune was thraste on His hed,
> Unbecasten Hym with a cry and on a Croys slowen.[1]

Beholding such scenes, late medieval readers were expected to feel – and indeed were guided by writers and artists to feel – powerful emotions.[2] But if graphic depictions of the Crucifixion could be sure to elicit strong emotion, which emotions were evoked – and which subject positions readers were thereby called to inhabit – depended much on context, genre, and audience.[3] Even an apparently simple emotion – compassion – was variously and complexly determined. For instance, devotional literature testifies to complexly differentiated religious postures, especially in the ways in which a reader/viewer imaginatively beholds Christ's suffering. In her recent and provocative book, Sarah McNamer has argued that the earliest meditational texts encouraging compassionate identification were written for (and possibly by) women, who were led through cultural scripts of perception to engage in a "protective and ameliorative action of beholding" Christ's suffering.[4] By contrast, many Franciscan texts register significant ambivalence about men as subjects directly beholding Christ's suffering, and they tend to afford their male readers a more mediated and distant relation to the suffering body of Christ.[5] Examining a range of texts, McNamer identifies a consistent tendency to "arrest rather than foster feeling," and to cultivate a more stoic disposition for its male readers.[6]

A similar ambivalence about masculine vulnerability to bodily pain and emotional distress can be discerned in the literary narrative that is the subject of this essay, the *Siege of Jerusalem*. The *Siege* narrative, although focused primarily on the Roman military campaign against Judea, represents the crucifixion of Christ at several critical junctures, and visualizations of this event – both literal and imaginative – work to inspire the conversion of Romans to Christianity and to spur the newly converted to take up a holy war against the Jews of Jerusalem some forty years after Jesus' death. Despite its critical function, visualization of Christ's suffering is carefully delimited. The poem confines acts of direct, empathetic beholding to women such as Veronica and to clerics who inhabit an anomalous gender position.[7] While the *Siege* avoids representing secular male characters directly beholding Christ's Passion, it does not, however, cultivate a stoic disposition, as McNamer's account might be taken to predict. Instead in characters such as Waspasian and Titus, the *Siege* models an aristocratic masculine *habitus* centered on the careful management of affect. As this essay will show, the poem suggests that normative aristocratic masculinity entails both the vigilant regulation of sorrowful, compassionate feelings and the continual cultivation/incitement of anger at the indignities suffered by Christ. While most of the *Siege* narrative is devoted to depicting the conduct of its Roman Christian protagonists, the poem also offers remarkably detailed portraits of Jewish suffering and affective response.[8] Perhaps the most important scene thematically – and certainly the most gruesome – is the crucifixion of the Jewish leader, Caiaphas, alongside his two clerks. With its graphically detailed portrait of their physical torments, the scene could conceivably work to elicit sympathy for Jewish suffering. But, as Roger Nicholson has persuasively argued, the poem's emphasis on the non-redemptive character of Jewish suffering not only tends to affirm an anti-Jewish ideology of Christian supercession, it also advances an anti-Semitic view of Jews as "refuse and pollution," casting them as a people who are "doomed to carnality and ruin."[9] Central to this dynamic, Nicholson argues, is the depiction of Caiaphas' suffering on the cross as "nothing but suffering itself," while Christ's bodily suffering is celebrated as a sacrificial act that enables a redemptive transcendence.

Where Nicholson reads the ambivalence attending the *Siege*'s depiction of carnality with recourse to a psychoanalytic account of subject formation, I will attempt to locate the ambivalent depiction of affect within the currents of late medieval philosophy and theology and what is sometimes referred to as faculty psychology. By mapping the ways in which emotion is felt – through and as acts of perception, cognitive discernment, and will – we can better appreciate how the poem works to position Jewish and Christian characters in relation to their own bodily suffering as well as the suffering they behold in others. Where Jews are cast as incapable of governing their sense appetites and are consistently overwhelmed by the distress they feel as beholders/sufferers of violence, Christians are distinguished by their ability both to contain the passions of the sensitive soul (specifically the paired emotions, pleasure and distress) and to cultivate the irascible emotion, anger. This binary is complicated, however, by the poet's presentation of his Christian protagonist's capacity to feel pity, an emotion understood in the late Middle Ages to be aroused "by the suffering, distress and grief" felt in respect to another.[10] Although a sharp division between the affective disposition of Jew and Christian is something the poem works hard to establish – and to naturalize – the *Siege of Jerusalem* also entertains the possibility that the very pity deemed central to the late medieval Christian prince threatens the performance of religious difference and undermines Christian claims to political, juridical, and historical superiority.

Passions of the Sensitive Soul

We might begin by noting that the *Siege* presents two types of emotional distress in the poem. The first is the distress felt in respect to a character's own bodily state. Throughout the *Siege*, the most striking depictions of Jewish distress center on the experience of starvation. As the residents of Jerusalem are cut off from supplies, with "nother fisch ne flesch freke on to byte, / Bred, browet ne brothe, ne beste upon lyve, / Wyn ne water to drynke bot wope of hemself," hundreds of Jews within the city "fellen doun for defaute flatte to the grounde, / Ded as a dore-nayl eche day" (1072–4).

Ravaged by hunger, one particular Jewish woman, Marie, is driven to turn her son, "hire own barn that ho bare," into a ghastly roast of "rigge and rib," all the while lamenting her state "with rewful wordes" (1082–3).

To fully appreciate the poet's designs in rendering such portraits of Jewish bodily suffering and emotional distress, it is necessary to turn briefly to the source tradition. For the story of Marie – or as she is alternatively named, Mary – occurs in all of the *Siege*'s source texts (as well as in manuscript illustrations of the Destruction of Jerusalem), providing an opportunity to gauge the thematic interests of the *Siege* poet.[11] In Josephus' original historical narrative, Mary is identified as a Jewish refugee who had generously used her own supplies to feed her fellow-besieged Jews. When the Roman blockade begins to have its effect, famine grips the city, but despite the huge loss of life, the governing Jewish elite refuses to surrender. Driven by hunger, but also filled with righteous indignation against the failures of the Jewish leadership, Mary contemplates killing her own child to feed herself and her neighbors:

> "Poor baby, in the midst of war, famine and civil strife, why should I preserve you? There will be slavery with the Romans, if we are alive under them; but the famine is beating out even slavery, and the rebels are harsher than both. Be food for me and for the rebels a fury . . ."[12]

Offering an astute reading of the political reality, Mary justifies killing her child as a means both of saving her own life and sparing her child the dehumanizing fate of the defeated.[13] In Josephus' rich account of emotional distress, Mary is driven by bodily appetite, but she also labors to make sense of her condition and to anticipate the effects of her action.[14]

In the *Siege of Jerusalem* Mary's character has been radically re-imagined. Her speech to her son focuses entirely on her physical discomfort and emotional distress:

> "Sone, upon eche side our sorow is alofte:
> Batail aboute the borwe our bodies to quelle,
> Withyn hunger so hote that negh our herte brestyth."   (1084–6)

Overcome by "a wode hunger" (1093), Mary is afforded no rational assessment of her situation and her actions are given no purposeful end.[15] Her only motive for killing her child is appetite itself, and she is represented as utterly overcome by emotional distress. Indeed, the *Siege* poet treats her as an exemplum of bestial incontinence: "as wolves they ferde; / The wyght waried on the woke alle his wombe-fille." A figure of dietary rapacity,[16] the wolf both suggests the incapacity of Jews to govern their own sensible appetites and the violence that might be expected when Jewish bodily suffering elicits feelings of extreme distress.

It is not just bodily distress that overwhelms the Jewish characters. Throughout the poem, Jewish characters are shown experiencing a second type of distress, one that attends the perception of the suffering of others. Maria's cannibalism, for instance, is depicted as causing great anguish amongst the Jewish civic leaders who, smelling meat roasting within her home, rush in, hoping to procure food. As they see Maria gnawing on the flesh of her child,

> ... alle their blode chaungeth.
> Away they went for wo, wepyng ech one
> And sayn: "Alas! In this lif how longe schul we dwelle?
> Yit beter were at o brayde in batail to deye
> Than thus in langur to lyve and lengthen our fyne." (1096–1100)

Maria's desperate act of cannibalizing her own child devastates the Jewish leaders; despairing at the prospect of yet more months of suffering, they yearn for their own deaths.

The self-consuming force of Jewish distress is given its most powerful and multi-layered depiction as the Jews of Jerusalem witness the torture and crucifixion of the Jewish high priest Caiaphas and his clerks, who have been captured in battle and condemned to death. Waspasian strategically locates the gallows, so that those defending Jerusalem's walls watch helplessly as their religious leaders are tortured and executed:

> The lered men of the lawe a litel bynythe
> Weren tourmented on a tre, topsailes walten
> Knyt to everech clerke kene corres twey,
> That alle the cité myght se the sorow that they dryven. (709–12)

This is an often-invoked scene in criticism of the poem and one that has occasionally been read as a sympathetic account of Jewish suffering.[17] In favor of this reading, we might note that Jewish grief bears some similarity with that experienced by mourners of Christ's death in late medieval literature and art. In pulling at their hair and swooning – "Somme hente here heere and fram the hed pulled, / And somme doun for deil daschen to grounde" – the Jewish spectators register emotional distress in familiar bodily gestures (713–16).

At the same time, the particular nature of the Jewish emotional response seems designed to perform Jewish difference:

> The Jews walten over the walles for wo at that tyme,
> Seven hundred slow hemself for sorow of here clerkes
> Somme hent here heere and fram the hed pulled,
> And somme doun for deil daschen to grounde. (713–16)

As the Jewish men experience distress – their vital spirit constricting and heat withdrawing into their hearts – they lose the power of their limbs and collapse.[18] Physiologically, they are no longer manly martial subjects fighting fiercely on the battlefield; they are like romance heroines fainting at the sight of violence they are powerless to resist. Indeed, the only agency they seem able to exercise is their own destruction. Understood theologically, the destructive sorrow of the Jews provides an instructive contrast to the spiritually enriching sorrow of the Christian faithful. Christian readers – especially those who had meditated upon Christ's Passion in their own devotional practice – must have registered the dramatic difference between the Jewish response to Caiaphas' crucifixion and their own affective experience of imaginatively beholding Christ's suffering.

At the same time that Jews are shown being overwhelmed by their feelings, the Roman Christians are depicted in ways that suggest they are able to control their emotional response to physical pain. Thus, for example, when at the end of the third day of battle, the Christian knights return wounded to their tents, the poet observes "though they wounded were was no wo nempned / Bot daunsyng and no deil" (854–5). The ability of the Christian men-at-arms to suppress distress works its own kind of healing, for the men find themselves in the morning "freschere to fight than at the furst tyme" (862).

The importance of managing the emotions is also registered in the narrative's account of the conversion of the Roman leader, Waspasian, and his son Titus. In both instances, becoming Christian involves the careful management of an emotional response to Christ's Passion.[19] That management is made easier by the highly mediated manner through which Christ's suffering is represented and experienced. Within the *Siege* narrative, no Christian character ever directly witnesses the torture or crucifixion of Christ;[20] rather his suffering is witnessed indirectly as characters look upon the veil of Veronica (who, the poet reports in rehearsing her legend, had herself seen Jesus on the road to Calvary, and captured his image on her veil when she reached out to wipe his face). Veronica's veil, like any relic, mediates the salvific power of Christ's suffering, making it available to believers. Imprinted with the bloodied face of Jesus, Veronica's veil serves, then, both to link secular men-at-arms to Christ's suffering and to distance them from that suffering and the distress it can evoke.

This complex dynamic is played out in the narrative account of the conversion of Waspasian who, at the opening of the poem, is depicted as suffering an infested nasal cavity that no physicians have been able to heal. Looking upon Veronica's veil and beholding Christ's suffering provokes "wepyng and wo and wryngyng of hondis / With loude dyn and dit for doil of Hym one" (251–2). Waspasian's distress at the sight of the suffering Christ is registered, but it is also quickly pushed aside, as the poet turns immediately to Waspasian's healing, and declares joyfully that, "Than was pyping and play, departying of stryf" (257). We find the same pattern at work in the poet's account of the veil's power in an earlier scene in which Veronica's veil heals a multitude. Here, a group of badly wounded men-at-arms kneel before Veronica's veil and are immediately rendered healthy and whole (165–72). In the *Siege of Jerusalem*, the miraculous power of Veronica's veil not only serves to demonstrate the benevolent, efficacious nature of Christian devotion, but also acts as an emotional solvent: for these Roman men, the carefully mediated beholding of Christ's suffering works to dissolve distress and preclude despair.

While distress is given the most fulsome treatment by the *Siege*, it is not the only emotion shown to have a dangerous power to overwhelm. Pleasure or joy, which was traditionally paired with distress in scholastic accounts of the emotions, is also shown to threaten the control of the Christian aristocrat.[21] This is realized most dramatically when Titus experiences joy at the news that his father, Waspasian, has been elevated to the imperial throne. He is immediately afflicted with a deadly paralysis:

> And Titus for the tydyng hath take so mychel joye
> That in his synwys soudeynly a syknesse is fallen.
> The freke for the fayndom of the fadere blysse,
> With a cramp and a colde caught was so hard
> That the fyngres and feet, fustes and joyntes
> Was lythy as a leke and lost han here strengthe.
> He croked agens kynde and as a crepel woxen,
> And whan they sey hym so, many segge wepyth.   (1027–34)

Titus' paralysis is consistent with popular medical understandings of the somatic manifestation of emotions, and it suggests the literal power of emotions to do harm. Given such portraits, we might at first conclude that the poem seeks to promote a Stoic Christian *apatheia* against an excessive Jewish emotionality. But, as we will see, other emotions – especially feelings of anger – don't produce the same kind of anxiety when they are experienced by the Roman Christian princes. What then about the nature of distress and pleasure might have provoked such anxieties?

For scholastic thinkers, delight (or pleasure) and distress (or sadness) were most commonly classified as concupiscible passions of the sensitive soul. In a tradition reaching back to Stoic philosophers, the emotions (*passio*) were distinguished in terms of their formal object or orientation.[22] Consequently, a broad distinction was made between emotions that were understood to involve a simple movement towards the end of human happiness or well-being and those that involved a movement away from painful or harmful objects. To return then to the *Siege*, the passion of delight experienced by Titus can be understood as a function of the appetitive power that naturally seeks good things, while the distress which so frequently overwhelms Jewish characters can be seen as a function of the appetitive power being repelled from bad or painful things.

As movements of attraction or repulsion, neither passion was believed to be directly caused by the will. According to most scholastic writers, the passions of the sensitive soul had a hybrid nature, one that Peter King has described as "partly perceptual, partly volitive."[23] In other words, as passive potencies of the sensitive appetite, pleasure and distress were feelings that were not taken to be entirely matters of choice; to a significant degree, these passions happened to an individual. The fourteenth-century Franciscan Duns Scotus observes:

> We should note that the concupiscible has to do with something agreeable or disagreeable of itself, so that on its part nothing more than apprehending such is required for an act of delight or sadness, or pursuit or flight to follow.[24]

This helps to explain, in part, why so many scholastic philosophers opted to treat these emotions as natural and thus not inherently sinful.[25] That said, as far back as Anselm, medieval theologians were quick to emphasize that humans could *choose* to orient themselves, not towards the end of well-being but, alternatively, towards the end, justice.[26] This freedom was considered to be distinctively human.

In the *Siege*, the conditions that move the Jewish characters to feel distress could well be seen as common to all human experience.[27] Starvation, illness, and wounding were well known during medieval siege warfare. Similarly, late medieval devotional practice had made graphic depictions of Christ's Passion commonplace, and there might be grounds for seeing Jewish distress at the crucifixion of their leaders as mirroring

Christian distress at Christ's suffering. It might then be construed as a sympathetic depiction of a compassionate beholding of suffering.

But I would argue that the *Siege* poet was raising such potential bonds of sympathy only in order to demonstrate their final inapplicability. Indeed, it seems likely that the *Siege* poet intended to register the experience of the Jews in the poem as the kind of "perception, movement, appetition and avoidance" common to "morally indifferent animals."[28] To fully appreciate this, we need to consider further theories of the human freedom to orient oneself towards an end, and thus, indirectly, to control concupiscent emotionality. The critical difference between the appetites and emotions of an animal and those of a human, as Augustine was keen to observe, was that humans could consent to or dissent from the actions and feelings that an emotion suggested. Thus Augustine terms emotions "volitions" in the *City of God*, for they are conditioned by humans' possession of a rational part of the soul as well as powers of intellect and will:

> For what is appetite or joy but will (*voluntas*) which consents to what we will (*volumus*)? And what is fear or distress but will which dissents from what we do not will (*nolumus*)? When this consent to what we will takes the form of pursuit, it is appetite, and when it takes the form of enjoyment of what we will, it is joy. In the same way, when we dissent from something that we do not will to happen, that will is fear, but when we dissent from something which happens and we do not will it to happen, that will is distress.[29]

Augustine's emphasis on will was intensified in twelfth-century philosophy, with its new focus on intentionality. As Edward Peters has explained, one effect of this emphasis was to turn both the sinner and the criminal into a "more deliberative actor, one more precisely responsible for his actions."[30]

We see this greater emphasis on the freedom of the will in a range of subsequent texts treating the emotions, but one particularly important way in which it changes the treatment of the emotions centers on philosophers' rejection of Augustine's sharp division between psychosomatic emotions and intellectual volitions.[31] In Scotus' work, for instance, we find the same taxonomic division between concupiscible and irascible emotions being applied to the intellectual level of the soul as well as to the sensitive part of the soul.[32] In keeping with Augustine, Scotus still classified emotions such as *dolor* as affective, non-voluntary phenomena of the sensitive level of the soul, but his account of the passions of the will also included emotions such as *tristitia*. (These two differently named but parallel feelings correspond to the single passion, "distress," that we find in earlier scholastic accounts.) What Scotus gained was a way to distinguish between a more fully agentive feeling of distress and a passion that almost inevitably followed upon the apprehension of a natural object of the senses. Importantly, Scotus believed that humans could learn to moderate those emotions that >pertained to the will through moral education or training of one's habits in a way that was not possible with the involuntary emotions of the sensitive soul.[33]

What do these complex accounts of emotion suggest about the Jewish spectators who are subjected to the sight of their leaders' death by torture? How does it enrich our reading of their response to see their distress as an emotion centered on apprehension, accompanied by bodily change, and subject to rational power and the free operations, or choice, of the will? To begin with, we can note that Jewish distress is presented in the *Siege* as a disordered response to the legitimate infliction of punishment on guilty bodies. Caiaphas is judged by Waspasian and his "domesmen upon deyes" to be liable for Christ's death, and his execution is framed as a legitimate punishment (697). Cognitively, the Jews who feel sorrow at his execution have either failed to discern correctly that the phenomenon they witness is conducive to justice (that is, their knowledge is defective or their reasoning is faulty), or they have discerned correctly the guilt of their leader but have failed to suppress the emotional feeling of distress at the sight of his suffering. They have followed their natural inclination to happiness/self-preservation, rather than exercising their moral freedom by willing an action that would be conducive to justice (in other words, their will is disordered and has chosen badly). However readers understood the deficiencies of Jewish intellect and will in these scenes, the narrative works to show that such sorrowful beholding of Caiaphas' crucifixion can only result in a self-destructive form of despair.

While the Jews of the *Siege of Jerusalem* are depicted as being overwhelmed by their feelings of distress, they are also positioned as being morally responsible for their actions. This is a critical matter, for it serves to make the common Jew responsible for a considerable portion of the suffering they experience in the war against the Roman Christians. For while the reaction to the revolting sight of Caiaphas' being flayed was not something any reader would say the Jewish spectators willed (that is, in no way is their despair being elicited voluntarily by their wills), Christian teaching was consistent in insisting that how a person behaved in response to an emotion was voluntary. Suicide, in particular, was consistently represented as a chosen behavior, a course of action that could be controlled.³⁴ Thus, in the poem, readers would be likely to understand that action as one for which the Jews were culpable.

This understanding of Jewish affectivity contributes much to the fantasy of just vengeance in the poem. For it allows medieval Christian readers to enjoy the violence of the poem inflicted upon Jewish leaders like Caiaphas while also avoiding guilt for feeling pleasure at the suffering of the common lot of Jews. In this poem, Jewish civilian deaths are not the fault of the Roman Christians who besiege Jerusalem so much as their own fault. At every turn, the Jews heap violence upon themselves; they are not in any important way portrayed as victims who deserve pity.³⁵

The Irascible Emotion: Anger

In casting Jews as incapable of governing their sense appetites and passions, the *Siege of Jerusalem* reinforces the perception of Jews as less than fully human.³⁶ It also provides a critical foil against which the masculine Christian subject is defined in the poem. In the sections that follow, I suggest how the emotional responses of Titus and Waspasian to suffering not only provided readers with a model of a virtuous *habitus* centered on the vigilant management of those emotions most commonly classified as concupiscible passions of the sensitive soul, but also celebrated a princely disposition centered on a particular species of anger often referred to as zealous anger.³⁷ Just as the poet's depiction of Jewish affect reinforces ideas about Jewish inferiority, so his depiction of the affect of the Christian princes is delineated in reference to their aristocratic social standing and their social duties as governors. Thus, in order to situate their anger, we need to consider it not simply as an abstract philosophical or theological concept which pertains to every individual, but as an emotion whose complex meanings depend upon socially constructed ideas about kingship, the roles and duties of princes, and the cultural context of religious warfare in which Christian governance operates in the *Siege of Jerusalem*.³⁸ Only once we situate the affect of Waspasian and Titus thus, can we fully appreciate the ends which are served by the poem's effort to differentiate the affect of Jews from that of the aristocratic Christian martial subject.

Unlike the Stoic who is committed to the goal of *apatheia*, to being as inured to pain as unperturbed by joy, Waspasian feels emotions strongly. He groans with delight at the sight of his newly cured son, Titus, and he cries aloud when the Pope brings Veronica's veil before his face and he asks to be healed: "Lo, lordlynges, here: the lyknesse of Crist / Of whom my botyng Y bidde for his bitter woundis" (249–50). Waspasian's apprehension of

Christ's injury inspires not compassionate feelings of sadness, as we might expect from the literature of affective piety, but rather a desire to avenge the unjust injury done to Christ. It inspires anger.[39] Anger plays an important role in Waspasian's martial leadership, and in many ways his affect as a military commander is traditional: he registers anger at the initiation of hostilities, and in a rallying speech before battle he stokes the anger of his men-at-arms with reminders of the injuries they have sustained.[40] Despite these traditional elements, the poet works hard to legitimize Waspasian as an imperial agent of vengeance, cognizant, it seems, that his anger might otherwise be deemed sinful.

A number of scenes work to define and legitimize Waspasian's anger, but the most important center on Waspasian's declaration of war. Upon arriving at the city of Jerusalem, Waspasian sends messengers to the Jews to demand their surrender. In this early scene, the *Siege* poet reinforces the justness of Waspasian's military campaign – a campaign that has already been presented as a divinely sanctioned war in the poem's prologue where Christ himself decides that it is time to avenge the "vyleny" on them who "His veynys brosten" (20). At the same time, the original source material had presented the war against Jerusalem in secular terms as one occasioned by the rebellion of Jerusalem, and subsequent medieval narratives retained this political motivation, centering it upon the failure of the Jewish city to pay the tribute owed their imperial Roman overlords. This is a fact rehearsed by the Roman senators and the emperor when they elect Waspasian commander (269–72), and to some degree the *Siege of Jerusalem* is comfortable with such a dual license for the war.

Both causes render Waspasian's war just. By sending messengers to the city and presenting yet another opportunity for the Jews of Jerusalem to recognize imperial authority over the city and to surrender without a violent siege, Waspasian ensures that his campaign is conducted with a proper aim; moreover, he meets Augustine's demand that recourse to violence be made only where no alternative means of achieving justice exists.[41] While the legality of Waspasian's conduct is apparent in this sense, the poem offers a more thorough inspection of the propriety of the desires propelling Waspasian to war, and it invites readers to consider (but also to reject) the possibility that the war against Jerusalem is motivated by a cupidinous desire for tribute.[42] Significantly, it is the Jews themselves who assume that Waspasian and his army seek the city's riches, asking "the cause of your comyng and what ye coveyte wolde" (344). The poet's strategic deployment of the moral vocabulary of covetousness highlights the troublesome implication borne by the source texts that this Roman imperial campaign is driven by the desire to secure wealth and power. Waspasian's response dissolves such anxieties. He charges his messengers to tell the Jews "that *alle* the cause of her come was Crist forto venge" (348, my emphasis), and he demands the surrender of only those Jewish leaders whom Augustine and other early Church Fathers isolated as the parties responsible for Christ's crucifixion. Cleansed of the potential taint of lucre, Waspasian declares that his intention is purely to avenge the death of Christ. Here Waspasian's anger assumes the character of that virtuous zeal of the prince praised by Gregory the Great in the *Moralia*. As Lester Little has observed, although Gregory excoriated irrational anger as a vice that stirred in the hearts of the impatient and the self-indulgent, he praised the zealous prince who sought to "marshal passion and thus focus energy to fight constructively against evil."[43] The Christian prince's orientation towards justice does much to help explain the positive valence of the irascible emotion, anger, throughout the *Siege* narrative. It also acts as an important restraint upon the disruptive power of concupiscible passions and their orientation towards well-being, which the poet consistently associates with the Jews of Jerusalem.

Despite its tendency to disparage Jews for their orientation towards well-being (an orientation that fits, theologically, with the association of Jews with the carnal and the literal), the *Siege* demonstrates an anxious regard for the physical and emotional well-being of its Christian aristocratic men. Zealous anger serves both to differentiate the Christian prince and to remedy the bodily ravages to which Christians and Jews are equally subject. Two scenes centered on Waspasian's son, Titus, illustrate this complex dynamic. The first highlights anger's role in Titus' conversion to Christianity. Like his father, Titus is presented at the very beginning of the *Siege* narrative as a non-Christian who suffers a debilitating physical ailment. Titus inquires about possible physicians with a ship-wrecked man, Nathan, who informs him that his painful and disfiguring facial canker might have been able to be healed by Jesus, whom he witnessed performing a range of miracles. Although this Jesus healed "ten lasares at a logge," the "croked and cancred," and "the dombe and the deve," he was hated, Nathan explains, by Jewish priests and princes, and killed (126–30). Titus' angry denunciation of those responsible for Christ's crucifixion immediately heals the young prince of his canker, and his immediate conversation, like his father's, is marked with a zealous vow to avenge the wrong, "to do the develes of dawe and Thy deth venge!" (188).

The second scene also begins with the Christian protagonist suffering a bodily affliction. Near the end of the *Siege of Jerusalem*, Titus learns that his father, Waspasian, has been elevated to the imperial throne. Titus is overwhelmed by the concupiscible emotion, joy, and afflicted by a deadly paralysis.[44] In narrating Titus' healing, the poet builds on ideas derived from medical texts that afforded anger, as an irascible emotion, the somatic power to come to the aid of a person overwhelmed by concupiscible emotions.[45] This healing power is realized in the remarkable remedy that the Jewish physician Josephus undertakes to heal Titus. Bringing a man whom Titus particularly hates before him, Josephus stokes the Christian prince's anger. This pushes the vital spirits out from Titus' heart and into his limbs, heating and drying them.[46] Here the *Siege* poet affords the irascible passion, anger, the power to overcome the concupiscible emotions and restore the bodily integrity and strength of the Christian prince.[47]

As I hope this analysis has convincingly demonstrated, a sharp division between Jew and Christian is something that the *Siege* narrative works hard to establish – and to naturalize. Nevertheless, the opposition is subject to considerable strain. Unable – or perhaps unwilling – to stabilize the demarcating lines between self and other, the poem includes several scenes in which emotionality threatens the subjective unity and coherence of its Christian aristocratic masculine subjects. And despite the poet's confidence in Christian claims to political, juridical, and historical superiority, the effort to claim a superior affective disposition is profoundly troubled by a quality that in the late fourteenth century had gained new importance as a princely attribute: pity.

"If Pité Measure Exceed"

While it was becoming increasingly common to assume and to assert that "pity renneth soone in gentile herte,"[48] the poets of late medieval England also expressed deep misgivings about princely pity and its capacity to undermine justice. John Gower, for instance, although eager to condemn bestial anger, bloodlust, and cruel vengeance, narrates several tales in the *Confessio Amantis* that illustrate the way in which pity clouds the judgment of secular authorities.[49] The concern with justice was, as we have seen, central to the *Siege* poet, and within the Vengeance of our Lord tradition it had so dominated that earlier poets and chroniclers consistently depicted Waspasian and Titus as refusing all pleas for mercy from the Jews.[50] Uniquely, the late fourteenth-century *Siege of Jerusalem* imagines the zealous Christian prince deviating for a moment from the course of unrestricted vengeance and allowing himself to feel distress at Jewish suffering and to let pity guide his action.[51]

Given the number of times the Christian princes have refused Jewish pleas for mercy, this moment comes as a dramatic shift in both attitude and course of action. The poet is consistent, however, in presenting the distress that inspires Titus' pity as an objectual state, that is, a psychophysical state elicited by sensory perception. Overwhelmed by the sight of Jewish corpses piling up outside the city walls and by a glimpse of the emaciated bodies of Jewish women – "Swounen, swallen as swyn, and som swart waxen, / Som lene on to loke as lanterne-hornes" (1149–50) – Titus calls for Josephus to preach to the surviving Jews, in an effort to spur their submission and request for forgiveness.[52] The preaching is effective, and the Jewish residents of the city pour out of the city and sue for grace.[53] But as soon as Titus has food brought to the emaciated captives, he learns that they cannot eat, for they have filled their stomachs with gems and other treasures from the Temple. Here the *Siege* poet once again imagines Jews as particularly prone to the concupiscible emotions, and once again, driven to enact their own destruction.

This portrait of Jewish incontinence is clearly meant to be a reassuring conclusion, a way of legitimizing the impending destruction of Jerusalem. Titus declares that he will now bring siege engines to bear on the city walls, and "Never pyte ne pees profre hem more" (1179). The Christian prince has learned a valuable lesson. But the ultimate test of Christian fortitude will come when the Christians breach the walls, and Titus enters the city as victor. His gaze registers the horrible suffering of the Jews of Jerusalem:

> Tytus into the toun taketh his wey:
> Myght no man stande on the stret for stynke of ded corses.
> The peple in the pavyment was pité to byholde
> That were enfamyned and defeted whan hem fode wanted. (1245–8)

Titus registers Jewish pain and suffering, but, this time, he does not succumb to distress, does not allow himself to act with pity: "Tytus tarieth noght for that, bot to the Temple wendith" (1253). Thus the masculine *habitus* of the Christian prince is celebrated for its capacity to govern the concupiscible feelings of distress and to orient martial anger towards the end of justice.

As we have seen, medieval accounts of the emotions situated feelings compositionally, in relation to bodily processes, cognitive acts, as well as volitional powers. Anger was a feeling firmly grounded in – if not absolutely naturalized as an attribute of – male bodies, especially in their capacity for heat and in their relative dryness. From the early decades of the fourteenth century, Jewish male bodies were increasingly associated with complexions and humoral conditions that were otherwise associated with women. Thus it was common to posit that Jewish men were subject to fluxes of blood, were more apt to be cold and moist, and were dominated by black bile and thus prone to melancholy.[54] Whether or not the *Siege* poet meant to feminize Jewish male characters, his depiction of Jews as incapable of governing their appetites and the passions of the sensitive soul aligns with the demonstration that both the Jewish leaders such as Caiaphas and the common residents of Jerusalem are morally culpable. Failing to confess or convert, they are shown to merit the punishment Jesus calls Waspasian to deliver. They do not deserve pity.

As Eric Auerbach emphasized in his study of the passions, "*pathos* originally meant sickness, pain, suffering."[55] As the *Siege of Jerusalem* anxiously dramatizes, all humans are subject to bodily harm and to the tempestuous movements of the emotions. In this poem, Christian difference is secured through the exercise of a *habitus* that contains the pleasure and distress born of the passions of the sensitive soul. More surprising, perhaps, it is also secured by anger, an irascible emotion held to be closer to reason and deemed more proper to the exercise of righteous authority and more appropriate as a manly response to the offense of evil-doers than pity. Navigating two threats to the Christian identity of the martial aristocracy – to masculine integrity *and* to religious superiority – the Middle English *Siege of Jerusalem* contributed to a tradition of literature in which the *zealous* avenging Christian prince enacts the fantasy of securing a safe distance from susceptibility to suffering, and a firm mastery of the passions of the sensitive soul.

Notes

1. *Siege*, ll. 9–18. Here and throughout I cite from the *Siege of Jerusalem*, ed. Michael Livingston (Kalamazoo, MI: TEAMS Medieval Institute Publications, 2004).
2. On the importance of "beholding" to devotional literature such as Nicholas Love's *Mirror*, see Sarah McNamer, *Affective Meditation and the Invention of Medieval Compassion* (Philadelphia, PA: University of Pennsylvania Press, 2010).
3. For a sophisticated account of the ways in which late medieval devotional texts and visual art imagine Jews' violent persecution of Christians, and the way in which terror and victimization become affective routes to an identity centered on compassionate feeling for Christ's suffering, see Anthony Bale, *Feeling Persecuted: Christians, Jews and Images of Violence in the Middle Ages* (London: Reaktion Books, 2010).

4. McNamer, *Affective Meditation*, 135.
5. Ibid., 90, and passim. For an insightful discussion of cross-gendered identification and the way in which male mystics took up the posture of bride and bridegroom, see C. D. Muir, "Bride or Bridegroom? Masculine Identity in Mystic Marriages," in *Holiness and Masculinity in the Middle Ages*, ed. P. H Cullum and Katherine J. Lewis (Toronto: University of Toronto Press, 2004), 58–78.
6. McNamer, *Affective Meditation*, 95. McNamer is, of course, not the first critic to suggest that a kind of "affective dissonance" (95) troubles depictions of the Crucifixion; the idea has been usefully investigated in relation to the Passion plays of York, Wakefield, and Digby in Richard L. Homan, "Mixed Feelings about Violence in the Corpus Christi Plays," in *Violence in Drama*, ed. James Redmond (New York: Cambridge University Press, 1991), 93–100. For a provocative account of efforts by Bernard of Clairvaux and other male writers to stimulate affectivity, in ways that might challenge McNamer, see Robert Mills, *Suspended Animation: Pain, Pleasure and Punishment in Medieval Culture* (London: Reaktion Books, 2005).
7. There is a substantial debate centering on whether medieval society constructed the clergy's gender as masculine. For an important critical intervention, see Jacqueline Murray, "One Flesh, Two Sexes, Three Genders?," in *Gender and Christianity in Medieval Europe: New Perspectives*, ed. Lisa M. Bitel and Felice Lifshitz (Philadelphia, PA: University of Pennsylvania Press, 2008), 34–51.
8. The vulnerability of Jewish bodies throughout the *Siege* narrative is all the more striking because of the way it contrasts with the impassibility of Christian bodies. Thus, for instance, the very battle that produces thousands of Jewish corpses, strewn across the field, leaves the Christian knights entirely unscathed (see *Siege*, 610–12). We can recognize here a pattern described by Lisa Lampert in a different literary context in which the contrast between "images of intact, incorruptible [Christian] bodies – and the permeable bodies of the doubting, defiling Jews" is part of a larger system of oppositions – literal vs. figural, carnal vs. spiritual, death vs. life – that aims to secure a "supercessionist view of the relationship between Judaism and Christianity." See Lampert, *Gender and Jewish Difference from Paul to Shakespeare* (Philadelphia, PA: University of Pennsylvania Press, 2004), 135, 54.
9. Roger Nicholson, "Haunted Itineraries: Reading *The Siege of Jerusalem*," *Exemplaria* 14,2 (2002), 479, 482.
10. See *MED*, "compassioun" 2a.
11. Ralph Hanna and David Lawton have argued that the *Siege* poet knew Josephus' text. See their "Introduction" to *The Siege of Jerusalem*, ed. Hanna and Lawton, EETS o.s. 320 (New York: Oxford University Press, 2003), xl–xlv. They were unaware, however, of a mid-fourteenth-century chronicle by John of Tynemouth that Andrew Galloway argues was the direct source. This text

includes the details cited here from Josephus (they appear as well in the *Legenda aurea*) as well as Ranulf Higden's added details. See Galloway, "Alliterative Poetry in Old Jerusalem: The *Siege of Jerusalem* and its Sources," in *Medieval Alliterative Poetry: Essays in Honour of Thorlac Turville-Petre*, ed. John A. Burrow and Hoyt N. Duggan (Dublin: Four Courts Press, 2010), 91.

12. Josephus, *The Jewish War, Books V–VII*, trans. H. St. J. Thackeray (Cambridge, MA: Harvard University Press, 1997), 6.204–7.

13. There is no explicit attempt in Josephus' text to link her act to the practice of Kiddush Ha'shem, a ritual form of self-inflicted "death in the sanctification of God's Name," enacted most famously by medieval Jews in 1096 at the Massacre at Mainz. In the twelfth-century chronicle account of Soloman bar Samson, the Jewish mother Rachel, failing to save her children from discovery by ransacking crusaders, acted with other "merciful women" who "slaughtered their children, doing the will of their creator." Cited in Simha Goldin, *The Ways of Jewish Martyrdom*, trans. Yigal Levin, ed. C. Michael Copeland (Turnhout: Brepols, 2008), 112–13. Such legitimizing and humanizing motives are absent from the *Siege*'s tale.

14. I follow here Mary Hamel, "The *Siege of Jerusalem* as a Crusading Poem," in *Journeys Toward God: Pilgrimage and Crusade*, ed. Barbara N. Sargent-Baur (Kalamazoo, MI: TEAMS Medieval Institute Publications, 1992), 180.

15. In another later medieval account of this incident, *Titus and Vespasian*, the Jewish mother Mary is responding to a direct command of God. A full-page manuscript illumination of the divinely commanded cannibalism by Mary and her companion Clarice is given in the Neville of Hornby Book of Hours, and illustrated as plate 8 of Kathryn Ann Smith's *Art, Identity and Devotion in Fourteenth-Century England: Three Women and Their Books of Hours* (Buffalo: University of Toronto Press, 2003), 12.

16. See *Siege of Jerusalem*, ed. Hanna and Lawton, 146, note 1079, for this identification.

17. See, for instance, Elisa Narin Van Court, "*The Siege of Jerusalem* and Augustinian Historians: Writing about Jews in Fourteenth-Century England," *Chaucer Review* 29,3 (1995): 227–48; and Alex Mueller, "Corporal Terror: Critiques of Imperialism in *The Siege of Jerusalem*," *Philological Quarterly* 84,3 (Summer 2005): 287–310.

18. These somatic effects are consistent with accounts given in medical texts such as the *Liber pantegni*. See Simo Knuuttila, *Emotions in Ancient and Medieval Philosophy* (New York: Oxford University Press, 2004), 212–23. Reflected here may also be what Peter Biller calls the "pro-racial thought" of late medieval scholastic texts, encyclopedia, and compendia. For instance, quodlibetical discussions from the Paris arts faculty began around 1300 to include disparaging discussions of Jewish characteristics, especially the dominance in their bodies of melancholia. See Biller, "Proto-racial Thought in Medieval Science," in *The Origins of Racism in the West*, ed. Miriam Eliav-Feldon, Benjamin Isaac, and Joseph Ziegler (New York: Cambridge

University Press, 2009), 172–4, and Biller, "A Scientific View of Jews from Paris around 1300," *Micrologus: Natura, Scienze e Societa Medievali* 9 (2001): 143–4, and for the relevant texts, 159–60. Does the *Siege* poet mean to represent Jewish melancholia? Possibly. However, melancholia was generally understood as a pathological condition (rather than properly speaking an occurrent emotional state). As a non-objectual somatic state, it was understood as a result of the humoral imbalance – specifically, an excess of black bile. For the *Siege* poet, however, Jewish distress seems to be a response to an object: it is quite pointedly distress *at* some externally perceived thing.

19. For a trenchant account of the way in which the depiction of Jewish corporeal excess and corruption participate in the performance of Christian identity, see Steven Kruger, *The Spectral Jew: Conversion and Embodiment in Medieval Europe* (Minneapolis, MN: University of Minnesota Press, 2006), especially the chapter, "Becoming Christian?"

20. Given his account of Jesus' ministry and crucifixion, Nathan, the merchant who meets with Titus, might well have been represented as a witness to the Crucifixion or to some moment in the Passion. I take the absence to be meaningful.

21. The pairing goes back to the centrality of delight and distress in the four-fold Stoic classification adopted by St Augustine and located within the irrational part of the soul; as passions of the sensitive soul, delight and distress were governed by the principle of appetition (versus the principle of cognition). In the thirteenth century, emotions were newly classified into contrary pairs of the concupiscible and irascible power. In Aquinas' treatment, for instance, the emotions are classified in pairs with "delight" and "distress" classified as a pair of concupiscible passions alongside "desire"/"aversion" and "love"/"hate." On their appetitive nature, see Thomas Aquinas, *Summa Theologica: The Emotions*, trans. E. D'Arcy, 1a2ae22–23 (New York: McGraw-Hill, 1975), 1a2ae q. 22, art. 2 and 3; for their pairing, 1a2ae q. 23. Although many scholastic thinkers classified the pair delight and distress as concupiscible passions of the sensitive soul, schemes varied. An earlier and more distinctive classification of the emotions was produced by the twelfth-century Englishman Isaac of Stella, for whom emotions of the concupiscible power included delight, while the irascible power was associated with distress. See Isaac of Stella, *Epistola de anima*, in *Three Treatises on Man: A Cistercian Anthropology*, trans. and ed. Bernard McGinn (Kalamazoo, MI: Cistercian Publications, 1977), chapters 5 and 6. The most influential taxonomy was that of Jean de la Rochelle (d. 1245), who held the Franciscan chair of theology at the University of Paris. See Jean's *Summa de Anima*, ed. J. G. Bougerol (Paris: Vrin, 1995), 2.104 and 2.107. His classifications greatly influenced subsequent scholastic treatments including those of Albert the Great, Bonaventure, and Aquinas. For a discussion of Jean's importance in medieval faculty psychology, see Peter King, "Emotions in Medieval Thought," in *The Oxford Handbook of Philosophy of Emotion*, ed. Peter Goldie (New York: Oxford University Press, 2010), 173–6, and Knuuttila, *Emotions*, 230–6.

22. For a succinct discussion, see King, "Emotions in Medieval Thought," 173–80; for an in-depth survey, see Knuuttila, *Emotions*.
23. King, "Emotions in Medieval Thought," 181; Knuuttila, *Emotions*, 135–6.
24. Duns Scotus, *Ordinatio III*, suppl. dist. 34, translated by Allan B. Wolter as "Moral Virtue and the Gifts and Fruits of the Spirit," in *Duns Scotus on the Will and Morality* (Washington, DC: Catholic University of America Press, 1986), 359.
25. After all, a person's natural inclination was towards his or her well-being, a perspective that Aristotle's reception reinforced. Jerome cited Jesus' own troubled thoughts on the eve of his Passion, as depicted in Matt. 26, as a sinless, natural human response to the prospect of suffering (see Knuuttila, *Emotions*, 194). In addition to Alan de Lille and Abelard, many Franciscan thinkers including William of Middleton and Alexander of Hales argued that if an emotion were experienced prior to the activity of reason and without the involvement of the will, there was no moral culpability. This view was, however, subject to considerable debate. Peter Lombard and Thomas Aquinas, for instance, argued otherwise.
26. Anselm of Lucca, *De Concordia Praescientiae et Praedestinationis et Gratiae Die cum Libero Arbitrio*, in *Anselm of Canterbury: The Major Works*, ed. and trans. Brian Davies and G. R. Evans (New York: Oxford University Press, 2008), 3.11.
27. Interpreting how the *Siege* poet might have understood such feelings is inevitably subject to uncertainty. The poet might have seen the distress of starvation as, strictly speaking, a *propassione* or pre-emotion, although when discussing questions of moral culpability Christian theologians might classify all the irascible and concupiscible feelings of the sensitive (i.e., irrational) part of the soul as *propassiones*. In such a classification, *passiones*, by contrast, were a product of rational deliberation and consent of the will.
28. Knuuttila, *Emotions*, 157–8.
29. Augustine, *City of God*, 14.6, cited in Knuuttila, *Emotions*, 159. I use the term "distress" throughout, and thus cite here Knuuttila's translation in preference to widely available editions of *City of God*, such as the Cambridge and Penguin editions, which use the term "grief" here. The Latin is *tristitia*.
30. Edward Peters, "Destruction of the Flesh – Salvation of the Spirit: The Paradoxes of Torture in Medieval Christian Society," in *The Devil, Heresy and Witchcraft in the Middle Ages: Essays in Honor of Jeffrey B. Russell*, ed. Alberto Ferreiro (Leiden: Brill, 1998), 138.
31. See Richard Cross, *Duns Scotus* (New York: Oxford University Press, 1999), 75–7; King, "Emotions in Medieval Thought," 180–2; and Knuuttila, *Emotions*, 206–69.
32. Knuuttila sees this as Scotus' most radical departure from the traditional account of emotions, though he also notes that Franciscan writers such as Bonaventure had also emphasized emotions of the will (*Emotions*, 268).
33. As Tobias Hoffmann notes, Henry of Ghent (who influenced Scotus greatly) similarly locates moral virtue in the will. See Hoffmann, "Henry of Ghent's

Voluntarist Account of Weakness of Will," in *Weakness of Will from Plato to the Present*, ed. Hoffmann (Washington, DC: Catholic University of America Press, 2011), 133. See also Knuuttila, *Emotions*, 268.
34. In canon law, as Alexander Murray observes in *Suicide in the Middle Ages*, Vol. 2: *The Curse on Self-Murder* (Oxford: Oxford University Press, 2000), "the wrongness of suicide" lay in its "consciously deliberate character" (248).
35. The idea that (only) guiltless suffering should stimulate pity goes back to Aristotle's *Rhetoric*, 2.8. On its centrality to late medieval literary depictions of pity, see J. D. Burnley, *Chaucer's Language and the Philosopher's Tradition* (Totowa, NJ: Rowman and Littlefield, 1979).
36. Peter the Venerable's remarks are apt here: "if any man is naturally endowed with the mental faculties to recognize the truth of Christianity and the Jews have not acknowledged that truth, then the Jews must not be human." Cited in Jeremy Cohen, *The Friars and the Jews: The Evolution of Medieval Anti-Judaism* (Ithaca, NY: Cornell University Press, 1982), 24.
37. Although the fourfold Stoic classification – "pleasure"/"distress," "desire"/"fear" – was widely known, an alternative taxonomy had been developed by the fourth-century bishop Nemesius of Emesa, in which "anger" was substituted for "desire." Nemesius' discussion of anger in *De natura hominis* draws much from Aristotle's account but also incorporates a Galenic understanding of the relationship of concupiscible and irascible power to physiological change. Nemesius' taxonomy was known both directly and indirectly through John Damascene's paraphrase in *De fide orthodoxa*. Knuuttila observes that his treatment of the emotions influenced thirteenth-century thinkers such as Isaac of Stella, Albert the Great, and Jean de la Rochelle (*Emotions*, 213–16, 228–37, 245–6).
38. Richard Newhauser calls for a socially constructionist perspective, one that emphasizes "the way in which those who use the vocabulary of emotions do so within socially restricted systems of duties and rights, obligations and conventions that serve as guidelines for the moral analysis of the terminology of emotions." See his "Introduction: Cultural Construction and the Vices," in *The Seven Deadly Sins: From Communities to Individuals*, ed. Newhauser (Leiden: Brill, 2007), 3.
39. Aristotle defines anger as "a desire, accompanied by pain, for a conspicuous revenge, on account of a perceived slight on the part of people who are not fit to slight one or one's own." See his *Rhetoric*, in *The Complete Works of Aristotle: The Revised Oxford Translation*, ed. and trans. Jonathan Barnes (Princeton, NJ: Princeton University Press, 1995), 2.2. 1378a31–3. On the subsequent reception of Aristotelian ideas in late antiquity, see David Konstan, *Pity Transformed* (London: Duckworth, 2001); on the medieval Christian reception of Aristotelian ideas of anger, see Richard E. Barton, "Gendering Anger: *Ira, Furor*, and Discourses of Power and Masculinity in the Eleventh and Twelfth Centuries," in *In the Garden of Eden: The Vices and Culture in the Middle Ages*, ed. Richard Newhauser (Toronto: Pontifical Institute of Mediaeval Studies, 2005), 371–92.

40. See Phyllis Moe's discussion of this literary trope in her Introduction to the *Bible en François*, in *The ME Prose Translation of Roger d'Argenteuil's Bible en françois*, ed. Moe (Heidelberg: Carl Winter, 1977), 28. Malcolm Hebron, in *The Medieval Siege: Theme and Image in Middle English Romance* (Oxford: Clarendon Press, 1997), argues that the motif is borrowed from heroic crusading literature into the *Siege* source tradition (122).
41. See Augustine, *City of God*, 19.7. In secular prose accounts of lordly power and authority, Barton finds an alternative to the "discourse of anger-as-sin," that emphasized the positive function of lordly anger as "the proper response to an unjust challenge to legitimate authority" ("Gendering Anger," 387).
42. On the requirement of just intentions, see Augustine, "Reply to Faustus the Manichean," in *A Select Library of the Nicene and Post-Nicene Fathers of the Christian Church*, ed. and trans. Philip Schaff (Grand Rapids, MI: Eerdmans, 1979), 22.74.300–1 and 22.79.303–4. For Augustine's concern with "lust for dominion," see Augustine, *City of God*, 4.4–5.
43. Lester K. Little, "Anger in Monastic Curses," in *Anger's Past: The Social Uses of an Emotion in the Middle Ages*, ed. Barbara H. Rosenwein (Ithaca, NY: Cornell University Press, 1998), 12. See also Barton, "Gendering Anger," who argues that princely anger – although it did attract censure – was also positively valued and deemed essential to the proper exercise of legitimate political authority, the punishment of "evil-doers," and the performance of princely masculinity.
44. For a similar and near contemporaneous account of paralysis, see John Trevisa's English edition of *De Proprietatibus Rerum*, Liber 7, "De Spasmo," Cap. 13, and "De Paralisi," Cap. 14: *On the Properties of Things: John of Trevisa's Translation of Bartholomaeus Anglicus De Proprietatibus Rerum,... A Critical Text*: Vol. 1, ed. M. C. Seymour et al. (Oxford: Clarendon Press, 1975).
45. This power derives from the fact that "the irascible emotions arise from the concupiscible" and thus "terminate them" (Knuuttila, *Emotions*, 214). One of the *Siege*'s source texts invokes the principle of contraries to make sense of anger's power to heal Titus' paralysis. See the legend of St James the Less, in Jacobus de Voragine's *The Golden Legend*, trans. William Granger Ryan and Helmut Ripperger (1969; Princeton, NJ: Princeton University Press, 2012), 267.
46. Duns Scotus offers this explanation of the somatic manifestations of anger: "the irascible at times suffers pain when it cannot vent its anger, namely when it has no power to vindicate itself ... the pain of the irascible makes one hot when the blood courses to the heart" (*Ordinatio III*, suppl. Dist. 34, trans. Wolter, 363). One of the earliest accounts of the way in which occurrent emotions produce inner movements and are accompanied by physiological change is Nemesius of Emesa's *De natura hominis*, which owes much to Galenic medical theory. Avicenna's understanding of the passions as "motive acts" that entail bodily change is another source of influence, important in

shaping the scholastic writings of both Jean de la Rochelle and Thomas Aquinas. See Simo Knuuttila, "Emotions in Medical Theories," in Knuuttila, *Emotions*, 212–26.

47. While moral treatises on the virtues and the vices commonly provided elaborate taxonomies of the emotions, so too did theological treatises on the soul that were absorbing new medical accounts of the emotions in the twelfth century. See, for instance, William of Saint Thierry's discussion of various types of anger in *De natura corporis et animae*, 2.8, in *Three Treatises on Man: A Cistercian Anthropology*, trans. and ed. Bernard McGinn (Kalamazoo, MI: Cistercian Publications, 1977), 138–40. There are no distinctions made here in the *Siege* between righteous and sinful forms of anger.
48. The line derives, of course, from Chaucer's *Knight's Tale*, line 1761.
49. Gower offers his most extensive remarks on the need to ensure that pity not exceed "measure," in *Confessio Amantis*, Vol. 3., ed. Russell A. Peck, Latin trans. Andrew Galloway (Kalamazoo, MI: TEAMS Medieval Institute Publications, 2004), VII.3520–31. More broadly, in late medieval England we find a growing concern that the King was dispensing pardons when, to return to Gower's plaint, the cause was not "reasonable." See Helen Lacey, *The Royal Pardon: Access to Mercy in Fourteenth-Century England* (York: York Medieval Press, 2009), for a discussion of literary as well as legal and political texts.
50. The relevant source texts are the *Bible en Francois*, Jacobus de Voragine's *Golden Legend*, and John of Tynesworth's chronicle.
51. This dynamic is comparable to that found in a number of tales told by Gower in Book VII of *Confessio Amantis*, including the paired stories of Saul and David. For a sophisticated reading of how the tensions between equity and pity are navigated by Gower, see Conrad van Dijk, "Giving Each His Due: Langland, Gower, and the Question of Equity," *Journal of English and Germanic Philology* 108,3 (2009): 310–35.
52. There are a number of ways to account for Josephus' exemption from the general portrait of abject Jewish bodies and incontinence, but I find none wholly satisfactory.
53. The military leaders, John and Simon, refuse Titus' offer of a truce, and apparently have stayed behind. They are represented throughout the narrative as truculent and obstinate.
54. Biller, "A 'Scientific' View of Jews," 137–68.
55. Erich Auerbach, "*Passio* as Passion (1941)," in *Time, History and Literature: Selected Essays of Erich Auerbach*, ed. James I. Porter, trans. Jane O. Newman (Princeton, NJ: Princeton University Press, 2014), 167.

CHAPTER 3

Engendering Affect in Hoccleve's Series

Holly A. Crocker

"[A]ny proposition about affect is also a proposition about the body, and a historical one at that."
Fredric Jameson, *The Antinomies of Realism*[1]

The speaker of modern poet Miller Williams' "Getting Experience" has a problem with which fifteenth-century poet Thomas Hoccleve was familiar: "He said I was crazy. / Everybody thought I was a little crazy." Yet Williams' narrator has a remarkably different reaction to this appraisal: "I just let them say I was. / Better [to] be thought mad than [to be] known for stupid."[2] In Hoccleve's *Series*, the speaker, Thomas, recounts his bout with madness by considering the social pressures attending re-entry into public life. As the speaker tells his friend, "Howe it wiþ me stood was in euery mannes mouþe."[3] Thomas' behavior is scrutinized, and his former colleagues whisper behind his back: "Alþou3 from him his siickness sauage / Withdrawen and passed as for a time be / Resorte [return] it wole" (1.86–8). Modern critics have been equally inquisitive about the reflexive reintegration that Hoccleve's poetry enables. Across the *Series*, if not the larger body of the poet's work, scholars agree that Hoccleve seeks to construct a coherent subject position from a fragmentary corpus of self-expression.[4] In assembling a unified self from textual scraps, Hoccleve uncovers the shifting, even "schizoid," contours of autobiographical poetry.[5] And the edges of subjectivity that emerge, from the bureaucratic self-effacement of Hoccleve's petitions (Knapp), to the masculine pacifism of his didactic self-portraiture (Lynch), document the daily vicissitudes that might define a man of middling station writing in bureaucratic London in early fifteenth-century England.[6]

Indeed, the workaday masculinity of Hoccleve's clerkly persona is well-documented in the *Series*. As Isabel Davis argues, "By Hoccleve's time – the early fifteenth century – labour and labouring communities have become the natural subjects of masculine autobiography: work defines the masculine self."[7] And as Matthew Boyd Goldie details, "One of the most striking aspects of Hoccleve's *Complaint* is the tangible, even 'raw' presence of the city and its inhabitants."[8] Less closely accounted for, however, are the affects that galvanize this gendered assemblage. In his efforts to prove he is fully recovered, the speaker of the *Series* experiences a variety of feelings, most of which do not qualify as emotions. He trembles, he seeks to hold a steady gaze, he is struck hot, then cold, by people's responses to him. We might link these somatic states to emotions – you will recall Mary F. Wack's influential connection of lovesickness to a variety of physical maladies in the Middle Ages.[9] But in what follows I argue that we need not do so. Instead, I maintain that certain affective responses are often more properly connected to specific identity formations.[10] Some affects bypass emotion altogether, and others hardly register in any expressive way. Yet, because they connect inward condition and outward presentation, affects play a crucial role in consolidating different identities in late medieval culture. Affects are not simply pre-emotions, but refer to a broad range of somatic, psychic, and spiritual intensities that frequently remain unnamed.[11] As Fredric Jameson remarks, "affects or feelings which have not thus been named ... are absorbed into subjectivity in different ways that render them inconspicuous and indistinguishable from the named emotions they may serve to fill out and to which they lend body and substance."[12] In the *Series* the act of managing these states becomes an aesthetic endeavor that ultimately provides Thomas with a socially restored masculinity.[13] His restoration is not a matter of isolated artistic expression; instead, it is a dialogic practice of communal (self) creation that the friend explicitly connects to poetic composition.

Making a masculine identity in late medieval England, much like making an instructional poem, requires the careful compilation of diverse sources with established *auctoritas*. Scholars have nonetheless shown a marked preference for the particular, or the historical, in analyzing the *Series*. For instance, when Lee Patterson discusses Hoccleve's *Tale of Jereslaus' Wife*, he recalls the "hardheaded" marital negotiations of Humphrey, Duke of Gloucester, Hoccleve's addressee, to support his characterization of this reworking from the *Gesta Romanorum* as "a spectacularly tactless choice."[14] Hoccleve's failure to unify a fantasy of Lancastrian prestige reveals the individual as divided, a jumble of competing fragments that remain diffuse if not altogether unreadable. Although I will suggest this reading is too restrictive, not least for its topical focus, Patterson deserves credit for taking up sections of the *Series* that stand in uneasy relation to his emphasis on Hoccleve's emergent individuality. Many other "autobiographical" critics pass over three-fifths of this collection in silence, focusing instead on those self-revelations and confessional exchanges of *My Compleinte* and the *Dialoge with a Friend* that foreground the creation of an individuated subjectivity in the late medieval urban context in which Hoccleve lived, labored, and wrote.

To ignore other parts of the *Series*, I maintain, is to pass over the role of affect in the creation of a socially intelligible masculinity in late medieval London. These other entries, which represent the ways in which individual selfhood is subsumed by universalizing conventions, are equally crucial to the quotidian masculinity Hoccleve assembles across this textual gathering. The importance of these texts to publicly recognizable identity formations, however, has of yet been admitted only in limited, piecemeal fashion. In his use of Isidore of Seville, Hoccleve uncovers his debts to the Boethian tradition of the *Consolatio*.[15] With the moralized exempla, Hoccleve nods to penitential literatures of his day.[16] And through his translation of Henry Suso's *Lerne to Die*, Hoccleve acknowledges his investment in the *ars moriendi* that preoccupied many late medieval English artists.[17] Some of these analyses gesture to the autobiographical: since Thomas tells us he is fifty-three, it is appropriate that he turns to focus on overarching concerns with sin, death, and the efficacy of confession.[18] Yet even when D. C. Greetham acknowledges that all poems in the *Series* are equally subjective, or when Steven Rozenski, Jr., traces the amplified individuality in Hoccleve's rendering of Suso, these analyses produce a universalized self that is unified by its participation in timeless traditions that guarantee transcendence.[19]

The gender of the self passes away, since the majority of intellectual investment in these poems concerns the spiritual condition of the human soul in a universal framework of Christian transcendence.[20] Critics who focus on the social dimensions of the *Series* are right to see the scholarly response to these poems as too abstract. But this does not mean these entries should be ignored or read into historical events to the exclusion of spiritual interpretations. Rather, as Sarah Tolmie argues, Hoccleve's "admixture of the autobiographical and the religious-didactic creates a generic openness."[21] In the *Series*, social and spiritual are alloyed because, as J. A. Burrow observes, medieval masculinity has a moral valence, though it is one that derives almost exclusively from non-clerical discourse.[22] As Ethan Knapp remarks, masculinity for Hoccleve is "a sense of gender as an abstract category standing beyond the individual, and not simply made up from the accumulation of all individuals in a given category."[23]

Masculinities derive from social sources, in other words, but they transmit transcendent values that add up to more than a compilation of specific social traits. These values are frequently spiritual, but they are adapted from devotional discourse to become legible in social contexts. Hoccleve uses the penitential tradition, as Robyn Malo has recently reaffirmed, yet, as she notes, he expands this discourse in order to assemble a subjectivity with legitimacy in secular contexts that exceeds, and potentially defies, devotional discipline.[24] Confession airs the self, but revealing one's interiority might damn rather than save.

For all the bookishness of the *Series*, however, its recombination of social and spiritual requires more than a loose gathering of textual pieces. The binding force that makes these spiritual scripts intelligibly masculine in a specific social context is affect. As the sensations that precede narratives of self-identity, affects connect inner and outer sensitivities to fashion a masculinity that functions in the dense, socially and morally fraught milieu of late medieval London. The greatest threat to this masculinity, Thomas acknowledges in *My Compleinte*, is his former madness, or that "wilde infirmite" (1.40), which suggests an imbalance of the individual faculties. When Thomas claims, "my wit were hoom come aʒein" (1.64), he refers not just to his mental capacities; rather, to the extent that the wits, as E. Ruth Harvey remarks, are "the human powers which occupy the area between the body and the soul."[25] Because they connect sensation and intellect, such powers are socially significant. These capacities write themselves on the body, showing affect's power to join inner and outer conditions that can be read and interpreted by others.

As he understands, Thomas' recovery is moot without the social recognition that will validate his return to good health. The scrutiny he receives, though, is largely concerned with his bodily comportment. His peers claim "[he] loked as a wilde steer, / And so my looke aboute I gan to throwe. / Min heed to hie, another seide, I beer" (1.120–2). His gait, too, signals his instability: "Chaunged had I m[y] pace, somme seiden eke, / ... / My feet weren ay wauynge to and fro, / Whanne þat I stonde shulde and wiþ men talke" (1.127, 131–2). Even Thomas' glance betrays his unsteadiness: "And þat myn yen souʒten euery halke" (1.133). When he stands in front of his mirror, as Shannon Gayk points out, Thomas works to show that the movements of his eyes signal the fitness of his wits.[26] To prove that God has taken his sickness from him, Thomas must manage his bodily presentation in ways that conform to a set of social expectations that are explicitly gendered. For a man in the public eye, the friend explains, this means suppressing all memories of his infirmity: "Reherse þou it not ne it awake / Kepe al that cloos for thin honours sake" (2.27–8). According to the friend, men should exercise control over their wits, maintaining a calm governance that suppresses any visible forms of imbalance.

Rather than confirming his recovery, the friend claims all mentions of Thomas' former ailment will raise suspicions about its persistence. This is because madness is believed to be deeply lodged, as the friend emphasizes with an analogy suggesting its continued potency:

> Thogh a strong fyr þat was in an herth late,
> Withdrawen be and swept away ful cleene,
> Yit aftirward, bothe the herth and plate
> Been of the fyr warm, thogh no fyr be seene
> There as þat was, and right so I meene.
> Althogh past be the grete of thy seeknesse
> Yit lurke in thee may sum of hir warmnesse.   (2.309–15)

Mental illness connects Thomas' outer presentation and his inner psychology through a common circulation of bodily heat. It is true, then, that the description of Thomas' "wildness" accords in many respects with humoral medicine. What Gail Kern Paster describes as a "humoral body" depended on keeping the body's four elements – blood, phlegm, black bile, and yellow bile – in balance.[27] If the body were too hot this could manifest itself in a person's emotional temperature. Indeed, skeptics examine Thomas' complexion as a sign of his continued potential for sickness: "'Whanne passinge hete is,' quod þei, 'trustiþ this, / Assaile him wole aʒein that maladie'" (1.92–3).

Nevertheless, the friend does not recommend a physical or dietary regimen to regulate Thomas' temperament: he neither recommends foods that will cool the body, nor does he suggest physical practices that would moderate the body's heat. Instead, the friend connects Thomas' condition to what he writes. When he asks Thomas if he considered writing something besides the complaint that recalls his former illness, the friend is no happier to learn that Thomas thought about translating "a smal tretice, / Wiche Lerne for to Die callid is" (2.205–6). The friend is initially convinced that such a heady meditation, requiring as it does intense mental concentration, will bring back Thomas' infirmity. Instead the friend explores topics with Thomas that will restore him to his former self. Here again, these possible topics are gendered as well as affective. With the friend's guidance, Thomas considers translating a treatise on chivalry for Humphrey, Duke of Gloucester, but he decides against this project because the Duke supersedes all models of masculine prowess. He is also loath to chronicle the Duke's military exploits, because he fears he may reduce the Duke's magnificence through paltry representation: "To e[x]presse hem my spirit wolde han fere / Lest I his thank par chaunce mighte abregge / Thurgh vnkonnynge" (2.586–8). Between them Thomas and the friend agree that to write for Duke Humphrey is to address "good mateer and vertuous" (2.637). This decision makes a crucial connection between masculinity, affect, and ethics in the *Series*. By suggesting that worthy men manage their affects in particular ways, Hoccleve's poetic assemblage uncovers masculinity's moral dimension in late medieval culture.

When the friend tells Hoccleve's speaker he should, "Sumwhat now wryte in honour and preysynge / Of [women]" (2.673–4), it is not just because Hoccleve has been said to defame them in the past. There is also an association between masculine nobility and women's praise, so this subject is deemed fit for the elevated sensitivity of Thomas' primary audience, Duke Humphrey. But this topic's fitness is ultimately due to masculinity's ethical stature, and its fundamental connection to medieval affect theory. In medieval affect theory, unlike modern understandings, affects make up part of the soul. When the soul is well-ordered, its sensitive part, which includes the affects, is governed by its rational part. Its rational part is masculine, while its sensitive part is, you guessed it, feminine. Walter Hilton's *Scale of Perfection* translates the soul's order as it is articulated by Augustine in *De doctrina Christiana*:

> The overe is likned to a man, for it schulde be maister and sovereyne, and that is propirli the ymage of God, for bi that oonli the soule knoweth God and loveth God. And the nethere is likned to a woman, for it shulde be buxum to the overe partie of resoun, as a woman is buxum to a man.[28]

Spiritual order relies on gender hierarchy here and elsewhere in Middle English writings (*Sawles Warde* offers another familiar example).[29] Importantly, masculinity assumes an ethical valence, since it is responsible for governing the soul's sensitive capacities, including the affects. Masculinity is therefore as ethical as it is social; its stature, moreover, derives from a man's ability to order his soul so that the affects remain under reason's control.[30] This does not mean eradicating all affects. Rather, as the remaining poems in the *Series* affirm, it means cultivating affects that contribute to the soul's perfection and suppressing affects that work to the soul's detriment.

In the first exemplum Hoccleve took from the *Gesta Romanarum*, a version of the "Empress of Rome" story that also informs Chaucer's *Man of Law's Tale*, an endangered woman becomes a positive source of compassion within the ordered human soul. Though the Empress is wronged on many occasions – by the deceitful brother, the murderous steward, the faithless servant, and the rapacious shipman – her fidelity transforms her into a powerful healer who ultimately controls the fates of all those who wronged her. The ailments these men contract (leprosy, blindness, deafness, lameness, gout, and dementia), index the harms perpetrated against the Empress. Rather than taking revenge, the Empress only makes one demand: each man must confess his wrongs to receive healing mercy. Upon confession, the Empress' forgiveness is complete. This outcome is credited to her allegorical status as the soul, whose sensitive powers are responsible for its ethical fitness. When the Empress withdraws from the world, all the wits (sight, hearing, and so on) "by whiche the soule vexed was and troubled, been infect with dyuerse seeknesses" (3.1063). It is only when she's recovered by the Emperor – Christ's spousal figuration in this allegory – that the Empress is fully redeemed.

This narrative demonstrates masculinity's ideal relation to affect, and to feelings (including pity, fidelity, mercy, and forgiveness) traditionally associated with femininity in medieval culture. As Sarah McNamer has demonstrated, compassion is specifically connected to femininity in the Middle Ages.[31] Nevertheless, the *Series* establishes the importance of compassion in an elite masculine subject, such as Duke Humphrey. This is an argument Hoccleve has made before: as the *Regiment of Princes* avers,

> A prince moot been of condicioun
> Pitous, and his angyr refreyne and ire,
> Lest an unavysid commocioun
> Him chaufe so and sette his herte on fyre.[32]

It is not so much, then, that elite men experience feminine feelings. By allegorizing the soul using gender hierarchy, this narrative shows that powerful men manage feminine affects by maintaining rational control over those very feelings. If we wonder why Chaucer's Knight is described as being "as meeke as is a mayde" (I.69) or why his Theseus is noted for his response to the Theban widows, "This gentle duc doun from his coursersterte / With herte pitous, whan he herde hem speke. / Hym thoughte that his herte wolde breke" (I.952–54), Hoccleve's *Series* suggests these sensitivities remain masculine when they are directed by reason.[33]

It is only when such feelings get out of control, overwhelming the body through excessive intensity, that masculinity is depleted by such passions. Lovesickness, to return to an earlier example, was thought by some medieval thinkers to be caused by an imbalance between heart and soul.

In her account of Giles' Gloss on the *Viaticum*, Mary Wack explains, "no affect in the soul can take place without a 'suffering' or 'being affected' of the heart (*cordis passione*). But it then remains debatable whether the affect in the soul occurs because of the heart's being affected, or whether the heart's being affected results from the affect in the soul ... [but] illness or even death can result from excessive love or other emotion."[34] When *affectiones* are measured, when they remain under the control of the man who experiences them, then such feelings signal an appropriate, masculine connection between intellect and sensation, body and soul. The main goal, from the advice contained in *Dialoge with a Friend*, to the moralized conclusion of the *Empress of Rome* narrative, is for a man to govern the intensities that join inner and outer modes of sensation. Thomas' middling masculinity might have little in common with the elite gender a man such as Duke Humphrey was expected to assume; both men, however, share an investment in displaying visible control over the affective states that define their masculinities in specific social contexts.

Like the final two poems of the *Series*, the *Empress of Rome* narrative emphasizes the importance of managing affects that might threaten to get out of hand. It does so, unlike the rest of this poetic sequence, by linking feelings traditionally associated with femininity to the ethical stature of late medieval masculinity. With his translation of Henry Suso's *Horologium Sapientiae*, Hoccleve continues the pedagogical construction of masculinity that Thomas' exchanges with the friend establish in other parts of this poetic sequence. Rather than offering social advice, in *Lerne to Die* the central figure receives spiritual instruction from Sapientia and a dying Image of himself. This poem makes the preparation for death part of a rational response to the body's mortality. Earlier, the friend worried that this meditation on death would underscore the speaker's weakness; however, set alongside other narratives of governance, this entry comes to suggest the central figure's strength. As the disciple learns from Sapientia and the Image, he cultivates those feelings that are meant to accompany his reflections upon death. By means of direct address and appeal, the Image encourages the disciple to feel pity and compassion for his plight: "Reewe eek on me, yee alle, and pitee haue" (4.456). A little later, the disciple claims to respond to the Image's suffering: "Y see wel ynow / Thy torment and thy greuous passioun, / Of which myn herte hath greet conpassioun" (4.467–9). Notwithstanding the disciple's claim, the Image once again implores him to feel in response to his displayed suffering: "See how Y brenne. O reewe on my langour" (4.501). Appeals from the Image ask the disciple to feel in certain ways, much like the "emotional scripts" that

McNamer links to late medieval devotional literature.³⁵ Hoccleve's poem does more, however, than designate a specified range of appropriate emotions for a devotional subject. Like the others in the *Series*, this poem contributes to the formation of a masculinity that is in full control of all faculties, including those that are frequently suppressed in heroic treatments of male prowess. The central figure is not stronger than death; nor will any elite masculine subject escape death's grip. The rational reaction to the realization that "To wite and knowe þat man is mortel" (4.43) is to order body and soul in preparation for one's inevitable demise. Rather than deny those affects that are associated with death, the poem uses the young man's lack of preparation – along with the weeping, wailing, trembling, and suffering that signal his unreadiness – to recommend tranquil acceptance of death's inevitable triumph. Bringing such affects into intelligibility as emotions, then, prevents those feelings from overwhelming the masculine subject's control as he contemplates death. As Sapientia counsels, a man in control of his wits will realize that "God nat wole hyde / His mercy fro man" (4.326–7). Thinking on death should finally bring calm and control as well as belief and faith.

Taken together, *Lerne to Die* and the *Empress of Rome* detail the positive social effects of an ethical model of masculinity. This is not a manhood that asserts its power by means of physical force. Instead, its practice is gentle, and its core manifestation is a cultivated performance of self-control. Its affordances, moreover, are definite: this model of masculinity brings restitution, reconciliation, and healing. Socially it is a force for good because it binds subjects together. It would certainly seem, then, that Hoccleve was at odds with the Lancastrian program that equated martial strength, good governance, and elite manhood.³⁶ Henry V's war against France, though it might have promised a martial and dynastic expansion of territory and influence, on its face does not accord with the reparative masculinity Hoccleve advocates. I am less interested, though, in parsing the politics behind Hoccleve's apparent pacifism than I am in examining the affects that make the ethical masculinity he constructs socially intelligible (and potentially persuasive) in the specific social milieu of early fifteenth-century London.³⁷ Once again, Hoccleve reaches across lines of social station to mold an ethical manhood: by insisting on death, not renown, as the organizing experience of *all men's lives*, Hoccleve effectively sidesteps the uncomfortable political implications of this masculinity. Whether one is a clerk in the office of the Privy Seal, or steward of England in service to a martial king and brother, confronting the feelings that accompany death's inevitable approach is equally important for any man. There is no achievement – humble or heroic – that will prevent death from eclipsing a man's life: "Thow dye shalt . . . / Frendshipe, gold ne noon othir richesse / May thee deliure out of dethes duresse" (4.131, 132–3). Managing the affects that surround death's realization, or, cultivating the composure that arises from reaffirmed faith in the face of one's assured demise, is an individual endeavor with social implications. Becoming the kind of ethical subject recommended in *Lerne to Die* entails gestures of forgiveness, compassion, and pity that come to define the *Empress of Rome* narrative. Though the queen is wronged, injured, and betrayed, confession reconciles all members of this community through a collective, affective bond of healing.

Through these two poems Hoccleve avails himself of what Teresa Brennan characterizes as affect's "contagious" character.[38] As she argues, affects transfer between bodies, often without conscious recognition. Our sensory attunement to others means that we take on or react to the feelings of those around us even if we don't actively recognize ourselves as doing so. The idea that a person might be able to "smell fear" in another is just one example of affect's transmissive capacity, its ability to move into and through other bodies by means of sensory encounters that neither party consciously directs (Brennan identifies this process as one of "entrainment").[39] And, while I've been highlighting Hoccleve's emphasis on reason's control in the *Series*, intellect's managerial relationship with affect is not completely conscious, and never reaches comprehensive totality. The subjectivity Thomas endeavors to display, critics have noted, is never securely under his power. Although he works to marshal a coherent, functional masculine self, this creative assemblage also uncovers that identity's elusiveness, or the way its borders fail to coalesce with certainty or permanence. This version of male subjectivity is always provisional, always contingent. The affects extolled for this selfhood, including sympathy, suffering, and patience, are supposed to be catching. They are instructive for their ability to move between men's bodies – between Thomas and the friend, or between Hoccleve and Duke Humphrey. If reason governs these powers, it is at least in part on account of a poem like the *Series*. This poetic sequence operates in the same fashion as Sara Ahmed's "happy object," or an entity (material in her account) in which we invest certain affects.[40] The circulation of this object, in turn, allows for an expanded circulation of those feelings it carries and transmits. Because feelings in Ahmed's terminology are "sticky," they are picked up by those who come into contact with affect-laden things.[41] The affects of Hoccleve's poem are supposed to stick to Duke Humphrey in the same way that they stick to Thomas. Reason's control, then, is always an improvisation, since, at any moment, new affects might move the subject in ways that had yet to be anticipated.

In one sense, all this amounts to an acknowledgment of gender's performativity, or the ways that subjects play with and expand upon the cultural scripts of identity they seek to realize.[42] That said, the sequence's final poem, *Jonathas and Fellicula*, threatens to overwhelm the measure associated with masculinity, and potentially suggests the impossibility of a reparative manhood in this context. Although this poem is situated as an addendum – the friend asks Thomas to include it for the benefit of his "riotous" son – in Hoccleve's second translation from the *Gesta Romanarum*, masculine nobility once again results from the management of affect. Here, however, the positive force of feminine counsel is more distanced from the action of the tale. As a consequence, the young man's control risks looking more like unfettered revenge than composed rationality. The young man, Jonathas, does not heed his mother's advice to avoid "vnhonest wommen" (5.266), but remains devoted to the prostitute Fellicula even after she proceeds to "lose" two of the three magical gifts his dying father bequeathed to him. When he shows his beloved the "vertue" of his final gift – a cloth that transports its possessor to any place imagined – Fellicula waits for him to fall asleep then leaves Jonathas stranded in a land filled with wild beasts. In making his way back from this wasteland, Jonathas dips his feet into waters so hot that they remove his flesh and eats fruit that transforms him into a wretched leper; he then finds a second source of water, which "Restored [him], and made [him] al hool and fressh" (5.486), as well as a tree with fruit that cures him of his disease. Like the Empress from the first exemplum, Jonathas ultimately becomes a renowned healer, and when "this Fellicula – / The well of deceyuable doubleness ... was fallen into greet seeknesse" (5.589–90, 593), she implores Jonathas for help. He compels Fellicula to make confession, but after she divulges her theft of the magic ring, brooch, and cloth, Jonathas dispenses only destructive medicines to his former lover.

At the close of this tale, there is no restorative forgiveness. When Jonathas gives Fellicula the damaging water then the leprous fruit, "Hir wombe opned and out fil eche entraille / ... / Thus wrecchidly, lo, this gyle [deceiving] [wom]man dyde" (5.664, 666). There appears to be no room for the compassion that characterizes the Empress in the earlier exemplum. The tale's moralization seeks to recover the narrative's ethical valence, associating Fellicula with the dangers of the flesh. But what the tale addresses, which no other poems in the *Series* take on, is the challenge that violence poses to the masculine subject's ethical stature. Thomas dodges this problem earlier when he declines to catalogue Duke Humphrey's martial accomplishments; as he seems to realize, to detail acts of violence in anything but heroic, terms is to open those deeds to critique. Masculinity's incorporation of feminine affects – including compassion, mercy, and forgiveness – does not eliminate the link between masculinity and aggression. In acknowledging this connection, Hoccleve tackles what it means for men, especially elite men such as his patron, to be ethically responsible for the dispensation of violence in late medieval culture. By this I do not simply mean Hoccleve ponders how to assign moral culpability for using physical force; rather, in the *Regiment of Princes*, like the *Series*, Hoccleve evinces awareness that certain men are tasked with acts of aggression in the fulfillment of their social duties. The former poem urges the prince to "Let vertu thane therto yow excyte," even as it shows awareness that there will be specific circumstances (say, the burning of Lollard heretic John Badby) that require exercises of physical aggression against others, even less-powerful others.[43] To distance masculinity from violence altogether would not just make Hoccleve's poetry displeasing to elite masculine patrons such as Prince Henry or Duke Humphrey; more problematically, it would sever the affective circuit linking Hoccleve's poetry to a large swathe of late medieval men. There might be no need for physical aggression in performing the duties of clerk of the Privy Seal. Indeed, Hoccleve only reports his own anger and frustration at the petty mischaracterizations that attend his re-entry into public life: "and thanne my visage / Bigan to glowe for the woo and fere. / Tho wordis, hem vnwar, cam to myn eere" (1.91). Even so, Hoccleve still seeks to recognize the ways in which violence subtends masculinity in specific social contexts.

Rather than sanction physical aggression in all its forms, the allegorized *Jonathas and Fellicula* relates the proper dispensation of violence to the soul's spiritual condition. What this final story imagines, if we read it in relation to medieval notions of affective management, is the possibility of rational violence. Anger was treated as justifiable in certain circumstances, particularly for royal men, as Gerd Althoff and Paul Hyams demonstrate.[44] This is despite the fact that Lester K. Little shows that anger was thought of as a vice – one of the seven deadly sins – in religious writing.[45] On account of its grammatical gender (*ira*), but also because of its uncontrolled character, anger was often represented as a woman. In Kristi Gourlay's analysis of women's anger, moreover, women's humoral makeup was often thought to foster long-term anger – it smoldered in the colder, wetter tissues of the female flesh.⁴⁶ As a counterpoint to such thinking, Stephen White details the elaborate system of rules and conventions that were designed to control the anger of elite men.⁴⁷ Such men were not ruled by impulse, but followed a regimented system that made anger into a well-governed feeling. If anger is regulated, exercised like a purgative medicine, it can be a productive passion. Barbara Rosenwein sums up medieval thinking when she remarks, "[anger] was a sin, but a sin that could be turned into a virtue, monopolized by an aristocracy."⁴⁸ When Jonathas destroys Fellicula, then, it is meant to be a reasoned action founded on reflective wisdom.

This wisdom is hard-earned in the tale, gleaned through a course of painful and damaging experience that precedes Jonathas' restoration and vengeance. And, despite this narrative's explicit anti-feminism, this exemplum nevertheless associates reasoned governance with femininity. Through the figure of Jonathas' mother, Hoccleve's poem clarifies the young man's descent into error. When she warns him to guard the final gift (the magic cloth), she continues to advise him about the conduct of his life:

> Sone, thow woost wel no iewel is left
> Vnto thee now but the clooth precious,
> Which Y thee take shal, thee chargynge eft
> The conpaignie of wommen riotous
> Thow flee, lest it be to thee so greuous
> That thow it nat susteene shalt, ne bere.
> Swich conpaignie, on my blessing, forbere. (5.351–7)

The trouble with this association, however, is that it is altogether erased by the remainder of the tale. The mother's wisdom recedes into the background as the son executes his revenge against Fellicula. The tale's moralization, furthermore, makes no mention of the power of feminine wisdom to order masculine identity. Her function, then, is to offer a proleptic warning that clarifies the son's disordered condition. She offers no guidance pertaining to his recovery or revenge. When she disappears, so too does the measure that characterizes her earlier advice. Despite the friend's insistence that "To goode wommen shal it be no shame / Althogh þat thow vnhonest wommen blame" (5.62–3), the only role allowed for femininity by the conclusion of this narrative is that of the duplicitous, dangerous flesh.

Karen Winstead argues that the treatment of Jonathas' mother is in keeping with the broader anti-feminism of the *Series*, which discredits women's governance through its exempla.⁴⁹ If Fellicula's duplicity, malice, and wantonness rather obviously suggest femininity's dangerous disorderliness, the Empress' kindness, forgiveness, and gullibility indicate a feminine inability to distinguish friend from foe. Winstead's reading is valuable because it notices the ways that the *Series* cabins femininity's ethical power; though she doesn't put it this way, each narrative makes masculinity's governance of femininity ethically foundational to all human experience. Femininity, these narratives suggest, is central to masculine displays of affective management. By figuring the sensitive elements of the soul – good or bad – as feminine, medieval writings suggest men's outward displays of rationality rely on their ability to manage women. In parting I want to think about why Hoccleve might marshal anti-feminism across a narrative interested in assembling an ethical masculine subject. The idea that the *Series* is a misogynist joke does not square, mainly because this poetic sequence takes masculinity's production so seriously.[50] Thomas is desperate to show himself fit to re-enter masculine community; moreover, the friend's interjections and suggestions reveal the threat that affective mismanagement poses to that endeavor.

If we track this structure – masculinity's governance of femininity – across the three final poems of the *Series*, we witness its careful externalization. In the *Empress of Rome*, the feminine protagonist is securely identified as an element of the masculine subject's interiority: "His wyf is the soule" (3.981). Neither her suffering nor her perseverance is treated as part of any worldly deed; hers are spiritual travails, and her delivery is an action of "Cryst hir spowse" (3.1066). Indeed, we might see the friend's scramble to provide the tale's missing moralization as an effort to identify the Empress' power with internal capacities of the human soul, rather than worldly powers of an elite woman:

> Hoom wole Y walke and retourne anoon—
> Nat spare wole Y for so smal trauaille—
> And looke in my book. Ther Y shall nat faille
> To fynde [the moralization]. Of þat tale it is parcel,
> For Y seen haue it ofte, and know it wel.   (3.969–73)

Similarly, in *Lerne to Die* the disciple is counseled by the internalized power of Sapientia. When she seeks to offer the disciple concrete advice about how to prepare himself for death, she uses the Image of the young man to do so. Even if the Image is also insubstantial, he offers a tangible portrait of the worldly subject, the living man. And while death is also feminized in *Lerne to Die*, like Fellicula, death's force is imagined as an external hazard that the Image of the young man must learn to handle and endure. Those who enact positive ethical change in the world are, almost without exception, men. Jonathas' mother, in fact, provides the *Series'* only glimpse of women's positive moral power in the world. That such power is ultimately obscured dovetails with other instances across this poetic sequence, which makes feminine influence socially invisible in order to focus on masculine exploits.

Though it might seem strange, then, for Hoccleve to include a dedicatory address to the Countess of Westmoreland at the end of the tale of *Jonathas and Fellicula*, by so doing, he signals his participation in a widespread discourse that affirms the ethical stature of masculinity through the management of feelings associated with actual women. With this final address we see Hoccleve handling his female audience in a powerful fashion that he claims is beyond his ken in other parts of the poem. It would be hard, for instance, for the Countess of Westmoreland to reject Hoccleve's petition for favor, even if she objected to his characterization of women's deceptiveness, destructiveness, and greed. When Hoccleve worries that powerful women will condemn him as "The double man … That hony first yaf and now yeueth galle" (5.40, 41), the friend reassures him by placing the ethical onus of his composition upon women:

> For, Thomas, thow shalt vndirstonde this:
> No womman wole to theeward maligne
> But switch oon as hath trode hir shoo amis,
> For, who so dooth, ful suspect is the signe.
> The vertuous womman good and benigne
> Noon encheson but good may han to thee
> For this tale. Wryte on, par charitee.   (5.64–70)

Only those women who are themselves at fault will object to his representation of feminine perfidy. Virtuous women, by contrast, will prove their worth through their approval of Thomas' writing. By positioning his writing as a test of women's ethical fitness, Hoccleve establishes Thomas' self-control through his ability to steer the responses of women readers. Their responses, and his ability to direct their feelings, demonstrates his governance over the affective possibilities of his composition.

Accordingly, the friend goes so far as to claim that good women will feel grateful for Thomas' willingness to uncase feminine deception, since, by exposing those women who are "nakid / Of honestee, and with deshonour blakid" (5.74–5), the *Series* clarifies the exemplary moral stature of virtuous women. When Hoccleve directs his final poem to the Countess of

Westmoreland, therefore, he replicates the ethical coercion the friend outlines for Thomas: following the established logic of the poem, the Countess' protest would reveal her culpability. The Countess' feelings, then, are already under Hoccleve's control, for she is offered no affective room to respond to this poem other than that which has already been specified through the friend's exchange with Thomas. Were she to feel hemmed in by Hoccleve's plea for favor, that would be no surprise; dispensing neutralizing praise to women is how the *Series* obscures women's ethical influence. In a fashion that is similar to the treatment of the mother in *Jonathas and Fellicula*, when Hoccleve identifies an exemplary woman, doing so precipitates her erasure. She could never call attention to herself or assert her ethical power with the kind of social independence reserved for men across this poetic sequence. Femininity's positive moral impact, whether as an element of the human soul or a component of a man's life, remains hidden, rendered invisible if not altogether interior. Directing the affects associated with women is a display designed to affirm masculine rationality. Hence, by founding masculinity on an ethical structure that requires feminine governance, Thomas not only shows his regained rationality, but Hoccleve also establishes his mastery over the affective management his *Series* expounds.

Notes

1. Fredric Jameson, *The Antinomies of Realism* (London: Verso, 2013), 34.
2. Miller Williams, *Why God Permits Evil* (Baton Rouge, LA: Louisiana State University Press, 1977), 49.
3. Thomas Hoccleve, *The Series*, 1.45. All quotations from the *Series*, cited by poem and line number, are taken from Hoccleve, *"My Compleinte" and Other Poems*, ed. Roger Ellis (Liverpool: Liverpool University Press, 2001).
4. J. A. Burrow, *Thomas Hoccleve* (Aldershot: Variorum, 1994), 25ff., claims the *Series* is held together by the authorial "I." A. C. Spearing, *Medieval Autographies: The "I" of the Text* (Notre Dame, IN: University of Notre Dame Press, 2012), suggests this position is less individual and stable, more formal and experimental, than others admit: "[Hoccleve] removes the subject from a stable selfhood, which is then perceived as unattainable and perhaps illusory; and it is a subjectivity subjected to the knowledge or speculation of others, founded from the beginning in the awareness of being alienated from itself" (181–2).
5. See Antony Hasler, "Hoccleve's Unregimented Body," *Paragraph* 13 (1990): 164–83, and Jeremy Tambling, "Allegory and the Madness of the Text: Hoccleve's Complaint," *New Medieval Literatures* 6 (2003): 223–48, for readings of Hoccleve's fragmented persona.

6. See Ethan Knapp, *The Bureaucratic Muse: Thomas Hoccleve and the Literature of Late Medieval England* (College Park, PA: Pennsylvania State University Press, 2001), and Andrew Lynch, "'Manly Cowardyse': Thomas Hoccleve's Peace Strategy," *Medium Aevum* 73,2 (2004): 306–23.
7. Isabel Davis, *Writing Masculinity in the Later Middle Ages* (Cambridge: Cambridge University Press, 2007), 142. Matthew Clifton Brown, "'Lo, Heer the Fourme': Hoccleve's *Series, Formulary,* and *Bureaucratic Textuality,*" *Exemplaria* 23,1 (2011): 27–49, argues that Hoccleve's interest in bureaucratic identity is formal in this poem, and constitutes part of his effort to authorize a secular poetic persona.
8. Matthew Boyd Goldie, "Psychosomatic Illness and Identity in London, 1416–1421: Hoccleve's *Complaint* and *Dialogue with a Friend,*" *Exemplaria* 11,1 (1999), 26.
9. Mary F. Wack, *Lovesickness in the Middle Ages: The "Viaticum" and its Commentaries* (Philadelphia, PA: University of Pennsylvania Press, 1990).
10. I have begun to elaborate this position across a series of articles. See Holly A. Crocker, "Affective Politics in Chaucer's *Reeve's Tale*: 'Cherl' Masculinity after 1381," *Studies in the Age of Chaucer* 29 (2007): 225–58; "Communal Conscience in William Tyndale's *Obedience of a Christian Man,*" *Exemplaria* (Special issue: *Conscience and Contestation, Langland to Milton*, ed. Paul Strohm) 24,1 & 2 (2012): 143–60; and "John Foxe's Chaucer: Affecting Form in Post-Historicist Criticism," *New Medieval Literatures* 15 (2015 for 2012): 149–82.
11. Brian Massumi, *Parables for the Virtual: Movement, Affect, Sensation* (Durham, NC: Duke University Press, 2002), 27–8, insists that affects are not pre-emotions. For a historical account of the relation between affect and emotion, see Simo Knuuttila, *Emotions in Ancient and Medieval Philosophy* (New York: Oxford University Press, 2004); Michel Meyer, *Le Philosophe et les passions: Esquisse d'une histoire de la nature humaine* (Paris: Hachette, 1991); and Thomas Dixon, *From Passions to Emotions: The Creation of a Secular Psychological Category* (Cambridge: Cambridge University Press, 2003), 1–61.
12. Jameson, *Antinomies of Realism*, 34.
13. In this I follow Eleanor Johnson, *Practicing Literary Theory in the Middle Ages: Ethics and the Mixed Form in Chaucer, Gower, Usk, and Hoccleve* (Chicago, IL: University of Chicago Press, 2013): "By 'aesthetic' I mean that which is perceptible to the senses, and, by extension, I mean the literary devices, forms, topoi, tropes, and styles by which a work engages its readers' sense perceptions" (3).
14. Lee Patterson, "'What is Me?': Self and Society in the Poetry of Thomas Hoccleve," *Studies in the Age of Chaucer* 23 (2001), 448.
15. See A. G. Rigg, "Hoccleve's Complaint and Isidore of Seville," *Speculum* 45,4 (1970): 564–74. For a view of Hoccleve's debts to Boethius as part of an aesthetic strategy that is socially engaged, see Johnson, *Practicing Literary Theory*, 203–4.

16. The classic articulation of the importance of penitential literature remains Eva M. Thornley, "The Middle English Penitential Lyric and Hoccleve's Autobiographical Poetry," *Neuphilogische Mitteilungen* 68 (1967): 295–321.
17. See Christina von Nolcken, "'O, why ne had y lerned for to die?': *Lerne for to Dye* and the Author's Death in Thomas Hoccleve's Series," *Essays in Medieval Studies* 10 (1993): 27–51. See also David Lorenzo Boyd, "Reading through the *Regiment of Princes*: Hoccleve's *Series* and Lydgate's *Dance of Death* in Yale Beinecke MS 493," *Fifteenth-Century Studies* 20 (1993): 15–34.
18. See J. A. Burrow, "Autobiographical Poetry in the Middle Ages: The Case of Thomas Hoccleve," *Publications of the British Academy* [1982] 68 (1983): 389–412.
19. D. C. Greetham, "Self-Referential Artifacts: Hoccleve's Persona as a Literary Device," *Modern Philology* 86,3 (1989), 245. See also Steven Rozenski, "'Your Ensaumple and Your Mirour': Hoccleve's Amplification of the Imagery and Intimacy of Henry Suso's *Ars Moriendi*," *Parergon* 25,2 (2008): 1–16.
20. Dyan Elliott, "Rubber Soul: Theology, Hagiography, and the Spirit World of the High Middle Ages," and Elizabeth Robertson, "Kissing the Worm: Sex and Gender in the Afterlife and the Poetic Posthuman in the Late Middle English 'A Disputacion betwyx the Body and Wormes,'" both in *From Beasts to Souls: Gender and Embodiment in Medieval Europe*, ed. E. Jane Burns and Peggy McCracken (Notre Dame, IN: University of Notre Dame Press, 2013), 89–120 and 121–54 respectively, trace the ways the soul takes on a feminine gender in medieval accounts. Hoccleve is equally invested in gendering the soul, as I mean to show here, but his affective management depends on a gender hierarchy.
21. Sarah Tolmie, "The Professional: Thomas Hoccleve," *Studies in the Age of Chaucer* 29 (2007), 353.
22. J. A. Burrow, "Versions of 'Manliness' in the Poetry of Chaucer, Langland, and Hoccleve," *Chaucer Review* 47,3 (2013): 337–42.
23. Knapp, *The Bureaucratic Muse*, 71.
24. See Robyn Malo, "Penitential Discourse in Hoccleve's *Series*," *Studies in the Age of Chaucer* 34 (2012): 277–305.
25. E. Ruth Harvey, *The Inward Wits: Psychological Theory in the Middle Ages and the Renaissance* (London: Warburg Institute, 1975), 2.
26. See Shannon Gayk, *Image, Text, and Religious Reform in Fifteenth-Century England* (Cambridge: Cambridge University Press, 2010), who stresses the visual aspects of Thomas' reform.
27. Gail Kern Paster, *The Body Embarrassed: Drama and the Disciplines of Shame in Early Modern England* (Ithaca, NY: Cornell University Press, 1993), 1–22.
28. Walter Hilton, *The Scale of Perfection*, ed. Thomas Bestul (Kalamazoo, MI: TEAMS Medieval Institute Publications, 2000), Book II, chap. 12, ll. 663–6.
29. *Sawles Warde*, in *Medieval English Prose for Women: Selections from the Katherine Group and "Ancrene Wisse,"* ed. Bella Millett and Jocelyn Wogan-Browne (Oxford: Clarendon Press, 1990), 86–109.

30. Karen Smyth, "Reading Misreadings in Thomas Hoccleve's *Series*," *English Studies* 87,1 (2006), 14, 19, characterizes the narrator's struggle as the struggle to submit to Reason (as he does at the end of *My Compleinte*). See also Johnson, *Practicing Literary Theory*, 206–13, for an analysis of Hoccleve's use of Boethian form in his submission to Reason.
31. Sarah McNamer, *Affective Meditation and the Invention of Medieval Compassion* (Philadelphia, PA: University of Pennsylvania Press, 2010), 11, 43–53, 119–49.
32. Thomas Hoccleve, *The Regiment of Princes*, ed. Charles R. Blyth (Kalamazoo, MI: TEAMS Medieval Institute Publications, 1999), ll. 3102–105.
33. Geoffrey Chaucer, *The Knight's Tale*, in *The Riverside Chaucer*, ed. Larry D. Benson, 3rd edn (Boston, MA: Houghton Mifflin Co., 1987). All citations given parenthetically to fragment and line numbers.
34. Wack, *Lovesickness*, 78.
35. McNamer, *Affective Meditation*, 1–21.
36. John M. Bowers, "Thomas Hoccleve and the Politics of Tradition," *Chaucer Review* 36,4 (2002): 352–69, suggests the lack of attention to Hoccleve is due in part to his political choices, which influenced his poetic writings. See also Ruth Nissé, "'Oure Fadres Olde and Modres': Gender, Heresy, and Hoccleve's Literary Politics," *Studies in the Age of Chaucer* 21 (1999): 275–99, who connects Hoccleve's advocacy of peace (or war) to issues of masculinity and kingship.
37. For an excellent treatment of the politics that potentially informs Hoccleve's formal choices (and his reception thereby), see Bowers, "Thomas Hoccleve."
38. Teresa Brennan, *The Transmission of Affect* (Ithaca, NY: Cornell University Press, 2004), 51–73.
39. Ibid., 52, where Brennan remarks: "Entrainment is a name for the process whereby human affective responses are linked and repeated."
40. Sara Ahmed, "Happy Objects," in *The Affect Theory Reader*, ed. Melissa Gregg and Gregory J. Seigworth (Durham, NC: Duke University Press, 2010), 29–51.
41. See Sara Ahmed, *The Cultural Politics of Emotion* (New York: Routledge, 2004), 44–9, where she argues that feelings become associated through their "sticky" circulation.
42. Judith Butler, *Undoing Gender* (London: Routledge, 2004), claims that gender's performativity involves "a practice of improvisation within a scene of constraint" (1).
43. Hoccleve, *Regiment*, 2915. The mention of John Badby occurs earlier, ll. 281ff.
44. On rulers and anger, see Gerd Althoff, "*Ira Regis*: Prolegomena to a History of Royal Anger," and Paul Hyams, "What Did Henry III of England Think in Bed and in French about Kingship and Anger?," both in *Anger's Past: The Social Uses of an Emotion in the Middle Ages*, ed. Barbara H. Rosenwein (Ithaca, NY: Cornell University Press, 1998), 59–74 and 92–124 respectively.
45. See Lester K. Little, "Anger in Monastic Curses," in *Anger's Past*, ed. Rosenwein, 9–35.

46. See Kristi Gourlay, "A Pugnacious Pagan Princess: Aggressive Female Anger and Violence in *Fierabras*," in *The Representation of Women's Emotions in Medieval and Early Modern Culture*, ed. Lisa Perfetti (Gainseville, FL: University Press of Florida, 2005), 133–63.
47. See Stephen D. White, "The Politics of Anger," in *Anger's Past*, ed. Rosenwein, 127–52.
48. Rosenwein, *Anger's Past*, 5.
49. See Karen A. Winstead, "'I am al other to yow than yee weene': Hoccleve, Women, and the *Series*," *Philological Quarterly* 72,2 (1993): 143–55.
50. Ibid., 152–3. Anna Torti, "Hoccleve's Attitude Towards Women: 'I shoop me do my peyne and diligence / To wynne hir loue by obedience,'" in *A Wyf Ther Was: Essays in Honour of Paule Mertens-Fonck*, ed. Juliette Dor (Liège: Université de Liège, 1992), claims that "by Hoccleve's time women had begun to play an active role in everyday life . . . [so] he could not avoid paying tribute to the status women had won for themselves" (273).

CHAPTER 4

Becoming One Flesh, Inhabiting Two Genders: Ugly Feelings and Blocked Emotion in the Wife of Bath's Prologue and Tale

Glenn D. Burger

Geoffrey Chaucer's Wife of Bath opens her autobiographical Prologue with a vigorous challenge to male authority:

> Experience, though noon auctoritee
> Were in this world, is right ynogh for me
> To speke of wo that is in mariage.[1]

Finally, she promises, we will hear the subaltern speak in her own voice as she talks back to an anti-feminist clerical tradition that for too long has tamped down women's natural tendencies. The Wife follows with a full-throated defense of a woman's right to use her body to its fullest and to marry multiple times, displaying such affective intensity that it seems she must indeed be communicating the embodied truth of a woman's lived experience. We hear a voice, we think we see a body. Yet what is really represented by this virtuosic performance of female affect?

First, what we witness in the Wife's performance of selfhood is, in the end, a set of rhetorical effects rather than biological fact.[2] There is no real woman's body to be discovered beneath the Wife's rhetorical clothing. Instead, performing female sexuality as a compulsion to *maistrie* foregrounds an all too familiar set of clerically authored clichés. Rather than the promised transgressive reinscription of subaltern femininity as biological action in the world, the Wife's identification of "female" as unruly affect, pure and simple, fits all too readily into a script used by a medieval anti-feminist tradition to produce forms of socialized emotion – for example, "the wo that is in mariage" – that stabilize sex/gender difference and maintain the dominance of clerical masculinity and virginity. As rhetorical performance, the Wife's self-presentation at the opening of the Prologue reproduces what appears to be a circular argument – between wives and husbands, laywomen and celibate clergy, orality and literacy, personal experience and traditional authority – that seems to preclude any possibility for actual change and innovation in the world. Yet, while the Wife presents the desire for *maistrie* as the truth about sexual relations, her performance of "what women want," here, in fact functions as a kind of rhetorical bait and switch. For such a vivid representation of the "wo that is in mariage" does not express the material complexity of the social experimentation that is taking place in the married estate in the period, especially in how it is charting new ways for sex/gender relations to be re-imagined, and with that, for the bourgeois and gentry household to model new forms of social and state relations. Thus, the Wife's performance importantly both attracts and repels its readers, especially readers from a similar social position to the Wife, that is, part of newly empowered and higher status "middling" groups of bourgeois, gentry, or would-be gentry subjects.

This essay explores the complex interplay of affect and emotion in the *Wife of Bath's Prologue and Tale* in order to understand just how they intervene in a broader discussion of female conduct, marital affection, and social innovation taking place in the later Middle Ages. Comparing and contrasting Chaucer's text with *Le Ménagier de Paris (The Good Wife's Guide)*, a contemporary conduct text and household book ostensibly written by an older husband for his young wife, I argue that in the first instance the Wife's autobiographical Prologue functions as a kind of anti-conduct book, her life story similar to the exemplary stories of bad women found in contemporary conduct texts. At the same time, the Wife's audience remains caught up in the affective intensity of her negative emotions. This bifurcated position we inhabit in relation to her performance, especially the account of the final domestic quarrel between Alisoun and her fifth husband, Jankyn, forces us in the Prologue to experience the married estate in more complexly material terms, not simply as an already socialized emotion, the "wo that is in mariage," but as what Sianne Ngai calls "ugly feelings," that is, the "affective gaps and illegibilities, dysphoric feelings, and other sites of emotional negativity" that result in "ambivalent situations of suspended agency."[3] As a result, to an extent not taken up in contemporary conduct literature for women, we are encouraged to explore from below the anxieties raised by bourgeois and gentry attempts to develop new ethical subject positions based on heterosexual desire and married relations. In turn, the Wife's Tale occupies a similarly unstable relationship with contemporary conduct literature for women and the social innovation it makes possible. The Tale presents a mirror image to the stabilizing reconfiguration of masculine and feminine articulated in a conduct text such as the *Ménagier*. If the latter text reconfigures gender as a way of authorizing emergent subject positions, the Wife's Tale, especially the final bedroom debate between rapist knight and loathly hag, pushes the kind of social innovation imagined in such conduct texts to its logical limits in challenging, even utopian ways.

Disabling Sex Difference: "Maistrie" and "The Wo that is in Mariage"

If we accept the logic of the Wife's argument at face value, her desire for *maistrie* simply manifests a biological compulsion hardwired into men and women. It is, therefore, a kind of irrepressible innate emotional state, common to both men and women, but one which women are "naturally" more prone to manifest. Her need to seek *maistrie* thus does not distinguish her in essential ways from her "natural" opponents – husbands, clerics, any man put in authority over her – and thereby denies the validity of a traditional male-dominated power structure for the married estate as somehow representing a transcendent social order instituted by God. As a result, she argues, it is this innate desire for *maistrie* that essentially contours her embodiment in the world. It constitutes a kind of affective "skin," demarcating the boundaries of who she really *is* as a woman and wife, boundaries that reinforce sex difference as the defining category of identity but that also affectively connect her in cycles of attraction and repulsion with her various audiences.[4]

However rhetorically satisfying this argument about *maistrie* may be for the Wife as a mode of self-identification – showing the pleasures of "winning" arguments with clerics and husbands alike and getting truly to "be herself" as a woman – in fundamental ways it remains, in real-world social terms, largely a feeling with no place to go. Yes, the Wife's performance of the return of the repressed in traditional masculinist medieval culture provides us with a vivid experience of female embodiment. But such an experience of female embodiment as all biology all of the time fits too easily into longstanding medieval scripts about sex/gender difference that privilege the dominance of traditional forms of masculinity and chaste sexuality. So long as we remain within the tight dramatic focus that the Wife's performance encourages, we begin and end with the return of the repressed, that is, the inherent "wo that is in mariage" because of this biological imperative to *maistrie*. And for anyone not wanting a complete reversal of things as they are the links that the Prologue makes between the Wife's compulsion to seek *maistrie* over men and the inevitability of experiencing *wo* in marriage, between her affective skin and the production of negative emotion, implicitly work to reinforce the need to maintain an already existing asymmetrical power divide between men and women, husbands and wives, vernacular subjects and Latinate authority. From the point of view of social stability – in an age committed to the notion that the basic order of things cannot fundamentally change – if *maistrie* really is all that women want, then surely they do *need* masculine control; if *wo* is all that marriage, the defining feature of lay life, can offer, then clerical celibacy really does provide the best way of realizing one's full potential as a human being. We can enjoy the carnivalesque escape from reality offered by the Wife, but a "properly" disciplined reader, faced with a female presence whose social effects are recognizable only as *wo*, is "naturally" encouraged to turn instead to already existing models of affect management: away from negative emotions such as anger, pride, lust, greed, and towards positive ones such as composure, humility, purity, charity; away, in short, from the negative feelings produced by the Wife's emphasis on "the body" and towards the empowering subject position best exemplified by clerical masculinity.

Rather than marking the truth about a pre-social reality, then, the Wife's affective display in her rhetorical debates with clerical and husbandly authority models the *wo* that is wife as *itself* the disabling socialized effect of a clerically dominated textual culture that privileges a certain form of celibate masculinity. And rather than giving us a new kind of truth felt in the body, the Wife's display of authentic selfhood actually sets in motion a kind of smoke and mirrors operation allowing socialized emotion, and an ideological construct deeply imbricated with clerical misogyny, to masquerade as the kind of pre-social affect involved in simply "doing what comes naturally." The Wife's performance, then, does not take us *beyond* clerical anti-feminist accounts of female "experience" as she promises, but itself works to reproduce the structural binaries undergirding clerical authority: male/female, masculine/feminine, celibate clerical/married lay, textual/oral, Latinate/vernacular, authority/experience, and so on. Masculinity in such a sex/gender system necessarily offers the best model for rising above the constraints of embodiment. And marital relations, which bring masculinity into intimate contact with an abject feminine, therefore constitute a site of woeful emotional negativity and offer little conceptual room to maneuver in the medieval symbolic.

But something unexpected is also taking place alongside the cycle of compulsion/repulsion that the Wife's performance foregrounds as the inevitable product of sex/gender relations, something, I argue, that is at the heart of what we find truly challenging and affecting about our experience of the Wife. Her presentation of woman's nature as unstable fleshliness *also* represents lay experience more generally as essentially an experience of the emotion *wo*. In her autobiographical account of marriage, the married estate, with its looser, less constrained social structures, constitutes a natural space for the play of lay desire and thus for feminine, biologically driven modes of embodiment. As she notes when describing her need to marry for a fifth time, and to a man half her age:

> For certes, I am al Venerien
> In feelynge, and myn herte is Marcien.
> Venus me yaf my lust, my likerousnesse,
> And Mars yaf me my sturdy hardynesse.   (III.609–12)

At every point when the Wife emphasizes the biological in this way, she defines the need for sexual activity and *maistrie* within marriage as natural, quintessentially female urges, and then links such urges to a more general lay impulse to take part in commercial exchanges and to seek material and social advancement. "If I wolde selle my *bele chose*, / I koude walke as fressh as is a rose" (III.447–8), she notes, presenting herself simply as a good bourgeois subject who has taken to heart the experiential lessons learned from married life with her first three husbands. The Wife's performance thus foregrounds the intertwining of both female *and* lay as similarly abject categories within a social system that has traditionally privileged celibate masculinity as the ideal human behavior and that therefore has conjured up female fleshliness as its threatening Other.

As a result, the homologies that the Wife establishes between female embodiment and the lay married estate interpellate lay readers of the Tale in profoundly destabilizing ways. If such readers accept the Wife's affective encounters with them at face value, without any examination of their social construction and material contexts, they either allow themselves to be subsumed within an abject, yet insurgent feminine subject position *or* within a masculinity accepting the dominance of clerical celibacy. Yet neither of these subject positions matches the complexly entangled identities being developed by newly empowered laymen and laywomen from within the married estate.

Beginning with the renewed emphasis on marriage as a sacrament undertaken by canon lawyers and theologians in the twelfth and thirteenth centuries, and disseminated more widely across Europe and among the laity by preachers in the thirteenth and fourteenth centuries, the reconfiguration of marriage as sacrament had penetrated all levels of Western European society by the later Middle Ages, as studies of marriage litigation have demonstrated. Marriage as sacrament was thus primarily conceived not as a contract between families to transfer land, belongings, and social status, as it had been throughout much of the early Middle Ages, but instead as a contract between man and woman whose informed consent – expressed when they pronounced the words of present consent in the wedding ceremony – was the essential marker of a valid sacramental marriage. Along with a new emphasis on the importance of the couple's informed consent and marriage as sacrament, medieval canon law, theology, and preaching during this period also stressed growth in marital affection as a goal. At the same time, changing economic and social conditions across Europe underscored the value that companionate relations in marriage could offer and accorded increasing importance to the managerial role that a wife could be called upon to play in the late medieval bourgeois, gentry, or noble household.[5]

Viewed from the perspective of these changes taking place in the later Middle Ages in the married estate and its representational power, the Wife's autobiographical Prologue constitutes more a dis-abling backward glance (to a long-established sex/gender system that offers only limiting subordinate options for laymen and laywomen) than a presentist, forward-looking snapshot of "things as they are" in late medieval society. Thus, I argue, a contemporary layman (or laywoman) from the same emergent "middling" group as the Wife would probably not choose to identify with her self-presentation as fleshliness out of control. But neither could he (or she) any longer simply buy into longstanding medieval modes of identification that subsume lay experience within "universal" models privileging celibate cleric or knightly aristocratic masculinities. Such lay readers are thus encouraged to stand uneasily *beside* the Wife, at once inside and outside the tight focus of voice and body that her performance enacts. Not unlike actual late medieval gentry and bourgeois husbands and wives, such readers inhabit a productively unstable situation *in between* innovative, empowering understandings of the married estate and traditionally dismissive accounts of marriage as a distant second to virginity. In doing so, they must adopt a different, more hybrid form of affect management than that provided by traditional clerical or aristocratic sex/gender systems that privilege male celibacy or the masculine erotics of *fin'amor*.

Late medieval conduct literature for women provides one notable genre charting this experimentation with the social that is taking place in the development of a sacramental and companionate understanding of married estate.[6] In the *Ménagier de Paris* (c. 1393), for example, marital affection functions as a kind of emotional "skin" contouring the differently gendered, embodied identities of good wife and good husband at the same time as it works to connect them in socially productive ways. If we read the *Wife of Bath's Prologue and Tale* in light of such a text, we can see how her Prologue functions as a kind of anti-conduct text, a mirror image of a male-authored text such as the *Ménagier*; further, the Tale puts in play a bold reinscription of the social engineering imagined by such contemporary conduct literature, with a woman now in the leadership role the *Ménagier* assigns to the husband. As I argue below, especially in the intimate domestic debates between husband and wife that close the Prologue and Tale respectively, Chaucer pushes to its limits the ability of conduct literature to mine the potential of marital relations to reconfigure the sex/gender system, and with that, the relationship of the individual with the social.

Reorienting the Sex/Gender System: The Ménagier de Paris, Female Conduct, and Marital Affection

I have written at length elsewhere about how conduct texts for women offer a particularly rich nexus in which to take up the hybrid nature of the married estate and its potential for developing socially innovative gendered and sexualized subject positions.[7] This genre, offering textual authority to laymen in their familial roles of father and husband, also works to construct powerful emotional communities through an embodied display of individual self-restraint. The programmatic attention to one's own conduct and that of one's spouse instilled through such texts functions as a kind of affect management machine for its readers, and thereby works to reorient lay desire and gender roles within the married household.

The *Ménagier de Paris*, for example, articulates the immaterial labor of devotion and affect management that good wives and husbands can achieve within the affective contract and conjoined body of the married estate. It textualizes this transformation of desire – from simple sexual satisfaction to chaste restraint – as a set of performative reading practices that can be repeated by any husband or wife. Such practices, if followed properly, the text promises, will necessarily produce a self-restrained spouse productively laboring to make herself good. The subject positions of good wife and husband are thus no accidents of nature but manifestations of something truly universal, self-identifications capable of competing with those of clerical or courtly subjects. In authorizing the work of conduct in this way, this literature demonstrates the surplus value accruing to such immaterial labor on the part of laymen and laywomen. The prologue to the *Ménagier*, for example, dramatizes the text's point of origin as that moment during the week following their wedding when the much younger wife asks her husband if – in the absence of any family – each night in the privacy of their bedchamber he will correct her mistakes so that she can amend her behavior and become a better wife. He replies to her:

> My dear, because you were only fifteen years old the week we were married, you asked that I be indulgent about your youth and inexperience until you had seen and learned more. You expressly promised to listen carefully and to apply yourself wholeheartedly to preserving my contentment and love for you (as you so prudently said following advice from, I do believe, someone more wise than yourself), beseeching me humbly in our bed, as I recall, that for the love of God I not rebuke you harshly in front of either strangers or our household, but that I admonish you each night, or on a daily basis, in our bedroom, and that I remind you of your errors or foolishness of the day or days past and that I chastise you, if I should want to. You said that you would not fail to improve yourself according to my teaching and correction, and you would do everything in your power to behave according to my wishes. That pleased me so much, and I praised and thanked you for what you said, and I have since remembered it often.[8]

In doing so the *Ménagier*'s prologue dramatically illustrates the kind of affective contract that such conduct literature argues is crucial in creating ethical subjects necessary to manage productive households. It is this kind of affect management in order to intensify the desire to express marital affection to one's spouse, not sexual consummation nor the simple production of children and heirs, which will fully consummate the marriage and bring to completion the words of present consent given during the wedding ceremony.[9]

Paradoxically, however, the performativity of conduct also ensures that its readers can only achieve universality by incorporating the particularities of their uniquely gendered, sexed, classed material circumstances into the performance of self-restrained, chaste desire within the one flesh of the married estate. Unlike the clerical authors the Wife of Bath argues against, the husband in the *Ménagier* does not expect his wife to be a passive recipient of some pre-existent authority he ventriloquizes for her. Instead her request for instruction, which is the outgrowth of the individual consent she has provided in the marriage vow, elicits a pedagogy that the author has tailored to her (and his) material circumstances. Because she is very young, her husband does not expect her to give up all youthful pursuits. Instead, he will provide her with a text various enough to adapt to her changing circumstances as she ages and grows in wisdom. He thus imagines her, as she matures, using his library, herself taking on his role as advisor to young women or daughters in her care, even marrying another man after his death. Furthermore, at the beginning of the lengthy second half of the book, which exhaustively covers the minutiae of day-to-day household governance, the author notes the ultimate goal of such an attention to conduct and proper self-formation in the wife: "next to your husband, you should be mistress of the household, commander, inspector, governor, and sovereign administrator."[10]

In such texts, however, the conduct of the good wife does not remain a matter confined to the domestic, interpersonal relations of the married household. These texts also need to find ways of expressing in the public sphere the value of the good wife's immaterial labor if the married household's productive affect management is to become fully social. The *Ménagier* is notable for its obsession with the material "facts" that will demonstrate the orderliness of the good wife's own embodiment and that of the complex household she administers: shaping how she walks, talks, dresses, socializes; instructing her in the hiring, control, and punishment of servants; providing information about every detail of shopping, catering, and housekeeping. In describing the embodied presence of the good wife and the domestic sphere in this way, such texts provide a skin for marital affection, construct, if you will, a new emotional framing of how such embodied sober self-restraint can find a point of entry into the social. No longer simply an inferior, debased state below an idealized celibacy, marriage in late medieval conduct texts for women put lay husbands on a par with, or even above, celibate clerics, and gave wives the opportunity for a chaste status previously available only to virgin nuns. As a result, the conjunction of a self-controlled husband and good wife could not only anchor a new household unit but also provide a model for civic society dramatically different from previous aristocratic or clerical ones. And affect management within marriage, expressed especially clearly through the conduct of good wives and husbands in a new kind of couple-centered household, became a powerful signifier of the good that could be produced by lay, married relationships.

Exploring Marriage's Ugly Feelings and Blocked Emotion: Standing beside the Wife in the Prologue

As even this brief account of late medieval marriage and conduct literature for women makes clear, the Wife's representation of *maistrie* and "doing what comes naturally" is radically at odds with changes taking place in the married estate and the sex/gender system it could imagine. Rather than expressing the truth about marriage in the period or about the feminist agency she has achieved by mastering five husbands, the rhetorical performance of "woman" with which she opens the Prologue demonstrates only the limited instrumentality given the feminine by an objectifying clerical anti-feminism. In the Wife's account (which is that of clerical anti-feminist tradition), the married estate, and the gendered relations it makes possible, can only attest to a recurring experience of stalemate rather than real debate and fruitful speculation. What I have been describing in the larger performance arena of the Wife's Prologue, however, suggests that something more complex in affective terms is taking place in the Wife's argument about the married estate. If, as I am suggesting, we stand beside the Wife in a way that encourages a double vision of clerical anti-feminist and conduct literature accounts of the married estate and what inter-gender lay relations might be capable of, then the Prologue encourages a more profoundly materialist analysis of the affects generated by the married estate: both the socially effective manifestations of marital affection found in conduct texts and the potentially negative or socially ineffective emotions arising out of the hybrid location of married laymen and laywomen. We are therefore encouraged to linger in the profoundly ambiguous position that the married estate occupies in this period, and as a result, to experience the affective states of medieval marriage (and "middling" lay experience more generally) not simply as negative emotion ("the wo that is in mariage") but as less completely socialized, subaltern, blocked emotion. This turn to a materialist experience of the "ugly feelings" produced by living as sexed and gendered married men and women – roles at once power-filled and subaltern for emergent groups in this period – finds its fullest representation in the domestic argument between Alisoun and her fifth husband, Jankyn, that ends the Prologue.

The content of the argument in certain ways reprises the debates between the Wife and male authorities at the beginning of the Prologue. But the materialist mode of representation here highlights the importance of attending to the role that *embodied* cognition in understanding "what women want." As a result, we are pushed to engage with the complexity of "ugly feeling" occasioned by the hybrid positions the married estate makes possible, rather than simply to accept as "natural" the scripted set of affects and movement to socialized emotion encouraged by the rhetorical debate with clerical authority at the beginning of the Prologue.[11] The Wife's argument with Jankyn occurs neither in the unlocalized public sphere of scholastic debate nor in the intimate space of bedroom sex, but instead in a domestic space neither completely private nor completely public.[12] In her encounter with her fifth husband, we once again find the Wife affected by and affecting a clerical anti-feminist tradition. But here we see a specific individual, Jankyn her clerk-husband, reading from a collection of stories of wicked wives he has in his possession. Jankyn's action is reminiscent of those moments of marital affection in the *Ménagier* where the young wife asks her husband to give her daily guidance each night in their bedchamber or where the husband searches his library to find material suitable for educating and advising his young wife. But the situation here foregrounds crucial differences between Chaucer's representation of Jankyn's husbandly "concern" for his wife's conduct and the *Ménagier*'s. Here there is no young wife asking for advice, nor does Jankyn, as concerned husband, read passages from the book selected and adapted to the specific needs of his wife's current situation. Instead, the scene of wifely (and lay) education represented here presumes the value of rote learning as Jankyn simply channels the voice of textualized clerical authority. Reading and listening here are not depicted as manifestations of or incitements to marital affection, as they were in the *Ménagier*. At the same time, the scene of reading we witness here does not remain static; instead we watch the disembodied voice of clerical authority that Jankyn evokes become material within the particular spaces inhabited by this couple. The violent interactions between Jankyn and Alisoun force us to see him simultaneously as clerk *and* husband, to hear the voice of clerical anti-feminism *and* to see the body of lay bourgeois masculinity in dissonance with each other. And most spectacularly, we see the conjoined body of the sacrament of marriage – man and woman come together as one flesh – symbolically ripped asunder by acts of verbal and physical violence, just as the leaves of Jankyn's book are literally torn in the Wife's attempts to throw it in the fire. We witness how the sexes here are kept apart rather than brought together in the kind of chaste affection imagined by conduct texts.

Jankyn's embrace of a clerical rather than husbandly point of view here keeps him from seeing or hearing the full possibility inherent in the present moment, dis-abling any possibility for affective reading and incitement of marital affection. In the Wife's Prologue, the physical violence that Jankyn and Alisoun inflict on each other, just like Jankyn's inattentive reading from the book and Alisoun's vengeful attempts to destroy it, materializes the ugly feelings and blocked emotions that characterize such failed domestic situations and thus indicates, in Ngai's words, the "affective gaps and illegibilities, dysphoric feelings, and other sites of emotional negativity" that result in "ambivalent situations of suspended agency."

Beating a wife (or an equivalent violent reining in of wifely loss of control) is occasionally advocated by conduct texts as an extreme example of marital affection. But such husbanding of the wife is there presented as a necessary, unwanted action brought about by a wife's extreme behavior or a husband's lack of attention to the physical and moral needs of his wife. In the section on wifely obedience in the *Ménagier*, for example, the text includes a story drawn from *The Seven Sages of Rome* about a beautiful young wife married to an old husband. Because he does not have sex with his wife, she decides to take a lover. Her mother advises her to test her husband first. The wife first cuts down her husband's favorite fruit tree, saying she did so to make a fire to dry him when he returned home cold and wet. The husband does nothing because she did it apparently out of concern for his well-being. Next, she kills her husband's favorite greyhound in front of him, explaining she did so because the dog muddied clothes and created more laundry. Her husband lets her off again when she pretends to be distressed that she has angered him. Finally, during the Christmas feast the wife pulls on the tablecloth so that everything on the table is overturned. Her husband says nothing until the next day when he tells her that she has bad blood and must be bled. She faints while that is occurring. When she awakes she calls for her mother and tells her that she no longer desires to take a lover because her husband has bled her so much that "I think I shall never enjoy my body." Restored to a humoral balance, the wife is now ready to listen to her mother's advice and vows never to neglect or anger her husband again.[13] Thus, when the Wife literally tears pages out of Jankyn's book or when Jankyn later burns it at her request, the book (and the tradition of celibate authority it embodies) is itself disabled in ways that parallel the disabling inflicted on the Wife when Jankyn boxes her ears and causes her partial deafness.

Thinking about the dis-abling of the conjoined body of the married estate in this way – as "less a single kind of act than an ecological field" – can also give us a different perspective on Alisoun's own disabling deafness that results from the domestic dispute with Jankyn. Lee Patterson has described the Wife's deafness as "an evidently enabling handicap; unable to hear the overbearing discourse of male superiority in all its authority, the Wife reproduces instead a parody that inscribes and legitimizes female difference."[14] I would say exactly the opposite. Recently there has been growing interest in bringing the insights of contemporary disability theory to bear on the Wife's deafness, that is, a desire to forestall rendering her deafness as a metaphor for limited understanding or as a shield against the discourse of patriarchal culture, and to focus instead more literally on the significance of her deafness as physical deafness.[15] I think it is also important – without simply turning the Wife's into metaphor – to consider how her disability is in crucial ways not just a matter of biological inheritance, something she was born with, but also a somatic marker of the disabling effects of the social on the body. Mikee Delony, for example, has argued that we must consider how the female body itself is something the Middle Ages viewed as inherently disabled. I want to extend that to think about the disabling effects of a clerical anti-feminism on the "one flesh" brought into being in the married estate.

The Wife's deafness, I argue, is a disabling that exists in the gap between the individual and the social, between the sexes, between inner and outer, between public identities and inner feelings. Her disability is a feature of her affective "skin" and the play of feeling that it initiates – in its representation of the connections between individual and social in embodied, affective terms, and more generally in the affective relations that are shown between Wife and pilgrimage auditors and put in place between Wife as character and Chaucer's readers. They, as much as the Wife, are caught up in the ugly feelings generated by hybrid gender relations that can find no productive emotional representation. They see and feel the impact of the social on the body, the Wife's impact on our experience; they materially respond to the hybridity of the married estate represented in her fight with Jankyn, and experience the disabling "ugly feeling" and blockages of conflicting representations of what "really" is happening in this moment.[16] As such, her deafness bears witness to the power of a clerically defined sex/gender system to deform and disempower the "one flesh" of the married estate. To that extent, it is a shared disability between the Wife and Jankyn; as Sara Ahmed reminds us, the skin created by affective contact "connects as well as contains."[17]

The Wife's deafness, then, parallels the "ugly feelings" that the reader witnesses as he/she stands beside the Wife's performance of *maistrie* and *wo* as positive emotional experiences for the subaltern subject. It lingers as a stubborn remainder alongside the Wife's "happy" account of a chastened Jankyn listening to his wife and burning the book of wicked wives in the fire at her request. The materialist analysis that I have been arguing structures how we experience the affective politics of the Prologue, also suggests that we should reconsider just how much the romance Tale that follows really does complete or supersede the Wife's autobiographical account of herself here. I argue instead that the Tale should be seen as itself positioned *beside* the Prologue, entangling present and past, autobiography and romance, in unexpected ways. If the end of the Prologue functions as a kind of disabling, anti-conduct text that exposes the limits of a clerically defined sex/gender system, the Tale, despite its conjoining of romance elements and rape, ultimately turns to the kind of intimate script developed for husbands and wives in late medieval conduct literature as a way to focus on the value of marital affection and the conjoined body of the married estate in developing new emotional states of being in the world.

Two Bodies, One Flesh: The Skin of Marital Affection in the Wife of Bath's Tale

The rape of the maiden by the "lusty bachelor" that opens the *Wife of Bath's Tale* is reported in such a matter-of-fact way – he saw her, he took her, he left her – that it provides a perversely masculine mirror image to the Wife's bombastic claim in her Prologue that she is "al Venerien," and by extension, that female behavior is simply the result of biological urges. Moreover, such biological and social determinism concerning the rapist knight is matched by the dispassionate, almost mechanical imposition of legal justice that follows his actions. Lying between these mechanistic accounts of individual action and its place within the social, however, are a succession of apparently agential emotional interventions. After the report of the rape, there was "swich clamour / And swich pursute unto the kyng Arthour" that the knight is threatened with the loss of his head "by cours of lawe" (III.889–90; 892). Then, the intercessory pleading of the queen and her ladies for mercy leads Arthur to turn the knight over to the queen to decide his fate.[18] Very quickly, "doing what comes naturally" appears to give way to personal choice and deferral of judgment as the knight must choose between immediate beheading or the choice of a year's quest to find out what it is that women want. The narrative arc of the Tale's romance quest plot thus would appear to emphasize a dialogic method – male violence and deafness to women's feelings versus an attention to what women really want, a mechanistic rule of law versus the ladies' affective appeal to noble pity – and a circular structure that demonstrates masculine maturation and its ability to change.

The romance plot here reduces a highly developed, socially powerful aristocratic discourse of *fin'amor* to its most basic elements. A knightly masculinity that self-identifies largely through violent action is productively contained by a femininity expressed largely as embodied affect. The rapist knight is taught an important lesson about sociality through such mastery by a woman and is therefore equipped to express a more fully *chivalric* aristocratic identity in the world. In this way, the Tale provides a kind of corollary to the Wife's engagement with a dominant clerical sex/gender system in her Prologue. Here too a dominant sex/gender system – now aristocratic – enacts its own kind of essentializing sex difference. But rather than moving us and the knight forward into a more mature understanding and re-formation of chivalric masculinity, the effect of the romance narrative is to reassert the social as it already is. The question "what do women want" thus elicits a univocal response that re-inscribes mastery as the only possibility. While the violence of the knight may be contained by his reincorporation into the social, and female voices may gain the appearance of being heard, in fundamental ways the ritualized performance of gender and class continues unchanged by the romance testing of the knightly anti-hero.

But like the playful plotting of *Sir Gawain and the Green Knight* – where the *real* test of Gawain turns out not to be the physical threat of beheading that he moves towards as his future and the climax of the romance narrative, but rather the conspiracy conducted by Bertilak through his wife in the bedroom scenes and Gawain's acknowledgment of fear – the actual plot of the *Wife of Bath's Tale* concerns the return of the repressed in the form of another "wyf" who will not go away. "A fouler wight ther may no man devyse" (III.999), the old woman that the knight encounters, and especially the woeful intimacy she forces on the knight by insisting that he marry her, condenses the repressed othering of female embodiment at the heart of both clerical and aristocratic sex/gender systems. The affective encounter she establishes with the knight is in marked contrast to the controlled emotion represented by the earlier "clamor" of a people contained by the rule of law, or by the stylized femininity of the ladies' emotional plea for mercy. Instead, the old woman – who we and the knight comfortably thought of as a native informant happy to be the agent of aristocratic control – here is able to step outside such a limited instrumentality for her "kind."

As so much of the Tale does, the wedding night encounter of young husband and old wife reworks the narrative material of the Wife's Prologue in unexpected ways, notably as it explicitly takes up the question of "the wo that is mariage." In the Wife's Prologue such *wo* was worked out in terms of a clerical sex/gender system that privileged (male) celibate subject positions. Now *wo* is expressed in terms of an aristocratic model of dynastic marriage that so frequently creates woe for the female brides chosen to transfer property or for the male subjects of *fin'amor* seeking modes of affective expression outside the bonds of marriage. The Wife's account of how to establish a successful married household shows the young aristocratic husband dis-empowered and dis-abled in ways we might normally associate with a young wife's position within an arranged marriage. A natural member of the ruling class – by virtue of aristocratic birth and gender – is initially forced into the position of the subordinate and gives voice to the "ugly feelings" that must have been felt if not easily voiced by young wives such as May, in Chaucer's *Merchant's Tale*, married to distinctly unattractive old men:[19]

> So wo was hym, his wyf looked so foule.
> Greet was the wo that the knyght hadde in his thoght.
> Whan he was with his wyf abedde ybroght;
> He walweth and he turneth to and fro. (III.1082–5)

But, of course, the knight's explosion of affect at this point is notably different from the situation of a May or other young wives placed in similar situations. Theirs would be versions of Ngai's "ugly feelings," blocked emotions that have no socialized mode of expression and therefore can only be expressed indirectly. And not surprisingly, perhaps, the knight here finds an emotional script readymade and at his disposal, adopting the "wo that is in mariage" language that the Wife of Bath quotes at the beginning of her Prologue. The knight here can be forthright in his disgust, partly because, as an aristocratic knight, he has access to such socialized forms of emotional release as his birthright. Whereas the old "wyf" here insists:

> For thogh that I be foul, and oold, and poore
> I nolde for all the metal, ne for oore
> That under erthe is grave or lith above,
> But if thy wyf I were, and eek thy love. (III.1063–6)

The knight indignantly responds:

> "My love?" . . . "nay, my dampnacioun!
> Allas, that any of my nacioun
> Sholde evere so foule disparaged be!" (III.1067–9)

But the knight's second emotional outburst cannot so easily be explained away simply as the manifestation of inherent class privilege or concern for shame to his family name.

The knight erupts into violent emotion now because he has been provoked by his new wife's needling accusation that he is not living up to the reputation of Arthur's court, and by her enjoyment of the irony that a man and a class usually in control is here immobilized by a subaltern subject such as herself. As a result, the knight is pushed to give voice to the ugly feelings produced by the experience of disempowerment:

> Thou art so loothly, and so oold also,
> And therto comen of so lough a kynde,
> That litel wonder is thogh I walwe and wynde.
> So wolde God myn herte wolde brest! (III.1100–03)

The wife's needling of the knight may appear on the surface simply to mirror the enjoyment of an old husband with a new trophy wife, the kind of wedding night "bliss" that Chaucer's Merchant mocks in his story of January and May. But unlike the objectifying enjoyment that January shows on his wedding night, demonstrating how May is nothing but flesh to be controlled and shaped to his enjoyment, the wife's comments here also develop an affective connection – albeit one initially "ugly" – between her and the knight that insists on the possibility of an affective contract rather than simple mastery and control – "I am youre owene love and youre wyf" (III.1091) – and through that connection the possibility that the "gilt" (III.1096) he accuses her of can be "amended" (III.1097). To that extent the wife here seems more like the concerned husband of a conduct text such as the *Ménagier*, intent on bringing his less mature spouse to a greater degree of self-awareness.

If the knight begins by clinging to a gendered and classed identity that blinds him to what is actually in the room with him, that lets him and us see only the degradation of engagement with alternative forms of embodiment, the wife's engagement with him as wife opens up other lines of affective communication and argument. Notably, she shows him how true amendment of his supposedly shameful condition by being married to her "belongs to the domain of free will and choice,"[20] and depends upon his embrace of a married love that is "a moral obligation," one which he as a husband can be persuaded to take up by her arguments about the value of poverty, low birth, and lack of beauty. In doing so she echoes many of the strategies and methods of a conduct text such as the *Ménagier* by emphasizing the performative nature of conduct and the importance of intimate scripts developed by means of careful choice from the options presented to one and equally carefully adapted to the needs of an intimate interlocutor. Thus, by the end of the Tale, the knight accepts a new nature in which masculine and feminine can "companion" one another in unpredictable and innovative ways.[21] His obsession with woman as (abjected) body is transformed into a self-restrained desire for the benefits of marital affection entered into of his own free will and choice. By assenting to this kind of affect management, the knight is shown a way to bring personal consent to a marriage that on the surface looks like simple coercion and a space in which the only affect possible is the abjecting one of "ugly feelings." Like the *Ménagier*'s fifteen-year-old wife, who on the first night of marriage, begs her older husband to instruct her, sparing no punches, the knight in the Wife's Tale on his marriage night begs for counsel from the old woman he has been forced to marry, and willingly accepts that, in doing so, his wife displays true marital affection.

The increase in marital affection that the old woman's bedchamber lecture initiates thus provides a truer consummation for the performative "I take you" of the marriage ceremony than actual sexual activity could. Both he and the Wife's readers are encouraged to recognize how, without such an incitement to desire the increase of marital affection, the union of young knight and old woman threatens to be as dehumanizing as the rape that starts the Tale. Notably, there is no book (real or symbolic) used by the old woman here to beat the knight into submission, as in the scene between Jankyn and the Wife of Bath at the end of her Prologue. Instead the performative reading practices used by the old woman to construct the married bedroom as scene of instruction adapts the disembodied authority of the book to construct instead, in Sarah McNamer's terms, an individualized "intimate script" that will permit true self-transformation.[22]

The newly conjoined body of the married estate, however, is represented at the end of the Tale not as an *organism* – how the *Ménagier* fantasizes husband as "head" and wife as "lower" appendage, if still a sovereign viceregent in the household – but as a *becoming-flesh*.[23] And the final transformation of the "loathly hag" into a young beauty should therefore be thought of as such a manifestation of affect and the virtual rather than an actual bodily fulfillment of male fantasy or romance completion, or as a magical transformation of symbolic content (the way Griselda in the *Clerk's Tale* may look like a poor peasant on the outside but "really" is noble to the core).[24] Once again, the affective skin that contours "wife" here connects as well as contains, this time to enabling rather than disabling effects. The transformation of sagging flesh into desirable fleshliness, of ugly feelings and blocked agency into intimate script and personal emotive,[25] renders visible the intensification of marital affect wrought by the wife's interventions, her ability to reform and instill alternative desire for self-restraint in the previously violent knight, to create a new affective skin connecting husband and wife.

The virtual, however, is not the real, and the return of the Wife of Bath's voice of *maistrie* at the end of the Tale reminds us of the fraught and tortuous path through which new affective relations connect to the social:

> And thus they lyve unto hir lyves ende
> In parfit joye; and Jhesu Crist us sende
> Housbondes meeke, yonge, and fressh abedde,
> And grace t'overbyde hem that we wedde.
> And eek I pray Jhesu shorte hir lyves
> That noght wol be governed by hir wyves;
> And olde and angry nygardes of dispence,
> God sende hem soone verray pestilence! (III.1257–64)

In contrast to the opening of the Prologue, however, the Wife of Bath's "voice" here cannot achieve the dematerialized "out of time and space" quality it had in the opening monologue, and because of that, cannot wipe out the transformative voice and affective force of the Tale's wifely presence. Or put another way, the affective "skin" of *maistrie* cannot simply substitute itself for the "skin" of marital affection that has transformed loathly hag into beautiful wife and rapist knight into companionate mate. So too, in this final transformative moment of the Tale, we inhabit two discursive registers and two conceptual fields without being able to settle fully in either: that is, both the *fantasy* of romance transformation (where the inner truth of a hero or heroine's character can magically be made manifest on the body and in the world) and the *real* performative of sacramental transformation (where two bodies can become one flesh, or bread and wine, the flesh and blood of Christ). Together, knight rapist/husband and loathly hag/beautiful bride, or loathly hag and Wife of Bath, are brought beside each other in a way that comprises "a wide range of desiring, identifying, representing, repelling, paralleling, differentiating, rivaling, leaning, twisting, mimicking, withdrawing, attracting, aggressing, warping, and other relations."[26] Only in such a way can we begin to experience fully both the "ugly feelings" *and* the transformative potential of late medieval marriage as social experiment.

Notes

1. Geoffrey Chaucer, *The Canterbury Tales*, in *The Riverside Chaucer*, ed. Larry D. Benson, 3rd edn (Boston, MA: Houghton Mifflin Co., 1987), III.1–3. All future references to the *Tales* will be to this edition and will be given parenthetically (by fragment and line number) in my text.

2. This observation, of course, is not a new one. It builds on a longstanding feminist interest in exploring the Wife as a product of patriarchal discourse. As Elaine Tuttle Hansen noted in the early 1990s, attempting to distinguish her feminist revisionary argument from a long tradition, extending from the fifteenth to the late twentieth century, of reading the Wife as a "woman whose opinion is accepted as authoritative": "More than any other well-known literary character, [the Wife of Bath] is frequently compared with historically real personages, from Christine de Pisan to Simone de Beauvoir. Where treated as a fictive character, she is often read in a sociological and historical context, as a sign of Chaucer's empathy with real women and/or understanding of feminine power; a realistic, historically plausible foil to the idealized views of femininity found in prescriptive texts of the period; possibly even 'a truly practicing feminist'; and indubitably a survivor and a spokeswoman." In contrast, Hansen argues "that the Wife's discourse in the *Prologue* and *Tale* belies her apparent garrulity, autonomy, and dominance. At this level of interpretation she paradoxically represents not the full and remarkable presence with which modern readings have tended to invest her, or even some feminine strategy of negativity and subversion that might be glimpsed through the text, but a dramatic and important instance of woman's silence and suppression in history and in language." *Chaucer and the Fictions of Gender* (Berkeley, CA: University of California Press, 1992), 26–8. For a somewhat different, influential reading of the Wife's representation of woman's silence and suppression, one that views her as mimicking the operations of patriarchal discourse and beginning to make a place for the feminine, see Carolyn Dinshaw, *Chaucer's Sexual Poetics* (Madison, WI: University of Wisconsin Press, 1990), 113–55.
3. Sianne Ngai, *Ugly Feelings* (Cambridge, MA: Harvard University Press, 2005), 1.
4. My thinking about *maistrie* as an affective "skin" here is indebted to Sara Ahmed's insight in *Queer Phenomenology: Orientations, Objects, Others* (Durham, NC: Duke University Press, 2006), that "the skin connects as well as contains": "Phenomenology hence shows us how objects and others have already left their impressions on the skin surface. The tactile object is what is near me, or what is within my reach. In being touched, the object does not 'stand apart'; it is felt 'by' the skin and even 'on' the skin. In other words, we perceive the object as an object, as something that 'has' integrity, and is 'in' space, only by haunting that very space; that is, by co-inhabiting space such that the boundary between the co-inhabitants of space does not hold. The skin connects as well as contains" (54).
5. For general discussion of these changes, see Glenn D. Burger, *Chaucer's Queer Nation* (Minneapolis, MN: Minnesota University Press, 2003), 60–77, and *Conduct Becoming: Good Wives and Husbands in the Later Middle Ages* (Philadelphia, PA: University of Pennsylvania Press, 2017), 16–30; David D'Avray, *Medieval Marriage: Symbolism and Society* (Oxford: Oxford University Press, 2015); Martha Howell, *The Marriage Exchange: Property,*

Social Place, and Gender in Cities of the Low Countries, 1300–1550 (Chicago, IL: University of Chicago Press, 2009), and "The Properties of Marriage in Late Medieval Europe: Commercial Wealth and the Creation of Modern Marriage," in *Love, Marriage, and Family Ties in the Later Middle Ages*, ed. Isabel Davis, Miriam Muller, and Sarah Rees Jones (Turnhout: Brepols, 2003), 17–61; Rüdiger Schnell, "The Discourse on Marriage in the Middle Ages," *Speculum* 73,3 (1998): 771–86; and Michael Sheehan, *Marriage, Family, and Law in Medieval Europe: Collected Studies*, ed. James K. Farge (Toronto: University of Toronto Press, 1996). For a discussion of marriage practices in late medieval England, see Shannon McSheffrey, *Marriage, Sex, and Civic Culture in Late Medieval London* (Philadelphia, PA: University of Pennsylvania Press, 2006). For discussions of marriage in late medieval English literature, see Burger, *Conduct Becoming*; Cathy Hume, *Chaucer and the Cultures of Love and Marriage* (Cambridge: D. S. Brewer, 2012); Emma Lipton, *Affections of the Mind: The Politics of Sacramental Marriage in Late Medieval English Literature* (Notre Dame, IN: University of Notre Dame Press, 2007); Conor McCarthy, *Marriage in Medieval England: Law, Literature and Practice* (Woodbridge, Suffolk: Boydell Press, 2004); and M. Teresa Tavormina, *Kindly Similitude: Marriage and Family in Piers Plowman* (Cambridge: D. S. Brewer, 1995).

6. Some of the earliest examples of the genre, the *Speculum Dominarum* (written c. 1300 by the Franciscan monk, Durand de Champagne, for Queen Jeanne de Navarre, wife of Philippe IV le Bel) or the late thirteenth-century *Enseignment à sa fille Isabelle* of Louis IX, adapt the model of *speculum principis* to that of female ruler. Others use the model of the mirror of virtues and vices – the anonymous mid- to late thirteenth-century *Miroir des bonnes femmes*, or Watriquet de Couvin's late thirteenth-century *Mireoir as dames*, or the anonymous fifteenth-century *Miroir aux dames*, for example – to compile collections of moralizing, exemplary stories of good and bad women from secular and biblical history. Less often, more thoroughly secular texts such as Robert de Blois' *Chastoiement des dames* (or *The Ladies' Instruction*) approach questions of moral conduct and *courtoisie* for ladies primarily in terms of the proper management of their physical appearance and of their social interactions with the men who surround them. The most fully developed examples from the period – the late fourteenth-century *Livre du Chevalier de la Tour Landry* and the *Ménagier de Paris* – also provide more complex, personalizing narrative frames for the didactic material, and incorporate a wide range of advice material drawn from family history, fabliaux, literary texts, and material culture, as well as more common moral and theological content from classical and scriptural sources. See Burger, *Conduct Becoming*, 75–140.
7. See Burger, *Conduct Becoming*, esp. 1–32, 191–7.
8. *The Good Wife's Guide (Le Ménagier de Paris): A Medieval Household Book*, ed. and trans. Gina L. Greco and Christine M. Rose (Ithaca, NY: Cornell University Press, 2009), 49. Further references in English will be from this translation and edition and given parenthetically in my text. ["Chiere seur,

pour ce que vous estans en l'eage de quinze ans et la sepmaine que vous et moy feusmes espousez, me priastes que je espargnasse a vostre jeunesse et a vostre petit et ygnorant service jusques a ce que vous eussiez plus veu et apris; a laquelle appreseure vous me promectiez d'entendre songneusement et mettre toute vostre cure et diligence pour ma paix et amour garder (si comme vous disiez bien saigement par plus sage conseil, ce croy je bien, que le vostre) en moy priant humblement en nostre lit, comme en suis recors, que pour l'amour de Dieu je ne vous voulsisse mie laidement corrigier devant la gent estrange ne devant nostre gent aussi, mais vous corrigasse chascune nuit, ou de jour en jour, en nostre chambre et vous ramenteusses les descontenances ou simplesses de la journée ou journees passees et vous chastiasse s'il me plaisoit; et lors vous ne fauldriez point a vous amender selon ma doctrine et correction et feriez tout vostre pouoir selon ma voulenté, si comme vous disiez. Si ay tenu a grant bien et vous loe et scay bon gré de ce que vous m'en avez dit, et m'en est depuis souventesfoiz souvenu."] *Le Mesnagier de Paris*, ed. Georgine E. Brereton and Janet M. Ferrier, trans. and notes Karin Ueltschi, Lettres Gothiques (Paris: Livre de Poche, 1994), 22. Future references to the French text are from this edition.

9. How marital affection signifies in the Middle Ages varies widely, and as a category, marital affection operates very differently from medieval *fin'amor* and modern romantic love. Marital affection, expressed most simply, was whatever worked to counter behavior that excessively corrected or mistreated a spouse. Beyond that, marital affection frequently described a spouse's care of the other's bodily needs – suitable dress and proper nourishment for wives, and for the husband, a peaceful, well-run home. But a developing understanding of the importance of the third good of the sacrament of marriage, its indissolubility or *sacramentum* (as opposed to the other two goods – offspring, or *proles*, and fidelity, or *fides*), led theologians to attach increasing importance to the transforming effects of grace throughout all aspects of the marriage, and hence to the *affective* dimension of this goal of increased marital affection. As Aquinas puts it, husband and wife are united not just in a fleshly union but also in a partnership of the whole range of domestic activity. Reorienting marriage in terms of individual consent and a growth in marital affection even led some churchmen to employ an unusually egalitarian language for such unions; Guibert de Tournai, for example, pronounces: "So if you want to get married, marry an equal" ("Unde si vis nubere, nube pari"), Paris, Bibliothèque nationale de France, lat. 15943, fol. 144va; quoted in David D'Avray and M. Tausche, "Marriage Sermons in *ad status* Collections of the Central Middle Ages," *Archives d'histoire doctrinale et littéraire du moyen age* 47 (1981), 129. In this sermon, Guibert distinguishes between two kinds of love in marriage: *dilectio carnalis* and *dilectio socialis*. He defines the latter as "the love which husband and wife owe to each other, because they are equal and partners" ("qua debent se coniuges diligere, quia pares sunt et socii"), BN lat. 15943, fol. 144vb; quoted in D'Avray and Tausche, "Marriage Sermons," 114. Equally important though – as D'Avray notes – for twelfth- and thirteenth-century preachers on marriage:

married love is also "a feeling which belongs to the domain of free will and choice ... In their view married love was a moral obligation and one which married people could be persuaded by arguments to fulfill." See D'Avray, "The Gospel of the Marriage Feast of Cana and Marriage Preaching in France," in *The Bible and The Medieval World: Essays in Memory of Beryl Smalley*, ed. Katherine Walsh and Diana Wood (Oxford: Blackwells, 1985), 216. Initially conceived largely in terms of caring for a spouse's bodily needs, by the later Middle Ages, marital affection was also understood in more profoundly affective ways: as the need to help a spouse to remedy personal failings, and thereby to develop a fully ethical subject position in the world.

10. "[A]pres vostre mary, vous devez ester maistresse de l'ostel, commandeur, visiteur, et gouverneur et couverain administreur" (440).

11. I am indebted to Eve Kosofsky Sedgwick's generative discussion of "the irreducibly spatial positionality of *beside*," in her *Touching Feeling: Affect, Pedagogy, Performativity* (Durham, NC: Duke University Press, 2003). She notes that as a critical term, *beside* offers: "some useful resistance to the ease with which *beneath* and *beyond* turn from spatial descriptors into implicit narratives of, respectively, origin and telos. *Beside* is an interesting preposition also because there's nothing very dualistic about it; a number of elements may lie alongside one another, though not an infinity of them ... Its interest does not, however, depend on a fantasy of metonymically egalitarian or even pacific relations, as any child knows who's shared a bed with siblings. *Beside* comprises a wide range of desiring, identifying, representing, repelling, paralleling, differentiating, rivaling, leaning, twisting, mimicking, withdrawing, attracting, aggressing, warping, and other relations" (8). As her model for such spatial positionality, Sedgwick cites Esther Newton's study in *Mother Camp: Female Impersonators in America* (Chicago, IL: University of Chicago Press, 1972), of the performances of female impersonators in relation to the floor plans of two drag clubs. Newton's attention to what was happening in the "multisided interactions among people 'beside' each other in a room" underlines, in Sedgwick's words, "Newton's continuous assumption that drag is less a single kind of act than a heterogeneous system, an ecological field whose intensive and defining relationality is internal as much as it is directed toward the norms it may challenge" (*Touching Feeling*, 9). In the *Wife of Bath's Prologue and Tale*, the Wife's opening monologue presents a voice and body apparently *beyond* traditional constraints and able finally to speak its truth, or alternately an experience *beneath* the radar of dominant discourses and here exposed in ways that textual, clerical culture is not interested in. Similarly, her narration of a succession of marriages establishes a temporality within the Prologue that turns that beneath and beyond into an implicit narrative of origin and *telos*: the Wife of Bath's female presence must ultimately be able to outperform canny bourgeois businessmen or a clerk like Jankyn; what the Wife of Bath wants must be what every woman wants. But the final scene with Jankyn, although ostensibly yet another iteration of the pursuit of *maistrie* on the part of the Wife, replays previous representations of the married state as "less a single kind of act than a heterogeneous system, an ecological field."

12. Curiously, it matches the location chosen by a manuscript illuminator of the *Ménagier* to illustrate the opening of that text. The illuminator resituates the bedchamber discussion between the *Ménagier*'s husband and wife to their upstairs private parlor, and presents them properly clothed and seated next to each. The color miniature of the *Ménagier* couple is found in Paris, Bibliothèque nationale de France, ms fonds français ms 12477, f. 1r, reproduced in black and white in *The Good Wife's Guide*, ii.
13. *The Good Wife's Guide*, 132–6. In another story in the same section on wifely obedience (119–20), the husband tells his wife the story of a married couple who quarrel with each other incessantly, each claiming to be the worthier, wiser, and nobler in lineage. Eventually the wife insists on a written contract for the marriage: all of her rights are written down, point by point, with all of the obligations she owes to her husband, and on the other hand, her husband's rights and obligations to her are also clearly listed. "With that," the narrator continues, "they should be able to live together in love – or if not in love, at least in peace" (119). One day, going on pilgrimage the couple must cross over a ditch by means of a narrow plank. The husband, crossing first, sees that his wife is frightened. So, he returns, takes her by the hand, and leads her across the plank. As he does so, he falls in the water. Drowning, he asks his wife to use her staff to draw the plank towards the bank to save him. She replies that she needs first to consult the marriage contract to see if it says she must do so. Since it does not mention such a situation, she leaves him to drown and goes on her way. Eventually a passing lord rescues the husband. When the lord learns what has happened, he has the wife pursued, seized, and burned. The story's negative example underscores the need for the kind of *affective* contract and true parity that we see entered into in the *Ménagier*'s prologue (and called for by Guibert de Tournai in his sermon; see note 9 above); an affective contract at the heart of medieval sacramental understandings of marriage.
14. Lee Patterson, *Negotiating the Past: The Historical Understanding of Medieval Literature* (Madison, WI: University of Wisconsin Press, 1987), 6, note 6.
15. See Mikee Delony, "Alisoun's Aging, Hearing-Impaired Female Body: Gazing at the Wife of Bath in Chaucer's *Canterbury Tales*," in *The Treatment of Disabled Persons in Medieval Europe: Examining Disability in the Historical, Legal, Literary, Medical, and Religious Discourses of the Middle Ages*, ed. Wendy J. Turner and Tory Vandeventer Pearman (Lewiston, NY: Mellen, 2011), 313–45; Tory Vandeventer Pearman, "Disruptive Dames: Disability and the Loathly Lady in the The Tale of Florent, the Wife of Bath's Tale, and the Weddynge of Sir Gawain and Dame Ragnelle," in The Treatment of Disabled Persons, ed. Turner and Pearman, 291–312; and Edna Edith Sayers, "Experience, Authority, and the Mediation of Deafness: Chaucer's Wife of Bath," in *Disability in the Middle Ages: Reconsiderations and Reverberations*, ed. Joshua R. Eyler (Farnham: Ashgate, 2010), 81–92.
16. Jonathan Hsy (in "Bound Codex as Prosthesis: Bookbinding as Site of Theory," a paper given to the New Chaucer Society Congress, Reykjavik, 2014) has argued for a connection between the Wife's disability and the

disablement of Jankyn's book. This suggests fruitful points of comparison between the Wife's deafness as the mark of a disabling sex/gender system that discounts the affective experience of the lay married estate and the book of tradition as it encounters the material contexts from which its authoritative "voice" emerges. In contrast, we might think of the extent to which conduct texts for women use clerical writing about women but adapt it to the quite different end of proving the good in woman and the married estate, often by bringing clerical models alongside sometimes competing or contradictory knowledges drawn from personal or family experience.

17. Ahmed, *Queer Phenomenology*, 54. See also, Isabel Davis, "Cutaneous Time in the Late Medieval Literary Imagination," in *Reading Skin in Medieval Literature and Culture*, ed. Katie L. Walter (New York: Palgrave Macmillan, 2013), who notes that "Alisoun is book-like: she is made out of 'skin' that has been preinscribed by others" (111).

18. Although these outbursts appear as an unmediated affective response to the cynical exercise of male power that takes place in the rape, neither the clamor of the people nor the intercessory pleas of the queen and her ladies could be called manifestations of individual affect. Instead, they are stock forms of socialized (and gendered and classed) emotion following social, rather than intimate scripts, and leading to the re-establishment of a pre-existing social order momentarily threatened by the excesses of a chivalric masculinity trained to cultivate violent forms of self-expression. For a discussion of the intercessory role of Queen Anne in Richard II's court, see Paul Strohm, *Hochon's Arrow: The Social Imagination of Fourteenth-Century Texts* (Princeton, NJ: Princeton University Press, 1992), 95–119.

19.
>And Januarie hath faste in armes take
>His fresshe May, his paradys, his make.
>He lulleth hire; he kisseth hire ful ofte;
>With thikke brustles of his berd unsofte,
>Lyk to the skyn of houndfyssh, sharp as brere–
>For he was shave al newe in his manere—
>He rubbeth hire aboute hir tendre face, . . .
>He was al coltish, ful of ragerye,
>And ful of jargon as a flekked pye.
>The slakke skyn aboute his nekke shaketh
>Whil that he sang, so chaunteth he and craketh.
>But God woot what that May thought in hir herte,
>Whan she hym saugh up sittynge in his sherte,
>In his nyght-cappe, and with his nekke lene;
>She presyeth nat his pleyyng worth a bene.
>
>(*Canterbury Tales*, IV.1821–7, 1847–54)

20. D'Avray, "Gospel of the Marriage Feast of Cana," 216.

21. After the old wife's bedroom lecture, when the knight is given the choice between having his new wife old, ugly, and faithful, or fair and potentially open to outside affairs, the knight responds:

> I put me in youre wise governance;
> Cheseth youreself which may be moost plesance
> And moost honour to yow and me also . . .
> For as yow liketh, it suffiseth me.   (III.1231–3;1235)

The knight's choice here has parallels both with the young wife's desire for guidance from a more experienced husband in the *Ménagier* and that husband's implicit recognition of the need for self-restraint and an ability to share authority with a wife who is sovereign administrator of the household. In other words, it implies a level of crossing of gender boundaries undertaken to a limited degree in a conduct text such as the *Ménagier* but here imagined in far broader terms. It is, after all, a *husband* here feeling "like a wife" and in the process, it is implied, better learning to be a husband. Perhaps because of this intensification of the potentiality for change in social relations, at the same time, the transformation of old wife into young, beautiful woman also calls into question the actuality of such a change in the day-to-day experience of men and women. It raises the question of whether, when there is talk of real choice or greater equality in married relations, there is ever the possibility of true equality, and whether sufferance is always part of the social.

22. Sarah McNamer, *Affective Meditation and the Invention of Medieval Compassion* (Philadelphia, PA: University of Pennsylvania Press, 2010), has characterized the affective meditations she examines as "intimate scripts": "They are quite literally scripts for the performance of feeling – scripts that often explicitly aspire to performative efficacy. Many are scripted as first-person, present-tense utterances, designed to be enacted by the reader. Others work through interpellation, hailing the reader as 'you' and directing affective response, even prescribing the gestures that will generate compassion ('behold him,' 'embrace him'). Still others stage detailed, vividly imagined scenes from the Passion and cast the reader as feeling eyewitness and participant. The participatory, performative character of these texts is often enhanced through the use of apostrophes and exclamations, deictic rhetoric ('here,' 'there'), and the regular use of the dramatic present" (12).

23. See Pearman's argument in *Disruptive Dames*, 309, about the loathly hag's ability to transform as effecting a larger social transformation:

> Instead of being condemned to being old, ugly, and disabled, Chaucer's hag *chooses* to appear in this guise in front of the knight [in the bedchamber discussion] . . . The hag's decision to take the shape of a disabled, old woman in order to influence a man marks the imperfect

body as a powerful body. According to Beidler, this hag does not need the knight to break a spell. "Rather, *he* needs *her* to effect his transformation from a 'lusti bacheler' into a more sensitive, more generous, more noble knight". The hag, however, influences more than just one knight. Despite the knight's fears that one so loathly would degrade 'any of [his] nacioun' (1068), which signifies both his familial line and his fellow citizens, it is clear that she seeks to transform the courtly structure itself when she compares herself to 'any lady, emperice, or queene, / That is bitwixe the est and eke the west' (1246–7). In the hyper-feminized court of the tale, the loathly lady hastens the tale's role reversal, which 'scrambles the semiotics of the family [and the disabled] body, and confounds gender role restriction' [Carter] while also advocating for a disruption of the court itself. Chaucer's hag, thus, escapes the limits of the narrative's attempt to normalize her by clinging to the productive qualities of the somatic memory of her former body. As such, the hag makes clear that her prostheticization is illusory. The hag seeks to transform the body politic in the same way that she shape-shifts her own body; in this way, the old, infertile body produces something new."

Pearman quotes here from Peter G. Beidler, "Transformations in Gower's Tale of Florent and Chaucer's Wife of Bath's Tale," in *Chaucer and Gower: Difference, Mutuality, Exchange*, ed. R. F. Yeager (Victoria, BC: University of Victoria, 1991), 109, and Susan Carter, "Coupling the Beastly Bride and the Hunter Hunted: What Lies Behind Chaucer's *Wife of Bath's Tale*," *Chaucer Review* 37,4 (2003), 340, respectively.

24. As Brian Massumi notes in *Parables for the Virtual: Movement, Affect, Sensation* (Durham, NC: Duke University Press, 2002), "The body is as immediately virtual as it is actual. The virtual, the pressing crowd of incipiencies and tendencies, is a realm of *potential*. In potential is where futurity combines, unmediated, with pastness, where outsides are infolded and sadness is happy (happy because the press to action and expression is life). The virtual is a lived paradox where what are normally opposites coexist, coalesce, and connect; where what cannot be experienced cannot but be felt – albeit reduced and contained. For out of the pressing crowd an individual action or expression *will* emerge and be registered consciously. One 'wills' it to emerge, to be qualified, to take on sociolinguistic meaning, to enter linear action-reaction circuits, to become a content of one's life – by dint of inhibition" (30–1).

25. William Reddy, *The Navigation of Feeling: A Framework for the History of Emotions* (Cambridge: Cambridge University Press, 2001), has articulated an influential theory of emotives, that is, "first-person, present tense emotion claims" that are "similar to performatives (and different from constatives) in that emotives do things to the world ... Emotives are themselves instruments

for directly changing, building, hiding, intensifying emotions, instruments that may be more or less successful." Reddy uses the concept of an emotive to analyze how groups can be bound together to form emotional "regimes" tied to state formation and hegemony (or its opposite) (104–5).
26. Sedgwick, *Touching Feeling*, 8.

CHAPTER 5

Accounting for Affect in the Reeve's Tale

Brantley L. Bryant

This essay asserts that both Chaucer's *Reeve's Tale* and documents of manorial practice allow us to explore the affects of accounting in late medieval agriculture.[1] The rigorous account-keeping and surveillance that drove manorial agriculture, I contend, made the manor a site for the textual exploration of affective intensity, and therefore a site that begs more attention from medieval affect studies. The document that most directly represents the sheer extent of manorial surveillance is the yearly account produced by a reeve. This exhaustive yearly reckoning was a distinctive and, in Chaucer's time, relatively recent form of bureaucratic observation, and does not go unnoticed in the *Canterbury Tales'* social imagination. The *Canterbury Tales* defines its story-telling Reeve by his accounting, and the *Reeve's Tale* explores the connection of this manorial management to affective control. In doing so, the Tale invites comparison with both the compositional form of the yearly manorial account and with the evidence of affect in manorial management recorded in the extant treatises from medieval England about the duties of manorial laborers: *The Seneschaucy, Walter of Henley,* and *The Husbandry*.[2] This essay will first argue that Chaucer focuses our attention on the affects of manorial surveillance through his assignment of a fabliau, a genre about circulation, to a Reeve defined as remorselessly managerial, enacting surveillance in the combination of tale and teller. The essay then compares the workings of affect in the Tale, in the circumstances of the yearly account, and in the practical treatises. In the Tale and manorial texts, we can discover a shared investment in the affective dimensions of surveillance, a special interest in the affective life of the medial figures who manage property and persons, and an attention to the feelings provoked by an accounting system that renders interchangeable humans, non-human animals, plants, and objects. The "malice of Chaucer's Reeve" is well known, and could simply be attributed to the Reeve's humoral composition as "colerik"; but attention to the distressing affects of the late medieval English manor can suggest an important context for why choler might be associated with the Reeve in the first place.³

Manorial documents have been of interest largely to historians reconstructing crop yields or techniques of agricultural production.⁴ Literary scholars can, however, use these seemingly matter-of-fact texts to investigate the kinds of subjectivity and affective relations imagined for manorial workers, as in recent work by Rosemary O'Neill and William Rhodes.⁵ Here I follow Lisa H. Cooper, who has proposed that critics should "consider whether insistently practical texts ... might be said to have a poetics."⁶ This essay explores ways that recent scholarly interests in documentary form and in affect can be productively combined.⁷ The concept of affect, as Holly A. Crocker defines it, "a non-rational, bodily force that contests individualist accounts of human agency" and "informs our affiliations without, or sometimes even in opposition to, our rational consent," is especially apt for theorizing the reactions of subjects, real or fictional, within systems of constraint and enforcement; dwelling on affect draws attention to conjunctions of manorial documents with the well-known dramatization of callous irrationalities in the *Reeve's Tale*.⁸ When we imagine medieval affect, the intensities of religious devotion or the sighs of amorous rapture might first come to mind. This essay will propose the equal importance of the affects of the manor, a nexus of social, legal, and economic forces that, in Mark Bailey's words, "touched and influenced the lives of common people in the Middle Ages, probably more than any other secular institution."⁹

Managing the Fabliau

The General Prologue emphasizes the Reeve's managerial labor, his account-giving, and the dread that he inspires, encouraging a reading of his tale in the context of manorial accounting and affect (I.587–622). The Canterbury Reeve is an account-maker *par excellence*, skilled at observing the movement of grain on the manor ("gerner" and "bynne"), estimating agricultural production ("the yeldyng of ... seed"), keeping livestock, and monitoring the behavior of other workers ("bailiff," "hierde," and "hyne").¹⁰ This management, the Reeve's "governynge," produces the "rekenynge" that he delivers to his lord: the yearly manorial account. Almost all of the details in the description of the Reeve in the General Prologue description either explain or depend upon his giving of the account (600–2), the mention of which stands directly in the middle of his portait. Even the Reeve's home in Norfolk links him to manorial accounting, since Norfolk manors were known for exhaustive manipulation of agricultural production for profit.[11]

The Reeve's production of a "rekenynge" positions him both as surveyor and surveyed in a system interested in controlling affect and controlling *through* affect. He can give his account because of his own keen observation and calculating mind, yet he is himself observed by the "auditor" who checks his account and who hopes to "wynne" from pointing out the Reeve's errors. Although the Prologue, at first glance, stresses the Reeve's success, the very mention of the "auditor" and the possibility of falling into "arrerage" shows the Reeve caught in a system larger than himself. Dread is noted as central to the accounting process. The other manorial workers fear the Reeve's surveillance as much as the plague itself, or "the deeth"; they are "adrad of hym as of the deeth" (605).[12] While the dread named here is specifically the reaction of subordinates to the Reeve, the word, working through suggestive contagion, reveals the centrality of fear and suspicion to this imagined manorial system. The "deeth" of that line rhymes surprisingly with the "heeth" of the next line where the Reeve has built his "wonyng," suggesting the alignment of the fear the Reeve creates with the position he occupies.[13]

Further investigation of manorial accounting in this period displays interweavings of management, surveillance, and affect similar to those in the Reeve's description. A reeve, indeed, stands out as an ideal figure for a writer like Chaucer, interested in the relationship of accounting to subjectivity.[14] English manors during Chaucer's time were business-like, by no means the quaint organic communities of the popular imagination.[15] Landholders maximized their profit and their control of laborers by exploiting elaborate technologies of management and accounting, carried out by networks of clerical and peasant officials. A land-owning lord would maintain a steward to oversee multiple manors, each manor run by a reeve or bailiff who would supervise lesser offices from dairymaid to shepherd. Production, sale, profit and loss would be tracked by tally-sticks and memory, regulated by checks and counter-checks, all eventually incorporated into the yearly account.[16] The entire system relied on a reeve's constant surveillance of labor and resources and his production of the manorial "rekenynge."[17]

We will soon see how manorial treatises touch on the affective dynamics of this constant observation. The manorial account itself, though, provides an immediate, if surprising, textual analogy for the *Reeve's Tale*. The Reeve, we are told, gives the yearly "rekenynge," and exploration of the tense collaborative production of the "rekenynge" document suggests ways that the fabliau of the *Reeve's Tale* is connected to the Reeve's previous documentary compositions.

Manorial accounts are a "dynamic record" of the struggles of different subjects to narrate the life of the manor, produced after intense surveillance, under intense surveillance, in potentially contentious collaboration, and subject to excruciating review.[18] The production of the account involved a reeve in difficult negotiations between power and subjection, speech and writing. Since reeves were largely illiterate, the account was written out in Latin by a clerk who was hired by the reeve. In this process, the reeve, who spoke to the clerk and provided the clerk with records, was the central conduit between the life of the manor and its recording in a formal document. A passage in one account makes this aspect clear, noting that a section is omitted because "the reeve died before he said anything about the fodder given to the oxen."[19] The same clerk who wrote the account was also, paradoxically, expected to look out for any wrongdoing by the reeve, as illustrated by a set of instructions for accounting clerks from a 1380 manuscript that warns the account-makers about tricks that a reeve might try to play.[20] According to Dorothea Oschinsky, this text shows that the clerk, "although engaged by the reeves, considered it his principal function to safeguard the lord's interests."[21] The first drawing-up of the account must have been an extreme labor, taking between three and ten days.[22] The account was then thoroughly examined by professional auditors, who engaged in a back-and-forth with the reeve and the accounting clerk, marking totals and determining any amounts for which the reeve might be responsible through fraud or negligence. The exacting and conflictual labor, and its high stakes (the reeve's reputation and finances depended on the account), imply a process charged with affect. A similar process, though differing in setting, procedure, and the social status of the participants, inspired an anguished early fifteenth-century poem: a set of Latin verses describe an Exchequer audit as a confusing series of hellish tortures.[23]

The very form of the manorial account, as it came to be standardized, carries an affective charge and resembles the structure of the *Reeve's Tale*. The manorial account's shape expresses its intense degree of surveillance and its exclusive concern with loss and gain. Although there are some variations, the late medieval English manorial account has a set format. It begins with a heading that includes the reeve's name, putting emphasis on his responsibility in the process. It then consists of ordered totals of "receipts" and "expenditure," including balances.[24] Money received or expended goes on the front of the account roll, and crops and livestock are accounted for on the back, each with orderly subheadings. This "rekenynge" covers almost every aspect of manorial life imaginable. One account from 1321 lists the following entries, among many others: fines from meetings of the manorial court; the exact value of ale given to customary workers; the wages of thatchers fixing the cow-shed's roof; the yields of wheat, barley, peas, vetches, and oats; and the loss of two cart horses from murrain.[25] These individual items become, in the account, part of a totalized numerical calculation of value. To twenty-first-century readers, this basic accounting format (list, in, out, balance) seems quite familiar, but it is worth considering the affective resonances of such a document: the account transforms a wide variety of things and experiences into a set of numbers designating cash value. Manorial accounting was a comparatively new, and exuberantly embraced, technology of control in Chaucer's time. Starting at a few large estates in the early thirteenth century, these accounting techniques spread throughout England to play a key role in the agile administration of manorial production.[26] The account's list of receipts and expenditures, I claim, provides an analogy to the *Reeve's Tale*'s own precise accounting for bodies, motions, and value. We can see a formal connection in the broadest sense, a poetics, or shaping of texts, that is interested in representing perceived objects at a high level of detail, in considering the nuanced position of intermediate agents working with the goods of another, and in equating a wide variety of goods by calculation.

When the account's formal ambitions to shape reality are transposed into a narrative fiction, affective intensity emerges even more clearly. Just as Chaucer's Reeve is defined by his participation in manorial accounting, his tale explores the affective resonances of that practice. If the life of the manor, its surveillance and relentless accounting, both produced and tried to control affect, then it is fitting that a tale told by a Reeve explores the frustrating affects of managing goods and people. Reading for affect, defined by Steele Nowlin as "the initial visceral responses that 'precede' emotion and the feelings that occur before their narrative interpretation by the mind as emotions," is especially useful for charting the reactions of subjects to a system of manorial production.[27] Subjects under constraint and surveillance, involved in busy production, are not given time for the kinds of processed articulations of emotion found in the *Knight's Tale* or *Troilus and Criseyde*, but in their exclamations, decisions, and reactions, their experiences can be read. Neither the *Reeve's Tale* nor manorial documents have much room for the elaborate examination of emotion, but they make space for the discussion of affect. In an arresting example of the regulation of bodies, force, and intensity, the treatise *Walter of Henley* asks a lord to examine his shepherd's relationship with the sheep he tends. A shepherd, the treatise writes, must not be too prone to anger (*irrous*), since he might beat the sheep and cause them to die. The lord is encouraged to watch the sheep as they walk with the shepherd, "and if the sheep avoid [the shepherd] then it is not a good sign that he is affectionate towards them" (*e les berbis vunt eschiwant dunqe nest pas bon sygne qil seit deboneyre a eus*).[28] My work here proposes that affect, bodily reaction, shout and cry and blow, are especially important topics to examine in relation to the regulation of late medieval English agricultural labor and in the texts that directly or indirectly describe it.

In the *Reeve's Tale*, Chaucer focuses on the affective consequences of manorial reckoning by creating a mismatch between the teller's position as middleman in a surveying bureaucratic system and the fabliau genre's teeming and uncontrollable abundance. The *Reeve's Tale*'s genre allows it to display the clash of the rigidity of accounting with the typical fluidity of fabliau economies. Simon Gaunt defines the "prime motivation of the [Old French] fabliaux" as "an interest in mutability, coupled with a mistrust of fixed hierarchies," and Holly A. Crocker notes that the "arousing multiplicity" celebrated by fabliaux allows them to "explore the ways that bodies infuse one another, often by embracing social and sexual divisions that are meant to preclude such congress."[29] In economic terms, Christian Sheridan observes that the Old French fabliaux depict the interaction of multiple economic systems, and points out that fabliau victors deftly negotiate these differences.[30] The fabliau form of the *Reeve's Tale* is therefore ironically significant. The Tale's genre leads readers to expect flow, mutability, and the "infusion" of bodies, but this customarily freewheeling genre is recast in the accounting interests of a supervisory manorial official. The resulting Tale sketches out the affective consequences of the redirection of free flow into regulated system: pleasures and pains of observation, strange distress, and a pervasive note of contempt.[31]

Form and Affect in the *Reeve's Tale*

There is no manor, of course, in the *Reeve's Tale*. The text does not directly represent manorial life so much as evoke situations of agricultural management in which accounting's affective dynamics can be explored. The text's setting shows this indirect evocation. The mill evokes a reeve's work, since milling, and rights to milling, were central aspects of manorial production.[32] The clerks' Cambridge college at first seems less directly tied to accounting, but J. A. W. Bennett has noted that the college mentioned in the Tale produced "recruits for the civil service" whose training would presumably include account-making.[33] Aleyn and John, we can imagine, are the kinds of clerks who might go on to work as manorial account-writers or auditors. P. D. A. Harvey, for example, mentions a reeve's clerk named Robert Molendinarius who, after training at Oxford, returned to the manor of his birth to serve as a "freelance" compiler of reeves' yearly accounts.[34]

The *Reeve's Tale* and the documents that detail manorial accounting both explore three key affects of manorial economy, which we can label: *the feeling of surveillance, the distress of mediality*, and *the contempt of combination*.[35] Each of these is associated with formal effects in the *Reeve's Tale*, particular ways the narrative is shaped. The Tale portrays the "feeling of surveillance," the affective force of strict observation of gain and expenditure, exploring the connection of that observation to intensity, interest, and surprise. The *Reeve's Tale* also explores the "distress of mediality" by depicting the strained subjectivity of those who account on behalf of others, showing the intensities triggered when an intermediary in a system fails to manage another's goods. Finally, the Tale instills in its readers "the contempt of combination": it explores the consequences of including people, actions, and things in one flatly composite monetary total. Taken all together, these aspects of the *Reeve's Tale* help account for the "malice" so often remarked upon by readers.

The Feeling of Surveillance

Manorial accounts are produced within a network of surveillance, in which the reeve monitors the behavior of others and is in turn monitored. Andrew Jeffrey Morris claims that the manor (as imagined in treatises) is a "pre-Foucaultian" place of "obsessive voyeurism and display," and the texts support this point.[36] The treatise *The Seneschaucy* uses the Anglo-Norman word *veer* to describe the reeve's observation.[37] *Veer* means "to see," but also has a range of meanings that stress the *relationship* established between bodies through sight: "to supervise," "to keep watch on, "to understand," "to inspect."[38] The treatise's injunctions to the reeve to *veer* encourage affective investment with the manor and its objects and inhabitants. According to *The Seneschaucy*, the reeve must *veer* that manorial workers get up in the morning and, at the end of the day, must *veer* that the animals are folded in the right places for manuring.[39] One passage superbly illustrates the intensity and particularity of a reeve's observation. The text states that, during the threshing and winnowing of grain, "The reeve should take care that threshers and winnowers do not take corn and carry it away in their dress, boots, shoes, and pockets or in sacks and bags hidden near the grange" (*E prenge garde le provost, ke nul batur, ne nule ventresse ne prengne del ble pur aporter en seyn, ne en huise, ne en soulers, ne en burse pantenere, ne en sak, ne en sakelet musce pres de la grange*).[40] Like *veer*, the expression "take care," *prenge garde*, emphasizes the personal and affective dynamic of observation.

The exactingly detailed manorial account textualizes this omnipresent and intrusive "seeing" and "taking care," its capacious list penetrating all the spaces of the manor, from the fields and plots of land, to henhouse, stable, and larder. Accounts expressly rely on the reeve's efforts on behalf of the lord, on his instinctual loyalty as the force that will encourage and verify this constant seeing. A passage in the treatise *The Husbandry* describes the giving of account in terms that evoke both confession (as Morris has observed) and the fealty oath: "[H]e who will render the account ought to swear that he will render true account and ... will not enter anything on his account roll except what he spent, honestly and to the lord's advantage" (*deyt celuy qe rendra acounte iurer de rendre leal acounte, e ... ne ryen ne mettra en sun roule for ceo qe il ath leaument despendu a pru le seygnur*).[41]

The *Reeve's Tale* enacts the intense profit-driven surveillance of manorial accounting through its relation of observation and affect. The narrator shows a preoccupation with justification and truth-telling, in which the Tale itself becomes equivalent to an account. After an opening that describes the mill's location, he adds, "And this is verray sooth that I yow telle" (I.3924). This line emphasizes the act of declaring details to others, the loyal positioning of narrator as accounter and hearers as auditors. Whether we read the emphasis on "verray sooth" as loaded with anxiety or crackling with pleasure (at the exactness of the facts that will embarrass the miller, perhaps), the line calls attention to the affective charge of surveillance. The pleasure of truth-telling reappears a little later, bearing both erotic charge and patronizing disdain; describing Malyne's physical features, the Reeve stresses his accuracy and precision by stating, "But right fair was hire heer; I wol nat lye" (I.3976).

The *Reeve's Tale* creates its world through an aggressive accumulation of detail and observation. Just as a manorial reeve takes care to see the grain in threshers' boots, so the narrating Reeve points out the weapons in Symkyn's belt, pouch, and hose (I.3930–3). Elizabeth Edwards has identified a strong "visuality" in the Tale that draws attention to observation, calculation, and precise detail.⁴² Although visuality is arguably an aspect of many tales, the *Reeve's Tale* takes special care to enact and represent attempts at perfect visual surveillance and their attendant pleasure or distress. A crucial analogy for the form of manorial accounting is in a passage given special attention by Edwards: Aleyn and John's plan to sit each at one end of the machinery of the mill. This constitutes a narrative enactment of the tracking of receipts and expenditures in the account. It is also affectively marked. Irma Taavitsainen has theorized that "interjections and exclamations" are special markers of affective intensity, "surge features of personal affect."⁴³ Anticipating this moment, both clerks use oaths to express their enthusiasm about the project of coordinated seeing. John shows a lively eagerness to "se howgates the corn gas in" and "[h]ow that the hopur wagges til and fra," swearing "by [his] fader kyn" (I.4037–9). Aleyn joins him, swearing "by [his] croun," that he will enjoy the "disport" of seeing the meal fall into the trough (I.4041–3). To Taavitsainen's observation, I would add that the clerks' swearing here registers and transfers intensity without being attached to a developed, intellectualized, "emotional" message – or even a clear motivation. Although the miller presumes the clerks are insincerely performing their enthusiasm as part of a "wyle," the Tale itself does not explain the reason for their "nycetee" (either "nonsense" or "cunning" in *MED*).⁴⁴ We never know if their exuberance is "authentic" or not, and, by never allowing us to see the reason for the clerks' exclamations, the text conveys only the pleasurable intensity of observation (I.4046–7).

A comparison with fabliau analogues drives home the distinctiveness of the *Reeve's Tale*'s preoccupation with observing circulation. Fabliaux deal with exchange, but the *Reeve's Tale* represents currency, material goods, and bodies as they circulate *within systems patrolled by account*. The Tale's fabliau analogues differ from it significantly by dwelling on essentially "free" agents who exchange without observation. In the Old French "The Miller and the Two Clerks," the clerkly protagonists exist largely outside of institutions; their wheat is borrowed, not owned by their college. In the Middle Dutch "A Moral Tale about Two Clerics" and in the much earlier "Gombert and the Two Clerks" the clerks arrive at the mill while traveling, unencumbered by obligations or affiliation.⁴⁵ By contrast, the *Reeve's Tale* imagines its characters within a bounded economic system. The material and institutional circumstances of the Tale (the organization of the college, the nature of the mill, and the relations between them) are specified to a degree of detail unknown in similar fabliaux: a miller with "sokene" over a specific area lives "nat fer" from a Cambridge college complete with manciple and warden, and the two sites are locked together in systemic competition (I.3921, 3987). In the *Reeve's Tale*'s manorial-managerial fabliau, everything is seen and tracked – at least eventually.

Both the *Reeve's Tale* and manorial treatises emphasize the feelings of surveillance. The manorial system provides an example of what Sara Ahmed calls "affective economies," situations in which "affect does not reside positively in the sign or commodity, but is produced as an effect of its circulation."[46] Drawing from biological studies, Teresa Brennan similarly notes the "entrainment" of affect, "the process whereby human affective responses are linked and repeated."[47] These theoretical insights clarify the world of managerial bureaucracy imagined by Tale and account, in which affects are not so much the possessions of individuals as the intensities that cross subjective boundaries, sparked by the mandated close observation of circulation; the feelings of surveillance in the *Reeve's Tale* are, to reframe Ahmed's term, "economic affects."

The Distress of Mediality

The Tale focuses readers' attention on the affective reponse to moments when supervised circulation fails: the loss of another's goods. As noted, the Tale defines its characters through their relationship to institutions: the clerks to their college and the miller to the makeshift family dynasty of the "person of the toun," a kind of corrupt outgrowth of "hooly chirche" (I.3943, 3986). This institutional setting emphasizes the characters' position as medial agents who manage on behalf of others, figures equivalent to the reeve in manorial systems.

Mediality, the status of standing between an authority and other workers, the condition of monitoring the goods of others, is characteristic of a reeve's role as described by manorial texts and enacted in the account. In manorial accounting, the account maker must render an accurate account or suffer a penalty, but the account-maker is only indirectly in control of the creation of the document. As noted above, the relation of lord and servant in accounting is given a strongly affective cast.[48] The treatise *Walter of Henley*, describing the view of account (a midway step in yearly account production), depicts the making of an account as a test of loyalty. The account can often detect the fraud, the text says, that occurs when "bailiffs and reeves by themselves or others make merchandise of the money of their lord to their [own] profit and not to the profit of their lord, and this is not loyalty" (*seriantz e provostz par eus e par autres funt marchandies de deners lur seygnur a lur prue e ne mye au pru lur seygnur, e ceo nest pas leaute*).⁴⁹ *Walter* goes on to give directions to the reeve about how to think of his master's property. In this striking passage, we find what might be called a manorial version of the "intimate scripts," or "scripts for the performance of feeling," that Sarah McNamer explores in devotional literature.⁵⁰ *Walter* instills intricately divided feelings. The treatise commands a reeve to divide his subjectivity and imagine the feelings of his lord alongside his own: "Those who have care of the things of another ought to feel four things by reason: to love their lord, and fear him, and in regards to profit they ought to think that the thing is their own, and in regard to expense [they ought to think that] the thing is that of another" (*Ceus qe autrie chose eyent en garde iiii chose deyvent aver par resun: de amer lur seygnur, e doter le, e qant a pru fere dussent penser qe la chose est lur, e qant a despenses fere qe la chose est autrie*).⁵¹

The *Reeve's Tale* plays out the affective consequences of this split subjective sovereignty: the "love" for institution or benefactor twinned with "fear," the quest for "profit" (*pru*) from another's goods, and the searing alienation when disaster reveals that the goods in one's halfway-possession have always been those of "another" (*autrie*). The Tale establishes its opposed characters as occupants of medial positions. The clerks Aleyn and John bring the grain as sworn agents of the warden of their college, filling in for the sick manciple (another accountant figure). They are given "leve" by the warden to go to the mill, and they "leye hir nekke" that they will protect the college's grain (I.4007, 4009). Symkyn, despite his seemingly independent status, is a medial agent himself, answering (in one of the equivalences that show the misogyny of the Tale's accounting) to the parson for his wife and daughter as the "thing[s] ... of another." As Edwards puts it, "Symkin, bristling with weapons, guards his wife's and daughter's chastity as the lock boxes of the church's goods."⁵² It is the parson father-in-law, in equivalent position to a manorial lord, who makes the larger strategic decisions about the marriage of Malyne, "his hooly blood," while Symkyn merely supervises (I.3980, 3985).

The Tale evokes the distress of mediality in two key moments in which affect overwhelms the narrative. Each moment is brought about by the loss of "property" that the characters paradoxically consider, according to the dynamics explained in *Walter*, both their own and another's. The clerks are brought to a high pitch of affect by their loss of the warden's horse, while Symkyn is brought to a similar state by hearing of the sexual violation of Malyne.

In the case of Aleyn and John, their horse becomes a kind of objective correlative for their intermediate status. The horse is the property of the warden of the college, an institutional possession, but the narrative leaves that fact undefined until the horse is lost. The creature is first called simply "an hors," then labeled the "clerkes hors," and later, when John goes to look for it "his hors" (I.4017, 4060, 4071). When the horse runs off, however, John's exclamations note its doubled ownership, saying first "[o]ure hors is lorn" but then "*our wardeyn* has his palfrey lorn" (I.4073, 4075, emphasis mine). As before, exclamations mark moments of intensity. This realization occurs in a sequence of dialogue that Taavitsainen has identified as especially full of affect-loaded words such as "[e]xclamations, swearing, short imperative forms with direct address, and non-standard speech."[53] Nowlin has pointed out the special importance of "allas" as an affect-word in his study of Chaucer's *Legend of Good Women*, and, in this moment of medial distress in the *Reeve's Tale*, the text repeats "allas" to tie together the characters' interactions. "Allas," says John when he first realizes the horse is gone. "Allas," responds the miller's wife. "Allas," says John again when he runs off to catch the horse, and "Allas," John exclaims once more after having returned (I.4075, 4080, 4109).[54] These circulating markers of distress surround the unpleasant reminder of the instability of medial possession.

At the Tale's climax, a burst of affective intensity again occurs when Symkyn realizes he, too, has lost the "property" of another. When Aleyn unwittingly informs Symkyn of his sexual relations with Malyne, Symkyn's reaction is both affective and also couched in language that draws attention to the parson's control. His reaction is notably not motivated by any affectionate bond or sympathy, but by Reeve-like possessive logic. Exclamations and threats show Symkyn's intense response: "false harlot," he says, calling Aleyn a "false traitour! False clerk!" (I.4268–9). Just as John's dialogue switches from "oure hors" to "our wardeyn," Symkyn's dialogue reveals the dynastic connection at its end: "Who dorste be so boold to disparage / My doghter, that is come of swich lynage?" (I.4271–2). Upon recognizing the "other" who possesses by ending his line with the "lynage" that metonymically defines Malyne, Symkyn springs immediately and "despitously" into violence. Symkyn's resort to physical violence exemplifies Crocker's claim that, in this Tale, "affect moves between bodies, precipitating an unmediated, uninitiated, and often-unwanted form of contact."[55] Two of the most affectively marked passages of the Tale explore the distress of a figure in the middle of an exacting system of surveillance. In the Tale's interest in proscribing and limiting the role of medial figures, it matches the broader formal ambition of the manorial account to track the management of another's goods.

The Contempt of Combination

The last connection between the *Reeve's Tale* and manorial accounting sheds additional light on a much-noted aspect of the tale. Chaucerians have consistently observed the disconcerting effect of the *Reeve's Tale*'s presentation of grain, money, and sexuality as interchangeable.[56] Edwards productively connects these debasing equivalencies to issues of "just exchange," but we can also see connections with the aggressively combinatory method of the manorial account.[57]

Manorial accounting relentlessly includes and flattens. The standard format, as we have seen, places a wide variety of different things, actions, and creatures within one textual-numeric calculation, quantifying the qualitative. Looking over manorial accounts, a reader is struck by the transformation of the materiality of life into the ciphers of monetary value. So drastic is this transformation that it sometimes employs its own fictions, including the practice historian P. D. A. Harvey labels the "fictitious sale." If the auditors determined that an animal died because of a reeve's neglect, they would mark the animal on the final account not as dead but as sold, in order to make sure that the reeve would be held accountable for the monetary value.[58] The *Reeve's Tale* similarly combines a wide variety of activities into one system and consistently performs calculations and appraisals. Aleyn thematizes this calculation when he announces his intended sexual assault of Malyne by saying, "gif a man in a point be agreved, / … in another he sal be releved" (I.4181–2).[59] Although Aleyn associates this principle with "lawe," his statement encapsulates the logic of manorial accounting calculations, which look for balance in "a point" from "another" source. Manorial accounts reduce the circle of the year, the life of things, the labor of human and non-human animals, into one bottom line that lists either how much the lord must pay the reeve (*et sic excedit*) or how much the reeve owes the lord (*et sic debet*). When the debts are paid on the account the reeve is declared, in a word key to the *Canterbury Tales*, "quit" (*et sic quietus est*).[60]

In the Canterbury Reeve's own attempt to "quyt the Millere in [his] tale," the *Reeve's Tale* itself concludes by performing an elaborate "rekenynge" (I.4324). The Reeve puts the actions, items, and characters into a balance that shows an "*et sic debet*" for Symkyn:

> Thus is the proude millere wel ybete,
> And hath ylost the gryndynge of the whete,
> And payed for the soper everideel
> Of Aleyn and of John, that bette hym weel.
> His wyf is swyved, and his doghter als. (I.4313–17)

The inclusion of the "soper" especially attests to the text's commitment to formally evoking manorial accounting. Although the supper was noted, it hardly seemed an important part of the revenge game between miller and clerks. Still, the accounting at the end of the Tale details *all* of the losses Symkyn sustains, placing the expense of the supper alongside the loss of the wheat and the sexual violation of two women, all of which are rendered chillingly equivalent through their position in an itemized list.[61]

The *Reeve's Tale* shows the interpersonal and affective consequences of such combination. Silvan Tomkins' exploration of the affect of contempt well describes the moments in the Tale when characters "account" for each other. Tomkins theorizes contempt as "the negative affect linked with individuation and hate."[62] "[C]ontempt," Tomkins writes, "strengthens the boundaries and barriers between individuals and groups and is the instrument par excellence for the preservation of hierarchical, caste, and class relationships."[63] Paradoxically, in the Tale, despite the jamming together of different kinds of experiences into a calculation of value, characters strive to maintain their distance from one another. They express their contempt through calculation. Aleyn says of Symkyn, "I counte hym nat a flye" (I.4192). John, lying in bed and imagining the judgment of others, accounts himself as inert matter, a bag of chaff: "I lye as a draf-sak in my bed" (I.4206). Passages such as these suggest that an examination of affect and account in the Tale can also open up possibilities for wider ethical and ecological examination. The Tale's anthropocentric disgust with animality and materiality is entwined with its affects of manorial accounting.[64]

The Tale's accounting also connects with views of gender. The ugliest example of calculating contempt is shown in John's objectification of Malyne. As he thinks of Aleyn's actions, John tells himself, "Yet has my felawe somwhat for his harm; / He has the milleris doghter in his arm" (I. 4203–4). In the affective world of the Tale's accounting, people become things. Malyne is, for John, "somwhat," a word used for an "unspecified thing," a "deed," or a "sum of money."[65] In the *Summoner's Tale*, for example, "somwhat" is the word used for the mysterious donation that the churl Thomas intends to make to the friar (III.2129). Critics have repeatedly noted the disturbing objectification of women in the Tale; for example, Crocker observes that Symkyn "treats the women like inert tools" and the clerks "view the women as passive instruments."[66] It is clear that the world of manorial accounting presumes a masculine subject, and also clear that its techniques and forms lend themselves readily to misogynistic objectification.[67]

"A Jape of Malice in the Derke"

The *Reeve's Tale* fills the dubiously trustworthy Cook with "joye" when he contemplates the "jape of malice in the derk" suffered by the miller, but later readers have often felt *off* about the narrative (I.4338).[68] Something of the Tale's *off*-ness comes from its evocation of the affects of manorial accounting, affects which prove, on the whole, to be negative. Here my argument aligns with Crocker's detailed tracing of the Tale's negative affect in relation to gender, class, and politics; the Tale, according to Crocker, examines "the ways in which social oppression fans out to divide members of a community who might otherwise find common ground."[69] Similarly, the Tale explores the oppressive nature of manorial accounting, not simply representing but affectively and formally enacting bureaucracy's troubled feelings. Once the freely circulating fabliau genre is pinned down by the specifics of manorial accounting, the more expansive erotics and resistant possibilities that readers have encountered in the *Miller's Tale* condense into the meanness of Symkyn's darkened house.[70] Nowlin argues that Chaucer's exploration of affect, poetic invention, and gender in the *Legend of Good Women* "makes cultural narratives *feel wrong* – not only ethically wrong but affectively *incorrect*, mismatching emotional and narrative understandings to the affects they would represent."[71] A similar kind of enacted critique, I would suggest, is at work in the *Reeve's Tale*, a text that implicates the reader in a very *wrong* experience by expressing the affects of a figure bound within a system of detailed accounting.

The examination here has been, by necessity, speculative. I have used a capacious definition of affect, drawing from the diverse theories and approaches currently in circulation, though attending always to the distinction of affect as unprocessed, bodily, and complicated with respect to agency, as opposed to processed, intellectualized emotion; tellingly, the narrative of the *Reeve's Tale* gives little space to the consideration of emotion. Since I work synthetically with historical materials and have leapt quickly from text to text to make my points, the conclusions here beg correction and further elaboration from specialist historians. If, however, this provocation opens more connections between medieval literary studies, the history of agricultural labor, and the theory of affect, then its ambitions will be happily realized. We can, I assert, "read" feeling in the manorial production of Chaucer's time, both as a way of more richly understanding the affective world of the *Reeve's Tale* and as a way of allowing the textual records of the manor to speak about the lived experience of those who made them.

Notes

1. I am grateful to Myra Seaman for organizing the panel at the 2012 New Chaucer Society Congress on which an early version of this project appeared; to Holly A. Crocker and Glenn D. Burger for their kind editorial guidance; to the members of the Medieval Writing Workshop at the University of Wisconsin-Madison 2013, hosted by Lisa H. Cooper and Jordan Zweck; and to Alexis Kellner Becker for sharing invaluable expertise in discussion of this project.
2. In Dorothea Oschinsky, ed., *Walter of Henley and Other Treatises on Estate Management and Accounting* (Oxford: Clarendon Press, 1971).
3. Ross G. Arthur, "'Why Artow Angry': The Malice of Chaucer's Reeve," *English Studies in Canada* 13,1 (1987): 1–11.
4. A notable early exception is the dissertation by Andrew Jeffrey Morris, "Representing the Countryside in Fourteenth-Century England," PhD Diss., University of Minnesota, 2005, key for my work here, which analyzes manorial treatises alongside literary texts. Morris, however, does not analyze the *Reeve's Tale* itself. See also David Stone, *Decision-Making in Medieval Agriculture* (Oxford: Oxford University Press, 2005), 14.
5. Rosemary O'Neill, "Counting Sheep in the C Text of *Piers Plowman*," *Yearbook of Langland Studies* 29 (2015): 89–116, and William Rhodes, "Medieval Political Ecology: Labour and Agency on the Half Acre," *Yearbook of Langland Studies* 28 (2014): 105–36. Appearing in print after the initial drafting of this chapter, these articles read the treatises alongside Langland and are broadly consonant with my project here. I note the most relevant overlaps.
6. Lisa H. Cooper, "The Poetics of Practicality," in *Middle English: Oxford Twenty-First Century Approaches to Literature*, ed. Paul Strohm (Oxford: Oxford University Press, 2007), 492.
7. For recent studies of the intersection of documentary practice and poetry in the late Middle Ages, see Andrew Galloway, "The Account Book and the Treasure: Gilbert Maghfeld's Textual Economy and the Poetics of Mercantile Accounting in Ricardian Literature," *Studies in the Age of Chaucer* 33 (2011): 65–124, and Emily Steiner, *Documentary Culture and the Making of Medieval English Literature* (New York: Cambridge University Press, 2003). I take inspiration from Ethan Knapp's discussion of Thomas Hoccleve's scribal labor and its relation to his poetry's "irresolvable fragmentation of the self," in *The Bureaucratic Muse: Thomas Hoccleve and the Literature of Late Medieval England* (College Park, PA: Pennsylvania State University Press, 2001), 163. On Chaucer and bureaucracy in general, see Jenna Mead, "Chaucer and the Subject of Bureaucracy," *Exemplaria* 19,1 (2007): 39–66.
8. Holly A. Crocker, "John Foxe's Chaucer: Affecting Form in Post-Historicist Criticism," *New Medieval Literatures* 15 (2015 for 2013), 151–2.
9. Mark Bailey, *The English Manor, c. 1200–c. 1500* (Manchester: Manchester University Press, 2002), 1–2. Note Rhodes' observation in "Medieval Political Ecology," based on his reading of Walter, "that the dynamic interactivity of the

agrarian ecosystem merges physical processes, social relations, and individual affective states" (116).

10. All citations of Chaucer are from *The Riverside Chaucer*, ed. Larry D. Benson, 3rd edn (Boston, MA: Houghton Mifflin Co., 1987). Morris on this passage notes that in some ways Chaucer's Reeve is "an ideal reeve" ("Representing the Countryside," 79). See also Alcuin Blamires, "Chaucer the Reactionary: Ideology and the General Prologue to *The Canterbury Tales*," *Review of English Studies* n.s. 51,204 (2000), 531–2.

11. Bruce M. S. Campbell, "The Livestock of Chaucer's Reeve: Fact or Fiction?," in *The Salt of Common Life: Individuality and Choice in the Medieval Town, Countryside, and Church*, ed. Edwin Brezette DeWindt (Kalamazoo, MI: Medieval Institute, 1995), 305.

12. On this line, see Blamires, "Chaucer the Reactionary," 532.

13. For a similarly close investigation of the logic of rhyme words, see Rita Copeland's examination of a Middle English verse couplet, in "*Pathos* and Pastoralism: Aristotle's *Rhetoric* in Medieval England," *Speculum* 89,1 (2013), 115.

14. On Chaucer and accounting in general (including a short discussion of the Reeve), see R. H. Parker, "Accounting in Chaucer's *Canterbury Tales*," *Accounting, Auditing, & Accountability Journal* 12,1 (1999): 92–112. Critics note the relation of manorial economy to the *Reeve's Tale* but have not put pressure on the connections between manorial accounting and affect: see Richard B. McDonald, "The Reve Was a Sclendre Colerik Man," in *Chaucer's Pilgrims: An Historical Guide to the Pilgrims in the Canterbury Tales*, ed. Laura C. Lambdin and Robert T. Lambdin (Westport, CT: Praeger, 1996); Paul A. Olson, "'The Reeve's Tale': Chaucer's 'Measure for Measure,'" *Studies in Philology* 59,1 (1962): 1–17; and William F. Woods, "The Logic of Deprivation in the 'Reeve's Tale,'" *Chaucer Review* 30,2 (1995): 150–63. Elizabeth Edwards' examination of Aristotelian principles of exchange in the *Reeve's* and *Miller's* tales, in "The Economics of Justice in Chaucer's Miller's and Reeve's Tales," *Dalhousie Review* 82 (2002): 91–112, has been an especially key source for my analysis here.

15. Stone, *Decision-Making*, 3–6. Morris, in "Representing the Countryside," applies ideas of Weberian rationality and Foucauldian discipline to the manor, seeing it as "partitioned, mechanized, and obsessively observed" (3). There is a diachronic aspect that invites further research: direct seigneurial control of manors became more or less viable and intensive over time. See, for example, Bailey, *The English Manor*, 105–6.

16. See Morris, "Representing the Countryside," 31; Stone, *Decision-Making*, 9–14; and Bailey, *The English Manor*, 100, 107–9. On the variety of separate items included in systems of manorial accounting, see also O'Neill, "Counting Sheep," 95–7. For manorial accounts, I rely upon Bailey, *The English Manor*; H. S. Bennett, *Life on the English Manor: A Study of Peasant Conditions, 1150–1400* (Cambridge: Cambridge University Press, 1962), 153–92; Bruce M. S. Campbell, *English Seigniorial Agriculture, 1250–1450* (Cambridge: Cambridge University Press, 2006), 26–37; Noël Denholm-Young, *Seigniorial Administration in England* (New York: Barnes and Noble, 1964), 120–61; and

P. D. A. Harvey, ed., *Manorial Records of Cuxham, Oxfordshire, circa 1200–1359* (London: Oxfordshire Record Society, 1976), especially the section "Accounts and Other Manorial Records," 12–83.
17. O'Neill also examines the "exacting surveillance" detailed in manorial texts and suggests that the impossibility of achieving such a level of surveillance is used thematically by Langland ("Counting Sheep," 95, 109).
18. See Harvey, ed., *Manorial Records*, 43, and Morris, "Representing the Countryside," 47–8. Morris notably connects the manorial account to confession (48).
19. Harvey, ed., *Manorial Records*, 44. The example is on page 455: *quia prepositus decessit antequam aliquid dixit de prebenda boum.* The translation is Harvey's, slightly adapted.
20. Ibid., 44–5; Oschinsky, ed., *Walter of Henley*, 231–2.
21. Oschinksy, ed., *Walter of Henley*, 232.
22. Harvey, ed., *Manorial Records*, 44 and note 63.
23. R. L. P. George and M. Dorothy, "Verses on the Exchequer in the Fifteenth Century," *English Historical Review* 36,141 (1921): 58–67.
24. This description is closely paraphrased from Harvey, ed., *Manorial Records*, 19. See also Bailey, *The English Manor*, 100–4.
25. Bailey, *The English Manor*, 120–40 (fines, 122; ale for workers, 124; crops grown, 132–6; cart horses, 136).
26. On the spread of accounts, see Harvey, ed., *Manorial Records*, 17–18, 20–1. On the use of accounts by lords, see Stone, *Decision-Making*, 14.
27. Steele Nowlin, "The Legend of Good Women and the Affect of Invention," *Exemplaria* 25,1 (2013), 17. I rely partially upon Nowlin's synthesis of Sara Ahmed's and Brian Massumi's definitions of affect in my own use of this variable term.
28. Oschinsky, ed., *Walter of Henley*, 336–7. See also Morris, "Representing the Countryside," 46–7.
29. See Simon Gaunt, *Gender and Genre in Medieval French Literature* (Cambridge: Cambridge University Press, 1995), 235, and Holly A. Crocker, "Introduction: Provocative Body of the Fabliaux," in *Comic Provocations: Exposing the Corpus of Old French Fabliaux*, ed. Crocker (New York: Palgrave Macmillan, 2006), 4.
30. Christian Sheridan, "Conflicting Economies in the Fabliaux," in *Comic Provocations*, ed. Crocker, 97–111.
31. On "containtment" and "constraint" in the Tale, see Woods, "Logic of Deprivation," 160. Tamarah Kohanski, "In Search of Malyne," *Chaucer Review* 27,3 (1993), notes the Tale's manipulation of fabliau expectations: "[The Tale] gives strict readers of fabliau exactly what they want while at the same time undercutting the assumptions under which they read" (234).
32. Laura C. Lambdin and Robert T. Lambdin, "The Millere Was a Stout Carl for the Nones," in *Chaucer's Pilgrims: An Historical Guide to the Pilgrims in the Canterbury Tales*, ed. Lambdin and Lambdin (Westport, CT: Praeger, 1996), 271–80.

33. J. A. W. Bennett, *Chaucer at Oxford and Cambridge* (Oxford: Oxford University Press, 1974), 93.
34. Harvey, ed., *Manorial Records*, 37–9.
35. Morris identifies three methods of control in *Walter of Henley* that have not guided my argument here but do offer an interesting comparison: "normalizing judgments (in the form of calculations), heirarchical [sic] observation, and examination (in the form of the hearing of account)" ("Representing the Countryside," 32).
36. Ibid., 3, 38.
37. The treatises provide a general background to cultural ideas about manorial organization, and so offer productive comparison even if we cannot identify a direct debt to them in Chaucer's work. They were composed mostly in the late thirteenth century, and they circulate in later manuscripts, although it is difficult to define precisely how well-known they would be to Chaucer's readers; see Oschinsky, ed., *Walter of Henley*, 7–9. Although Harvey (*Manorial Records*, 33) claims that the treatises themselves were "seldom copied after 1300" and that they describe older techniques of estate management, it is clear that the *general* practices of organization and accounting they describe were practiced during Chaucer's time. In fact, Harvey observes that centralized management of multiple estates declined in this period, and so the role of reeves became, if anything, even more important and fraught than the treatises describe (34). Also see Rhodes, "Medieval Political Ecology," note 25, and O'Neill, "Counting Sheep," note 2. O'Neill observes that the "larger system of ethics" embodied in these documents also manifests in the "well-known 1388 *Redde Rationem* sermon" of Thomas Wimbledon (90). I thank Alexis Kellner Becker for discussion of this issue.
38. *Anglo-Norman Dictionary* on the *Anglo-Norman Online Hub* (www.anglo-norman.net), s.v. "veer." Note Morris' discussion in "Representing the Countryside" of practices of "oversight" in *The Seneschaucy* (68–9).
39. Oschinsky, ed., *Walter of Henley*, 274–7.
40. Ibid., 276–77. Translations are by Oschinsky unless otherwise noted.
41. Ibid., 418–19. Morris, "Representing the Countryside," convincingly argues for the connection of *Walter* to penitential discourse (19, 21, 23). This passage of the treatise does not describe a reeve's duty, but probably that of a manorial steward. Nevertheless, as the sole accounter of a manor, Chaucer's Reeve would be in a similar position. Chaucer's depiction of the Reeve, I maintain, is more an occasion for an investigation of manorial accounting than an exact representation of the precise responsibilities given to a historical reeve.
42. Edwards, "Economics of Justice," 103–4.
43. Irma Taavitsainen, "Narrative Patterns of Affect in Four Genres of the *Canterbury Tales*," *Chaucer Review* 30,2 (1995), 205. For Taavitsainen's discussion of oaths in the *Canterbury* fabliaux, see 203.
44. *MED*, s.v. "nicete, n."
45. The Old French and Middle Dutch tales are printed in Robert M. Correale and Mary Hamel, eds., *Sources and Analogues of the Canterbury Tales* (Cambridge:

D. S. Brewer: 2002), vol. 1, 28–67. For "Gombert and the Two Clerks," see Larry D. Benson and Theodore M. Andersson, eds., *The Literary Context of Chaucer's Fabliaux* (New York: Bobbs-Merrill Company, 1971), 88–99.
46. Sara Ahmed, *The Cultural Politics of Emotion* (New York: Routledge, 2004), 45.
47. Teresa Brennan, *The Transmission of Affect* (Ithaca, NY: Cornell University Press, 2004), 52.
48. Note also O'Neill's discussion in "Counting Sheep" of the "all-encompassing ethical system" of stewardship (97).
49. Oschinsky, ed., *Walter of Henley*, 340. My translation.
50. Sarah McNamer, *Affective Meditation and the Invention of Medieval Compassion* (Philadelphia, PA: University of Pennsylvania Press, 2010), 12.
51. My translation, based on Oschinsky and with reference to the *Anglo-Norman Dictionary* on the *Anglo-Norman Online Hub* (www.anglo-norman.net). See the discussion in Morris, "Representing the Countryside," 88–91.
52. Edwards, "Economics of Justice," 103.
53. Taavitsainen, "Narrative Patterns," 202.
54. Nowlin, "Legend of Good Women," 25.
55. Holly A. Crocker, "Affective Politics in Chaucer's *Reeve's Tale*: 'Cherl' Masculinity after 1381," *Studies in the Age of Chaucer* 29 (2007), 251. The affective possibilities of the fight are intensified when we consider Woods' observation in "Logic of Deprivation" that in this scene "the streams of pronoun references begin to merge, until it is hard to know who is hitting whom" (157).
56. Edwards, "Economics of Justice," 94–6; Kohanski, "In Search of Malyne," 235.
57. Edwards, "Economics of Justice," 91. Rhodes, "Medieval Political Ecology," 108, 115–16, emphasizes the ecological knowledge based on lived experience encoded within manorial account documents, whereas I stress here the reductive potential of manorial account-making.
58. Harvey, ed., *Manorial Records*, 52.
59. Edwards, "Economics of Justice," 94–6.
60. Bailey, *The English Manor*, 104.
61. Jenna Mead, "Chaucer and the Subject of Bureaucracy," 56–60, observes a similar equivalence at work in the account book that records Chaucer's 1360 ransom. Although my examination leaves the historical Chaucer's connections with accounting unexamined, it is clear that the *Reeve's Tale* could be considered alongside Chaucer's own involvement with accounting documents.
62. Silvan Tomkins, "Shame-Humiliation and Contempt-Disgust," in *Shame and Its Sisters: A Silvan Tomkins Reader*, ed. Eve Kosofsky Sedgwick and Adam Frank (Durham, NC: Duke University Press, 1995), 139.
63. Ibid., 156.
64. For the ethics of imagining "inert matter," see, for example, Jane Bennett, *Vibrant Matter: A Political Ecology of Things* (Durham, NC: Duke University Press, 2010).

65. *MED*, s.v. "som-what, pron."
66. Crocker, "Affective Politics," 243.
67. The larger gender dynamics of manorial accounting, especially as they relate to this tale, could indeed suggest a confirmation of the views of some critics that the women in the *Reeve's Tale* somehow escape, trouble, or critique the "accounting" of the system. See Edwards, "Economics of Justice," 106–7, 111 (though Edwards does not see this escape as liberatory); and Kohanksi, "In Search of Malyne," 235–6.
68. I am thankful for the insights of the papers from my Sonoma State University Spring 2012 "Chaucer and Affect Theory" class in shaping this essay. As one student observes, the *Reeve's Tale* "explores what happens to audience affect when anger replaces play in a narrative meant to be humorous."
69. Crocker, "Affective Politics," 229.
70. Critics often find a more liberatory and capacious world in the *Miller's Tale* in contrast to the *Reeve's*. See, for example, Woods, "Logic of Deprivation," 151, and Edwards, "Economics of Justice," 97–9.
71. Nowlin, "Legend of Good Women," 31.

CHAPTER 6

Affect Machines
Sarah Salih

Parameters

"Thou shalt not make to thyself a graven thing, nor the likeness of any thing that is in heaven above, or in the earth beneath, nor of those things that are in the waters under the earth," the Commandment says; and yet medieval Christians practiced, and debated, "a piety characterized by intense awareness of the power of the material."[1] They were deeply invested in material things that were sacralized by virtue of their functions as repositories and triggers of affect. Religious practices are rich examples of networks, as articulated by Bruno Latour: "Action is not done under the full control of consciousness; action should rather be felt as a node, a knot, and a conglomerate of many surprising sets of agencies that have to be slowly disentangled."[2] Such agencies include material things as well as humans: "*any thing* that does modify a state of affairs by making a difference is an actor ... things might authorize, allow, afford, encourage, permit, suggest, influence, block, render possible, forbid and so on."[3] Humans, affects, institutions, material things both artifactual and natural are all actors with a contribution to make to complex activities such as worship.

In the context of worship, material objects become affect machines when human attention affords them spiritual power. Attention here is that which enables stickiness, to use Sara Ahmed's term: "Affect is what sticks, or what sustains or preserves the connection between ideas, values, and objects."[4] "Attention" names a two-way process, either stimulating or stimulated by affect: one may make an active decision to pay attention, or it may be experienced as a hailing from an external agent, as when a thing "catches" one's attention. Attention is an embodied experience. Hans Belting observes the inescapable embodiment of perception:

> The human being is the natural *locus of images*, a living organ for images, as it were. Notwithstanding all the devices that we use today to send and store images, it is within the human being, and only within the human being, that

> images are received and interpreted in a living sense ... [O]ur bodies themselves constitute a place, a locus, where the images we receive leave behind an invisible trace ... We see images with our corporeal organs ... But the final outcome is not an analysis but a synthesis.[5]

"Images" here includes all kinds of perceptible phenomena: encounters with them involve a moment of contact, in which the observed rubs off on the observer and perpetuates itself within them. Belting's analysis is entirely compatible with medieval theorizations of the senses. Medieval sight may be imagined as extramission or intromission, but in either case the transmission of sensation is a form of bodily contact.[6] As Suzannah Biernoff puts it: "carnal vision extends the appetite and attributes of the flesh beyond the boundaries of individual bodies. Sight lends the flesh an intersubjective dimension; it literally carries carnality outside the viewer's corporeal envelope and into the world: even into other bodies."[7]

The Book of Wisdom tells us that idolatry originated as an attempt to externalize intolerable affect by the construction of an image to be looked upon:

> For a father being afflicted with bitter grief, made to himself the image of his son who was quickly taken away: and him who then had died as a man, he began now to worship as a god, and appointed him rites and sacrifices among his servants.
>
> Then in process of time, wicked custom prevailing, this error was kept as a law, and statues were worshipped by the commandment of tyrants.[8]

The image of the son is constructed in order to manage an excess of affect, to distract the bereaved father from his grief and comfort him with the image's presence to his senses. Yet placing affect in a material thing has unintended consequences. Material objects carry memory because they are ideally suited to prolong affects beyond a human lifespan. "[N]o interaction is *synchronic* ... Time is always folded," argues Latour: material things bring their many pasts into any given present, because "Action has always been carried on thanks to shifting the burden of connection to longer- or shorter-lasting entities."[9] The Book of Wisdom's example demonstrates that such networks of action are open-ended; the material object, the image, was transformed from a memorial to an idol, both influencing and influenced by the actions of people around it.

This origin story appealed to medieval writers, who named several persons as the inventors of such idolatry.[10] John Lydgate, in his *Troy Book*, exchanges the roles of father and son, but lays emphasis on the work done by complex and intense feelings. In this version, Ninus mourns his father Belus:

> An ymage dide make
> To be worschipte only for his sake—
> Al of brent gold, be fals affeccioun,
> And sette it vp for consolacioun,
> And for a mynde and a memorial,
> Vn-to þe whiche, with herte, wil, and al,
> Of ygnoraunce and of fleschly love
> He dide honour, as to God above,
> In his templis, most of excellence,
> And made his peple to do reuerence.[11]

Lydgate brings out the affective agency of the image, which actively consoles and reminds, and the experiential, embodied complexity of Ninus' feelings for it. The institution of a temple and a regular round of activity around the statue both disperses the mourning throughout society and prolongs it by making it a ritual practice. Affective attention inducts the material object into a network, enlivening it. However, this is an open network, and thus unstable; Shannon Gayk argues that "Lydgate claims that this false memory based on misplaced affection ultimately led to an entire culture's fall."[12] Affect machines, once set in motion, make new connections: "A wickid spirit, folkis to be-gyle, / In þis ydole entrid to abyde" (II.5540–1). This narrative, derived from St Augustine's *City of God*, solved the riddle of how paganism might be understood both as the worship of demons, and also as the worship of merely material things.[13] The affective energy around the statue attracts the demon and gives it the opportunity to enter into the network and appropriate the attention for itself.

Discussions of idolatry trace the outcomes and after-effects of such contacts between humans and images, demons and images: idols are conceived as demanding particularly troublesome forms of attention. The Old Testament denounces idols as insensate material things that nevertheless exercise agency over their worshippers:

> The idols of the gentiles are silver and gold, the works of the hands of men.
> They have mouths and speak not: they have eyes and see not.
> They have ears and hear not: they have noses and smell not.
> They have hands and feel not: they have feet and walk not: neither shall they cry out through their throat.
> Let them that make them become like unto them: and all such as trust in them.[14]

Attention to idols, this passage suggests, is dangerous; the incapacities of idols rub off on and stick to their viewers, making them less than fully human. Agency and sensory capacity are exchanged, or pooled, between viewer and viewed. The pagan persecutors of hagiography, for example, are raging automata, their strings easily pulled by saints bent on martyrdom. Chaucer's St Cecilia provokes her pagan by pointing to his idol's inertia and his own insensibility:

> That ilke stoon a god thow wolt it calle.
> I rede thee, lat thyn hand upon it falle
> And taste it wel, and stoon thou shalt it fynde,
> Syn that thou seest nat with thyne eyen blynde.[15]

The relation of idol and worshipper may be specifically conceived as an erotic mingling. It is already sexualized in the Old Testament's denunciations of other religions, in what Robin Lane Fox calls "the vicious threesome, idolatry, adultery and the jealousy of a cuckolded God."[16] An image derived from the *bibles moralisées* imagines gazing at an idol as an erotic act (Fig. 1).

The idol's beauty, it seems, is erotically stimulating to viewers, appealing directly to their bodily sensations, seducing them into likeness to it: the idol makes the viewer its puppet.

Attention works in both directions: excessive affect, originating in the observer, may also rub off on the observed. Chaucer's Parson explains: "be it wyf, be it child, or any worldly thyng that he loveth biforn God, it is his mawmet, and he is an ydolastre."[17] In *A Revelation of Purgatory*, the visionary sees the spirit of her dead friend lamenting that she has been damned for excessive love of her "mawmettes," her pet cat and dog, who have been transformed into her guards and tormentors.[18] Idolatry, in these deliberately provocative statements, is not confined to pagans, but is a widespread human capacity, to which everyone is susceptible. The excess of the observer corrupts the observed, transforming an ordinary wife, child, or cat into that sinister agential thing, a "mawmet."

In late medieval England, affective attention to devotional art was debated, cultivated, and feared. As Sarah McNamer suggests, performative scripting is a rich source of affect in medieval writing.[19] The mendicant priest Pauper gives the layman Dives extensive instruction in the script he is to use to pay attention to the crucifix:

> And, as Seynt Bernard byddyȝt, take heid be þe ymage how his heid is bowyd doun to the, redy to kyssyn the and comyn at on wyt the. See how hese armys and hese hondys been spred abrod on þe tree in tokene þat he is redy to fangyn the and halsyn the and kyssyn the and takyn the to his mercy. See how his syde was openyd and his herte clouyn in too in tokene þat his herte is alweys opyn to the, redy to louyn the and forȝeuyn the.[20]

Affect Machines 143

Figure 1 Worship of Baal-Peor. Paris: Bibliothèque nationale de France, ms lat 9471, f. 235.

The viewer is thus instructed to construct a mutually affective relation to the crucifix: not only does he adore it, but he sees it adoring him back. Once more, the viewing situation is sticky: attention animates the image and makes it, in its yearning desire, resemble the spectator. The mutual attention of crucifix and viewer unsettles any difference between human and object, wood and flesh. The artifactuality of the crucifix fades out of sight. The lyric:

> Whan Ich se on rode
> Jhesu mi lemman
> And beside him stonde
> Marie an Johan
>
> . . .
>
> Wel ow Ich to wepen
> And sinnes forleten,
> Yif Ich of love can[21]

is ambiguous as to whether it imagines a visionary experience or gazing at an artwork, most likely the rood group, "that most universal of images . . . found in every church throughout the land."[22] The experience of attention to a crucifix opens up time and place: even an artifactual crucifix is able to make a connection with the past.

Performative scripts such as the instructions and the lyric emphasize the intensity of attention to images; theorizations of the practice emphasize its regulation. The past mattered to the present. In a debate with more than two sides and a certain amount of common ground, the devotional practices of the present day were analyzed with reference to ancient idolatry. The idea of idolatry was used to mark troublesome responses to imagery, and to guard the boundaries between licit and illicit uses of images. Reginald Pecock argues that the term was used too imprecisely to be anything more than an opportunistic insult: "Ful ofte haue y herd men and wommen vnwiseli iuge and diffame ful scherpli weel nyȝ alle Cristene to be ydolatrers, and al for the hauyng and vsing of ymagis. And ȝit whanne it hadde be askid of hem what ydolatrie is, forsothe thei couthe not seie neither feele what it is in his trouthe."[23] His indignation, however, shows that the slur hurt. His and other defenses of engagement with images relied on an assessment of the precise flavor of the attention directed to them, whether *latria* or *dulia*.[24] *Dives and Pauper* argues, ingeniously, that images are shod in silver not because of the sensual appeal of the metal, but to make them strong enough to withstand devotional handling.[25] Both arguments differentiate image devotion from idolatry by arguing that its affect is regulated by devotional scripts that guard against excess and impropriety.

Wycliffite critiques of images argue instead that devotional practice is characterized by the excessive and poorly aimed attention that constitutes worshippers as idolaters and images as idols. The *Lanterne of Liȝt* argues that affective relations with images should be considered to be in breach of the First Commandment: "neiþir knele to hem. ne kisse hem / neiþir putt feiþ hope ne trist in oo ymage."²⁶ To travel to, vow to, kneel to a specific image is to invest it with agency and personality, to allow it to control the bodies of its devotees; agency continually passes back and forth between person and thing. Wycliffite polemic recognizes and resists the agency of such images: it attempts to reinstate a boundary and a hierarchy between person and artifact. As one writer argues, the problem is precisely that people attribute agency to items which, s/he insists, are in themselves only inert matter:

> summe lewid folc wenen þat þe ymagis doun verreyly þe myraclis of hemsilf, and þat þis ymage of þe crucifix be Crist hymsilf, or þe seynt þat þe ymage ys þere sett for lickenesse. And þerfore þei seyn "þe swete rode of Bromholme", "þe swete rode of Grace", "þe swete rode at þe norþe dore", "oure dere Lauedy of Walsyngham", but nouȝt "oure Lauedy of heuene", ny "oure lord Iesu Crist of heuene", but cleuen sadly strokande and kyssande þese olde stones and stokkis.²⁷

In this analysis, the devotees' attention fails to stick to the statues or to make them agential objects. These Christs do not love their viewers back: affect is poured into artifacts but goes nowhere, powering no circuit. The critique adopts the biblical denunciation of idolatry to scorn the perverse eros of people lavishing affection on unresponsive materials. Yet scorn, too, is a kind of attention, and the passage vividly conveys the intensity of image devotion. McNamer suggests that Wycliffite critiques of images may themselves be driven by affective anxiety:

> Could it have been that the ubiquitous image of Christ on the cross, an image so many Middle English lyrics cast as that of Christ the lover – leaning down to embrace and kiss the mediator-as-beloved, and demanding passionate compassion in return – had become a threat to sexual identity for certain categories of readers in late medieval England?²⁸

This argument implies that the critiques recognized the reality of affective, even erotic, engagement with artifacts, and that such engagement might stick with and change the observer. This writer's derision of the devotees is not, primarily, an analysis of the inadequacy of their understanding of the relation between image and prototype, but an emotive revulsion from their behavior, and an invitation to readers to join in the scorn.

In Ancient Troy

While this debate continued, John Lydgate stepped back to describe pagans constructing an enviably effective affect machine that evaded the taint of idolatry. In the *Troy Book*, Hector's death provokes an outpouring of grief so violent that it threatens to hold up the narrative itself:

> And al her wo for to specifie,
> A large boke it wolde occupie,
> ȝiffe eche þinge I shulde in order telle-
> I trowe it were to longe for to dwelle. (III.5561–4)[29]

The sight of Hector's body is sticky: Priam and others who look on it become deathlike themselves, "cold as any stoon, / Inly desyrous for to deie anoon" (III.5533–4). Meanwhile, in a frenzy of grief, women "Furiously ronne to and fro" (III.5516). This riot of sorrow is channeled, or congealed, into an extraordinary material object, a machine constructed of human and mineral parts, powered by and generating affect. Hector's body is displayed in an elaborate Gothic shrine, which is also a kind of life-support machine.[30] The body is plumbed into a circulation of balm, which acts like a vegetable soul to keep the body minimally alive (III.5686):

> And at his hede of gold was an ourne,
> Þat was filde with bawme natural
> Þat ran þoruȝ pipes artificial,
> Þoruȝ nekke & hed in-to many place,
> Penytrable by veynes of þe face,
> Þat þoruȝ vertu & force of þe lycour
> He was conserued lifly of colour. (III.5677–82)

Grief is transformed, via money, labor, and artisanal expertise – "What it cost þe kyng wil spare nouȝt" (III.5599) – into a network of oratory, tabernacle, golden angels, crystal steps, jewels, spices, oil lamps, balm, ebony, the dead body of Hector, and the live bodies of the priests who maintain a constant round of prayer. The whole is a materialization of affect, "riche werke, noble & excellent, / Of hertly loue" (III.5743–4). Hector's body is an attention-attracting object. Although apparently inert, it invites bodily engagement from those around it. The body is in a tabernacle, within an oratory, surrounded by a parclose, within a temple; so approaching it is a gradated process of moving through a series of enclosures, with consequent building-up of feeling (III.5613–18, 5718). It appeals to various senses and guides people's movements. It offers "degres, men by to ascende" (III.5639); the vapors of balm smell delightful:

"For þe flavour more holsom was & soote / Þan þe odour of spice, gomme, or rote" (III.5703–4). It also protects the viewers from more troubling feelings, such as revulsion from the "odour and abomynacioun" of a decaying body (III.5593). This elaborate construction allows the mourners to undo their initial obsessive sticking to the body. While Hector's body is preserved by the circulation of balm and lit by inextinguishable lamps (III.5708–10), his memory is preserved by an annual cycle of ritual memorial activity, when the mourners renew their grief, "Ful pitously with her heer [to-]torn, / Mornyng in blak & knelynge ay a-forn / Þe dede cors" (IV.535–7). Their grief is not much reduced in intensity: the memorial perpetuates affect rather than assuaging it. But it is allocated a time and a place – in the temple, at the anniversary – that hygienically seal it off from the public spaces of the city's everyday life. This scene generates a further link in the chain of affects: Hector's killer, Achilles, falls in love with his victim's sister, Polyxena, when he watches her mourning at the funeral anniversary (IV.551–636). The memorial seems at first to stop time, keeping body and grief equally fresh, but Achilles is a new element in the network, and his participation in it plays a part in the eventual destruction of the city, the memorial included. The assemblage is designed as a perpetual-motion machine of affect, powered by and generating mourning, but is halted – eventually – by the brute force of historical inevitability.

The preserved body in its enclosure is not, exactly, an idol, and so not compounded in the text's denunciation of "false goddes"

> And her statues of stokkes & of stoon,
> In whiche þe serpent & þe olde snake,
> Sathan hymsilf, gan his dwellinge make. (IV.6932–3)

Although the scenario is identical to that of the Book of Wisdom's origin of idolatry, as a grieving father erects a memorial to a fallen son, there is no demon here. The monument does include a statue of Hector, "[of] massyf gold" (III.5649), but its centerpiece is undoubtedly the embalmed body, which seems not to be a space where a demon might enter. In the *Iliad*, the gods might intervene to preserve a body incorrupt, as when Thetis "through the nostrils of Patroklos … distilled / ambrosia and red nectar, so that his flesh might not spoil."[31] But decorum forbids the appearance of the gods in person in the Troy books of the Christian Middle Ages, so Lydgate's account is of a triumph of technology and the harnessing of the properties of materials. Balm prevents the body from decay, and a parclose of indestructible ebony protects the oratory. Hector is more like, though not identical to, a relic: a class of thing whose combination of fragile human tissue and incorruptible precious metal is ideal to provoke affect and to perpetuate it through time. Lydgate, of course, had a personal investment in the custody of miraculous royal bodies, and the policing of appropriately affective responses to them. His *Life of St Edmund* tells an incident from the history of his own abbey, of how an impious lord glanced at St Edmund's shrine with "fals dysdeyn voyd off deuocion"; was struck down "[as] a demonyak, vexyd with a gost" – that is, himself becoming an idol-like shell for a demon – and was cured at last only by appeals to the saint's finer feelings, his "benygnyte" and "pite."[32] Edmund's shrine includes defenses against inappropriate forms of attention: such Christian artifacts, the anecdote implies, are sufficiently alive to police their reception.

Hector's preserved body shows how a relic is imagined: as a thing that orchestrates a circuit of affect whilst itself remaining constant and self-identical, immune to change and decay. Lydgate's narrative shares the Trojans' grief at Hector's death in terms calculated to stimulate affect, especially if a reader chooses to voice them and thus place themselves amongst the mourners. Lydgate's Prologue to the *Troy Book* specifies, amongst other things, the affect its readers should anticipate: its privileged reader, Prince Henry, is instructed to take an active, manly kind of "Ioye" in contemplating the exemplars of chivalric heroism (l. 79). The poem is therefore engaged in transmitting affect through time. The embodiment of sight means that visual images may intensify such a transference of affect. Illuminated *Troy Book* manuscripts disappointingly duck the challenge of visualizing Hector's shrine: the luxury John Rylands manuscript shows instead a fine but conventional funeral scene with a black-draped coffin carried into a Gothic chapel; the Digby manuscript an armored figure lying in state, overseen by a small statue.[33] However, the undead body of Hector is depicted in a late fifteenth-century Burgundian tapestry, now in the Burrell Collection (Fig. 2).

The tapestry's subject is specified as the *Anniversary of Hector's Funeral*, an identification borne out by the presence of lay mourners in the foreground. It must surely have been a deliberate choice of subject: not just an image of Hector, or even of the memorial, but an image of the annual commemoration of his death. It is impossible to prove, but irresistible to suspect, that its owners felt themselves to be continuing that commemoration by commissioning the tapestry. Pecock happened to light upon the example of a tapestry of Hector to proclaim the sheer commonsensical obviousness of the gulf between representation and presence: "thou wolt perauenture seie to me in descryuyng the storie peintid or wouun in thin halle or chaumbre, '. . .

Figure 2 *Anniversary of Hector's Funeral*. Glasgow: Burrell Collection

here Hector of Troie throwith doun a knyt.' . . . schal y bere thee an hond that thou trowist . . . Hector to be quyk in thi clooth?"[34] But this particular tapestry does seem to have presence; its formal features give the image a very direct address. Depth is clearly marked in the perspectival lines of the tabernacle and the arrangement of mourners in front of the body, which is itself in front of the shrine: it would be easy to see this image as opening up a window into ancient Troy. The view takes us within the enclosure, so any room where the tapestry is hung might be imagined to be the Temple of Apollo. The viewer, standing in front of the tapestry, is placed with the mourners in the foreground, and on the same scale, for these are life-sized figures. Identification is made smoother by the placing of the family as if on a medieval monument, with the men to Hector's right and the women to his left.[35] The tapestry thus reaches through time and space to allow its viewers an affective identification with ancient Trojans. It is both a representation of an affect machine, and one in its own right. Ahmed argues that the stickiness of objects of attention is essential to the formation of group identities: "the social bond is always rather sensational. Groups cohere around a shared orientation toward some things as being good, treating some things and not others as the cause of delight."[36] Adherence to Hector's body as a cause of delight realizes the legendary descent of Northern Europeans from Trojans. Hector's undecayed body in this tapestry is a synecdoche of the transmission of the Matter of Troy into medieval European culture.

In Medieval England

Encounters between people and artworks continued to be powerful producers of an affect that constituted the artifacts as things that themselves produce energies. Images and people might mingle on equal terms. In liturgical dramas, Christ might be played by the figure from the church's crucifix, and interact with human performers: "It was not unusual to find monks or even lay people actually playing the roles of Joseph of Arimathea, Nicodemus, and an attendant as they took the wooden image of Christ from the cross and placed it in the lap of the man who played the Virgin Mary."[37] The success of the drama depended on this charged physical contact between person and image. The *Croxton Play of the Sacrament* testifies to the power of such an appearance. In this play Jesus appears, apparently, not in the body of a human actor, but as an "image," "A chyld apperyng with wondys blody: / A swemfull syght ytys to looke vpon."[38] The result of gazing on this emotive sight is a profound and permanent personal transformation: the Jews whose scientific curiosity had prompted them to attack the Host convert to Christianity "with great devocion / With repentant hart."[39] The process of bonding and identification takes in the audience too: their investment in the sight of the image needs to be strong enough to bind them in Christian community to these converts from another country and century.

Margery Kempe, traveling from Jerusalem to Rome, fell in with a party traveling with a devotional image of the Christ-child:

> And þe woman the which had þe ymage in þe chist, whan þei comyn in good citeys, sche toke owt þe ymage owt of hir chist & sett in worshepful wyfys lappys. & þei wold puttyn schirtys þerup-on & kyssyn it as þei it had ben God hym-selfe. &, whan þe creatur [Kempe] sey þe worshep & þe reuerens þat þei dedyn to þe ymage, sche was takyn with swet deuocyon & swet meditacyons þat sche wept wyth gret sobbyng & lowde crying.[40]

Like the liturgical dramas, this practice relies on the intimate contact of person and image, but is removed from the structuring framework of the church building and ritual year. Viewed externally, the women's behavior might be derided as a delusional embracing of "stones and stokkis." Told from the devotee's point of view, lavishing attention on a figurine as if it were God is so rich an experience as to equate to direct access to God. Kempe seeks out the image to pay attention to it, and is also ambushed, "takyn" with its affect-generating power. The women treat it as if it were God; it holds God's place in this network, and the affect it generates is equivalent to that which would be produced by God himself. Kempe had had regular personal visionary contact with God, but found his presence mediated through the image overwhelming, because the embodied sight somehow confirmed her previous visions. When "sche sey with hir bodily eye lych as sche had be-forn wyth hir gostly eye," she wept, sobbed, and cried "so wondirfully & mythtyly þat sche was nerhand ouercomyn."[41] Encounter with the image brings such affective overload that it threatens to make her into an insensible image of God's power, and she takes the image's place as the passive object of the women's attentions, as they put her to bed and comfort her. The image bonds the women – the pilgrim who owns it, Kempe, and the Italian women they visit – into an affective community: as Kathy Lavezzo argues, "its fondling and passage from wifely lap to wifely lap ... renders it a medium through which these women homosocially bond."[42] Michael Camille points out that in this scene the women themselves become image: "[a] living Virgin and Child group is created for and from female beholders."[43] They become art, while their attention enlivens the image.

The erotic intensity of such practices was a target for satire. The power of images to attract and perpetuate desire is parodied in a bawdy visual joke, in the form of a badge, featuring three phallus-creatures bearing a crowned vulva on the approximate location of their shoulders (Fig. 3).

Figure 3 Phallic procession badge. Collection Van Beuningen Family

Its intended meaning is unknown, but Malcolm Jones makes the plausible suggestion that:

> this may be seen as a satirical proto-Protestant attack on a Catholic procession in honour of the Virgin Mary, whose image, perhaps in the form of a crowned statue of the Queen of Heaven, and surrounded by a rayed

"glory" or mandorla – itself a vulvate shape, of course – was paraded through the streets.⁴⁴

The badge identifies both devotees and image as objects and subjects of desire, erect phalloi and open vulva. In this satirical rendering, such a network, rather than offering an enriching of experience, reduces its participants to mere blind organs. But it confirms too the stickiness of the devotional object, showing the network of the image and its devotees molded into a single object, sharing the same material and level of reality.

Coda: In London, Just Now

It is odd to write about affect, a force at once so elusive and visceral, as if it were any other scholarly topic. If affect is embodied, surely an inquiry into it should use other registers than academic prose? This thought prompted me to seek out an experimental embodied encounter with the medieval past, one that might echo, however faintly, the late medieval encounters with affect machines. So I went looking for St Etheldreda's hand. An incorrupt hand of St Etheldreda, or Æthelthryth, the Anglo-Saxon princess and founding abbess of Ely, is kept as a relic in the medieval Catholic church of St Etheldreda's, Ely Place, formerly the chapel of the Bishops of Ely's London palace, and a few minutes' walk from the Strand campus of King's College.⁴⁵ According to the church's website, the hand had managed to bypass the Reformation, and, it was implied, offered contact with the medieval Catholic past:

> A special relic was also given to the Church [in the 1870s]. It was a piece of the uncorrupted hand of St Etheldreda. The hand, removed in Norman times, had been kept during the Persecution in a secret hiding place on the Duke of Norfolk's estate. The relic now lies in the jewel cask to the right of the high altar.⁴⁶

St Etheldreda's, a startlingly quiet and secluded medieval church in the heart of a busy commercial and legal district, and yards from a major traffic junction, produces a powerful sense of stepping outside the time and place of the mundane city. It commemorates the Reformation, but also, by virtue of being a medieval Catholic church in post-Reformation England, generates an alternative history in which it never happened. And it is certainly a place that demands affective attention. The hand in its reliquary was quite a distance from the nearest viewing position, and unavailable for close inspection: on reflection, I was quietly relieved to have evaded this unpredictable encounter with medieval materiality. My attention was seized

Figure 4 St Swithun Wells. London: St Etheldreda's Church, Ely Place

instead by a series of hyper-realistic polychrome statues of the English Martyrs of the Reformation along the wall (Figure 4).

The church's information gives no art-historical details of their dates or makers, focusing instead on the individuals represented: Pecock would have applauded the attention to prototype in preference to image. The verisimilitude of these statues asks viewers to respond to them as presences rather than artifacts. They, along with the invisible presence of the hand and a number of other images in the church, energetically try to trigger an effect that might induct visitors into forming an identification with a persecuted English Catholic community; into mourning the martyrs as the medieval viewers of the tapestry mourned Hector. They would certainly repay the kind of affective attention I have described in relation to the real and imaginary medieval artifacts. Many visitors, of course, will have come to the church impelled by other kinds of curiosity – historical, aesthetic, touristic – but all are hailed by the statues, waiting in the church to ambush their attention. Their affect may thus be unpredictable, exceeding the observer's anticipation and control. Making the visit showed me something that was not apparent from the textual examples; an ambivalence of spectatorial feeling. I felt addressed by the statues, but also doubtful that it was really me they wanted to talk to: it was not an easy feeling to name. I did not, I found, particularly want them to stick to me once I had left the heterotopic zone of the church. But stick they did, and along with them a persistent unease at being found wanting by the things that offer contact with the past.

Notes

1. Exodus 20:4; Caroline Walker Bynum, *Christian Materiality: An Essay on Religion in Late Medieval Europe* (New York: Zone Books, 2011), 18.
2. Bruno Latour, *Reassembling the Social: An Introduction to Actor-Network Theory* (Oxford: Oxford University Press, 2005), 44.
3. Ibid., 71–2.
4. Sara Ahmed, "Happy Objects," in *The Affect Theory Reader*, ed. Melissa Gregg and Gregory J. Seigworth (Durham, NC: Duke University Press, 2010), 29. "Objects" in Ahmed's analysis here includes, but is not limited to, material things.
5. Hans Belting, *An Anthropology of Images: Picture, Medium, Body*, trans. Thomas Dunlap (Princeton, NJ: Princeton University Press, 2011), 37–8.
6. See Suzanne Conklin Akbari, *Seeing through the Veil: Optical Theory and Medieval Allegory* (Toronto: University of Toronto Press, 2004), 21–36, for details of the extramission and intromission theories.
7. Suzannah Biernoff, *Sight and Embodiment in the Middle Ages* (Basingstoke: Palgrave Macmillan, 2002), 41.
8. Douay-Rheims Bible, Wisdom 14:15–16.
9. Latour, *Reassembling the Social*, 200–1.
10. See John Daniel Cooke, "Euhemerism: A Medieval Interpretation of Classical Paganism," *Speculum* 2,4 (1927), 404–6.
11. John Lydgate, *Troy Book*, 3 Parts, ed. Henry Bergen, EETS e.s. 97, 103, 106 (London: Kegan Paul, Trench, Trübner, 1906, 1908, 1910), Part 2, Book II, ll. 5527–36. All citations are to this edition, with line numbers given in the text.
12. Shannon Gayk, *Image, Text, and Religious Reform in Fifteenth-Century England* (Cambridge: Cambridge University Press, 2010), 133.
13. Augustine of Hippo, *Concerning the City of God against the Pagans*, trans. Henry Bettenson (Harmondsworth: Penguin, 1972), VIII.24. See also Sarah Salih, "Idol Theory," *Preternature* 4,1 (2015): 13–36.
14. Douay-Rheims Bible, Psalm 113:4–8.
15. Geoffrey Chaucer, *The Canterbury Tales*, in *Riverside Chaucer*, ed. Larry D. Benson, 3rd edn (Boston, MA: Houghton Mifflin Co., 1987), VIII.501–4.
16. Robin Lane Fox, *The Unauthorized Version: Truth and Fiction in the Bible* (London: Penguin, 1992), 320.
17. *The Parson's Tale*, in *The Riverside Chaucer, Canterbury Tales*, X (1)855.
18. Marta Powell Harley, ed., *A Revelation of Purgatory by an Unknown Fifteenth-Century Woman Visionary* (Lewiston, NY: Edwin Mellen, 1985), ll. 628–30.

19. Sarah McNamer, "Feeling," in *Middle English: Oxford Twenty-First Century Approaches to Literature*, ed. Paul Strohm (Oxford: Oxford University Press, 2009), 246.
20. *Dives and Pauper*, ed. Priscilla Heath Barnum, EETS o.s. 275, 280 (London: Oxford University Press, 1976), vol. 1, 84–5.
21. Thomas G. Duncan, ed., *Medieval English Lyrics, 1200–1400* (Harmondsworth: Penguin, 1995), 119.
22. Richard Marks, *Image and Devotion in Late Medieval England* (Stroud: Sutton, 2004), 10.
23. Reginald Pecock, *The Repressor of Over Much Blaming of the Clergy*, Vol. 1, ed. Churchill Babington (London: Longman, Green, Longman, and Roberts, 1860), 149.
24. See, for example, *Dives and Pauper*, ed. Barnum, vol. 1, 102.
25. Ibid., 101.
26. *The Lanterne of Li3t*, ed. Lilian M. Swinburn, EETS o.s. 151 (London: Kegan Paul, Trench, Trübner, 1917), 85.
27. Anne Hudson, ed., *Selections from English Wycliffite Writings* (Toronto: University of Toronto Press, 1997), 87.
28. McNamer, "Feeling," 248.
29. The narrative is not original to Lydgate, but, like the rest of the *Troy Book*, is translated from Guido delle Colonne's *Historia destructionis Troiae*.
30. Paul Strohm, in "Sovereignty and Sewage," in *Lydgate Matters: Poetry and Material Culture in the Fifteenth Century*, ed. Lisa H. Cooper and Andrea Denny-Brown (New York: Palgrave Macmillan, 2008), identifies the technology as "life support" (63).
31. *The Iliad of Homer*, trans. Richmond Lattimore (Chicago, IL: University of Chicago Press, 1951), 19.38–9.
32. *John Lydgate's "Lives of Ss Edmund and Fremund" and the "Extra Miracles of St Edmund," Edited from British Library MS Harley 2278 and Bodleian Library MS Ashmole 46*, ed. Anthony Bale and A. S. G. Edwards (Heidelberg: Universitatsverlag Winter, 2009), ll. 3306–46.
33. Manchester, John Rylands English MS 1, f. 109v; Oxford, Bodleian MS Digby 232, f. 110. See Lesley Lawton, "The Illustration of Late-Medieval Secular Texts, with Special Reference to Lydgate's *Troy Book*," in *Manuscripts and Readers in Fifteenth-Century England: The Literary Implications of Manuscript Study*, ed. Derek Pearsall (Cambridge: D. S. Brewer, 1983), 59, note 62 (for a discussion of these images), and 56–8 (for a table comparing the illustrative choices of six *Troy Book*s). Some continental illustrators attempt to depict the whole assemblage: see E. R. Truitt, *Medieval Robots: Mechanism, Nature, and Art* (Philadelphia, PA: University of Pennsylvania Press, 2015), plates 22–3.
34. Pecock, *Repressor of Over Much Blaming*, 149.
35. See Corine Schleif, "Men on the Right – Women on the Left: (A)Symmetrical Spaces and Gendered Places," in *Women's Space: Patronage, Place, and Gender in the Medieval Church*, ed. Virginia Chieffo Raguin and Sarah Stanbury

(Albany, NY: State University of New York Press, 2005), 207–49, on this polarity.
36. Ahmed, "Happy Objects," 35.
37. David Freedberg, *The Power of Images: Studies in the History and Theory of Response* (Chicago, IL: University of Chicago Press, 1989), 286.
38. Norman Davis, ed., *The Play of the Sacrament*, in *Non-Cycle Plays and Fragments*, EETS s.s. 1 (London: Oxford University Press, 1970), l. 712 s.d., ll. 804–5.
39. *Play of the Sacrament*, ll. 928–9.
40. *The Book of Margery Kempe*, ed. Sanford Brown Meech and Hope Emily Allen, EETS o.s. 212 (London: Oxford University Press, 1940), 77–8.
41. Ibid., 78.
42. Kathy Lavezzo, "Sobs and Sighs between Women: The Homoerotics of Compassion in *The Book of Margery Kempe*," in *Premodern Sexualities*, ed. Louise Fradenburg and Carla Freccero (New York: Routledge, 1996), 186.
43. Michael Camille, *The Gothic Idol: Ideology and Image-Making in Medieval Art* (Cambridge: Cambridge University Press, 1989), 237.
44. Malcolm Jones, *The Secret Middle Ages: Discovering the Real Medieval World* (Stroud: Sutton, 2002), 255.
45. Thanks to Sadaf Najib, who told me about the hand.
46. "History of the Church", *St Etheldra*, www.stetheldreda.com/index.php/history-of-st-etheldredas/.

CHAPTER 7

Witnessing and Legal Affect in the York Trial Plays

Emma Lipton

Meditations on the Passion by Richard Rolle, Nicholas Love, the Pseudo-Bonaventura, and others have played a key role in the characterization of medieval affect as devotional and individualistic. For example, Sarah McNamer's influential book, *Affective Meditation and the Invention of Medieval Compassion*, is centered on "affective meditations on the Passion," which she characterizes as "a private drama of the heart," a body of texts that "teach their reader, through iterative affective performance, how to feel."[1] Although recent work has drawn attention to the collective nature of emotion, this model of inward devotion continues to be seen as crucial to understanding medieval drama.[2] A representative example of this conventional wisdom is Clifford Davidson's assertion that the York plays are "congruent with the intense spirituality that is found in such writings as Nicholas Love's adaptation of the popular Latin *Meditations on the Life of Christ*." For Davidson, the "plays were designed to promote emotional involvement with the events being staged."[3] Davidson cites Love's insistence on identifying personally with Christ on the cross: "such identification [must] be felt 'inwardly' in one's thoughts through 'trewe ymaginacion and inwarde compassion of the peynes and the passion'" of Christ.[4] In this way, Davidson and others argue, medieval drama participates in the construction of a subjectivity generated by the individual's experience of emotion.

This essay proposes that the legal theory of witnessing provides an alternative way to consider medieval affect and to understand the affectivity of late medieval religious drama.[5] Drawing on the work of contemporary theorists Sara Ahmed and Sianne Ngai, I argue for a model of "legal affect" poised between the social and the individual.[6] Late medieval religious plays are not, in McNamer's words, "a private drama of the heart," but a public affective experience.

As I will demonstrate, the plays employ legal ideas of witnessing to explore the relationship between individual perception and the collective experience of emotion. Medieval practices such as allowing prosecution by reputation and requiring multiple witnesses made even a witness' first-hand perceptions social. Medieval legal theorists understood the somatic elements of witnessing to be affected by socially generated emotions such as love and hate. The plays' legal affect can be seen as an alternative to a confessional discourse that framed even the social emotion of envy in individual terms, since the plays deviate from their sources in their emphasis on legal concepts of witnessing.[7]

The centrality of legal witnessing to late medieval culture has yet to be fully recognized by critics, despite a number of important recent studies on the relationship between medieval law and literature.[8] Better known in recent scholarship as a watershed in the history of confession, the Fourth Lateran Council also catalyzed a major shift in legal practice by promoting the witness trial and effectively outlawing the ordeal and trial by battle.[9] This emphasis on eyewitness testimony in the courts led to the wide participation of the community in legal culture as victims, neighbors, and jurors, ensuring that legal concepts of evidence were not, in Lorna Hutson's words, "esoteric professional doctrine," but widely diffused through society.[10] Although earlier scholars located a shift in authority from church courts to secular courts in the sixteenth century, historians Marjorie McIntosh and Shannon McSheffrey have shown that local courts gained jurisdiction and authority as early as the late fourteenth century.[11] For this reason, we can see legal concepts of witnessing as culturally central at the time of the York plays, believed to have been staged as early as 1376 and performed through the late 1500s.

Often seen as the focus of the affective practices of late medieval religious culture, the Passion was also depicted legalistically in late medieval sermons and confessional manuals and was even referred to in legal treatises. A representative sermon by Bishop Brunton of Rochester, for example, uses the trial of Christ to comment on false judges, identified as "the powerful men of the world today," arguing that they are swayed by earthly concerns: "it is the same with the Justice of the English as it was with the Justice of the Jews at the time of Christ's passion."[12] The Passion is often specifically linked to problems of witnessing and false speech. The confessional text *Jacob's Well* claims that false swearing, including "whanne men seryn fals wytingly, & beryn fals wyttnesse" is "werse than iewys" when they crucified Christ.[13] The legal problems illustrated by the condemnation of Christ are frequently depicted as relevant to the contemporary practice of law. In *De legibus et consuetudinibus Angliae*, the influential legal theorist Henry Bracton uses the story of the Passion to warn judges to explore the intentions of witnesses, who might be swayed by negative emotions to pave the way to false justice.[14] Reflecting this legalistic version of the Passion, the York plays contain an extended sequence of five pageants devoted to the trial of Christ in contrast to only one pageant devoted to the Crucifixion. The York plays' depiction of the Passion specifically engages the blending of perception and emotion, and of individual and social elements that constituted the medieval act of witnessing.

Drawing on the discussion of witnessing in late medieval legal treatises, the first part of this essay will argue that medieval witness theory constructs a model of "legal affect." In contrast to the depiction of false witnessing in confessional discourse as an individual sin, legal witnessing is simultaneously personal and collective. The second portion of this essay will use the York trials of Christ as a case study, demonstrating that the plays enlist a model of affect based on legal witnessing. By casting the audience simultaneously as witnesses to the play and to the trials of Christ, the York plays construct "legal affect" as dramatic theory. The plays use legal ideas of witnessing to shape an ethics of affect that is, like the drama itself, potentially civic and communal, in contrast to the clerical discourse of confession focused on individual conscience or the devotional tradition of "affective piety" more commonly associated by critics with medieval drama. In this way, I argue against the prevailing wisdom that the trials of Christ in medieval drama are primarily a criticism of the corruption of contemporary legal practices.[15]

Witnessing and Legal Affect

Jacques Derrida famously claimed that "testimony is always autobiographical: it tells, in the first person, the sharable and unsharable secret of what happened to me, to me, to me alone, the absolute secret of what I was in a position to live, see, hear, touch, sense and feel."[16] In this well-known passage, Derrida makes witnessing the quintessential example of a subjectivity defined by unique first-hand sensory experience. Similarly, in another influential account, Giorgio Agamben asserts: "to be a subject and to bear witness are in the final analysis one and the same."[17] Indeed, as Andrea Frisch has argued, the "paradigm of witnessing-as-experiential knowledge" is often tied to "the consolidation of the modern subject."[18] By contrast, medieval legal theory and practice, although focused on the somatic elements, did not construct witnessing as a private discourse of uniqueness or individualism. Instead, witnessing was seen as an affective testimony poised between the collective and individual, an idea that is demonstrated in the York plays' use of legal affect in the construction of civic identity.

While accounts of medieval witnessing have tended to describe a teleological progression from ordeal and proof by battle to modern eyewitnessing, in both secular and ecclesiastical courts of late medieval England, more "modern" notions of witnessing as first-hand experience existed at the same time as "traditional" modes of proof which relied on the group rather than the individual, and on knowledge of character rather than sensory perception.[19] These included compurgation, in which people testified to their faith in the reliability of a defendant, and prosecution by *mala fama* or reputation. These modes of witnessing were designed to establish what Richard Firth Green terms an "ethical truth" based on social consensus, rather than on an individual's first-hand experience of the facts, suggesting that medieval witnessing was collective and even intersubjective.[20]

By the time that the Fourth Lateran Council officially outlawed the ordeal in 1215 and established witness procedure as the official policy of the ecclesiastical courts, the theory of witnessing was already well established by both canonists and civil law theorists.[21] According to legal historian Charles Donahue, there was relatively little innovation after the twelfth century, when treatises on witnessing proliferated and became sources for later witness theory. Following Gratian's *Decretum*, these texts claimed that asserting vocal testimony was the best form of proof, superior to either written documents or bodily proof of ordeal or battle.[22] One influential treatise was Tancred's *Ordo* from *Libri de iudiciorum ordine* (c. 1215), which outlines the standard overall form for the course of judgment.[23] Tancred's *Ordo* required that witnesses be examined to see if they were telling the truth about events that they saw and heard for themselves.[24] Preference for eyewitness testimony was widely evident in a variety of specific subsequent legislation, such as the 1316 Statute of Glavelet, which specified that witnesses testify in court to their "own sight and hearing" (*de pleno visu et auditu*).[25] According to legal historian Richard Helmholz, witness depositions became, in practice, the most common form of proof in late medieval English church courts.[26]

Although this emphasis on what an individual saw and heard might seem to confirm Derrida's idea of the witness as a mode of subjectivity, a standard requirement for at least two witnesses demonstrates that witnessing was not understood as an individualized activity. In his analysis of marriage cases in York, Charles Donahue claims that even the number of witnesses on each side could play a role in the case.[27] Court records often do not give the full depositions of witnesses who repeat previous testimony; the clerk simply indicates that they repeat.[28] Thus, even witnessing based on first-hand experience was understood as a collective act. Furthermore, witnesses were allowed to discuss the matter with each other before they testified, accounting for some of the notable agreement in cases.[29] The fact that slaves, women, those under fourteen years old, the poor, the infamous and the criminal may not testify indicates that social status played a role in witnessing. Similarly, children and domestics could not testify, nor could friends and enemies of the accused. All of these rules indicate that the role of the witness was constructed in social terms.[30]

The standard oath used for medieval witnesses shows the belief that witnessing was affected by socially generated emotions. For example, Tancred's *Ordo* instructs:

> Tale iuramentum debent praestare testes generaliter: quod ipsi dicent indici vel ei, cui iudex hoc commiserit inquirendum, totem veritam, quam sciunt de quaestione, super qua inducuntur, usque ad finem litis, quotiens interrogabuntur; et nullam falsitatem interponent; *et pro utraque parte veritatem dicent et quod nec pretio, nec amicitia, nec private odio, seu commodo aliquot, quod inde habituri sint ad dicendum testimonium ipsum accedent.*
>
> Witnesses must generally give an oath of this kind: that they speak to the investigator (or to him whom the judge may have here appointed as the investigator) the whole truth that they know about the question for which they are led in until the end of the trial, however many times they are interrogated. [They swear] to introduce no falsehood and to tell the truth for both parties. *They are also to swear that they do not come to bear testimony for a price or out of friendship, or for private hate, or for any benefit they might receive.*[31]

Historian Paul R. Hyams has argued that the formula at the end of this passage, with its mix of emotional and financial motives, recurs in routine administrative records and documents throughout the late Middle Ages, and may have derived from Gratian's widely circulated *Decretum*.[32] As the passage above illustrates, the list structure of the standard witness oath gives grammatical equivalence to price, friendship, private hate, and benefit. The terms "pretio" (price) and "commodo" (benefit), which refer to exchanges of capital, are implicitly compared to the emotions of "amicitia" (friendship) and "odio" (hate), suggesting that those emotions circulate between people. As contemporary theorist Sara Ahmed argues, emotions, especially hate, "work as a form of capital: affect does not reside positively in the sign or commodity, but is produced as an effect of its circulation ... 'the subject' is simply one nodal point in the economy rather than its origin and destination."³³ Instead of depicting emotion as privatized self-expression, Ahmed argues that emotion is a "social form." Ahmed's theory of emotion helps us see that medieval witnessing was not a discourse of individuality as Derrida and other witness theorists would have it, but a circulation of affect that illustrates the "sociality of emotion."³⁴

Despite the existence of treatises promoting the eyewitness, in practice, medieval courts gave the reports of neighbors and first-hand experience similar weight. Neighbors testified not from what they had seen, but to what the community believed. *Tractatus de legibus et consuetudinibus regni Angli qui Glanvilla vocatur* ("Glanville"; c. 1189) was the earliest common law treatise to propose a trial as a possible alternative to battle, in which the neighborhood is called to testify to what they already know. Glanville explains:

> Ad scientiam autem eorum qui super hoc iurant inde habendam, exigitur quod per proprium uisum suum et auditum illius rei habuerint noticiam, uel per uerba patrum suorum et per talia quibus fidem habere teneantur ut propriis.
>
> The knowledge required from the jurors is that they shall know about the matter from what they have personally seen and heard, OR from statements which their father made to them in such circumstances that they are bound to believe them as if they had seen or heard for themselves.³⁵

In other words, jurors could either be eyewitnesses themselves or they could judge the words of others to be reliable. In contrast to modern procedure in which jurors are selected for presumed impartiality and lack of prior knowledge about the case, in late medieval law, witnessing required interpreting the evidence. In late medieval court practice, the collective knowledge of the neighborhood was widely accepted, especially in difficult cases. For example, in a marriage case from York, the deposition includes the following statement: "The whole neighborhood testifies to this, and it is well known to all."³⁶ In a case heard before the archbishop of Canterbury's court of audience, when the judge wanted to supplement the allegations of both parties, he "decided to inquire by thirteen or twelve men from among the faithful neighbors of the [parties] who were not suspect to either, as to which of the parties was guilty of the aforesaid dissension and dispute."³⁷ As such, witnessing was often defined as a collective act of observation, which blended the communal with the perceptual.

The collective aspect of witnessing enabled social emotions such as hate or greed to become part of witnessing. In a passage from his mid-thirteenth-century English legal treatise, Henry Bracton shows how the emotions of individuals can move through a social chain to influence jurors and negatively affect their ability to promote proper justice. The title of this section is "Diligenter inquirendum a quibus didicerint id quod dicunt quia quidam mentiuntur per odium, quidam propter cupiditatem" ("Careful inquiry must be made from whom they have learned what they say, for some lie from hatred, some from greed").[38] The use of the plural "they" and "some" indicates that acts of testimony are collective while the references to "hatred" and "greed" convey emotional content. The passage begins by advising that the judge "debet inquirere ... a quo vel a quibus illi duodecim didicerint ea quae veredicto suo proferunt de indictato, et audita super hoc eorum responsione de facili perpendere poterit si dolus subfuerit vel iniquitas" ("ought ... to inquire ... from what man or men the twelve jurors have learned what they put forward in the *veredictum* from one of their fellow jurors; having heard their answer he may readily decide if any deceit or wickedness lies behind it").[39] In its use of "man or men," this passage also moves between plural and singular agency. Personal motivation is detached from the individual when it becomes part of legal procedure in the form of the *veredictum*. Bracton next traces the process by which one person's deceit becomes integral to a collective act of witnessing:

> Dicet forte aliquis vel maior pars iuratorum, quod ea quae ipsi proferunt in veredicto suo didicerunt ab uno ex coniuratoribus suis, et quilibet interrogatus dicet forte quod illud didicit ab alio tali, et sic descendere poterit interrogatio et responsio de persona in personam usque ad aliquam vilem et abiectam personam, et talem cui non erit fides aliquatenus adhibenda.

> For perhaps one or a majority of the jurors will say that they learned the matter put forward in their *veredictum* from one of their fellow jurors, and he under interrogation will perhaps say that he learned it from such a one, and so by question and answer the judge may descend from person to person to some low and worthless fellow, one in whom no trust must be in any way reposed.[40]

Information is passed along a chain of people who then collectively employ it in an act of witnessing. The language of this passage, with its vacillation between "one or a majority" of jurors, also suggests that witnessing is simultaneously an individual and collective action.

The passage concludes with a representative example that links the collective act of witnessing to the circulation of misinformation colored by hatred and other emotions:

> Evenit quidem quandoque quod dominus tenentem suum indictat, vel indictare facit et ei crimen imponi ob cupiditatem terram suam habendi in dominico, vel vicinus vicino propter odium et huiusmodi.

> It sometimes happens that a lord accuses his tenant, or causes him to be indicted and a crime imputed to him, through a greedy desire to secure his land ... or one neighbor accuses another through hatred and the like.[41]

The emotions of "greedy desire" and "hatred and the like" defining improper witnessing in this passage are social crimes experienced in relationship to "tenant" or "neighbor." The emotion of hatred threatens to form a social bond that undermines or competes with the vision of community and neighbor defined by proper witnessing, reflecting Ahmed's argument that hatred plays an active role in creating the collective. Indeed, this description of the circulation of the misinformation generated by the emotions of the "lowly fellow" resembles Sara Ahmed's account of the ways in which emotions themselves are "sticky." She argues: "emotions are not 'in' either the individual or the social, but produce the very surfaces and boundaries that allow the individual and the social to be delineated as if they were objects. The objects of emotion take shape as effects of circulation."[42] In other words, counter to modern notions of objective legal procedure and ethics, the medieval law of witnessing shows that, as Ahmed has written, "emotion and perception are not easily separated."[43]

Bracton ties his concern about the effect of affect in legal witnessing specifically to the biblical trial of Christ, warning judges who value their reputations to inquire into witnessing of this nature so "that it not be said, 'Jesus is crucified and Barabas delivered'" ("ne dicatur Ihesus crucifigitur et Barabas liberatur").[44] Medieval legal theory links problems of witnessing to biblical precedent and suggests that the Passion of Christ should not just be seen as an instance of an individualized affective piety, but as a crucial example of the risks of emotion in witnessing, as affect can circulate in exchanges of testimony.

Confessional Manuals and False Witnessing

The centrality of witnessing to late medieval culture is evident not just in legal texts, but also in confessional handbooks. Like legal texts, confessional handbooks link problematic emotion to legal witnessing, but they represent false witnessing as a private problem of regulating a person's emotion rather as an integral part of public collective acts of testimony. In confessional handbooks false witnessing is consistently associated with the sin of envy and identified as a motive for the condemnation of Christ. In the fourteenth-century *Book of Vices and Virtues*, for example, envy is defined as "whan a man werrieþ anoþer mannes gostly good, as þe Iewes werriede Ihesu Crist for þe good þat he dide."[45] In *Fasciculus Morum*, the "evil Jews who preferred the thief Barabbas to Christ" ("pessimis Iudeis qui latronem Baraban Christo pretulerunt") represent flatterers, a subset of envy.[46] Indeed, *Fasciculus Morum* includes an extensive account of Christ's Passion in the section on Envy.[47] These texts and sermons tie the Passion to the individual sin of envy, rather than the more collective view of emotions we saw in Bracton and other legal theorists' discussions.

Not only is envy associated with the trials of Christ, it is also often broadly linked with false witnessing in confessional texts. For example, *Handlying Synne* described the evil consequences of false witnessing in practical legal terms: "wyl men swere falsely a sawe, / And bere wytnes of swyche a fals / To make a man hang be þe hals."[48] In this passage the false words of men lead to severe legal punishment. Similarly, the same text depicts the Fifth Commandment against false witnessing in legalistic terms: "false traitours & feloune, – þat falslyche, for enuye, / On here neghburs wyl gladly lye."[49] "Traitours" and "feloune" allude to crimes, while "neghburs" invokes the legal definition of witness in the period. Similarly, Bracton's concern that "one neighbor accuses another through hatred and the like" reflects the same equation between witness and neighbor bound by chains of emotion.[50] Like witnessing, envy was depicted as a fundamentally social sin committed against neighbors in confessor's handbooks, as a perversion of *caritas*, the Christian imperative to love. As Jessica Rosenfeld has argued, envy is "an inwardly experienced sin that is also necessarily social" because it is defined as a rejection of compassion, "a simultaneous emotional and behavioral refusal of the command to love one's neighbor."[51] Confessional texts construct witnessing in the same terms as envy. *Fasciculus Morum*, for example, instructs that "if you love your neighbor, you will not ... give false witness."[52]

Although confessional manuals have a striking resemblance to legal treatises in their discussion of false witnessing in terms of *amicitia* and in the context of the biblical trial of Christ, unlike legal treatises, they connect the love and hate of false witnessing to a discourse of selfhood rather than to collective emotion. The *Book of Virtues and Vices*, for example, warns about "fals justises and juges, þat hongeþ more touward þat o syde þan þat oþere for ȝiftes, or for bihestes, or for biddynges, or for loue or for hate, or for drede, and delaien and tarien þe quereles wiþ wrong, and makeþ men spende grete."[53] This has a striking similarity to the witness oath discussed above. In contrast to the Bracton passage, where love, hate, and money moved through a chain of people ending with the judge, here, although the emotions are experienced in relationship to others, the fault is ascribed to the justices as individuals. Similar terms are invoked in a long passage from Chaucer's *Parson's Tale* that warns against false witnessing "for ire, or for meede, or for envy," ending with the exhortation: "Ware yow questmongeres and notaries!"[54] The use of the second-person pronoun asks the listener to self-identify as a "questmonger," or false witness, and thus take personal responsibility for the emotions of false witnessing. Similarly, the commentary on legal abuse in *Jacob's Well* lists twelve kinds of abuse of the law under the category of "couvetousness," and these are characterized by a list of people who are evildoers, including false plaintiffs, false pleaders, solicitors, secretaries, false witnesses, and judges who do "more wrong than evynhed in jugement, for auantage."[55] This passage ascribes fault to bad individuals who occupy roles in the legal system rather than to the collective or to the structures of the legal system itself.[56] While recognizing envy and covetousness as social sins, the text ascribes responsibility for the experience of these emotions to the individual, in contrast to "legal affect" that is generated more collectively.

Medieval confessional texts do what Sianne Ngai has observed in a modern context: they make envy a matter of the individual psyche. "Instead of seeing it as a way to respond to social disparities," she explains, "we tend to perceive envy as designating a passive condition of the subject rather than the means by which the subject recognizes and responds to an objective relation."[57] According to Ngai, this subverts a potential for political engagement. She argues "that the dominant cultural attitude toward this affect converts its fundamentally other-regarding orientation into an egocentric one, stripping it of its polemicism and rendering it merely a reflection of deficient and possibly histrionic selfhood."[58] By framing false witnessing as an individual experience of envy, medieval confessional texts are similarly resistant to social change. By contrast, as I will argue, the York trial plays reject confessional discourse and embrace legal ideals of witnessing to promote civic values.

Legal Affect and the York Trial Plays

Given this common association of envy in the confessionals with the Jews who condemn Christ and with legal crimes more generally, it is notable that the York trial plays do not give it a central role. This is an important omission given the persistent association of legal corruption with envy and covetousness in the confessionals. Furthermore, the sources for the York plays, including the *Northern Passion*, the *Gospel of Nicodemus*, and Jacobus de Voragine's *Legenda aurea*, all ascribe envy to the canon lawyers Anna and Caiaphas and to Pilate, in their condemnation of Christ.[59] The York trials plays do not entirely omit the discourse of sin, instead associating confessional discourse with the morally suspect figures of Pilate and his wife Procula and assigning to them the more emphatically individualistic sin of pride. In fact, the York plays replace confessional discourse that depicts legal abuses as a problem of individual self-regulation with a legalistic model of witnessing that treats affect as public and social. Furthermore, the play associates confessional discourse with the corruptions of church and state while it uses a legalistic model of witnessing to embody civic virtues and values.

In "Christ Before Pilate I: The Dream of Pilate's Wife," Pilate's boasting rant employs a confessional discourse of emotion. The play begins, not with the trial of Christ, but with a soliloquy by Pilate that deviates from the play's immediate sources and serves as a prologue addressed to the audience. In a long speech that establishes his authority to judge the Jews, Pilate alludes to his pride four times in the space of seven lines, concluding, "I haue schewid you in sight, / Howe I am prowdely preued 'Pilatus.' / Loo, Pilate I am, proued a prince of grete pride" (18–20).[60] This passage equates "I" with an abstract expression of vice, participating in the dynamics of self-definition key to the confessional. Indeed, pride is perhaps the quintessential example of self-directed emotion. According to *Fasciculus Morum*, pride is "love of one's own superiority" ("amor proprie excellencie"), and includes "pride in one's power and rank" ("superbiendum in potencia") and "pride in the nobility of our blood" ("de generis nobilitated"), characterizations specifically invoked by the speech of the York Pilate.[61] As the short passage above indicates, Pilate is relentless in his repetition of the first person singular, the grammatical expression of his pride. By focusing on pride in contrast to the sin of envy more commonly associated with this biblical story in sermons, confessional manuals, and in the sources for the York plays, the trial plays emphasize the individualistic element of the confessional.

The play frames the confessional discourse of Pilate's opening speech politically through the invocation of the language of the Divine Right of kings. It ascribes the discourse of the confessional to Pilate in this moment when he also expresses his tyranny. Immediately before the passage quoted above, Pilate invokes his pedigree, asserting "[S]ir Sesar was my sier and I soethely his sonne, / That exclent emperoure exaltid in hight" (10–11). He claims that his name comes from his mother's parents, using his genealogy as "grounde ... To justifie and juge all þe Jewes" (24). By linking his genealogy to his role as judge, York's Pilate refers to the idea, common in legal treatises and mirrors for princes, that the king embodies the law in his divine person. Hoccleve's *Regiment of Princes*, for example, asserts that "A kyng is maad to keepen and maynteene / Justice" (2514–15).[62] Pilate initially hesitates to condemn Christ, seeming to uphold his role as just ruler. He asserts that "His liff for to lose þare longes no lawe, / Nor no cause can I kyndely contryue / [Why þat] he schulde lose þus his liffe" (435–7). After discovering that Christ claims kingship and is thus a threat to his own power, Pilate condemns him. In doing so, York's Pilate fits the familiar paradigm of a tyrant who values his own singular profit over the common good. John of Salisbury's widely circulated *Policraticus*, for example, asserts that what distinguishes a king from a tyrant is that the former is "obedient to law ... because the authority of the prince is determined by the authority of right."[63] The play's portrait of Pilate thus rejects the paradigm that the king is an image of divine justice on earth, by linking legal corruption with the monarchy and aristocratic genealogy. This passage suggests the dangers of understanding law as personal expression rather than social act. By linking Pilate's assertion of royal prerogative to pride, the play shows the potential for an individualized view of emotion to have an implicit politics, linking it to the uses of law for monarchical power rather than justice.

The play not only associates Pilate with the penitential sin of Pride, it also employs a discourse of confessional internality in its depiction of the temptation of his wife, Procula. While in bed, Procula is visited in a dream by the Devil, who tries to get her to prevent Christ from being unjustly judged. The Devil seeks to save Christ for the wrong reason; he is worried that Christ's death will bring redemption. He tells Procula that she should save Christ or her "richesse shall be refte" (174), attempting to persuade her to save Christ to protect her possessions. Although Ruth Nisse has argued that this scene should be understood in the context of women's visionary literature, it also invokes a conventional use of dreams of the Devil to describe evil desires and internal motivations.[64] *Handlying Synne* warns that some dreams "beyn the fendes temptacyoun."[65] *Fasciculus Morum* links the Devil to sleep itself: "when the devil attacks man, he does ... things similar to what people do when they want to rest and sleep." Just as people shut the door, turn out the light, and seek quiet when going to sleep, the text instructs, so the devil closes the window of the soul, extinguishes the light of God, and stops man's ears to God's word.[66] When York's Procula reports that she has had a "dream," the Devil's speech can be read as an abstract representation of Procula's state of mind, as an abbreviated *psychomachia*. Even the Devil's speech is framed as testimony to Christ's power. Although Diabolus calls Him "gentilman, Jesu, of cursednesse he can" (160), he is forced to recognize that "Be any syngne þat I see, þis same is Goddis sonne" (161). Whereas in Towneley's "Last Judgment" juridical procedure is figured as diabolic in contrast to the truly just and merciful jurisdiction of God's representative, the priest, over the soul, the York play inverts that paradigm by associating the Devil with the discourse of the confessional.[67]

The York play replaces confessional language with a legal discourse of witnessing. Whereas the legalism of the York trial plays has been widely noted, the plays' particular preoccupation with witnessing and the extent to which they draw on the specific legal understanding of contemporary witnessing has not previously been examined.[68] The York trials of Christ do not so much illustrate the sin of envy as they portray the perils of false witnessing. "Christ Before Annas and Caiaphas" recasts Peter's betrayal as a failure to bear witness for Christ, a role instead taken up by Malchus, who testifies to the miracles Christ has performed.[69] Christ himself calls Caiaphas a "wronge wittenesse" (329) when the canon lawyer accuses him of being a traitor. Similarly, Annas and Caiaphas bear false witness against Christ in "Christ Before Pilate I," when they bring him before Pilate the judge, but the Beadle testifies to the miracles he has seen Christ perform. The Beadle is a figure for civic law who instructs Pilate's wife Procula in what "langis to our lawes" and whom Pilate acknowledges as a repository of legal knowledge: "he knawis all oure custome" (71). In "Christ Before Herod," Herod acts as judge while others are enlisted to "beris wittenesse" (376) against Christ. "Christ Before Before Pilate 2: The Judgement" features Annas and Caiaphas acting as witnesses and then offering to provide a crowd of people who, they claim, will provide additional "witnesse" (106, 110) to the false traitorous acts of Christ. In contrast to penitential texts that treat false witnessing as a branch of envy, the York pageants separate the two, depicting the condemnation of Christ as the effect of a public act of false witnessing.

In "Christ Before Pilate I," Caiaphas alludes to the collective aspect of contemporary practice of witnessing. Deflecting attention from his own motives, he claims he can find others who can testify against Christ, enacting an act of witnessing by many people at the same time: "the greeteste" number of people "of þis werke beres witnesse" (510–12). Caiaphas suggests that the sheer number of witnesses should play a role in the condemnation of Christ. As we have seen, the mere number of witnesses on a particular side did play a role in court cases of the period. Furthermore, Caiaphas' words treat perception and recollection as potentially collective acts, reflected in such practices allowing testimony by reputation.

The York trial plays engage the specific terms of the witness oath not to testify "for a price or out of friendship or for private hate."⁷⁰ In "Christ Before Annas and Caiaphas, " Annas tells Caiaphas they should bring Christ to Pilate and tell him "how ye hym hate" (342), and ask if he will "helpe hym or haste hym to hyng" (343), demonstrating the role of hate in false justice. In "Christ before Pilate I," Annas explains that Christ "werkis whane he will, wele I wote, / And þerfore in herte we hym hate" (420–1). In the same play, Pilate quizzes the two lawyers about their "entente" (498) and repeatedly accuses them of "malice" (483–5), and of lying for a "price" (455). Similarly, in "Christ Before Pilate 2," Pilate accuses Caiaphas and Annas directly of being false witnesses motivated by "hatred" (122, 325). They attempt to testify against Christ and are rejected by Pilate in terms that reflect the legal concern with witnessing being tainted by emotions:

> þer witnesse I warande þat to witnesse ȝe wage,
> Some hatred in ther hartis agaynes hym have hent,
> And purpose be this processe to putt doun þis page. (121–3)

This passage echoes the terms of Bracton's warning when he advises judges against witnesses who hate, lest it lead to the miscarriage of justice.

Although Pilate initially rejects Caiaphas' and Annas' testimony on the grounds of their hatred, the play's depiction of Pilate's change of heart traces the terms of Bracton's warning for judges against the ways false witnessing generates emotion through a chain of people. Pilate asks, "what harmes has þis hatell here haunted? / I kenne to co[n]vyk hym no cause" (292–3), and later "why suld I deme to dede, þan, withoute deseruyng in dede? / But I haue herde al haly why in hertes ȝe hym hate / He is fautles in faith" (324–6). When Caiaphas responds that he claims to be king (329), Pilate immediately promises violent punishment "for wo to he be wepyng" (338), which indicates that the canon lawyers' hatred has generated a similar emotion in Pilate. In this way, the play recognizes the ways in which emotions can be "sticky" and take shape in the circulation between people. Like Bracton, the play characterizes the circulation of emotion in acts of false witnessing as responsible for the condemnation of Christ, linking the biblical trial to contemporary witness theory.

Although both confessional and legal texts use the trials of Christ to discuss the failures of contemporary witness trials, the York plays also draw on legal discourse to generate an idealized affective model of witnessing. In "Christ Before Annas and Caiaphas," Peter refuses to testify for Christ, claiming "I saw hym neuere are" (129) and "I was neuere with hym in werke þat he wroght / In worde nor in werke" (154–5). In these lines, Peter simultaneously eschews both his role as eyewitness and as compurgatory witness who might testify to Christ's character, an act Malchus identifies as a perversion of "oure lawe ... Thus hath he denyed hym thryes" (160–1). These lines construct Peter's betrayal as a refusal to bear witness, and identify witnessing as a rejection of both perception and bonds of affection. Instead, Malchus performs this public role of witness, asserting "I schall preve to ȝou pertly, and telle you my tale" (134). Taking on the role of an eyewitness, Malchus says "I was presente with pepull whenne prese was full prest" (135). He reports on the miracles of healing that Christ has performed, asserting "of tokenyng of trouth, schall I telle yowe" (139). In this last phrase, Malchus claims that perception has a role in conveying larger theological truths to the local community.

In "Christ Before Pilate I," the Beadle plays a similar role, testifying that he has seen Christ working miracles on the way to Jerusalem. The canon lawyers Annas and Caiaphas try to persuade Pilate to condemn Christ, warning him that Christ is a threat to their laws. Like Malchus in the other play, the Beadle accuses Annas and Caiaphas of being "false frawdes" (241), identifying them as bad witnesses. In this way, the Beadle plays the role of a good judge who roots out bad witnesses before they have an adverse effect on the community and its legal process. The Beadle himself is a good witness, in that he is not moved by hate or price but by "wirschippe ... for wytes þat wer wiser þan I ... worshipped þe full holy on hy / And with solempnité sang *Osanna*" (311–15). In this case, not hate but worship is generated in a chain of emotion passed between people. In his gloss, the Beadle's words merge with those of the men he has seen and heard sing "Hosanna." This passage reflects a contemporary legal ideal of witnessing in which eyewitnesses could be individual or communal, especially in cases of defamation, a term explicitly invoked in this play. Responding to Pilate's command to get Christ, the Beadle prefaces his witnessing speech by saying that he is "fayne [moued in myn herte]" (307), identifying his emotion as a source for his testimony. The play draws attention to the ways that legal discourse of witnessing provided a theory of affect in which both emotion and somatic experience are poised between the collective and the individual.

The legal theory of witnessing serves as both an agent of civic community and a model for the drama itself.[71] The plays establish a parallel between witnessing the drama and watching a trial. For example, in "Christ Before Annas and Caiaphas," when Malchus says "I schall preue to ȝou pertly, and telle you my tale" (134), he addresses both those present within the play and the larger audience on the streets of York. Furthermore, in his emphasis on telling the tale "pertly," or openly, Malchus constructs his act of witnessing as a public act of telling, as opposed to either a private meditation or a documentary approach to proof. The Beadle's act of narrating Christ's past actions makes him a model for the York drama which itself tells Christ's life. The play establishes the Beadle's acts of witnessing as a model for the urban audience, who participate collectively in a somatic and emotional experience of the play, and, like the Beadle, act as witnesses to biblical events. If the Beadle acts as a model for proper witnessing, he also invokes the work of the actor who voices his speech, itself a somatic and emotional act of witnessing. By inviting the audience to witness, the play signals that its own medium can potentially embody the truth by speaking not just to what the audience sees and hears but to what they know as neighbors and members of the community, drawing on legal affect for dramatic theory.

The famous passage in the York play of the "Crucifixio Christi," when Christ invites the audience to behold his suffering body, can be seen as an invitation to the audience to bear witness. Christ says:

> Al men þat walkis by waye or strete,
> Takes tente ȝe schalle no trauayle tyne.
> Byholdes myn heede, myn handis, and my feete,
> And fully feele nowe, or ȝe fyne,
> Yf any mournyng may be meete,
> Or myscheue mesured vnto myne.   (253–8)

In this passage, Christ addresses the audience directly, asking the viewers to act as eyewitnesses to his Crucifixion and experience somatically ("fully feele") what they see. By calling on "al men" passing on the street to "byholdes" his crucified body, York's Christ invites the audience, who would have been watching the pageants in the streets of York, to bear witness collectively and publicly, rather than privately as individuals. In her analysis of Nicholas Love's *Mirror of the Blessed Life of Jesus Christ*, Sarah NcNamer has argued that the term "behold" has a gendered meaning in which the Virgin's "holding" of Christ's body "establishes a foundation for the compassionate beholding" of Christ's body in the Passion.[72] By calling on "al men," however, this passage of the York play unsettles any association of "beholding" with female compassion, perhaps instead evoking the court's bias for male witnesses. Thus, although this scene is often read as a quintessential example of medieval drama's engagement with an individualized and feminized tradition of late medieval "affective piety," legal affect provides an alternative model consonant with the public and corporate element of performance.

Indeed, by calling on those "þat walkis by waye or strete," Christ's speech locates the audience's collective act of beholding in the urban neighborhood, mapping the spatial element of legal definitions of medieval witnessing onto the space of performance. Fashioning the urban audience to the York plays as witnesses draws on the legal construction of the witness as a representative of the community pulled from the neighborhood.[73] The law of witnessing constructs community based simultaneously in affective social ties and geographical space, asking us to think of the city, in the words of sociologist Georg Simmel, as a "sociological fact that is conceived spatially."[74] As many scholars have demonstrated, the plays were also a communal experience, performed by local guildsmen in the streets of medieval York. Indeed, as Sarah Beckwith has argued, the pageants of York may be seen as a ritual marking the territory of the city.[75] Whereas Beckwith and others have focused on the plays' engagement with the corporate symbolism of the Eucharist, the "legal affect" of witnessing, itself defined by the "neighborhood," provides an alternate way to theorize late medieval religious drama and its relationship to the city.

This essay has argued that witness theory, which was culturally central during the period in which the York plays were staged, is crucial to understanding the affective experience of late medieval religious drama. In contrast to the private meditations outlined by Nicholas Love and others, the York plays engage a legal model of witnessing that blends somatic aspects of first-hand experience with collective knowledge of character and reputation. Like Bracton's description of the emotions of a chain of witnesses, the plays show how emotions are generated like capital, by circulating among people. The York trial plays construct their own audience as a community of neighbors acting as virtuous witnesses, like Malchus and the Beadle within the plays, who defend the law against corrupt ecclesiastical and royal authorities. The "legal affect" of witnessing, defined by the "neighborhood," thus provides a new theory of late medieval religious drama that blends individual and social, emotion and perception.

Notes

1. Sarah McNamer, *Affective Meditation and the Invention of Medieval Compassion* (Philadelphia, PA: University of Pennsylvania Press, 2010), ix, 2.

2. See, for example, Stephanie Trigg's introduction to a recent volume devoted to emotion, "Introduction: Emotional Histories – Beyond the Personalization of the Past and the Abstraction of Affect Theory," *Exemplaria* 26,1 (2014): 3–15.
3. The fact that this citation is from a teaching edition of the plays is further evidence for its conventional nature. See Clifford Davidson, "Introduction," in *The York Corpus Christi Plays*, ed. Davidson (Kalamazoo, MI: TEAMS Medieval Institute Publications, 2011), 10.
4. Ibid., 10. For other examples of the meditational tradition exemplified by Nicholas Love as central to the drama, see Richard Beadle, "'Devoute ymaginacioun' and the Dramatic Sense in Love's *Mirror* and the N-Town Plays," in *Nicholas Love at Waseda*, ed. Shoichi Oguro, Richard Beadle, and Michael G. Sargent (Cambridge: D. S. Brewer, 1997), 1–17; Gail McMurray Gibson, *The Theater of Devotion: East Anglian Drama and Society in the Late Middle Ages* (Chicago, IL: University of Chicago Press, 1989); and Jill Stevenson, *Performance, Cognitive Theory, and Devotional Culture: Sensual Piety in Late Medieval York* (New York: Palgrave Macmillan, 2010), esp. 5. Also see Sarah Beckwith, *Christ's Body: Identity, Culture and Society in Late Medieval Writings* (New York and London: Routledge, 1993), esp. 49–50.
5. On emotion as performative, see William M. Reddy, *The Navigation of Feeling: A Framework for the History of Emotions* (Cambridge: Cambridge University Press, 2001), and discussion in McNamer, *Affective Meditation*, 12.
6. Sara Ahmed, *The Cultural Politics of Emotion* (New York: Routledge, 2004), and Sianne Ngai, *Ugly Feelings* (Cambridge, MA: Harvard University Press, 2005).
7. For an opposing point of view, that the seven deadly sins provide an interpretive framework for the plays, see Sally Mussetter, "The York Pilate and the Seven Deadly Sins," *Neuphilologische Mitteilungen* 81 (1980): 57–64.
8. An important exception is Jamie K. Taylor's *Fictions of Evidence: Witnessing, Literature, and Community in the Late Middle Ages* (Columbus, OH: Ohio State University Press, 2013), which argues for the centrality of witnessing to late medieval literature and culture: "witnessing practices offered medieval vernacular writers a language and framework to examine the various ways devotional, moral, legal or ethical obligations to one's community might be understood" (2). Important examples of work on medieval law and literature include Richard Firth Green, *A Crisis of Truth: Literature and Law in Medieval England* (Philadelphia, PA: University of Pennsylvania Press, 1999); Emily Steiner, *Documentary Culture and the Making of Medieval English Literature* (New York: Cambridge University Press, 2003); Emily Steiner and Candace Barrington, eds., *The Letter of the Law: Legal Practice and Literary Production in Medieval England* (Ithaca, NY: Cornell University Press, 2002); and Ralph Hanna, *London Literature, 1300–1380* (New York: Cambridge University Press, 2005). None of these books, however, addresses the interaction between medieval law and drama or considers the law as a theory of affect.
9. See *Decrees of the Ecumenical Councils*, Vol. 1, ed. Norman P. Tanner (Washington, DC: Georgetown University Press, 1990), 244. Taylor makes this point in *Fictions of Evidence*, 16.

10. Lorna Hutson, *The Invention of Suspicion: Law and Mimesis in Shakespeare and Renaissance Drama* (Oxford: Oxford University Press, 2007), 3. Hutson argues that this shift did not happen until the sixteenth century. In contrast to my argument here, for Hutson, medieval drama is "sacramental ... not evidential" (5); she argues that late sixteenth-century commercial theater is the first evidential English drama.
11. See Majorie K. McIntosh, "Finding Language for Misconduct: Jurors in Fifteenth-Century Local Courts," in *Bodies and Disciplines: Intersections of Literature and History in Fifteenth-Century England*, ed. Barbara A. Hanawalt and David Wallace (Minneapolis, MN: University of Minnesota Press, 1996), 87–122, and McIntosh, *Controlling Misbehavior in England, 1370–1600* (Cambridge: Cambridge University Press, 1998). Also see Shannon McSheffrey, "Jurors, Respectable Masculinity, and Christian Morality: A Comment on Marjorie McIntosh's *Controlling Misbehavior*," *Journal of British Studies* 37,3 (1998): 269–78.
12. Sermon by Bishop Brunton of Rochester, MS Harl. 3760, f. 236. Cited by G. R. Owst, *Literature and Pulpit in Medieval England* (Cambridge: Cambridge University Press, 1933), 339.
13. *Jacob's Well: An English Treatise of the Cleansing of Man's Conscience*, ed. Arthur Brandeis, Part 1, EETS o.s. 115 (London: Kegan Paul, Trench, Trübner & Co., 1900), 153. This is because each act of swearing crucifies Christ repeatedly, in contrast to the Jews who only crucified him once.
14. *Bracton on the Laws and Customs of England*, ed. and trans. Samuel E. Thorne, 2 vols. (Cambridge, MA: Harvard University Press, 1968), vol. 2, 403–4; Latin text ed. George E. Woodbine.
15. See Pamela M. King, "Contemporary Cultural Models for the Trial Plays in the York Cycle," in *Drama and Community: People and Plays in Medieval Europe*, ed. Alan Hindley (Turnhout: Brepols, 1999), 200–16, and King, *The York Mystery Cycle and the Worship of the City* (Woodbridge, Suffolk and New York: D. S. Brewer, 2006), 184–203. King notes parallels between the Scrope trial (York's "man of God") and the York plays. Also, see Roger Nicholson, "The Trial of Christ the Sorcerer in the York Cycle," *Journal of Medieval and Renaissance Studies* 16,2 (1986): 125–69. On the York plays as a reflection of heresy trials, see Elza C. Tiner, "English Law in the York Trial Plays," *Early Drama, Art and Music Review* 18,2 (1996): 103–12, reprinted in *The Dramatic Tradition of the Middle Ages*, ed. Clifford Davidson (New York: AMS Press, 2005), 140–9; and Sarah Beckwith, *Signifying God: Social Relation and Symbolic Act in the York Corpus Christi Plays* (Chicago, IL and London: University of Chicago Press, 2001), 103–13.
16. Jacques Derrida, *Demeure: Fiction and Testimony*, trans. Elizabeth Rottenburg (Stanford, CA: Stanford University Press, 2000), 43.
17. Giorgio Agamben, *Remnants of Auschwitz: The Witness and the Archive*, trans. Daniel Heller-Roazen (New York: Zone Books, 2000), 158.

18. Andrea Frisch, "The Ethics of Testimony: A Genealogical Perspective," *Discourse* 25,1 & 2 (2004), 36. For a representative example of the association of witnessing with first-person testimony, see Mary B. Campbell, *The Witness and the Other World: Exotic European Travel Writing, 400–1600* (Ithaca, NY: Cornell University Press, 1988). Frisch notes that the eyewitness is often privileged in travel accounts.
19. For an example of the teleological view, see John Marshall Mitnick, "From Neighbor-Witness to Judge of Proofs: The Transformation of the English Civil Juror," *American Journal of Legal History* 32,3 (1988): 201–35.
20. Green, *A Crisis of Truth*, 100–6.
21. On the similarities of witness theory in ecclesiastical and common law, see Charles Donahue, Jr., "Proof by Witnesses in the Church Courts of Medieval England: An Imperfect Reception of the Learned Law," in *On the Laws and Customs of England: Essays in Honor of Samuel E. Thorne*, ed. Morris S. Arnold, Thomas A. Green, Sally A. Scully, and Stephen D. White (Chapel Hill, NC: University of North Carolina Press, 1981), 136, note 49; and R. H. Helmholz, *The Oxford History of the Laws of England*, Vol. 1: *The Canon Law and Ecclesiastical Jurisdiction from 596 to the 1640s* (New York: Oxford University Press, 2004), 316.
22. Donahue, "Proof by Witnesses," 129. Also see John W. Baldwin, "The Intellectual Preparation for the Canon of 1215 Against Ordeals," *Speculum* 36,4 (1961): 613–36, esp. 619–26.
23. In *Pilii, Tancredi, Gratiae libri de iudiciorum ordine*, ed. Friedrich Christian Bergmann (Gottingen: Apud Vandenhoeck et Ruprecht, 1842), 88–316. Hereafter cited as Tancred, *Ordo*.
24. "iudices hoc addunt adcautelam: quod ita dicent veritatem, sicut sciunt, quia quod sciunt per visum, dicent de visu, et quod per auditum, dicent de auditu; nec dicent de credulitate, quod sciunt pro certo, vel e contra" (Tancred, *Ordo*).
25. *The Statutes at Large from the Magna Carta to the End of the Reign of King Henry the Sixth*, Vol. 1, ed. Owen Ruffhead (London: Mark Baskett, 1769), 173. This statute concerns rents.
26. Helmholz, *Oxford History*, 328.
27. In "Proof by Witnesses," 149, Donahue notes a case in which multiple witnesses are used "to support the parties' position in the case rather than bring out the facts." For additional examples from York see Charles Donahue, Jr., *Law, Marriage, and Society in the Later Middle Ages: Arguments about Marriage in Five Courts* (New York: Cambridge University Press, 2007).
28. Donahue, "Proof by Witnesses," 138.
29. See Norma Adams and Charles Donahue, *Select Cases from the Ecclesiastical Courts of the Province of Canterbury, c. 1200–1301* (London: Seldon Society, 1981), 175.
30. Donahue, "Proof by Witnesses," 130–2.
31. Tancred, *Ordo*, section 3.9, 236. My translation and emphasis.

32. Paul R. Hyams, *Rancor and Reconciliation in Medieval England* (Ithaca, NY: Cornell University Press, 2003), 40–2. In a passage where Gratian explores the corruption of human judgment, he includes the perversion of judgment "from hatred or friendship or a gift or out of fear or by any other means whatever [*vel quolibet modo*]" or "from kinship, friendship, hostile hatred or enmities [*vel hostili odio vel inimicitiis*]." Gratian, *Decretum Magistri Gratiani*, ed. Emil Friedburg (Leipzig: Bernard Tauchitz, 1879), C II.3.78 dpc and C. ii.3.79.
33. Ahmed, *Cultural Politics of Emotion*, 46.
34. Ibid., 8.
35. *The Treatise On the Laws and Customs of the Realm of England Commonly Called Glanvill*, ed. G. D. G. Hall (London: Thomas Nelson and Sons, 1965), section 11.17, 33–4. Also see William Searle Holdsworth, *A History of English Law*, Vol. 1. (London: Methuen, 1903), 317.
36. Donahue, "Proof by Witnesses," 140.
37. Helmholz, *Oxford History*, 337. Furthermore, as Helmholz explains, the Fourth Lateran Council allowed trial by public rumor, in which the collective played the role of individual witness, "with the rumor providing the accusation and the outcry making the denunciation."
38. *Bracton on the Laws and Customs of England*, ed. Thorne, vol. 2, 404.
39. Ibid.
40. Ibid.
41. Ibid.
42. Ahmed, *Cultural Politics of Emotion*, 10.
43. Ibid., 6.
44. *Bracton on the Laws and Customs of England*, ed. Thorne, vol. 2, 404.
45. Lorens d'Orléans, *The Book of Vices and Virtues: A Fourteenth Century English Translation of the Somme Le Roi* . . ., ed. W. Nelson Francis, EETS o.s. 217 (London: Oxford University Press, 1942), 24.
46. *Fasciculus Morum: A Fourteenth-Century Preacher's Handbook*, ed. Siegfried Wenzel (University Park, PA: Pennsylvania State University Press, 1989), 171.
47. Ibid., 200ff.
48. *Robert of Brunne's Handlyng Synne*, ed. Frederick J. Furnivall, Part I, EETS o.s. 119 (London: Kegan Paul, Trench, Trübner & Co., 1901), 95.
49. Ibid., 49.
50. *Bracton on the Laws and Customs of England*, ed. Thorne, vol. 2, 404.
51. Jessica Rosenfeld, "Compassionate Conversions: Gower's *Confessio Amantis* and the Problem of Envy," *Journal of Medieval and Early Modern Studies* 42,1 (2012): 83–105.
52. "Si autem diligis proximum, tunc non committes . . . falsum testimonium . . .," *Fasciculus Morum*, ed. Wenzel, 177. On envy and neighbors, see 150–1, 156–7, 160–1, 172–3. Also see discussion on witnesses as neighbors in Taylor, *Fictions of Evidence*, 86–114.
53. Orléans, *Book of Vices and Virtues*, ed. Francis, 36. In the passage that precedes this one, false witnessing is associated with the sin of avarice: "false witnesses

and fals questmongers þilke it beþ that bynemeþ men here heritages, and doþ many oþer wronges, and so feele [many] wikkednesses and harmes þat no man my3t amende it; and aldoþ þei þat for gret couetise" (33). Even though the sin of *couetise* clearly affects others, it is nonetheless located within the individual.

54. Chaucer, *Parson's Tale*, in *The Riverside Chaucer*, ed. Larry D. Benson, 3rd edn (Boston, MA: Houghton Mifflin Co., 1987), 315.
55. *Jacob's Well*, ed. Brandeis, 130–1.
56. At least since Michel Foucault, modern criticism has emphasized this individualistic nature of medieval confessional discourse, identifying it as the *locus classicus* of medieval subjectivity, echoing the critical emphasis on witnessing as crucial to the construction of the subject.
57. Ngai, *Ugly Feelings*, 128.
58. Ibid., 129.
59. For example, in the *Northern Passion* when Pilate initially cannot find fault with Christ, "than the Jews bigan to cry / To him again with grete envy." See *The Northern Passion*, ed. Frances A. Foster, 2 vols., EETS o.s. 145 and 147 (London: Kegan Paul, Trench, Trübner & Co., 1916), vol. 2, 95. See also *The Middle-English Harrowing of Hell and Gospel of Nicodemus*, ed. William Henry Hulme, EETS e.s. 100 (London: Oxford University Press, 1907), and Jacobus de Voragine, *The Golden Legend*, trans. William Granger Ryan, 2 vols. (Princeton, NJ: Princeton University Press, 1993).
60. *The York Plays: A Critical Edition of the York Corpus Christi Play as Recorded in the British Library Additional MS 35290*, ed. Richard Beadle, 2 vols., EETS s.s. 23 and 24 (New York and Oxford: Oxford University Press, 2009), vol. 1, 256. All subsequent references will be to this edition, and line numbers will be included in the text.
61. *Fasciculus Morum*, ed. Wenzel, 37–8, 54–5, 54–7.
62. *Thomas Hoccleve: The Regiment of Princes*, ed. Charles R. Blyth (Kalamazoo, MI: TEAMS Medieval Institute Publications, 1999), 113.
63. John of Salisbury, *Policraticus: Of the Frivolities of Courtiers and the Footprints of Philosophers*, ed Cary J. Nederman (Cambridge: Cambridge University Press, 1990), 28–9.
64. In Orléans' *Book of Vices and Virtues*, envy is the sin that "makth a man or a woman most like to the deuel" (22). See Ruth Nisse, *Defining Acts: Drama and the Politics of Interpretation in Late Medieval England* (Notre Dame, IN: Notre Dame University Press, 2005), 47–74.
65. *Handlying Synne*, ed. Furnivall, 25.
66. "Et nota quod diabolus hominem invadens ... facit sicut solent homines facere quando volunt quiescere et dormire." *Fasciculus Morum*, ed. Wenzel, 602–5.
67. *The Towneley Plays*, ed. Martin Stevens and A. C. Cawley, 2 vols., EETS s.s. 13 and 14 (New York: Oxford University Press, 1994), vol. 1, 401–25.
68. See note 8 above.

69. The EETS edition of the play has the form "Caiaphas" in the title but "Cayphas" within the dialogue of the text. To avoid confusion I have used the form "Caiaphas" in the discussion that follows.
70. Tancred, *Ordo*, 236.
71. Olga Horner, analyzing the parallels between the York Resurrection Play and legal witnessing, argues that "arriving at the essential truth of the Resurrection was exactly like serving on a jury," since jurors, like the characters in the play, must make sense of conflicting accounts. Horner, "'Us must make lies': Witness, Evidence, and Proof in the York *Resurrection*," in *Medieval English Theatre* 20 (1998): 24–76.
72. McNamer, *Affective Meditation*, 137.
73. The law required jurors to be drawn from the "neighborhood" (*de uisneto*) because of their knowledge. See, for example, *Treatise On the Laws and Customs of the Realm of England Commonly Called Glanvill*, ed. Hall, 37 and 83. On the correlation between witness and neighbor, see Mike Macnair, "Vicinage and the Antecedents of the Jury," *Law and History Review* 17,3 (1999): 537–90, and Taylor, *Fictions of Evidence*, 86–114. The correlation between neighbor and witness can be found in a range of writings on the Eighth Commandment. See, for example, the discussion of false witnessing as a violation of the role of the neighbor in *Dives and Pauper*, ed. Barnum, EETS o.s. 280, vol. 1, part 2, 227. Pauper claims "he is a fals witnesse in deceyt of his neyhebore" (ll. 26–7).
74. Georg Simmel, "The Sociology of Space," originally published as "Sociology des Raumes," *Jahrbuch fur Gestzgeburg, Verwaltung and Volkswitschaft* 27 (1903): 27–71. Quoted in Sarah Beckwith, "Ritual, Theater, and Social Space in the York Corpus Christi Cycle," in *Bodies and Disciplines: Intersections of Literature and History in Fifteenth-Century England*, ed. Barbara A. Hanawalt and David Wallace (Minneapolis, MN: University of Minnesota Press, 1996), 72.
75. Beckwith, "Ritual, Theater, and Social Space."

CHAPTER 8

Affecting Forms: Theorizing with the Palis of Honoure

Anke Bernau

Gavin Douglas' dream vision allegory, the *Palis of Honoure* (1501), has been accused by critics of both formal and affective "excess" in ways that suggest a series of interrelations between the two. C. S. Lewis commented in 1944 that all of Douglas' "reading, too often in the form of *mere catalogue*, pours into his poem";[1] more recently, Douglas Gray feels that "[m]odern readers are overwhelmed – and often repelled – by [the poem's] plethora of allusion and decorative detail, long catalogues, and elaborate style."[2] Such critiques of the medieval poem, especially of its lists, and the challenge it poses to the (modern) reader are based on two aspects, both of which are associated (in the Middle Ages as well as today, though differently) with particular values: form (the sense that a list has little, if any, aesthetic value), and function (its often moral or didactic intent).[3] Both, it is suggested, cause the reader intense affective dis-ease. Yet lists have also been read critically as a sign of the medieval poet's own affective condition. Lewis argues, again in relation to Douglas, that they show that the "poet is still too delighted with the whole world of poetry, as he understood it, to control his delight. He is happily overwhelmed, like a surf-bather."[4] Here Douglas' *excess* of pleasure – the sign of which is his extensive use of lists – is read as a lack of poetic discipline and aesthetic judgment. Such criticisms, as I will show, find an echo in the poem's own exploration of the relation between history, affect, poetic discipline, and values – an exploration conducted precisely through the great number and variety of lists that make up most of the poem, and the figure of an affectively turbulent narrator.

This essay will look at the dream vision's two most conventional, yet seemingly opposed, narrative features – the authoritative catalogue on the one hand, and the emotionally troubled narrator on the other – from an "affective" perspective that allows us to rethink the way both have been read critically, using Douglas' poem as a test case.[5] In *The Particulars of*

Rapture: An Aesthetics of the Affects, Charles Altieri focuses on that which makes affect "resistant to reason's authority," and to treat "affective states as ends in themselves."[6] Altieri attempts here to acknowledge the differences (not just the synergies) between affect and reason, not least in order to make visible those affects that are not amenable to it (and which, he argues, have therefore received little critical attention).[7] Doing so, he suggests, allows us to "clarify different kinds of intensity" while resisting any straightforward or automatic equivalence between such affective states and generalizing or rationalizing explanations, or "moral terms."[8] Affects, that is, may challenge governing "values," whether these are (in a modern context) philosophical or scientific.[9] Drawing on Altieri's argument, I will suggest that the numerous lists that make up much of *Palis* function not only to *denote* established, authoritative poetic traditions and modes of being, related to a higher moral imperative, but also to *connote* the complex affective energies that color the encounters between these and the experience of a particular human subject (however stylized). The text's key claim for poetry, that it is a "joyus discipline," emerges as an uncertain and open-ended process that can mediate between different sets of relations (affective, as well as others), but that cannot guarantee a secure destination, moral transformation, or stable subject. That is, its instantiation through individuals like the dreamer-narrator always necessarily involves differentiation – particularities – that need to be accommodated for any given poetic voice to emerge at all. Through this process of particularization, the affective and authoritative aspects of poetic production, and their relation to history as well as to the moral demands of an absolute ideal such as "Honour," emerge as closely associated, but never as fixed, revealing a spectrum of affective positions that are sometimes, but not always, named.

Douglas' *Palis* knowingly participates in many of the dream vision genre's familiar motifs; Gregory Kratzmann has called it "a *summa* of nearly two centuries of writing in the genre of the vision allegory."[10] In the Prologue, the narrator finds himself in a beautiful garden on a glorious morning in May. Suddenly, an authoritative voice begins to sing, and it admonishes the followers of May (and Venus) to "glore and magnify" them (88). Overcome by the fear of not being able to do so, the narrator prays to Nature to "[c]onfort your man" (97) and prepares to leave the garden; before he can do so, a bright light suddenly shines on him, causing him to fall into an "extasy or swoun" (106). When he awakens, he finds himself in a nightmarish wilderness. In this visionary landscape, the dreamer first encounters, serially, the courts of Minerva,

Diana, and Venus, all of which are on their way to the Palace of Honor. Incensed at the mutability of Venus' court, the dreamer recites a poem attacking her; this incites the fury of the goddess and her followers. He is charged with treason and expects to die. The dreamer is saved by the arrival of the court of the Muses. Their leader, Calliope, convinces Venus to pardon him, promising her that he will, from now on, compose poetry in her honor. Calliope assigns the dreamer one of her nymphs to guide him, and he travels far and wide with the Muses before arriving by a hill near the Palace of Honor. In the final sequence of the vision, the nymph guides the dreamer towards the Palace. In its precincts is a garden, in which he sees Venus enthroned, and is invited to look into her mirror. Here, he sees all the deeds that men have performed on earth. Finally, he enters the hall of the Palace itself; through a chink in a closed door he catches a glimpse of the god of Honor, whose terrible brightness causes him to swoon again. The nymph mocks him for his faint-heartedness and offers to take him in to the garden of rhetoric to recover. Fear overcomes him yet again, and he falls into the moat surrounding the garden. He laments his awakening, and concludes with a poem in praise of Honor, which is followed by a dedication of the poem to James IV.[11]

In his 1966 study of the *Palis of Honoure*, Denton Fox points out that its "basic structural device ... is the list";[12] the poem's recent editor, David Parkinson, states that its lists are so pervasive that "imbedded within *The Palis* is the skeleton of a rather specialized encyclopedia," one that focuses in particular on "literature, history, and pastime from a courtly perspective."[13] In the Middle Ages (and earlier), the list was an immensely popular form, and was found in a wide range of different texts.[14] The list's close association with various kinds of moral and wisdom literatures has led scholars to concentrate in particular on their didactic function. Thus, Glenda McLeod argues that while "modern readers ... tend to look for entertainment, amusement, and originality," "[m]edieval readers ... wanted edification, a moral example to imitate, and ... ample erudition and facts. The catalogue could supply all of these needs."[15] Yet while it was most commonly associated with non-imaginative writing, the list is also used abundantly in late medieval dream visions. Stephen Barney attributes this to the genre's "dreamy logic," and concludes that in it, "[l]ist-making and story-telling become one."[16] The association of lists with important cultural knowledge also made them obvious candidates for inclusion in dream visions, a genre that was used by some authors to explore the nature of poetry itself.[17]

If lists are one staple feature of the dream vision genre, another is the hapless narrator-dreamer. Often read as comic figures,[18] their affective responses are portrayed as inappropriate: either too emotionally excessive, or intellectually inadequate, or morally suspect. Thus, in many dream visions, not least in *Palis*, the relationship of the narrator-dreamer to both knowledge and affect is presented as anything but straightforward. In *Palis*, the narrator occupies affective extremes from the start: at first, in the garden, his "sprete" is "rejoyst and confort" (59) by its beauty; soon, however, he is "[q]uakyng for fere" (99), because of the authoritative demand to produce suitable songs in praise of Venus. Before long he has fallen "in extasy or swoun" (106), as feeble "[a]s femynine" (108), and is assailed by "dredfull terrour" (117). And all this before we get to the vision itself! There are no lengthy lists in the Prologue – the only part of the poem to lack them – but the affective tone is clearly set here. From the outset of the poem, then, the dreamer is repeatedly plunged into intense states, mainly associated with fear. While this fear is not self-identical, affective dis-ease provides a consistent backdrop to the whole poem. Indeed (as in many dream visions), the poem ends where it began, though nothing is quite the same. The affective effects on the dreamer are all-encompassing (his heart, spirit, wit, "curage," brain, and body are all said to feel their force); at times the "surge" is so powerful that the dreamer's very sanity and life seem imperilled.

In their introduction to *Fear and Its Representations in the Middle Ages and Renaissance*, Anne Scott and Cynthia Kosso argue that medieval thinkers "seemed to embrace the idea of fear in all of its many forms." In contrast to contemporary culture, medieval culture regarded fear "as an emotion to be cultivated, harnessed, probed, explored, and exploited, not overcome and avoided." While their primary emphasis is on religious discourses, they note that, more generally, fear was valued "for its role in defining moments of personal awareness or motivating cultural and political change."[19] Yet in *Palis* it is difficult to see fear as enabling transformation. The dreamer's often inarticulate resistance, his inability to respond in a way that matches what the contents of the authoritative lists clearly require from him (what some critics have read as his "failure") – all of this leads to a sense of inertia: of affective intensity that freezes or blocks the subject. While the dreamer's affective condition can, and does, find expression in language (most explicitly in his inset laments and complaints),[20] it also *resists* language: most obviously when he swoons, but also when he stands silent and is commented on critically by others in the poem. It is not that every experience – or the vision as a whole – is thought by the dreamer

Affecting Forms: Theorizing with the Palis of Honoure

to be nightmarish; indeed, he often resorts to the inexpressibility *topos* as the only mode that can gesture towards the "heavenly" beauty of what he encounters. Nonetheless, this in no way prevents affective dis-ease. And while one may argue that such dis-ease is part and parcel of the dreamer's education (that is, affective discomfort as salutary in moral terms), it is not finally evident that it proves a successful didactic tool – or even what that might mean.

When the dream vision itself begins, lists and affect are placed in different forms of relation to one another, offering a textured exploration of the dreamer's fluctuating affect when confronted with each of the paths towards Honor represented by the three companies he sees passing by in the wilderness.[21] Here lists exemplify authoritative cultural information as well as potential modes of being – they enumerate and thereby characterize, respectively, the appearance, qualities, skills, and followers of Wisdom (Minerva), Chastity (Diana), and worldly Love (Venus). Lists and the dreamer's affective state are not, however, simply opposed to one another, for the dreamer *also* draws on the former to articulate the latter. Thus, the dreamer's affective experience is indicated explicitly, in his own lists, and implicitly, in his response to and description of others'.[22] His affective contours thus emerge gradually through this dance between form and feeling – a dance that relies on connotation as well as denotation, distance and closeness, juxtaposition and alignment.

When the narrator enters the nightmarish visionary landscape, it is one that both mirrors his affective state (his "barrant wyt" is matched by the "deserte terrybill"; 127, 136) and perpetuates it. Once he has surveyed his bleak and hostile surroundings, he launches into the first of his inset compositions: a lament addressed to Fortune, consisting of three stanzas, which includes a short list outlining actions that indicate his affective state ("I wepe, I wale, I plene, I cry, I plede"; 171), set within a longer description of the fickle nature of this "[i]nconstant warld and quheil contrarius" (163–92). By the end of this lament, a loud noise causes the dreamer to hide in a hollow tree-trunk, and the first of the three "courts" – that of Minerva (Wisdom) – approaches.

Among the list of this goddess' followers (240–64) we find the Sibyls, the Fates, figures from biblical as well as classical narrative, and "[c]lerkis divine, with problewmys curius" (249). Wisdom's followers are "stedfast" (209), prudent, and traditional, following always "[e]ftyr the feitis auld" (206). Their inward mode of being is indicated by their outward attire, their "constant weid," that "weil my spretis payit" (203). Wisdom is not necessarily an innate good, however. The figures of Ahithophel and Sinon precede the company and explain to the narrator that they misused their "wyt" "lewdly" (275), submitting "wysdome" to "desyre" (276). Yet while the narrator curses them for their misdeeds, his encounter with them provides him with the only emotional solace he can find in this wasteland, and he must admit: "[G]laid I wes that I with thaym had spokkyn. / Had not bene that, certis my hart had brokkyn / For megirnes and pusillamytee" (310–12). This human need and interaction offers emotional sustenance in the confusion brought about by the dreamer's loneliness in hellish surroundings. The members of Minerva's court are admirable, but they do not speak to him or otherwise engage him. There is no strong affective connection, and so he returns to his tree, alone. Here the lists describing Wisdom and the dreamer's affect diverge, even if they are not utterly opposed to one another. The list presents examples of an idealized condition that the dreamer can "see," and admire, from a distance, but one he evidently does not "feel" close to and does not (or cannot) join. His morally dubious interlocutors, themselves on the margins of this company, are his sole source of emotional comfort – even as he judges them.

Almost immediately the second company, that of the goddess Diana (Chastity), arrives. It is preceded by a "hart transformyt" (316), "rent" (317) by hounds. (This wounded "hart" appears in the same stanza as the dreamer's "hart," which would have broken without human interaction.) The dreamer knows that this is Actaeon, torn apart by his own dogs – we are thus introduced to the anger of affronted Chastity. The brevity of the list enumerating Diana's followers (it lasts for only one stanza) underlines the narrator's wry comment: "I not, bot few I saw with Diane hant" (336), and the style here is plainly enumerative, without rhetorical embellishment. The shortness of this list is indicative of Chastity's high-minded purity (there are few such virtuous individuals) as well as humorous (there are few such virtuous individuals). Diana's court passes by and this time there are no interlocutors who offer the dreamer any point of contact. Brevity (form) and "trew virginité" (335) (content, moral value) suggest virtue, exceptionality, and affective remoteness; the violent death of Actaeon warns powerfully against any kind of inappropriate lingering, and the dreamer expresses no wish to become a follower of Diana himself.

It is the third company that both captures the narrator's imagination and plunges him into the most emotionally fraught encounter thus far. For now Venus (Love) arrives, and *her* "rout" does not lack followers. From the moment the narrator hears the music announcing her arrival, there is an ambivalent disjunction between his affective condition and what he describes – and this is once more made evident through the use of lists.

A reference to his "dreidfull dreme" and "grysly fantasyis" (384) introduces us to the "sound ... of angellys" that herald Venus' coming (389). The "armony" (390) of her court, however, does not soothe him, for he is completely out of tune with it (391–6); the "joyous" response by those who would follow Venus is in stark contrast to his own condition: "This melody intonyt hevinly thus / For profund wo constrenyt me mak care" (398–9). Mourning (400), he begins to describe this "maist plesand court" (401) by firing off a list of questions that highlights simultaneously its aesthetic beauty and the intensity of his affective disconnection from it: "Quhat sang? Quhat joy? Quhat armony? Quhat lycht?" (403ff.).

Venus' court "so variabill" (484) operates under the aegis of an authority that is based on "erdly luf, quhilk sendill standis stabill" (485). In contrast to Diana's terse virtue and Minerva's uniform sobriety, Venus' restless abundance offers the poet-dreamer a wealth of gorgeous "matter" to work with, and causes him to respond most strongly in affective terms.[23] The description signals all of this through the number, length, and variety of lists that make up the description of Venus' court: of musical terms (490–507), famous biblical and classical musicians (508–25), her followers (534–43), the gear worn by the horses (546–9), famous lovers (562–97), and emotions experienced by her followers (601–2). The variety here is not least one of topic and vocabulary. Even so, Venus' adherents remain "innumerabill" (597), exceeding effortlessly the attempt to "capture" the size and variety of her court through enumeration. What holds this court together in unity *is* variety – a variety gathered and held by the force of worldly love.

The narrator's response, a "lay" (606) consisting of a short list outlining his emotional state, reasserts the gap which associates the joys of Venus with the narrator's woes: his "infinyte" "paynfull caris" (609) match her "innumerabill" followers precisely. His dismay does not even offer him the solace of moral superiority – he presents himself as utterly isolated and bereft of comfort. The extended lists that present, and perform, the variety of Venus' "rout" are thus counterpointed by this condensed list of woe. He acknowledges the power and allure of Love, even as he resists it fiercely.[24] The list form is used both to map the aesthetic variety and plenitude of the one, and to convey the distilled affective intensity of the other, illustrating their antagonism – but an antagonism that is more complex and ambivalent than simple opposition.

Venus and her followers respond to the dreamer's lament with outrage.[25] There follows a "mobbing scene,"[26] in which the goddess' retainers "torment" him with "teynfull play" (655); affective overload now defines both sides, but there is a clear power imbalance between them. Nonetheless, while he is "[s]ore abasyt" (685), the dreamer reacts feistily, refusing Venus' authority on the grounds that she is a woman, and he a "spirituall man" (697) – the first time his identity is thus explicitly stated. In an impassioned speech against clerics, Venus catalogues their negative qualities, thereby claiming the power to define how things are. Things are not looking good for the dreamer.

Lists in this part of the poem provide a range of affective "colorings," or "intensities" (to use Altieri's term), for the dreamer's basic state of terror. These intensities are profoundly connected to particular modes of being, to ways of knowing, and to particular values. Each one of the three courts that the dreamer sees represents a possible path to Honor – their desired destination is shared, even if their means of getting there differ considerably. While Wisdom provides a moment of possible, if incomplete, affective engagement for the dreamer, Chastity passes by without any connection. In contrast, the power of worldly Love is presented as an overwhelming and seductive force, to which the dreamer does not (cannot?) respond with anything but profound and fundamental affective resistance. At the same time, it requires of him the lengthiest, and most varied, of poetic descriptions. The lists associated with each court reveal the differences between them, and they also illustrate the level and intensity of relation between the dreamer and what each court represents.[27] Thus, while the dreamer's fear is always more or less present, it is not undifferentiated, shading off into loneliness, alienation, admiration, dismay, unwilling fascination, yearning, anger, and stubbornness. The variety of the lists allows the narrator's affective dis-ease to become something that fluctuates beyond the terms used to reference it explicitly; this suggests a more complex subjectivity – and a more problematic relationship to the discourses associated with each of the goddesses – than might otherwise be evident. This part of the poem, then, explores in depth the dread experienced by the narrator in the Prologue – the fluctuating condition of his "curage"[28] – in response to the cultural discourses available to him as a "spirituall" man who seeks also to become a poet. He does not "fit" in with any of them.

Before the court of the Muses arrives next, the dreamer already experiences emotional respite, despite his precarious situation. He does not know why he feels a lessening of his fear, but assumes that it is because God is looking after him as a result of "sum gude spretis" "intercessioun" (778, 779). Out of the woods comes a fourth "hevinly rout" (787), and the description of this one, too, consists of lists whose variety and length are comparable to those associated with Venus' court. The leader here is

Calliope, who speaks "of nobillis fatis" (875) in the "kyngly style" (877) that is "[c]heif of al wryt" (879). If the interplay between lists and affect thus far has situated the dreamer in relation to a range of possible modes of knowing, feeling, and being, offering a textured exploration of his troubled affective relationship to each, this next part, relating his encounter with the court of the Muses, describes a kind of "homecoming" – but one that nonetheless requires the dreamer's affective and poetic transformation. As well as finding an immediate affective "fit" with the court of Calliope, the dreamer is reconciled to Venus by the chief Muse; this reconciliation marks the dreamer's submission to poetic authority.

The Muses, "so blyith and glaid," "[r]ecomfort" the dreamer, causing the "joyus heit" to return to his "brest" (893, 890, 891). The poets that make up their following include those writing in the vernaculars (including English and Scots), and recent writers (such as Chaucer, Gower, Lydgate, Kennedy, and Dunbar; 916–24) are mentioned alongside long-deceased, classical ones. The emotional tenor of this "rout" is steadfast merriness. Yet Venus' court and that of the Muses are not opposed to one another: Calliope calls Venus "[s]yster" (943). Calliope's calm authority, however, offers a clear contrast to Venus' impassioned anger; while her reasons for arguing that Venus ought to pardon the dreamer-narrator belittle him (he is not worthy of the goddess' anger), Calliope's approach is skillful, taking account of Venus' touchy pride without giving in to it. Thus the sorrow and anger Venus feels because of the dreamer's "laithly ryme" (948) are contained and transformed by the chief Muse into mercy.

Calliope's words restore harmony all round: Venus is mollified and the dreamer tells us that his "febil gost" becomes "glad" (970). Venus modifies her affect in accordance with Calliope's argument and the dreamer, too, must radically alter his affective stance, at least as it is expressed in his poetry, in order to praise rather than criticize the goddess of Love. Both Venus and narrator reform themselves, and their relationship to one another, through Calliope's intervention. This allows Venus' "fame" to continue (the dreamer will now help to further it), and the narrator gets to live. In this scene, we witness the authority and majesty of poetry, as well as its ability to reconfigure affects, circumstances, and relations. Poetry becomes a condition of mercy and acts as mediator in emotionally charged conflicts: in exchange for his life, however, Calliope dictates the general subject matter and emotional tenor of what the dreamer is to compose.[29]

Venus confirms that she will "foryet" "all greif" (994, 993) if the dreamer will write a "breif / Or short ballat in contrare pane and wo" (994–5). His poetry is thus linked to the banishment of woe twice over: his own (for he lives), and Venus' (he makes good his former bitter critique). The poem he promptly produces is noticeably different from his previous two: while those expressed his troubled affective state in impassioned terms, here he tells himself what he must do, say, and feel. Each of the three stanzas performs this disciplining of his composition (and self) through the use of lists: the first addresses his own "[u]nwemmyt wit" (1015; which is said, rather dubiously, to be "[r]eleschit fre of servyce and bondage"; 1017), exhorting it to expel all sorrow and suffering. The second stanza poses a series of rhetorical questions, still addressed to his wit, which is now said to be "replenyst with plesance" (1031). Here the emotional coordinates are "hop," "esperance," "grace," "comfort," "gladnes," and "happy chance" (1025–33). He tells himself he must not be "dissolat," since he has had his "wyll" (1034). In the final stanza the dreamer continues the transformative process by telling himself sternly to: "Incres in myrthfull consolatioun, / In joyus swete ymaginatioun" (1035–6). This "ballat" performs the desired affective change to be brought about by Calliope's intervention; that is, the dreamer's relief at being rescued from Venus' ire, but also his obedience to the rules governing that release. Obeying Calliope means speaking (and, perhaps, feeling) differently. Whereas previously his affect determined his poetic expression, now poetic expression outlines the desired affective stance required of him. His new poem, then, seems to refute the affective impulse that motivated him before, and aligns itself obediently with Calliope's claim on him. This new position brings immediate poetic and social benefits, which are also personal, for he is able to recite his poem to acclaim at the center of Venus' court, no longer an isolated, vulnerable, frustrated "trespassor" (632).

Yet this cannot be read as a simple capitulation on the dreamer's part; he does not submit to Venus as a lover, but as a poet. When Calliope says to him at the end of his poem, "I stand content; thow art obedient" (1047), we are reminded again that he is acting at *her* behest. Poetic authority mediates his affective response to Venus, which is determined by his identity as a "spirituall man" (a denomination whose meaning stays rather vague, however). While he is both drawn to, and repelled by, Venus' court – drawn to its explosive aesthetic energy but repelled by the affective conditions that govern and result from that energy – poetry offers a possibility of relation. By rescuing the dreamer from Venus' vengeance, Calliope has shown herself to be indeed the leader of the "court of joyus disciplyne" (846), and poetry's joyous discipline offers the dreamer the possibility of a "joyus ... imaginatioun" (1036). Submission to Calliope – entering into relation with poetry – is a precondition for the kind of poetry that allows its maker to experience joy – a joy that is predicated on social acceptance and proper respect for Venus' authority, even if that authority is felt to be deeply problematic. At the same time, his obedience is predicated on an intrinsic affective ease – his affinity with the court of the Muses is evident *before* he knows who they are. He "fits" with them; belonging is submission to authority, but the *right* authority – that is, one with whom one has a profound affective connection.

In this scene, the poem draws on the interaction of list and affect in order to convey the dreamer's achievement of (at least momentary) affective ease within the court of the Muses, and his subjection to their "joyus disciplyne." In the intermediate space between Venus and dreamer, opened up by poetry, both benefit. At the same time, the dreamer must also use poetry as a tool of affective self-discipline. While his new alliances ensure his safety and secure him an illustrious audience, his "voice" at least must be radically altered. So even as lists illustrate the Muses' status and indicate the dreamer's glad submersion in their following, they also signal the affective reformation required by this association, a discipline that must be experienced as "joyus." There is room for doubt here. Since the dreamer only articulates the *possibility* of such joy in the form of a command to himself, expressing the idea of its fulfillment in the subjunctive, it is left unclear whether the transformation is really complete.

After travelling far and wide with the court of the Muses, the dreamer is led towards the Palace of Honor by a nymph assigned to him by Calliope. Along the way, he has to pass fiery gulfs, climb the dizzying heights of steep hills, and witness a shipwreck caused by raging tempests. The moral significance of these sights is explained by the nymph: all instances reveal the danger of worldly distraction, the importance of seeking honor and living virtuously. On this final journey, lists trace the increasingly uneasy relationship between the dreamer and the nymph, and introduce a movement in the poem towards an externalized, critical, view of the dreamer as he approaches Honor. The emphasis on the dreamer's moral education is introduced by an abrupt shift away from "syngyng, lauchyng, merines and play" (1252), back towards "fere," as the narrator anticipates having to recount the final stage of his vision. At this point the dreamer even imagines *himself* as a kind of failed list: "[T]he hundreth part all day / I micht not schaw, thocht I had tonges ten. / Thocht al my membris tongis were on raw / I wer not abill the thousand fald to schaw" (1259–62).[30] The rapid proliferation of one body part (ten tongues) is followed immediately by bodily disaggregation ("membris tongis . . . on raw"); the inability to articulate fully the plenitude experienced turns the dreamer into a series of grotesquely enhanced speaking parts that are still not adequate to the task. Considering the repeated use of lists to present all kinds of material throughout the poem thus far, gives its stated *failure* here added force. The final part of the poem, then, is introduced as touching upon that which cannot be approached through, or encompassed by, language. The absolute demands of Honor, if taken as a point of arrival rather than as a distant goal organizing the trajectory of one's journey, may put an end to language – and therefore poetry. Totalizing values are not conducive to the continuation of human and literary history, and the climax reveals the violence at the heart of Honor's demands on the (flawed) human subject.

As the dreamer approaches the Palace of Honor, lists chart the various shifts that its presence brings about. First, the dreamer describes it through an enumeration of its architectural features that indicates its splendor and the intensity of his appreciation.[31] Indeed, he gazes at it in delight for so long that the nymph chides him for being "prolixt" (1462) and for standing there, "stupefak" (1460).[32] This is the first time we "see" the dreamer through the nymph's eyes, and her criticism indicates the gap between his experience and her assessment of it, for to describe him as "stupefak" suggests a total *absence* of affective and cognitive engagement.[33] By telling him he is being "prolixt," she also seems to be critiquing his poetry – specifically, the description of the palace we have just read.[34] Next, they arrive in a garden situated outside the Palace of Honor, where they find Venus, enthroned, facing a mirror held up by "thre curius goldyn treis" (1474). What follows is the longest catalogue in the poem, outlining the whole sweep of human history reflected in the mirror. (This does not, however, stop the dreamer from stating at least twice that he cannot enumerate all that he sees in it, for fear of being "prolext"; 1650, 1663.) The mirror's powers are not temporally limited, but extend from the distant past to the "cumming of the Antecrist" (1701).[35] History is shown to topple ineluctably into narrative when the dreamer concludes by stating that the mirror displays "every famus douchty deid / That men in story may se, or cornakyll reid" (1693–4). From the start of the catalogue to the end, the mirror changes from being a window onto the past in its entirety (the deeds of every person), to being a collection of famous narratives recalling specific kinds of action ("famus douchty deid"). It is the catalogue that demonstrates through its formal features the variety of human history, its temporality (one damn thing after another) and its selectivity (that is, its composition). Furthermore, history is associated with particular affects and behaviors brought about by "warldly onfaithful brukkylnes" (1699): "miserie, … crewelté, … dreid, / Pane, sorow, wo, baith wretchitnes and neid, / ... gret envy, covatus, dowbilnes" (1696–8).³⁶ Yet the catalogue does not end here. With a sharp shift in tone, it moves incongruously in the final three stanzas from the coming of the Antichrist to the enumeration of "[p]lesand debaitmentis" (1702).

When the nymph tells the dreamer what the mirror signifies, she condenses the list into a three-line summary: the mirror means "nothing ellis till understand / Bot the gret bewty of thir ladyis facis / Quhairin lovers thinkis thay behald all gracis" (1762–4). The nymph's terse dismissal suggests that she considers all human history reducible to a "lover's" gaze. Since it is Venus' mirror that reflects human history and pastime, these realms are shown to be thoroughly imbued with her affective "coloring." This makes it hard to know exactly where the dreamer stands, and reminds us of his earlier dilemma: if Venus has all the (best) stories, what is he, as "spirituall" man, aspiring poet, and flawed human, to do? While we have seen him lament the "[i]nconstant warld" (165–92, also 610), we also know that he has been urged by Calliope to reconcile himself to Venus, both poetically and affectively. As an aspiring poet, he necessarily works in Venus' proximity; invested in both history and literature, which are shown to emerge out of earthly mutability, he is inevitably affectively involved, if not straightforwardly. This uneasy relationship is now tested in the face of Honor's absolute imperative.

By placing Venus' garden in proximity to, but not within, Honor's palace, the poem indicates a potentially close but uneasy relationship between the two. The difference between them becomes clear through yet another list, recited by the nymph, who explains the many personified virtues that work in and keep the Palace of Honor; these include Loyalty, Discretion, Humanity, Innocence, Devotion, Peace, Quiet, and many more (1783–1827). Instead of particular historical human actions, we have allegorical types. The dreamer pays close attention, but, as in the encounter with Diana, we are given no indication how – or if – he is moved. That he might be less than captivated by her exposition is suggested only when the nymph has finished, and the dreamer immediately moves on to describe his delight at the beautiful, ornately engraved gates of the palace. Here we see him captivated, joyous – and again, for the second time, the nymph chides him for his response, growing so impatient with his "dotyng" (1868) that she pushes him through the gates.

Parkinson argues that "Douglas's dream-poet notices the wrong things and is *affected in the wrong ways,*" judging him a "buffoon."³⁷ To do so, however, is to see him through the nymph's eyes, privileging her inhuman perspective. While the dreamer clearly does have a moral compass – he criticizes Sinon and Ahithophel and laments the mutability of Venus' court – he *cannot* see in the way that the nymph requires of him. This is made clear when he tells us that the Palace is so bright that he is blinded.[38] When the dreamer does finally catch a glimpse of the god of Honor, it undoes him: "In extasy, be his brychtnes, atonys, / He smate me doun and byrsyt all my bonys" (1923–4). While the Palace can be described, though with increasing difficulty, the god of Honor cannot: only two brief lines sketch the grim glory of his appearance (1921–2) before the dreamer is dashed to unconsciousness. The limits to affective experience and the limits of language coincide. While lists can both connote and denote, the immensity of this experience can only be indicated by a silence made all the more emphatic by coming after their linguistic plenitude.

The silence of the swoon is followed by a conversation that underscores the profound difference between the nymph and the dreamer – a difference characterized by divergent affective modes. Although she is concerned for his welfare, the nymph urges the dreamer to "[b]e myrry," as he regains consciousness, for "the werst is past" (1935). It is unclear what exactly she means by "the werst," and there is a sense that her meaning is unlikely to match his experience.[39] The discrepancy between her definition of what he has seen and his experience of it is summed up in her incomprehension that he could be "mysmaid" by such a "plesand sycht" (1938). Yet what exactly constitutes a "plesand sycht" – and for whom – remains unclear.[40] The dreamer's description of Honor's face as glorious, but also "grym" and "fyry" (1949), suggests his fearful awe. When he finally explains to the nymph that he his "wyt" and "spretis" were overcome by this encounter (1950), she laughs "rycht merylie" (1952) and promises not to "assay" him anymore with "sic plesance" (1954–5).[41] The relationship between fear and joy – the very definition of "plesance" – remains contested. The nymph shows her awareness of this when she refers to it as a mode of "assay."[42] This "assay," furthermore, does not simply cause the dreamer affective discomfort – it is so intense that it blasts his very bones. The poem does not really offer us a way of imagining how the dreamer could have responded differently; the experience is simply too absolute to be assimilated or adjusted to. While poetry represents a joyous discipline, what is demanded by Honor silences poetic language by causing an affective response so extreme that it threatens to undo the dreamer completely. The absoluteness of Honor's moral imperative is thus shown to be ultimately incompatible with the affective energies that are required for poetic production – at least as produced by *this* particular subject.

As noted above, it is not that the dreamer is *dishonorable*; he is, we might say, oriented towards honor. This is suggested when the dreamer questions the nymph about the people he saw in the hall of Honor's palace. The nymph lists the qualities of "true" honor (as opposed to "warldly honoring"; 1973), of the transformative powers of honor, and of those who serve in Honor's court (which includes the Nine Worthies, Sampson, Hercules, Hippolyta, and three Scottish kings). Had he lasted but a moment longer, she claims, he might have heard "the gret sentence diffinytive" and seen "the dreidful pane / Execute on trespassouris" (2054–6). This prospect excites the dreamer tremendously: "My spreit desyris to se thair torment fane" (2059). In articulating this disciplinary desire, the dreamer actively aligns himself with those who judge and punish trespassers against Honor, even as he cannot himself be one of Honor's direct champions. This is a clear shift from his earlier position, when he desired mercy for being a trespasser himself and cursed those who refuse to give it. In what one might term the poem's *affective* logic, the dreamer's sudden didactic enthusiasm seems somewhat surprising, although one could argue that being a trespasser against Venus (Love) is different from being a trespasser against "true" Honor.[43] What both examples share is that in each instance we witness the dreamer moving towards a relation with the divinity in question, through poetic mediation. Just as he cannot be a follower of Venus but is shown by Calliope how to respect and praise her, thereby evading her displeasure and its violence, so he cannot stand before Honor without being overcome. While the nymph's didactic explanations seemed to leave him unmoved before, now they bring his unspeakable experience into a framework that holds it and makes sense of it. Together, the experience of encounter (which results in "extasy") and exposition lead to a shift in the dreamer's "curage" – his desire to witness disciplinary action against Honor's trespassers. He thus confirms his orientation towards Honor (affectively and morally), while remaining at the threshold because of affective intensities (his fear).

As L. O. Aranye Fradenburg has argued, "bonds of attachment *always* discipline desire to some degree," because "we can only satisfy our needs through a *relationship* (hence, who is this being on whom my survival depends?)."[44] This is evidently the case here.[45] The nymph continues the education begun by Calliope, but the dreamer also reaches the limits of his (affective, cognitive, moral, poetic) capacity. When he awakens, the dreamer finds himself back in the beautiful garden in which he first swooned. But now its beauty is meaningless; he is "in pane" (2096) and "langyt sore for till have swounyt agane" (2097). What he regrets is not having entered the garden of rhetoric in which he had hoped to "fund sum parte" (2106); what grieves his "curage" most is that he missed out on witnessing how the trespassers against Honor were punished. Yet his regret seems motivated largely by the loss of *poetic* opportunity; the disciplining of the transgressors would have provided him with good "copy": "Glaidly I wald amyd thys wryt have brevyt, / Had I it sene, quhow thay were slane or schent" (2111–12). He resigns himself to concluding with a poem dedicated to Honor, which involves submitting himself to Honor's "devyse" (2142), while also requesting that his sorrow may be dispersed.

The verses that follow express the poet's submission to Honor, but his stated unhappiness and their heightened formal complexity underscore this unresolved situation. The internal rhymes that characterize these three stanzas are so insistent that poetic discipline, foregrounded thus, pushes the boundaries of language and form. If this is the language of one submitting to Honor, it is language marked primarily by control – a bravura performance that seems unsustainable. As the narrator says, he writes it in order to "mak ane end" (2114).[46] The dreamer's inability to gain a clearer view of Honor's discipline, or to gain entry to the garden of rhetoric because of his intense affective responses, cannot be read as being just – or even mainly – about loss or failure, as the existence of the poem suggests. The sheer variety of lists found throughout *Palis* celebrates the capaciousness of poetic language, which is articulated in relation to tradition as well as specific modes of being, but also always necessarily and productively in relation to particular affective perspectives and responses. Read through and in relation to lists, the dreamer's affective "surges" emerge as less quiescent (or ridiculous), more nuanced and poetically significant than has previously been suggested. The "intensities" that emerge shed light on the grounds of articulation itself – on the possibilities and limitations of affect *and* discipline, poetic as well as moral.[47]

Because the list exhibits an uneasy relationship to the narrative in which it is imbedded, due to its tendency to "stall" the narrative flow, Barney imagines it as a "dam" or even "an intruder."[48] Lists, that is, always raise the question of their relationship to the narrative whole: do they *serve* it, or *detract* from it? In their very form, they illustrate and map the (often productive) tensions between part and whole, digression and linearity, plenitude and discipline, resistance and movement. In this sense, lists in *Palis* can be read as representing the dreamer-poet's own multi-faceted relationship to the larger structures associated with authority, tradition, and specific values – a relationship that cannot be understood through simple opposition or alignment. At the same time, the limitations of the list form (towards which the list always gestures) are used to remind us of that which *cannot* be named, enumerated, or itemized; that which exceeds categories and escapes such linguistic order (hovering on the edges of articulation) – affects, but also absolute moral ideals.[49] Lists, in *Palis*, allow us to trace the particularities of affective energies and intensities; they raise the question of what must – and what cannot – be disavowed or reformed, in order to enjoy the rewards of a form that can be "joyous" as well as "disciplinary" (if not always at the same time). Paying attention to what is connoted as well as denoted allows us to expand our understanding of medieval affective discourses and to re-evaluate the affects and effects made possible by some of the most "conventional" medieval literary forms. But it also encourages us to review our own critical and affective responses – to the pains and pleasures of discipline as well as to the objects that we study and, sometimes, love.

Notes

1. C. S. Lewis, *English Literature in the Sixteenth Century excluding Drama* (Oxford: Clarendon Presss, 1954), 78; emphasis mine.
2. Douglas Gray, "Gavin Douglas," in *A Companion to Medieval Scottish Poetry*, ed. Priscilla Bawcutt and Janet Hadley Williams (Cambridge: D. S. Brewer, 2006), 151.
3. Glenda McLeod, in *Virtue and Venom: Catalogs of Women from Antiquity to the Renaissance* (Ann Arbor, MI: University of Michigan Press, 1991), notes that modern readers have "dismissed" their use by medieval authors "with charges of monotony, formlessness, and a general lack of artistry or point" (2). William J. Farell, in "Chaucer's Use of the Catalogue," *Texas Studies in Literature and Language* 5,1 (1963), argues that a poet's clumsy handling of the catalogue "kills whatever spark of attention ... the story itself might have enkindled," and associates ineffectual use of the catalogue form with "formula," "ordinary convention," "prolixity," "padding techniques," and a "mechanical" approach (70, 71). See also Stephen A. Barney, "Chaucer's Lists," in *The Wisdom of Poetry: Essays in Early English Literature in Honor of Morton W. Bloomfield*, ed. Larry D. Benson and Siegfried Wenzel (Kalamazoo, MI: Medieval Institute Publications, 1982), 189; and Nicholas Howe, *The Old English Catalogue Poems* (Copenhagen: Rosenkilde and Bagger, 1985), 13.
4. Lewis, *English Literature*, 78–9.
5. All references to the poem will be to *Gavin Douglas: The Palis of Honoure*, ed. David Parkinson (Kalamazoo, MI: TEAMS Medieval Institute Publications, 1992). Line numbers will be given parenthetically in the text.
6. Charles Altieri, *The Particulars of Rapture: An Aesthetics of the Affects* (Ithaca, NY: Cornell University Press, 2003), 4, 5. Aligning himself with Silvan Tomkins, Altieri defines "affect" as a "distinctive realm of experience," and

understands it as an "umbrella term," comprising feelings, moods, emotions, and passions (2–4, 72–88). The vocabulary of affect/emotion remains contested and complex. Following Altieri, I will be using the term "affect" here to refer to "the range of mental states where an agent's activity cannot be adequately handled in terms of either sensations or beliefs but requires attending to how he or she offers expressions of those states" (47–8). While I do not follow the exact subdivision of Altieri's terms, I do use "affect" as an "umbrella term" for a range of psychological experience that emerges from the reading of the poem that follows.

7. Altieri argues that approaches that seek to integrate affect (especially "passion") and reason result in "simplifying both domains and leaving the emotions far too little power to disrupt and to delight" (*Particulars*, 30). While there is no such clear division between powerful emotion and "reason" here (both belong to "wit" and "curage" more generally), I do think the poem resists straightforward or totalizing judgments of the dreamer's affect.

8. Altieri, *Particulars*, 5.

9. Altieri critiques attempts to theorize affect provided by contemporary neuroscience and "cultural constructivism" (*Particulars*, 34, 265 note 5); he sees both as being too keen and too quick to subsume affective textures and particularities within totalizing, flattening explanatory frameworks which often privilege "higher" cognitive functions. His aesthetic, phenomenological approach is rooted in Romanticism and modernism which, respectively, attempt to "dramatize the limitations of epistemic orientation" and "to make the nondiscursive and nonepistemic dimensions of art wield the same level of cultural force as did scientific and utilitarian argument." This is not an argument I can make in the same way of the medieval dream vision, of course. Yet the poem does explore the limits of certain kinds of cultural knowledge and modes of being, and it uses poetry to do so. Although Altieri is critical of readings that focus on historical context, he argues that "[m]apping kinds of affects" might "help us try modes of responsiveness to a range of art works that emphasize how history enters art rather than how art can be placed in historical contexts" (*Particulars*, 33). And while Holly A. Crocker has rightly reminded us that, in the Middle Ages, "affect" did not mean the same thing it does for contemporary criticism (they have "moral power" and "are not disturbances ... [or] ... para- or pre-emotions"), drawing on a medieval poem in conjunction with contemporary aesthetic theory highlights the various different, and distinctive, affective encounters and tensions between them (however incommensurable) that contemporary medievalists must negotiate – as the critical responses to Douglas' poem cited above suggest. See Crocker, "Medieval Affects Now," *Exemplaria* 29,1 (2017), 83.

10. Gregory Kratzmann, *Anglo-Scottish Literary Relations, 1430–1550* (Cambridge: Cambridge University Press, 1980), 105.

11. A brief overview of the poem's syntactical, linguistic, and rhetorical complexities can be found in David Parkinson's "Introduction," in *Gavin Douglas: The Palis of Honoure*, ed. Parkinson, 1–14 (5).

12. Denton Fox, "The Scottish Chaucerians," in *Chaucer and Chaucerians: Critical Studies in Middle English Literature*, ed. D. S. Brewer (London: Thomas Nelson and Sons, 1966), 198. See also Kratzmann, *Anglo-Scottish*, 127. Howe, *Old English Catalogue Poems*, points out that, "[a]lthough the list and the catalogue are not precisely identical, both are didactic strategies for ordering large quantities of material" (20). Farrell discusses seven types of catalogues in medieval writing; see "Chaucer's Use of the Catalogue," 68–9, 73–4, 75. For a discussion of the differences between the list and the catalogue, see *Princeton Encyclopedia of Poetry and Poetics*, s.v. "catalog." For further considerations of lists, see Robert E. Belknap, *The List: The Uses and Pleasures of Cataloguing* (New Haven, CT: Yale University Press, 2004), esp. 1–35; and Umberto Eco, *Infinity of Lists*, trans. Alastair McEwen (London: MacLehose Press, 2009).
13. Parkinson, "Introduction," 6. See also Priscilla Bawcutt's seminal work, *Gavin Douglas: A Critical Study* (Edinburgh: Edinburgh University Press, 1976), esp. 66. Both Fox, "Scottish Chaucerians" and Bawcutt argue that the lists successfully perform structural and rhetorical work in the poem.
14. See Barney, "Chaucer's Lists," 194, and Laura Hibbard Loomis, "'Sir Thopas': X. The Catalogue Lists, Nos. 88–100," in *Sources and Analogues of Chaucer's "Canterbury Tales,"* ed. W. F. Bryan and Germaine Dempster (Chicago, IL: University of Chicago Press, 1941), 550.
15. See McLeod, *Virtue and Venom*, 3. See also Howe, *Old English Catalogue Poems*, 202, and Kevin S. Kiernan, "The Art of the Descending Catalogue, and a Fresh Look at Alisoun," *Chaucer Review* 10,1 (1975), 1. While recent work on literary lists has challenged such assessments, it is still the case that *medieval* lists have not tended to be associated with the quality of imaginative play found in later examples. See, for instance, Francis Spufford, "Introduction," in *The Chatto Book of Cabbages and Kings: Lists in Literature*, ed. Spufford (London: Chatto and Windus, 1989), 1–23. For a recent formalist, transhistorical discussion of lists in literature, see Eva von Contzen, "The Limits of Narration: Lists and Literary History," *Style* (Special issue: *Lists*) 50,3 (2016): 241–60.
16. Barney, "Chaucer's Lists," 219–20, 206. See also Loy D. Martin, "History and Form in the General Prologue to the Canterbury Tales," *ELH* 45,1 (1978), 2; and J. V. Cunningham, "Convention as Structure: The Prologue to the Canterbury Tales," in *Tradition and Poetic Structure: Essays in Literary History and Criticism* (Denver, CO: Alan Swallow, 1960), 11–25.
17. On the parallels between the "oneiric" and the "poetic," see Steven Kruger, *Dreaming in the Middle Ages* (Cambridge: Cambridge University Press, 1992), 131, 133, 134. On dream vision poetry as "fiction about fiction," see Barry Windeatt, "Postmodernism," in *Chaucer: An Oxford Guide*, ed. Steve Ellis (Oxford: Oxford University Press, 2005), 406. See also, in relation to Douglas' poem, Kratzmann, *Anglo-Scottish*, 106; and Bawcutt, *Gavin Douglas*, 50. On the role of affect in cognitive processes as explored in a medieval dream vision, see Anke Bernau, "Feeling Thinking: *Pearl*'s Ekphrastic Imagination," in *The Art of Vision: Ekphrasis in Medieval*

Literature and Culture, ed. Andrew James Johnston, Ethan Knapp, and Margitta Rouse (Columbus, OH: Ohio State University Press, 2015), 100–23. In relation to Douglas' poem, see Johnston and Rouse, "Facing the Mirror: Ekphrasis, Vision, and Knowledge in Gavin Douglas's *Palice of Honour*," in *The Art of Vision*, ed. Johnston, Knapp, and Rouse, 166–83.

18. In relation to the dreamer in *Palis*, see, for instance, Gerald B. Kinneavy, "The Poet in *The Palice of Honour*," *Chaucer Review* 3,4 (1969): 280–303; Kratzmann, *Anglo-Scottish*, 121, 127; and David Parkinson, "The Farce of Modesty in Gavin Douglas's *The Palis of Honoure*," *Philological Quarterly* 70,1 (1991): 13–26. While describing the narrator figure as "comically faint-hearted" in another article, "Mobbing Scenes in Middle Scots Verse: Holland, Douglas, Dunbar," *Journal of English and Germanic Philology* 85,4 (1986), Parkinson also acknowledges the complexities of this "comic" representation by noting that "One may laugh, but the narrator insists on his own fear" (502, 504). In her consideration of Douglas' poem as an exploration of the ethical potential of poetry, Joanna M. Martin, "Responses to the Frame Narrative of John Gower's *Confessio Amantis* in Fifteenth- and Sixteenth-Century Literature," *Review of English Studies* 60,246 (2009), takes the dreamer's distress at face value (571–4).

19. Anne Scott and Cynthia Kosso, "Introduction," in *Fear and Its Representations in the Middle Ages and Renaissance*, ed. Scott and Kosso (Turnhout: Brepols, 2002), xi–xxxvii (xii). Key studies on fear in the Middle Ages are Jean Delumeau, *La Peur en Occident, XIVe–XVIIIe siècle: Une cité assiégée* (Paris: Fayard, 1978), and Peter Dinzelbacher, *Angst im Mittelalter: Teufels-, Todes- und Gotteserfahrung; Mentalitätsgeschichte und Ikonographie* (Paderborn: F. Schöningh, 1996). For a critique of these, see Barbara H. Rosenwein, *Emotional Communities in the Early Middle Ages* (Ithaca, NY: Cornell University Press, 2006), esp. 6.

20. On these see Parkinson, "Introduction," 6.

21. For a discussion of the tension between the "clarity" offered by the visual, and the powerful energy of affect – between *enargeia* and *energeia* – see Joseph Campana, "On Not Defending Poetry: Spenser, Suffering, and the Energy of Affect," *PMLA* 120,1 (2005): 33–48.

22. This is akin to the relationship between marvel and list as discussed by Michael Uebel, *Ecstatic Transformation: On the Uses of Alterity in the Middle Ages* (New York: Palgrave Macmillan, 2005), esp. 113.

23. A familiar association, as we know from Chaucer's *House of Fame* and Lydgate's *Temple of Glass*.

24. See also Bawcutt, *Gavin Douglas*, 55.

25. Steele Nowlin has recently argued in "The Legend of Good Women and the Affect of Invention," *Exemplaria* 25,1 (2013), that Chaucer's *Legend of Good Women* "generically assumes affect to be central to the fictional account of its invention" (17). I think this is also true of Douglas' *Palis*, though in different ways.

26. See Parkinson, "Mobbing Scenes."

27. Parkinson, "Farce of Modesty," argues that the contrast between "grand synthesizing catalogue[s]" and the "insecure poet" "implie[s] kinds of ambivalence: of the cleric towards Venus and Mars, of the Scots poet towards his Roman and English predecessors, of the courtier towards honour itself; no paragon can be assumed to be entirely safe" (14).
28. See *MED*, s.v. "corage," defined as: "The heart as the seat of emotions, affection, attitudes, and volition; heart, spirit; disposition, temperament."
29. There is sleight-of-hand here, for we are reading the "fuller" version of events leading up to the dreamer's praise of Venus. The poem thus stages submission to, and circumvention of, authority.
30. This echoes the Sibyl's lines in the *Aeneid* 6.625–7. See Douglas, *Palis*, ed. Parkinson, note to lines 1259–62, at 110.
31. On the relationship between lists and ekphrases, see Anke Bernau, "Enlisting Truth," *Style* (Special issue: *Lists*) 50,3 (2016): 261–79.
32. This term, and the description elsewhere in the poem of the dreamer's physiological responses to fear, match closely Thomas Aquinas' discussion of *stupor*, an extreme manifestation of fear which overwhelms the individual, preventing any engagement with that which has caused it. See Stephen Loughlin, "The Complexity and Importance of *timor* in Aquinas's *Summa Theologiae*," in *Fear and Its Representations*, ed. Scott and Kosso, 1–16, esp. 10–11. See also Geoffrey de Vinsauf's *Poetria Nova*, which uses fear to illustrate the mode of amplification called apostrophe; *Poetria Nova of Geoffrey of Vinsauf*, trans. Margaret F. Nims (Toronto: Pontifical Institute of Mediaeval Studies, 1967), 27–8, 32.
33. See *MED*, s.v. "stupefacte," as meaning "devoid of feeling, numb, anesthetized."
34. See *MED*, s.v. "prolix": "of writings, love-making, lengthy, protracted."
35. While it begins with the creation of the angels, and Lucifer's fall, there are no references to the events of the New Testament, or to more recent history.
36. These words, of course, recall the dreamer's earlier laments concerning the "[i]nconstant warld" (165–92; also 610).
37. Parkinson, "Farce of Modesty," 16, 19; emphasis mine.
38. Blindness here might indicate the possibility of a different way of seeing – one less tied to the body and the world – but, as the poem goes on to show, it is not a way of seeing that is possible for the dreamer or, by implication, for the poet.
39. She accuses him of having a "wyfis hart" (1937); this is the second time the dreamer's affective response is described as feminizing. The first time occurs in the Prologue (108).
40. The terms "plesance" and "plesand" come up repeatedly throughout the poem, and can refer to a wide range of things. See *MED*, s.v. "plesaunce."
41. Clearly, there is a gendered dimension to this relationship. The dreamer addresses the nymph in misogynistic terms, and she responds with anticlerical taunts (see 1941–4). Gender is a fascinating issue throughout, as it is

a fundamental aspect of the dreamer's identity, and structures his relationship to the goddesses and nymph, but I do not have space to discuss it here.
42. See *MED*, s.v. "assaien." It can mean: "To test or try the character or qualities of (a person)," to "subject (sb.) to trials or ordeals," or, "To assail or attack."
43. Parkinson, "Farce of Modesty," comments on this "unexpected" wish, and refers to the dreamer as a "toady" (21).
44. L. O. Aranye Fradenburg, "Beauty and Boredom in *The Legend of Good Women*," *Exemplaria* 22,1 (2010), 78. She concludes that "[o]ur bonds are social and economic arrangements; we do not survive without them." The poem ends with a dedication to James IV, reminding us of the conditions governing the production of courtly poetry.
45. Fradenburg argues that "discipline *is* a mode of enjoyment," one which is "not always pleasurable" or even "conscious." She states that "[b]y 'enjoyment' I mean everything we mean by terms like 'affect,' 'feeling,' 'emotion,' and 'drive'" ("Beauty and Boredom," 66; my emphasis).
46. Parkinson notes that "[i]nternal rhyme is a technique of closure in Older Scots verse" (Douglas, *Palis*, ed. Parkinson, 129, note to 2116–42).
47. On the association of the list with "disciplinary actions," see Matti Peikola, "The Catalogue: A Late Middle English Lollard Genre?," in *Discourse Perspectives on English: Medieval to Modern*, ed. Risto Hiltunen and Janne Skaffari (Amsterdam: John Benjamins, 2003), 105–35, esp. 118.
48. Barney, "Chaucer's Lists," 190.
49. As Altieri puts it: "[E]xpressive activity manifests a continual struggle between a sense of inchoateness and the forms of intelligibility provided by our social grammars" (*Particulars*, 19).

Afterword: Three Letters

Anthony Bale

> "Feelings can get stuck to certain bodies in the very way we describe spaces, situations, dramas. And bodies can get stuck depending on what feelings they get associated with."
> Sara Ahmed, "Happy Objects"[1]

The essays gathered in this volume reveal a rich and nuanced world of personal and interpersonal "feeling" in medieval sources. The cultural history of emotions as it is practiced here is not merely an exercise in spotting emotions in the past – joy here, heartbreak there – but rather a site for sophisticated discursive reflections on representation and subjectivity. In particular, we are now in a position to reject a history of emotions that strives for continuity (grand narratives of "affective piety" or "medieval fear," for instance) and instead examine differences in feeling across time, space, gender, and class. The essays here excavate the many expressive and interpretative possibilities of thinking with emotion and affect; the expressive multi-dimensionality of medieval subjectivity must now be acknowledged as we see that medieval emotional communities were many and their affective experiences diverse.

A cultural history of emotions is not simply the province of the social psychologist or the neuroscientist. The fact remains, as the essays gathered in this volume show, that when we talk about feelings in the past, we are usually talking about mediated feelings. Emotions come to reside in words, affects are exhibited in gestures and physical activities, and medieval texts are revealed to be a rich source for the ways in which both emotion and affect were communicated and transmitted. When we turn to affect as a critical category it is all too easy to look for something that connects us with the people in our sources: emotions clearly have a history, and affects are clearly linked to emotions, but does one of the contentions of this volume – that there are specific contextual valences of late medieval English affective culture – get us any closer to understanding what *feeling* is? If we try to move beyond the over-personalization of historical figures and their disclosed emotions, are we not in danger of asserting our presentist concerns onto our sources? And yet if we explore each source as its own disclosure of a moment of feeling, are we not in danger of one of the perils of micro-histories: that of producing ever more microscopic analyses that reduce human feeling to unconnected moments of mediated experience?

In this afterword, I will reflect on some of the themes and issues that have been covered by the essays in this volume, doing so through three medieval English letters. As Bryant's essay on manorial documents demonstrates, "non-literary" texts and documentary forms can be valuable sites for the recovery of affective transactions. Letters, whether historical or fictional, with their assumptions of intersubjective communication, are a productive place to look at how emotional situations are rendered into written documents in specific circumstances, and can help us explore the intersection of affect, feeling, and emotion.

Margaret Paston on Grief

One Christmas Eve, probably in 1459, the Norfolk gentry-woman Margaret Paston had a letter written to her husband John Paston I. The letter was started by one scribe and completed by another, so it is best thought of as a collaborative text. It is part of the extensive collection of letters circulating among members of the Paston family and their associates during the fifteenth century.

Margaret's letter begins with a discussion of grief and its effects, in the wake of the death of her relative Sir John Fastolf (1380–1459). In effect, the letter documents the social regulation of feeling in the context of mourning. The letter begins:

> Ryght wvrschipful husbond, I recomaund me on-to yov. Plese it yov to wete that I sent yovr eldest svnne to my Lady Morlee to haue knolage qwat sportys were husyd in here hows in Kyrstemesse next folloyng afryr the deceysse of my lord here husband. And sche seyd that þere were non dysgysynggys nere harping nere lvtyng nere syngyn, nere non lowed dysportys, but pleyng at the tabyllys and schesse and cardys, sweche dysportys sche gave here folkys leve to play, and non odyr.[2]

> Right worshipful husband, I recommend myself to you. It will please you to know that I sent your oldest son to my Lady Morley to know what sports took place in her house at Christmas, immediately following the death of my lord, her husband [i.e., Thomas, Lord Morley, who had died some years earlier]. And she said that there were neither disguisings nor harping nor luting nor singing, nor any loud recreations, just playing at the

tables [i.e., backgammon] and chess and cards, such recreations as she gave her people permission to play, and no others.

The letter appears on first sight to be a gossipy titbit, eschewing elaborate formal rhetoric and getting to the point in order to report that Margaret Paston had sent her son to see how Lady Morley had been "celebrating" Christmas. To gauge this, Paston checked on the "sportys" in Lady Morley's household: disguisings (masques or playlets), harping, luting, singing, and other "lowed dysportys" were clearly considered inappropriate, whereas quiet games of cards and chess were permitted.

Margaret Paston's letter is poised somewhere between the documentary (it is a letter about everyday things, and is part of the Pastons' bureaucratic interactions as a family) and the literary (insofar as it is a rhetorically constructed version of events). But such letters offer us a moment of emotional response in a textual frame, and they provide one way of approaching the issue of emotional authenticity in the distant past. Rather than offering a description of how somebody felt, the letter portrays the social comprehension of feeling, that which is now frequently called an "emotional practice" by historians of emotions.[3] "Emotional practices" are always conditioned by their social context, and are thus historically located; at the same time, "emotional practices" can only be retrieved through discourse, language, or enactment, and so letters, texts, poems, images, games, and all sorts of cultural media become highly valuable in gauging the construction of feeling. Margaret Paston, her son, her scribes, and Lady Morley were all real people with real feelings; but Paston's letter shows the conjunction of grief with a practical engagement with the world, in effect showing the culturally constructed and textually recorded movement from grief (the feeling) to mourning (the "emotional practice" of grieving). At the same time, we should be mindful of the letter's status as a bearer of emotions, able to effect an affective communication, in which one person was able to consider the feelings of another: here, "feelings" are not in the mind, but first in the physical activities of Lady Morley's household and then in the words on Margaret Paston's scribes' page.

Margaret Paston's letter discloses several levels of the regulation and surveillance of the performance of feeling: not only via Margaret Paston and the two scribes who wrote her letter, and her son who visited Lady Morley, but by Lady Morley herself, who "gave her folkys leve" to play certain games but not others. This letter narrates a premodern community of people concerned with reading each other's emotional states, judging emotional inclination by social performance, and generating something akin to what Crocker identifies in Hoccleve's writings as a "regimented system [of] well-governed feeling." An emotional regime is at work here, in which Lady Morley demonstrates to, and requires from, her household a kind of judicious sobriety which indicates a "proper" emotion and the need to perform that as, or in place of, emotion (such as grief, immoderate lamentation, depression, or other "emotions" of loss). Barbara Rosenwein has commented in an extended exploration of the Pastons' emotions that "[the] *lack* of emotions is also part of emotions history"; Rosenwein shows, in her survey of the Pastons' letters, that they valued "equanimity over passion."[4] But the members of Lady Morley's household are not inert: they are affected by their kinsman's death, but in a regulated way. One of the key insights of this volume is that affect is not anti-autonomous but can rather be read as part of the construction of a self-authorizing performance.

We gain from Margaret Paston's letter little sense of what we might today call "sadness," "grief," "angst," or personal loss. Rather, it seems that Margaret Paston wanted to see how Lady Morley had managed emotion and perhaps to model her own behavior on hers. In this sense, the letter is profoundly about the management of *emotions* – feelings that are displayed, mediated, or performed – rather than *affects* in the sense of pre-personal states in which an unformed but powerful drive achieves an embodied *and* mental state. The letter tells us how Lady Morley's household *emoted* rather than how its members were feeling, affectively; yet the performance of "appropriate" sports might be seen as an affective response to grief, just as tears or wailing might have been in other contexts. As Burger helpfully notes, affect is generally held to cross boundaries of the individual and the social, the oral and the textual, and the textual and the intimate; the "scene" of the gentry household performing its grief challenges us to consider where affect – the impulse to mourn – actually is. Conversely, emotion might be seen to be engendered in very specific and localized emotional communities and, in this case, the sense of emotion we gain from the letter is profoundly influenced by the specific class-based – and *arriviste* – concerns of the newly wealthy Paston family.

Margaret Paston's letter offers a glimpse of an emotional community: connecting ideas and feelings with physical activities, the *expression* of an emotion (grief at the death of Fastolf) itself becomes a kind of dramatic *tableau* or playlet, for the inquiring eyes of Margaret Paston's son, in a way that echoes Emma Lipton's discussion of a "community of neighbors acting as virtuous witnesses." We will never know how Lady Morley really felt about her late husband, or how her household felt about being asked to perform their grief during the Christmas holiday, but we do know that they entered into a social vocabulary of appropriate responses to grief. The letter shows that the "collective knowledge of character and reputation" described by Lipton in the dramatic performances at York could also be policed in "intimate" letters between kinsmen. So this letter demands of its readers a kind of witnessing of what, in Morley's household, appears to have been a well-managed collective experience, not unlike a dramatic production (and, perhaps, an extension of the public staging of formalized grief at the funeral). The household then became a "stage" for the performance of well-managed sobriety, in which Lady Morley's proper control over its members was displayed through their collective version of appropriate emotional response.

Lipton's essay in this volume is a particularly useful intervention in emotional history and affect studies inasmuch as Lipton urges us to expand our sense of how "individual perception and the collective experience of emotion" were mediated. If, as Lipton suggests we should, we properly understand medieval records of emotional performance as indebted to notions of witnessing, and attendant concerns of false speech and faulty performance, then we can begin to understand why the Pastons might have been so interested in checking on, and documenting, the social forms that Lady Morley's feelings took. Building on Lipton's argument, we might suggest that the Paston letter functions as a witness "to shape an ethics of affect" which is at once individual (to Lady Morley), social (to the gentry community of East Anglia at this specific moment), and civic or general.

What is the role of the letter – a communally written text – from Paston to her husband in remediating an emotional scene? Is this letter best considered a record of shared emotion or of leisure practices? A written source like this, then, is perhaps not especially useful in telling us how people felt, but it does tell us how people wished to appear to be feeling. As Trigg observes, medieval sources are not uncomplicated mirrors of how people "really felt" – but, Trigg continues, "the use and history of particular motifs and expressions [in literary texts] can be an important source for the mutable history of emotions and emotional expression." The meaning of emotions and affective states in premodern texts should never be taken to be self-evident; Margaret Paston's letter does not show emotion as residing in Lady Morley's mind but in the viewed bodies of the members of her household, yet this is clearly not an "affective" state in the sense of it being pre-linguistic or unconscious. It is clear from the letter that "grief" or "mourning" was attended by *enforced* social rituals, what Trigg describes as "established social norms and expectations";

a game of cards may seem to us no more or less respectful than the performance by a lute-player, but it clearly was. In other words, to convey the correct emotional state, emotions had to be *seen to be performed* in a socially governed way, with Lady Morley and Margaret Paston here both complicit in such emotional management.

Pandarus on Love

In book two of Geoffrey Chaucer's *Troilus and Criseyde*, as the eponymous love affair builds towards its climax, Pandarus, Troilus' mentor and confidant, offers his advice on how to write an effective – and affective – love letter. This famous scene is valuable in showing the use and abuse of emotional stylistics, as it appears to disclose a well-developed medieval theory of emotional manipulation. The three stanzas of Pandarus' advice are worth quoting in full, as they develop his theory of touching composition:

> "Towchyng thi letter, thou art wys ynough.
> I woot thow nylt it dygneliche endite,
> As make it with thise argumentes tough;
> Ne scryvenyssh or craftily thow it write;
> Biblotte it with thi teris ek a lite;
> And if thow write a goodly word al softe,
> Though it be good, reherce it nought to ofte.
>
> "For though the beste harpour upon lyve
> Wolde on the beste sowned joly harpe
> That evere was, with alle his fyngres five
> Touche ay o stryng, or ay o werbul harpe,
> Were his nayles pointed nevere so sharpe,
> It sholde maken every wight to dulle,
> To here his glee, and of his strokes fulle.
>
> "Ne jompre ek no discordant thyng yfeere
> As thus, to usen termes of phisik
> In loves termes; hold of this matere
> The forme always, and do that it be lik;
> For if a peyntour wolde peynte a pyk
> With asses feet, and hedde it as an ape,
> It cordeth naught, so were it but a jape."[5]

Pandarus' advice opens with an emphasis on what to avoid rather than what to include, as if emotional content can be too easily misconstrued or malformed.[6] The letter must not be written "dygneliche" (pretentiously, proudly), it must not make "tough," arrogant, or obstinate, arguments, it must not be too writerly, formal ("scryvenyssh"), or artful ("craftyly"). For Pandarus, the letter and its effects are thus constructed around a set of things that the letter *is not*, things that must not be said. Troilus' feeling of love-longing is taken for granted as the affective ground upon which the letter is written.

The first thing that Pandarus recommends for inclusion are not words, but tears with which to blot the letter a little – "biblotte it with thi teris ek a lite" – a contrivance designed to show the affective state of the *author*. Troilus' tears, a para-textual device, seem designed to show the physical "authenticity" of Troilus' emotions through appealing to physical (pre-linguistic) signs of emotion, even as these tears are artfully arranged. Ironically, the tear – sometimes a sign of humiliation, loss, pain, and one associated with women, but more often the sign of sincere compunction – becomes the mark of affective authorship. Pandarus then goes on to give a manifesto against expressive repetition and discord. Strikingly – and similarly to Lady Morley in Margaret Paston's letter – he does this in terms of music, as well as medicine and painting, rather than through verbal proficiency or emotional candor. Troilus must be neither like a harper playing on one string nor like someone who mixes lexicons of "phisik" (medicine) and love. There must be no "jompre" (haphazard arrangement, jumble) or unsettling hybridity. Ironically, as he is giving this advice, Pandarus' own language becomes more expressive and poetic, moving excitedly into flowing sentences and subordinate clauses, punctuated with discordant rhymes ("harpe"/"sharpe," "lik"/"pyk," "ape"/"jape") and ridiculous imagery which further provide Troilus with a negative example of correct emotive composition.

Throughout, Pandarus draws attention to the barely concealed craft of writing a love letter. Troilus' tears aside, emotions, in this letter, are largely absent, but the letter is, nonetheless, an "intimate script," to use a term from the history of emotions to describe "scripts for the performance of feeling."[7] It is taken for granted that, if the letter is properly executed, then it will have the correct effect on Criseyde (who is also absent from the letter, only implicitly and unflatteringly compared to a harp to be played or a surface for painting). This is a kind of intimacy that is paradoxically non-intimate due to its mechanic, social production. Barry Windeatt has described how, for Pandarus, "a letter is an essentially non-spontaneous, pre-considered statement, consciously designed to achieve maximum effect";[8] the letter is not an emotional outburst but a series of socially agreed gestures and synonyms, yet the letter has within it the affective power to move others.

What, then, is the emotional content of this imagined letter? The answer is in Troilus' reaction, where he reveals himself to be moved not by the letter as such but by the idea of writing the letter:

> This conseil liked wel to Troilus,
> But, as a dredful lovere, he seyde this:
> "Allas, my deere brother Pandarus,
> I am ashamed for to write, ywys,
> Lest of myn innocence I seyde amys,
> Or that she nolde it for despit receyve;
> Than were I ded: ther myght it nothyng weyve."

Troilus' reaction is replete with emotions and affective drives: "dred" (terror, anxiety), love, shame, "despit" (spite, contempt), and his often-repeated suicidal propensities ("than were I ded"). Chaucer depicts the letter's force as residing in fear, worry, and ambitions of the letter-writer, the terror not of self-disclosure but of being misunderstood, the shame of being rejected rather than the embarrassment of articulating one's feelings.

This letter is, foremost, a plot device in Chaucer's narrative poem. Indeed, this letter, and subsequent missives, will go on to play a significant role in the development of the characters' love affair. But here it is worth thinking about the letter as a vehicle of emotional deferral and intersubjective *misunderstanding*. Chaucer, through Pandarus, is discussing the way in which an "emotional practice" – the love letter – can be constructed and mobilized; emotion does not need to reside within the love letter, but can be created through it (as is shown by Troilus' reaction) and the unpredictable energy that resides in affective utterances and cultural forms. Literary emotional utterances may, as Bernau suggests, initiate and stimulate poetic invention, even as they might be shown as leading to a kind of emotional alienation and annihilation. Troilus' "dred" is a quite different state from the courtly love apparently encoded in Pandarus' advice, but it is nonetheless a vivid and violent emotional and affective reaction, albeit an unexpected one.

Both Margaret Paston's letter (a historical source) and Pandarus' (fictional) advice on constructing a love letter speak to one of the most dominant ideas in the recent history of emotions, that of Pierre Bourdieu's notion of "*habitus*."[9] *Habitus* – an unconscious, social disposition that informs and regulates everyday practices – emphasizes the communal construction and guiding of emotion, in ways that resonate in these letters. Whilst these letters show individuals crafting an emotional "self" in a way that may seem deeply at odds with *habitus*, we might say that in the letters of both Margaret Paston and Pandarus there is a strong sense of acceptable and communally held expressions of emotion – mourning and love – being inculcated and repeated. Both texts share a *social* sense of the construction and regulation of emotion: emotions are not translated from within but performed outwardly. In a way that foreshadows the writings of anthropologists and psychologists like Claude Lévi-Strauss and William James, might we go so far as to suggest that physical expression (or "affective reaction") *is*, in fact, the emotion?[10] Feeling might be the *consequence*, not the *cause*, of the emotive letter, which holds within it a distinctively textual power to transmit affective reactions. Or, to use McNamer's terminology of "intimate script" and emotional performance, their performative iteration (the sober game, the blotted love letter) as *emotives* makes the emotion they are scripting: as McNamer argues, "emotions can indeed be willed, faked, performance through the repetition of scripted words," but "through such manifest fakery" an emotion can come to be "true."[11]

Henry VIII on Anne Boleyn's Breasts

In the summer of 1528 Henry VIII, king of England, composed a letter in his own hand, possibly seated at the beautiful writing-desk often said to have been made for him.[12] The letter was composed for his then lover, Anne Boleyn, and dates from July 1528, when the king was still married to Catherine of Aragon and some five years before he would be married to Boleyn. It is amongst the letters between the couple now held by the Vatican in Rome, probably taken there by an agent of Rome, gathered as evidence against the king's later divorce of Boleyn. In the current context, this short letter offers a fascinating portrait of the king's expressive self, his emotional literacy, and the use of languages of emotion between the public and private realms. Moreover, it is useful in gauging the historical use of emotional language in the "courtly" world of a Tudor king and his educated mistress. Henry wrote:

> Myne awne sweth-hart, thes shall be to advertes yow off the grete elengnes [*loneliness*] that I fynde her syns your departyng, for, I ensure you, methynkyth the tyme lenger syns your departyng now last then I was wonte to do a hole fortnyght. I thynke your kyndnes and fervenes off love causyth it for other wyse I wolde not have thought it possyble that for so littyll a wyle it shulde have grevyd me but now that I am comyng toward yow methynkyth

my painnys bene halfe relesyed, and allso I am right well comfortyd in so muche that my boke makyth substantially for my matter, in wrytyng wheroff I have spente above iiii [h]ours thys day, whyche causyd me now to wrytte the schortter letter to yow at thys tyme bycause of summe payne in my hed, wyshyng myselfe (specially an evenynge) in my swethart harmys whose pretty dukkys [*breasts, dugs*] I trust shortly to cusse [*kiss*]. Wryttyng with the hand of hym that was, is, and shal be yours by his will, H[enricus]. R[ex].[13]

Troilus-like, Henry's letter is a reflection very much of the writer's concerns, rather than those of the recipient. Henry opens with a declaration of, or complaint about, his "elengnes," his loneliness, since Boleyn's departure; this feeling of loneliness is cleverly juxtaposed with his lover's "kyndnes" – her constancy, her affections – and the fervency of their love. Fulcrum-like, the middle of the letter moves from a (past-tense) disclosure of Henry's emotional loneliness to a (future-tense) statement of their coming physical reunion; his "painnys bene halfe relesyed," he is "comforted," tracing an emotional trajectory from solitude to anticipation. As with Troilus' letter, the *writing* of the letter has an effect on the author, not the recipient, as Henry's use of emotives moves the letter into its markedly somatic final stage.[14] Henry describes his headache from writing his own book (*A Glasse of the Truthe*, a tract against the validity of his marriage to Catherine of Aragon), he imagines himself in his sweetheart's arms, he longs to kiss her "dukkys" (her breasts), and he mentions that he is writing the letter with his own hand. Affect here is not disconnected from narration, but rather affect is the culmination, the result, of narration.

The letter is full of expressive strategies, in effect moving through feeling ("elengnes") via emotion and affect ("my painnys bene halfe relesyed") to physical sensation ("in my swethart harmys whose pretty dukkys I trust shortly to cusse"). We might well read it in the terms of "affect management" proposed by Burger, in which a range of emotional and physical feelings (what Burger calls "biological urges") are marshaled into something called – and calling attention to itself as – a "love letter." It is a fascinating and illuminating document, but how far can we say that it discloses Henry VIII's intimate proto-modern "self" rather than speaks to an older (*Troilus*-like) tradition of courtly rhetoric and intimate script? If affect is unconscious, physiological, and physical, as is generally suggested, how does it engage writerly and readerly emotion in this letter? That is to say, does emotional longing here trigger erotic reverie and embodied affective response, echoed in the physical labor of Henry's own handwriting, his headaches, and his somatic wishes to kiss Anne's breasts? As Salih comments, images, objects, and things – including letters – have a power "to attract and perpetuate desire" through their "sticky," affective communication; in this letter we see affairs of state comingling with a love affair, a world of longing and action that refuses modern ideas of "public" and "personal" realms. Henry's affective utterances traverse such realms, and the moment of the writing of this letter – during a period of national, political turmoil – is imbricated with his "intimate" wish to see Boleyn and her body. What governs the letter is its rhetorical appeal to generic formulae, and Henry's apparently un-ironic similarity to Chaucer's Troilus, moaning and groaning whilst composing courtly love-longing.

Letters like this pose productive problems in the interpretation of affective media from the past. "Originality" and "authenticity" are rarely appropriate words for understanding medieval texts, but such terms continue to suffuse our sense of what an emotional utterance should be. Both Pandarus' "ideal" letter and Henry's actual letter veer towards cliché, and Lady Morley's household appears to be under a strict emotional regime, even as each source asserts that bodies – the Morley household's games, Troilus' tears, Henry's libido – can be controlled and stimulated by emotion. There seems to be little that is "automatic" about Troilus' tears or Henry's erotic wooing: both are rhetorically framed, just as the mourners in Lady Morley's household were not *spontaneously* playing quiet card games but had been directed to do so. All three letters thus show how bodies can be ruled by formal emotions, rather than vice versa, bearing out Fredric Jameson's quotation, cited above by Crocker, that "any proposition about affect is also a proposition about the body, and a historical one at that." Even in the distant past, culture must therefore, to some extent, be understood to be able to *act* on the body; in each case, the flow of emotion, from feeling to embodied gesture, is mediated through the written word. In terms of how we understand Henry VIII's intimate self, his letter shows that the rhetorical communication, replete with feeling, was both the *outcome* of emotion and the vehicle for engendering an emotional response.

Authorship, Authenticity, and the Writing of Emotions

In the essays gathered in this volume we have encountered descriptions of a range of "feelings" – anger, love, zealous vengeance, shame, humiliation, jealousy, alienation, terror – but we have also seen the capacity of texts to *move* their audiences – in sources as diverse as the creepy embodied inventions described by Sarah Salih, or the systems of manorial management probed by Bryant.

Scholars of the past now see all kinds of media in which languages of feelings are expressed as important sources through which to construct a historically sensitive account of emotional subjectivity. On the one hand, letters appear to offer a perfect source for the history of emotions, as sites designed for the disclosure and communication of feelings, often presenting themselves as an intimate exchange. On the other hand, all letters are formalized by language, framed by convention, and fraught with potential miscommunication between the feelings of the author and the recipient. One of the difficulties of working with affective media is, as DeMarco suggests, the inherent instability of the contexts in which emotions are being evoked. Letters rely on norms of feeling, because they are concerned with communicating one person's state to another, yet they also foreground strong or aberrant emotions, as stylized records of notable feelings. The letter – and in particular the love letter – has been a foundational text in the western emotional landscape, as a place in which to assert and record moments of emotion. The letters by Margaret Paston and Henry VIII are called "historical sources," whereas Pandarus' advice on letter-writing is a "literary text," but all three participate in a shared enterprise of rendering an emotional state in a written communication through rhetorical and performative formulae; and all three are full of emotional management and rhetorical tricks which mediate not only emotion (performed feelings) but also affect (non-linguistic and feeling expressions tied to feeling).

Letters are understood to be key moments of intertextual articulation and, as intersubjective disclosures of emotion, they have been much discussed in the critical theory of authorship. The letter is central to Roland Barthes' *S/Z* and *A Lover's Discourse*, to Jacques Lacan's *Seminar on the Purloined Letter*, in Helene Cixous' *Love Itself in the Letterbox* ("all my soul's caressed tactile extremities were caressing the incessant trembling of the paper"),[15] and others. For Barthes, the love letter staged a "special dialectic," being "both blank (encoded) and expressive (charged with longing to signify desire)";[16] Barthes says that "[l]ike desire, the love letter waits for an answer; it implicitly enjoins the other to reply, for without a reply the other's image changes, becomes other."[17] For Lacan, the letter could be a key site "in which ... subjects relay each other in their displacement during the intersubjective repetition";[18] that is, the letter, and its movement between people, came to be a kind of displacement of subjectivity and emotion, through the deferral of the audience and through the retransmission of the letter. In the three letters I have briefly introduced above, letters are valuable precisely because of their struggling to find a mode of intelligibility between subjects, in which emotions and affects are rendered in a mutual comprehensible lexicon.

This mode of intelligibility helps us see how writings about emotion are often actually writings about something else: in Margaret Paston's case, about manners and decorum; in Troilus' case, about Pandarus' own voyeurism and manipulation, and the political situation between the Greeks and Trojans; and for Henry VIII and Anne Boleyn, about diplomacy, religion, and the regulation of marriage. Yet letters are also important as records of *what they leave out*: for it seems that to write down a feeling or to record someone else's affects was thought more significant than just expressing an emotion verbally. "Intimacy" is itself a historically and socially bounded concept, and it might be that the most everyday emotional utterances – like "I love you," "I'm frustrated," "I'm sad" – are rarely recorded, or thought worthy of being recorded, whereas those written down were done so with a sense of ceremony, longevity, or formal assertiveness.[19] Moreover, letters as emotional vehicles assert only the perspective of the author's emotional field, and have no guaranteed success in terms of the recipient. Both Troilus and Henry seem to be saying to Criseyde and Anne Boleyn respectively: "acknowledge my emotions," or "feel how I am feeling," because to *send* a written account of one's emotions to someone else is fraught with the missive's finding of its right audience. As Barthes suggests, the love letter is a contingent form, one which is not only expressive but solicits an answer; and without an answer, the love letter is empty, unrealized, an iteration not of love but of longing.

As the essays gathered in this volume amply show, medieval textualities were a rich site for the interrogation of feeling. What becomes clear through this collection is that it would be a mistake to think that medieval emotions are in some way predictable or unambiguous; the codified languages of gesture and iconography did not mean that feelings themselves were rendered in an unmodulated way. It is worth recalling that one of the distinctive pleasures of reading literature from the past is the ambiguity of "emotional" states. Feelings remain encrypted in languages of convention whilst the terminology of emotion has changed over time. At the same time, we continue, as a twenty-first-century community of readers, to feel an affective connection with writing from the past, and allow ourselves to be seduced by the wayward, unpredictable capacity of sources to evoke an affective reaction across time: do we not feel a kind of awful thrill – at once voyeuristic, prurient, and macabre – on reading

Henry VIII's words to his then paramour, whom he would execute just a few years later?

In the writing of the past we can discern how medieval people theorized their feelings, how they placed their reactions into emotional categories, and how they disclosed their desires and their subjectivities within frameworks of intelligent response and performance. Written sources are not only a valuable indicator of the social construction of emotion; in these sources, we see that medieval affects often resided neither in bodies nor minds, but in words.

Notes

1. Sara Ahmed, "Happy Objects," in *The Affect Theory Reader*, ed. Melissa Gregg and Gregory J. Seigworth (Durham, NC: Duke University Press, 2010), 39.
2. [Margaret Paston,] "To John Paston I," in *Paston Letters and Papers of the Fifteenth Century*, ed. Norman Davis (Oxford: Clarendon Press, 1971), 257. My translation.
3. See Monique Scheer, "Are Emotions a Kind of Practice (And Is That What Makes Them Have a History)? A Bourdieuian Approach to Understanding Emotion," *History and Theory* 51,2 (2012): 193–200.
4. Barbara Rosenwein, *Generations of Feeling: A History of Emotions, 600–1700* (Cambridge: Cambridge University Press, 2016), 215–21.
5. Geoffrey Chaucer, *Troilus & Criseyde*, in *The Riverside Chaucer*, ed. Larry D. Benson, 3rd edn (Boston, MA: Houghton Mifflin Co., 1987), II.1023–43.
6. The classic account of Chaucerian letter-writing and rhetorical formulae is Norman Davis' "The *Litera Troili* and English Letters," *Review of English Studies* 16,63 (1965): 233–44.
7. Sarah McNamer, *Affective Meditation and the Invention of Medieval Compassion* (Philadelphia, PA: University of Pennsylvania Press, 2010), 12.
8. Barry Windeatt, "'Love That Oughte Ben Secree' in Chaucer's *Troilus*," *Chaucer Review* 14,2 (1979): 116–31.
9. See, in particular, Scheer, "Are Emotions a Kind of Practice?" and Jan Plamper, *The History of Emotions: An Introduction*, trans. Keith Tribe (Oxford: Oxford University Press, 2015), 268–70.
10. See Plamper, *History of Emotions*, on theorists who have argued "that emotions were not something internal to the body; instead, physical expression was itself the emotion" (84–5).
11. McNamer, *Affective Meditation*, 13.
12. Now London, Victoria and Albert Museum W.29:1 to 9–1932, on display in the British Galleries.
13. Edited from the facsimile in *The Love Letters of Henry VIII*, ed. Jasper Ridley (London: Cassell, 1988), 64 (which includes a modern English translation on p. 65).

14. In this way, Henry's letter anticipates Roland Barthes' description in *A Lover's Discourse: Fragments*, trans. Richard Howard (New York: Hill and Wang, 1978), of the status of the writer of the love letter: "I have nothing to tell you, save that it is to you that I tell this nothing"; and then, quoting Goethe, "Why do I turn once again to writing? Beloved, you must not ask such a question, For the truth is, I have nothing to tell you, All the same, your dear hands will hold this note" (157).
15. Hélène Cixous, *Love Itself in the Letterbox*, trans. Peggy Kamuf (London: Polity, 2008), 73.
16. Barthes, *Lover's Discourse*, 157.
17. Ibid., 158.
18. Jacques Lacan, "Seminar on the Purloined Letter," trans. Jeffrey Mehlman, *Yale French Studies* 48 (1972), 39.
19. See further, Orest Ranum, "The Refuges of Intimacy," in *A History of Private Life*, Vol. 3: *Passions of the Renaissance*, ed. Philippe Ariès and Roger Chartier (Cambridge, MA: Harvard University Press, 1989), 207–63, on letter-writing and "significant" emotions in the early modern period.

Bibliography

Primary Sources

London, Victoria and Albert Museum W.29:1 to 9–1932.
Manchester, John Rylands English MS 1.
Oxford, Bodleian MS Digby 232.
Paris, Bibliothèque nationale de France, ms lat 9471.

Anselm of Lucca. "*De Concordia* (The Compatibility of God's Foreknowledge, Predestination, and Grace with Human Freedom)." In *Anselm of Canterbury: The Major Works*. Ed. and trans. Brian Davies and G. R. Evans. New York: Oxford University Press, 2008, 435–74.

Aquinas, Thomas. *On Human Nature*. Trans. and ed. Thomas S. Hibbs. Indianapolis: Hackett Publishing Co., 1999.

Summa Theologica: The Emotions. Trans. and notes E. D'Arcy, 19 Ia2ae22–23. New York: McGraw-Hill, 1975.

Aristotle. *Rhetoric*. In *The Complete Works of Aristotle: The Revised Oxford Translation*. Ed. and trans. Jonathan Barnes, Volume 2. 6th reprint, Princeton, NJ: Princeton University Press, 1995.

Augustine of Hippo. *Concerning the City of God against the Pagans*. Trans. Henry Bettenson. Harmondsworth: Penguin, 1972.

"Reply to Faustus the Manichean." In *A Select Library of the Nicene and Post-Nicene Fathers of the Christian Church*. Ed. and trans. Philip Schaff. Grand Rapids, MI: Eerdmans, 1979.

Benson, Larry D., ed. *King Arthur's Death: The Middle English Stanzaic Morte Arthur and Alliterative Morte Arthure*. Kalamazoo, MI: TEAMS Medieval Institute Publications, 1994.

Benson, Larry D., and Theodore M. Andersson, eds. *The Literary Context of Chaucer's Fabliaux*. New York: Bobbs-Merrill Company, 1971.

Boccaccio, Giovanni. *The Decameron*. Trans. Mark Musa and Peter E. Bondanella. New York: Norton, 1982.

Early English Versions of the Tales of Guiscardo and Ghismonda and Titus and Gisippus from the Decameron. Ed. Herbert G. Wright. EETS o.s. 205. London: Oxford University Press, 1937.

Boccaccio, Giovanni, and Vittore Branca. *Tutte le Opere Di Giovanni Boccaccio*. Classici Mondadori, Vol. 4. Milan: Mondadori, 1964–92.
Bracton, [Henry de]. *Bracton on the Laws and Customs of England*. Ed. and trans. Samuel E. Thorne. 2 vols. Cambridge, MA: Harvard University Press, 1968.
Chaucer, Geoffrey. *The Miller's Tale: A Variorum Edition of the Works of Geoffrey Chaucer*. Vol. 2, *The Canterbury Tales*, Part 2. Ed. Thomas W. Ross. Norman, OK: University of Oklahoma Press, 1983.
  The Riverside Chaucer. Ed. Larry D. Benson. 3rd edn. Boston, MA: Houghton Mifflin Co., 1987.
  Troilus and Criseyde: A New Translation. Trans. and ed. B. A. Windeatt. Oxford: Oxford University Press, 1998.
Correale, Robert M., and Mary Hamel, eds. *Sources and Analogues of the Canterbury Tales*. Cambridge: D. S. Brewer, 2002.
Dante Alighieri. *The New Life/La Vita Nuova*. Ed. and trans. Stanley Appelbaum. Mineola, NY: Dover, 2006.
  Decrees of the Ecumenical Councils. Vol. 1. Ed. Norman P. Tanner. Washington, DC: Georgetown University Press, 1990.
Dives and Pauper. Ed. Priscilla Heath Barnum. EETS o.s. 275, 280. London: Oxford University Press, 1976–80.
Davis, Norman, ed. *Non-Cycle Plays and Fragments*. EETS s.s. 1. London: Oxford University Press, 1970.
Douglas, Gavin. *Gavin Douglas: The Palis of Honoure*. Ed. David Parkinson. Kalamazoo, MI: TEAMS Medieval Institute Publications, 1992.
Duncan, Thomas G., ed. *Medieval English Lyrics, 1200–1400*. Harmondsworth: Penguin, 1995.
Fasciculus Morum: A Fourteenth-Century Preacher's Handbook. Ed. Siegfried Wenzel. University Park, PA: Pennsylvania State University Press, 1989.
The Good Wife's Guide (Le Ménagier de Paris): A Medieval Household Book. Ed. and trans. Gina L. Greco and Christine M. Rose. Ithaca, NY: Cornell University Press, 2009.
Gower, John. *Confessio Amantis*, Vol. 3. Ed. Russell A. Peck, Latin trans. Andrew Galloway. Kalamazoo, MI: TEAMS Medieval Institute Publications, 2004.
Gratian. *Decretum Magistri Gratiani*. Ed. Emil Friedburg. Leipzig: Bernard Tauchitz, 1879.
Harley, Marta Powell, ed. *A Revelation of Purgatory by an Unknown Fifteenth-Century Woman Visionary*. Lewiston, NY: Edwin Mellen, 1985.
Harvey, P. D. A., ed. *Manorial Records of Cuxham, Oxfordshire, circa 1200–1359*. London: Oxfordshire Record Society, 1976.
Henry VIII. *The Love Letters of Henry VIII*. Ed. Jasper Ridley. London: Cassell, 1988.
Hilton, Walter. *The Scale of Perfection*. Ed. Thomas Bestul. Kalamazoo, MI: TEAMS Medieval Institute Publications, 2000.

Hoccleve, Thomas. *The Regiment of Princes.* Ed. Charles R. Blyth. Kalamazoo, MI: TEAMS Medieval Institute Publications, 1999.
 The Series. In *"My Compleinte" and Other Poems.* Ed. Roger Ellis. Liverpool: Liverpool University Press, 2001.
Homer. *The Iliad of Homer.* Trans. Richmond Lattimore. Chicago, IL: University of Chicago Press, 1951.
Hudson, Anne, ed. *Selections from English Wycliffite Writings.* Toronto: University of Toronto Press, 1997.
Isaac of Stella. *Epistola de anima* [Letter on the Soul]. In *Three Treatises on Man: A Cistercian Anthropology.* Trans. and ed. Bernard McGinn. Kalamazoo, MI: Cistercian Publications, 1977, 155–77.
Jacob's Well: An English Treatise of the Cleansing of Man's Conscience. Ed. Arthur Brandeis. Part 1. EETS o.s. 115. London: Kegan Paul, Trench, Trübner & Co., 1900.
Jean de la Rochelle. *Summa de Anima.* Ed. J. G. Bougerol. Textes philosophiques du moyen âge, 19. Paris: Vrin, 1995.
John of Salisbury. *Policraticus: Of the Frivolities of Courtiers and the Footprints of Philosophers.* Ed. Cary J. Nederman. Cambridge: Cambridge University Press, 1990.
Josephus, Flavius. *The Jewish War, Books V–VII.* Trans. H. St. J. Thackeray. Reprint. Cambridge, MA: Harvard University Press, 1997.
Kempe, Margery. *The Book of Margery Kempe.* Ed. Sanford Brown Meech and Hope Emily Allen. EETS o.s. 212. London: Oxford University Press, 1940.
Langland, William. *William Langland's the Vision of Piers Plowman: A Critical Edition of the B-Text Based on Trinity College Cambridge MS, B.15.17.* Ed. A. V. C. Schmidt. London: Everyman, 1995.
The Lanterne of Li3t. Ed. Lilian M. Swinburn. EETS o.s. 151. London: Kegan Paul, Trench, Trübner, 1917.
Lydgate, John. *John Lydgate's "Lives of Ss Edmund & Fremund" and the "Extra Miracles of St Edmund," Edited from British Library MS Harley 2278 and Bodleian Library MS Ashmole 46.* Ed. Anthony Bale and A. S. G. Edwards. Heidelberg: Universitatsverlag Winter, 2009.
 Troy Book. Ed. Henry Bergen. 3 Parts. EETS e.s. 97, e.s. 103, e.s. 106. London: Kegan Paul, Trench, Trübner, 1906, 1908, 1910.
Malory, Sir Thomas. *The Works of Sir Thomas Malory.* Ed. Eugène Vinaver and P. J. C. Field. 3 vols. Oxford: Oxford University Press, 1990.
Le Mesnagier de Paris. Ed. Georgine E. Brereton and Janet M. Ferrier, trans. and notes Karin Ueltschi, Lettres Gothiques. Paris: Livre de Poche, 1994.
The Middle-English Harrowing of Hell and Gospel of Nicodemus. Ed. William Henry Hulme. EETS e.s. 100. London: Oxford University Press, 1907.
The Northern Passion. Ed. Frances A. Foster. 2 vols. EETS o.s. 145 and 147. London: Kegan Paul, Trench, Trübner & Co., 1916.
D'Orléans, Lorens. *The Book of Vices and Virtues: A Fourteenth Century English Translation of the Somme Le Roi of Lorens d'Orleans.* Ed. W. Nelson Francis. EETS o.s. 217. London: Oxford University Press, 1942.

Oschinsky, Dorothea, ed. *Walter of Henley and Other Treatises on Estate Management and Accounting*. Oxford: Clarendon Press, 1971.
[Paston, Margaret.] "To John Paston I." In *Paston Letters and Papers of the Fifteenth Century*. Ed. Norman Davis. Oxford: Clarendon Press, 1971, 257.
Pecock, Reginald. *The Repressor of Over Much Blaming of the Clergy*. Vol. 1. Ed. Churchill Babington. London: Longman, Green, Longman, and Roberts, 1860.
Pilii, Tancredi, Gratiae libri de iudiciorum ordine. Ed. Friedrich Christian Bergmann. Gottingen: Apud Vandenhoeck et Ruprecht, 1842.
Robert of Brunne's Handlyng Synne. Ed. Frederick J. Furnivall. Part 1. EETS o.s. 119. London: Kegan Paul, Trench, Trübner & Co., 1901.
Sawles Warde. In *Medieval English Prose for Women: Selections from the Katherine Group and "Ancrene Wisse."* Ed. Bella Millett and Jocelyn Wogan-Browne. Oxford: Clarendon Press, 1990.
Scotus, John Duns. *Ordinatio*. In *Duns Scotus on the Will and Morality*. Trans. Allan B. Wolter. Bk. III, suppl. dist. 34. Washington, DC: Catholic University of America Press, 1986.
Select Cases from the Ecclesiastical Courts of the Province of Canterbury, c. 1200–1301. Ed. Norma Adams and Charles Donahue. London: Seldon Society, 1981.
Sidney, Sir Philip. *The Major Works*. Ed. Katherine Duncan-Jones. Oxford: Oxford University Press, 2009.
Siege of Jerusalem. Ed. Michael Livingston. Kalamazoo, MI: TEAMS Medieval Institute Publications, 2004.
The Song of Roland. Ed. Dorothy L. Sayers. Harmondsworth: Penguin, 1957.
The Statutes at Large from the Magna Carta to the End of the Reign of King Henry the Sixth. Vol. 1. Ed. Owen Ruffhead. London: Mark Baskett, 1769.
The Towneley Plays. Ed. Martin Stevens and A. C. Cawley. EETS s.s. 13 and 14. 2 vols. New York: Oxford University Press, 1994.
The Treatise On the Laws and Customs of the Realm of England Commonly Called Glanvill. Ed. G. D. G. Hall. London: Thomas Nelson and Sons, 1965.
Trevisa, John. *On the Properties of Things: John of Trevisa's Translation of Bartholomaeus Anglicus De Proprietatibus Rerum, A Critical Text*. Vol. 1. Ed. M. C. Seymour et al. Oxford: Clarendon Press, 1975.
Vinsauf, Geoffrey of. *Poetria Nova of Geoffrey of Vinsauf*. Trans. Margaret F. Nims. Toronto: Pontifical Institute of Mediaeval Studies, 1967.
Voragine, Jacobus de. *The Golden Legend*. Trans. William Granger Ryan. 2 vols. Princeton, NJ: Princeton University Press, 1993.
The Golden Legend of Jacobus de Voragine. Trans. Granger Ryan and Helmut Ripperger. 1969; Princeton, NJ: Princeton University Press, 2012.
William of Saint Thierry. *De natura corporis et animae* [The Nature of the Body and the Soul]. In *Three Treatises on Man: A Cistercian Anthropology*. Trans. and ed. Bernard McGinn. Kalamazoo, MI: Cistercian Publications, 1977, 103–52.

The York Corpus Christi Plays. Ed. Clifford Davidson. Kalamazoo, MI: TEAMS Medieval Institute Publications, 2011.

The York Plays: A Critical Edition of the York Corpus Christi Play as Recorded in British Library Additional MS 35290. Ed. Richard Beadle. 2 vols., EETS s.s. 23 and 24. New York and Oxford: Oxford University Press, 2009.

Secondary Sources

Agamben, Giorgio. *Homo Sacer: Sovereign Power and Bare Life*. Trans. Daniel Heller-Roazen. Stanford, CA: Stanford University Press, 1998.

Remnants of Auschwitz: The Witness and the Archive. Trans. Daniel Heller-Roazen. New York: Zone Books, 2000.

Ahmed, Sara. *The Cultural Politics of Emotion*. New York: Routledge, 2004.

"Happy Objects." In *The Affect Theory Reader*. Ed. Gregg and Seigworth, 29–51.

The Promise of Happiness. Durham, NC: Duke University Press, 2010.

Queer Phenomenology: Orientations, Objects, Others. Durham, NC: Duke University Press, 2006.

Airlie, Stuart. "The History of Emotions and Emotional History." *Early Medieval Europe* 10,2 (2001): 235–41.

Akbari, Suzanne Conklin. *Seeing Through the Veil: Optical Theory and Medieval Allegory*. Toronto: University of Toronto Press, 2004.

Althoff, Gerd. "*Ira Regis*: Prolegomena to a History of Royal Anger." In *Anger's Past*. Ed. Rosenwein, 59–74.

Altieri, Charles. *The Particulars of Rapture: An Aesthetics of the Affects*. Ithaca, NY: Cornell University Press, 2003.

Anderson, Earl R. "'Ein Kind wird geschlagen': The Meaning of Malory's Tale of the Healing of Sir Urry." *Literature and Psychology* 49,3 (2003): 45–74.

Armitage, Simon. *Sir Gawain and the Green Knight: A New Verse Translation*. New York: W. W. Norton, 2007.

Arthur, Ross G. "'Why Artow Angry': The Malice of Chaucer's Reeve." *English Studies in Canada* 13,1 (1987): 1–11.

Auerbach, Erich. "*Passio* as Passion (1941)." In *Time, History and Literature: Selected Essays of Erich Auerbach*. Ed. James I. Porter, trans. Jane O. Newman. Princeton, NJ: Princeton University Press, 2014, 165–87.

Bailey, Mark. *The English Manor, c. 1200–c. 1500*. Manchester: Manchester University Press, 2002.

Baldwin, John W. "The Intellectual Preparation for the Canon of 1215 Against Ordeals." *Speculum* 36,4 (1961): 613–36.

Bale, Anthony. *Feeling Persecuted: Christians, Jews and Images of Violence in the Middle Ages*. London: Reaktion Books, 2010.

Barney, Stephen A. "Chaucer's Lists." In *The Wisdom of Poetry: Essays in Early English Literature in Honor of Morton W. Bloomfield*. Ed. Larry D. Benson and Siegfried Wenzel. Kalamazoo, MI: Medieval Institute Publications, 1982, 189–223.

Barthes, Roland. *A Lover's Discourse: Fragments.* Trans. Richard Howard. New York: Hill and Wang, 1978.
Barton, Richard E. "Gendering Anger: *Ira, Furor*, and Discourses of Power and Masculinity in the Eleventh and Twelfth Centuries." In *In The Garden of Evil: The Vices and Culture in the Middle Ages.* Ed. Richard Newhauser. Toronto: Pontifical Institute of Mediaeval Studies, 2005, 371–92.
Bawcutt, Priscilla. *Gavin Douglas: A Critical Study.* Edinburgh: Edinburgh University Press, 1976.
Beadle, Richard. "'Devoute ymaginacioun' and the Dramatic Sense in Love's *Mirror* and the N-Town Plays." In *Nicholas Love at Waseda.* Ed. Shoichi Oguro, Richard Beadle, and Michael G. Sargent. Cambridge: D. S. Brewer, 1997, 1–17.
Beckwith, Sarah. *Christ's Body: Identity, Culture and Society in Late Medieval Writings.* New York and London: Routledge, 1993.
  "Ritual, Theater, and Social Space in the York Corpus Christi Cycle." In *Bodies and Disciplines: Intersections of Literature and History in Fifteenth-Century England.* Ed. Barbara A. Hanawalt and David Wallace. Minneapolis, MN: University of Minnesota Press, 1996, 63–86.
  Signifying God: Social Relation and Symbolic Act in the York Corpus Christi Plays. Chicago, IL and London: University of Chicago Press, 2001.
Beidler, Peter G. "Transformations in Gower's Tale of Florent and Chaucer's Wife of Bath's Tale." In *Chaucer and Gower: Difference, Mutuality, Exchange.* Ed. R. F. Yeager. Victoria, BC: University of Victoria, 1991, 100–14.
Belknap, Robert E. *The List: The Uses and Pleasures of Cataloguing.* New Haven, CT: Yale University Press, 2004.
Belting, Hans. *An Anthropology of Images: Picture, Medium, Body.* Trans. Thomas Dunlap. Princeton, NJ: Princeton University Press, 2011.
Bennett, H. S. *Life on the English Manor: A Study of Peasant Conditions, 1150–1400.* Cambridge: Cambridge University Press, 1962.
Bennett, J. A. W. *Chaucer at Oxford and at Cambridge.* Oxford: Oxford University Press, 1974.
Bennett, Jane. *Vibrant Matter: A Political Ecology of Things.* Durham, NC: Duke University Press, 2010.
Berlant, Lauren. "About." *Supervalent Thought* (blog). https://supervalentthought.com/about/.
  "Cruel Optimism." In *Affect Theory Reader.* Ed. Gregg and Seigworth, 93–117.
  Cruel Optimism. Durham, NC: Duke University Press, 2011.
  The Female Complaint: The Unfinished Business of Sentimentality in American Culture. Durham, NC: Duke University Press, 2008.
Bernau, Anke. "Enlisting Truth." *Style* (Special issue: Lists) 50,3 (2016): 261–79.
  "Feeling Thinking: *Pearl*'s Ekphrastic Imagination." In *The Art of Vision: Ekphrasis in Medieval Literature and Culture.* Ed. Andrew James Johnston, Ethan Knapp, and Margitta Rouse. Columbus, OH: Ohio State University Press, 2015, 100–23.

Biernoff, Suzannah. *Sight and Embodiment in the Middle Ages*. Basingstoke: Palgrave Macmillan, 2002.
Biller, Peter. "A 'Scientific' View of Jews from Paris around 1300." *Micrologus: Natura, Scienze e Societá Medievali* 9 (2001): 137–68.
  "Proto-Racial Thought in Medieval Science." In *The Origins of Racism in the West*. Ed. Miriam Eliav-Feldon, Benjamin Isaac, and Joseph Ziegler. New York: Cambridge University Press, 2009, 157–80.
Bishop, Louise. "'Of Goddes pryvetee nor of his wyf': Confusion of Orifices in Chaucer's Miller's Tale." *Texas Studies in Language and Literature* 44,3 (2002): 231–46.
Blamires, Alcuin. "Chaucer the Reactionary: Ideology and the General Prologue to *The Canterbury Tales*." *Review of English Studies* n.s. 51,204 (2000): 523–39.
Bowers, John M. "Thomas Hoccleve and the Politics of Tradition." *Chaucer Review* 36,4 (2002): 352–69.
Boyd, David Lorenzo. "Reading through the *Regiment of Princes*: Hoccleve's *Series* and Lydgate's *Dance of Death* in Yale Beinecke MS 493." *Fifteenth-Century Studies* 20 (1993): 15–34.
Braidotti, Rosi. *Nomadic Subjects: Embodiment and Sexual Difference in Contemporary Feminist Theory*. New York: Columbia University Press, 1983; 2011.
  Nomadic Theory: The Portable Rosi Braidotti. New York: Columbia University Press, 2011.
Breen, Katharine. *Imagining an English Reading Public, 1150–1400*. Cambridge: Cambridge University Press, 2010.
Brennan, Teresa. *The Transmission of Affect*. Ithaca, NY: Cornell University Press, 2004.
Brown, Matthew Clifton. "'Lo, Heer the Fourme': Hoccleve's *Series*, Formulary, and Bureaucratic Textuality." *Exemplaria* 23,1 (2011): 27–49.
Burger, Glenn. *Chaucer's Queer Nation*. Minneapolis, MN: Minnesota University Press, 2003.
  Conduct Becoming: Good Wives and Husbands in the Later Middle Ages. Philadelphia, PA: University of Pennsylvania Press, 2017.
Burnley, J. D. *Chaucer's Language and the Philosophers' Tradition*. Totowa, NJ: Rowman and Littlefield, 1979.
Burrow, J. A. "Autobiographical Poetry in the Middle Ages: The Case of Thomas Hoccleve." *Publications of the British Academy [1982]* 68 (1983): 389–412.
  Thomas Hoccleve. Aldershot: Variorum, 1994.
  "Versions of 'Manliness' in the Poetry of Chaucer, Langland, and Hoccleve." *Chaucer Review* 47,3 (2013): 337–42.
Butler, Judith. *Bodies That Matter: On the Discursive Limits of "Sex."* New York: Routledge, 1993.
  Undoing Gender. London: Routledge, 2004.
Bynum, Caroline Walker. *Christian Materiality: An Essay on Religion in Late Medieval Europe*. New York: Zone Books, 2011.

Holy Feast and Holy Fast: The Religious Significance of Food to Medieval Women. Berkeley, CA: University of California Press, 1987.
Camille, Michael. *The Gothic Idol: Ideology and Image-Making in Medieval Art.* Cambridge: Cambridge University Press, 1989.
Campana, Joseph. "On Not Defending Poetry: Spenser, Suffering, and the Energy of Affect." *PMLA* 120,1 (2005): 33–48.
Camelot. R. J. Lerner and Frederick Loewe, dir. Joshua Logan. Hollywood: Warner, 1967.
Campbell, Bruce M. S. *English Seigniorial Agriculture, 1250–1450.* Cambridge: Cambridge University Press, 2006.
  "The Livestock of Chaucer's Reeve: Fact or Fiction?" In *The Salt of Common Life: Individuality and Choice in the Medieval Town, Countryside, and Church.* Ed. Edwin Brezette DeWindt. Kalamazoo, MI: Medieval Institute, 1995, 271–305.
Campbell, Mary B. *The Witness and the Other World: Exotic European Travel Writing, 400–1600.* Ithaca, NY: Cornell University Press, 1988.
Cannon, Christopher. "Proverbs and the Wisdom of Literature: *The Proverbs of Alfred* and Chaucer's *Tale of Melibee*." *Textual Practice* 24,3 (2010): 407–34.
Carruthers, Mary. "On Affliction and Reading, Weeping and Argument: Chaucer's Lachrymose Troilus in Context." *Representations* 93,1 (2006): 1–21.
Carter, Susan. "Coupling the Beastly Bride and the Hunter Hunted: What Lies Behind Chaucer's *Wife of Bath's Tale*." *Chaucer Review* 37,4 (2003): 329–45.
Cixous, Hélène. *Love Itself in the Letterbox.* Trans. Peggy Kamuf. London: Polity, 2008.
Clough, Patricia Ticineto. "Introduction." In *The Affective Turn.* Ed. Clough and Halley, 1–33.
Clough, Patricia Ticineto, and Jean Halley, eds. *The Affective Turn: Theorizing the Social.* Durham, NC: Duke University Press, 2007.
Cohen, Jeremy. *The Friars and the Jews: The Evolution of Medieval Anti-Judaism.* Ithaca, NY: Cornell University Press, 1982.
Cooke, John Daniel. "Euhemerism: A Medieval Interpretation of Classical Paganism." *Speculum* 2,4 (1927): 396–410.
Cooper, Lisa H. "The Poetics of Practicality." In *Middle English: Oxford Twenty-First Century Approaches to Literature.* Ed. Paul Strohm. Oxford: Oxford University Press 2007 (hardback), 491–505.
Copeland, Rita. "*Pathos* and Pastoralism: Aristotle's *Rhetoric* in Medieval England." *Speculum* 89,1 (2013): 96–127.
Crocker, Holly A. "Affective Politics in Chaucer's *Reeve's Tale*: 'Cherl' Masculinity after 1381." *Studies in the Age of Chaucer* 29 (2007): 225–58.
  "Communal Conscience in William Tyndale's *Obedience of a Christian Man*." *Exemplaria* (Special issue: *Conscience and Contestation, Langland to Milton.* Ed. Paul Strohm) 24,1 & 2 (2012): 143–60.

"Introduction: The Provocative Body of the Fabliaux." In *Comic Provocations: Exposing the Corpus of Old French Fabliaux*. Ed. Crocker. New York: Palgrave Macmillan, 2006, 1–14.

"John Foxe's Chaucer: Affecting Form in Post-Historicist Criticism," *New Medieval Literatures* 15 (2015 for 2013): 149–82.

"Medieval Affects Now." *Exemplaria* 29,1 (2017): 82–98.

Cross, Richard. *Duns Scotus*. New York: Oxford University Press, 1999.

Cubitt, Catherine. "The History of the Emotions: A Debate." *Early Medieval Europe* 10,2 (2001): 225–7.

Cunningham, J. V. *Tradition and Poetic Structure: Essays in Literary History and Criticism*. Denver, CO: Alan Swallow, 1960.

Cushman, Stephen, gen. ed. *The Princeton Encyclopedia of Poetry and Poetics*, 4th edn. Princeton, NJ: Princeton University Press, 2012.

Davidson, Clifford. "Introduction." In *The York Corpus Christi Plays*. Ed. Davidson. Kalamazoo, MI: TEAMS Medieval Institute Publications, 2011.

Davis, Isabel. "Cutaneous Time in the Late Medieval Literary Imagination." In *Reading Skin in Medieval Literature and Culture*. Ed. Katie L. Walter. New York: Palgrave Macmillan, 2013, 99–118.

Writing Masculinity in the Later Middle Ages. Cambridge: Cambridge University Press, 2007.

Davis, Norman. "The *Litera Troili* and English Letters." *Review of English Studies* 16,63 (1965): 233–44.

D'Avray, David. "The Gospel of the Marriage Feast of Cana and Marriage Preaching in France." In *The Bible and The Medieval World: Essays in Memory of Beryl Smalley*. Ed. Katherine Walsh and Diana Wood. Oxford: Blackwells, 1985, 207–24.

Medieval Marriage: Symbolism and Society. Oxford: Oxford University Press, 2015.

D'Avray, David, and M. Tausche. "Marriage Sermons in *ad status* Collections of the Central Middle Ages." *Archives d'histoire doctrinale et littéraire du moyen age* 47 (1981): 71–119.

Delony, Mikee. "Alisoun's Aging, Hearing-Impaired Female Body: Gazing at the Wife of Bath in Chaucer's *Canterbury Tales*." In *The Treatment of Disabled Persons in Medieval Europe: Examining Disability in the Historical, Legal, Literary, Medical, and Religious Discourses of the Middle Ages*. Ed. Wendy J. Turner and Tory Vandeventer Pearman. Lewiston, NY: Mellen, 2011, 313–45.

Delumeau, Jean. *La Peur en Occident, XIVe–XVIIIe siècle: Une cité assiégée*. Paris: Fayard, 1978.

Denholm-Young, Noël. *Seigniorial Administration in England*. New York: Barnes and Noble, 1964.

Derrida, Jacques. *Demeure: Fiction and Testimony*. Trans. Elizabeth Rottenburg. Stanford, CA: Stanford University Press, 2000.

Dinshaw, Carolyn. *Chaucer's Sexual Poetics*. Madison, WI: University of Wisconsin Press, 1990.

Dinzelbacher, Peter. *Angst im Mittelalter: Teufels-, Todes- und Gotteserfahrung; Mentalitätsgeschichte und Ikonographie.* Paderborn: F. Schöningh, 1996.

Dixon, Thomas. *From Passions to Emotions: The Creation of a Secular Psychological Category.* Cambridge: Cambridge University Press, 2003.

Donahue, Charles, Jr. "The Canon Law on the Formation of Marriage and Social Practice in the Later Middle Ages." *Journal of Family History* 8 (1983): 144–58.

  Law, Marriage, and Society in the Later Middle Ages: Arguments about Marriage in Five Courts. New York: Cambridge University Press, 2007.

  "Proof by Witnesses in the Church Courts of Medieval England: An Imperfect Reception of the Learned Law." In *On the Laws and Customs of England: Essays in Honor of Samuel E. Thorne.* Ed. Morris S. Arnold, Thomas A. Green, Sally A. Scully, and Stephen D. White. Chapel Hill, NC: University of North Carolina Press, 1981.

Dryden, John. "Passions, Affections, and Emotions: Methodological Difficulties in Reconstructing Aquinas's Philosophical Psychology." *Literature Compass* 13,6 (2016): 343–50.

Dryden, John. *The Poems.* Vol. 4. Ed. James Kinsley. Oxford: Clarendon Press, 1958.

Eco, Umberto. *The Infinity of Lists.* Trans. Alastair McEwen. London: MacLehose Press, 2009.

[Edsall, Mary Agnes.] "Affective Piety." Wikipedia, The Free Encyclopedia. Accessed January 25, 2017. https://en.wikipedia.org/wiki/Affective_ piety.

Edwards, Elizabeth. "The Economics of Justice in Chaucer's Miller's and Reeve's Tales." *Dalhousie Review* 82 (2002): 91–112.

Elliott, Dyan. "Rubber Soul: Theology, Hagiography, and the Spirit World of the High Middle Ages." In *From Beasts to Souls: Gender and Embodiment in Medieval Europe.* Ed. E. Jane Burns and Peggy McCracken. Notre Dame, IN: University of Notre Dame Press, 2013, 89–120.

Enterline, Lynn. *Shakespeare's Schoolroom: Rhetoric, Discipline, Emotion.* Philadelphia, PA: University of Pennsylvania Press, 2012.

Farrell, William J. "Chaucer's Use of the Catalogue." *Texas Studies in Literature and Language* 5,1 (1963): 64–78.

Fox, Denton. "The Scottish Chaucerians." In *Chaucer and Chaucerians: Critical Studies in Middle English Literature.* Ed. D. S. Brewer. London: Thomas Nelson and Sons, 1966. 164–200.

Fox, Robin Lane. *The Unauthorized Version: Truth and Fiction in the Bible.* London: Penguin, 1992.

Fradenburg, L. O. Aranye. "Beauty and Boredom in *The Legend of Good Women.*" *Exemplaria* 22,1 (2010): 65–83.

Freedberg, David. *The Power of Images: Studies in the History and Theory of Response.* Chicago, IL: University of Chicago Press, 1989.

Frisch, Andrea. "The Ethics of Testimony: A Genealogical Perspective." *Discourse* 25,1 & 2 (2003): 36–54.

Galloway, Andrew. "The Account Book and the Treasure: Gilbert Maghfeld's Textual Economy and the Poetics of Mercantile Accounting in Ricardian Literature." *Studies in the Age of Chaucer* 33 (2011): 65–124.

"Alliterative Poetry in Old Jerusalem: The *Siege of Jerusalem* and its Sources." In *Medieval Alliterative Poetry: Essays in Honour of Thorlac Turville-Petre*. Ed. John A. Burrow and Hoyt N. Duggan. Dublin: Four Courts Press, 2010, 85–106.

Gaunt, Simon. *Gender and Genre in Medieval French Literature*. Cambridge: Cambridge University Press, 1995.

Gayk, Shannon. *Image, Text, and Religious Reform in Fifteenth-Century England*. Cambridge: Cambridge University Press, 2010.

George, R. L. P., and M. Dorothy. "Verses on the Exchequer in the Fifteenth Century." *English Historical Review* 36,141 (1921): 58–67.

Gibson, Gail McMurray. *The Theater of Devotion: East Anglian Drama and Society in the Late Middle Ages*. Chicago, IL: University of Chicago Press, 1989.

Goldie, Matthew Boyd. "Psychosomatic Illness and Identity in London, 1416–1421: Hoccleve's *Complaint* and *Dialogue with a Friend*." *Exemplaria* 11,1 (1999): 23–52.

Goldin, Simha. *The Ways of Jewish Martyrdom*. Trans. Yigal Levin, ed. C. Michael Copeland. Turnhout: Brepols, 2008.

Gourlay, Kristi. "A Pugnacious Pagan Princess: Aggressive Female Anger and Violence in *Fierabras*." In *The Representation of Women's Emotions*. Ed. Perfetti, 133–63.

Gray, Douglas. "Gavin Douglas." In *A Companion to Medieval Scottish Poetry*. Ed. Priscilla Bawcutt and Janet Hadley Williams. Cambridge: D. S. Brewer, 2006, 149–64.

Green, Richard Firth. *A Crisis of Truth: Literature and Law in Ricardian England*. Philadelphia, PA: University of Pennsylvania Press, 1999.

Greetham, D. C. "Self-Referential Artifacts: Hoccleve's Persona as a Literary Device." *Modern Philology* 86,3 (1989): 242–52.

Gregg, Melissa, and Gregory J. Seigworth. "An Inventory of Shimmers." In *The Affect Theory Reader*. Ed. Gregg and Seigworth, 1–29.

Gregg, Melissa, and Gregory J. Seigworth, eds. *The Affect Theory Reader*. Durham, NC: Duke University Press, 2010.

Grosz, Elizabeth. *Volatile Bodies: Toward a Corporeal Feminism*. Bloomington, IN: Indiana University Press, 1994.

Hamel, Mary. "*The Siege of Jerusalem* as a Crusading Poem." In *Journeys Toward God: Pilgrimage and Crusade*. Ed. Barbara N. Sargent-Baur. Kalamazoo, MI: TEAMS Medieval Institute Publications, 1992, 177–94.

Hanna, Ralph. *London Literature, 1300–1380*. New York: Cambridge University Press, 2005.

Hanna, Ralph, and David Lawton. "Introduction." In *The Siege of Jerusalem*. Ed. Hanna and Lawton. EETS o.s. 320. New York: Oxford University Press, 2003, xiii–xcix.

Hansen, Elaine Tuttle. *Chaucer and the Fictions of Gender*. Berkeley, CA: University of California Press, 1992.

Harbus, Antonina. *Cognitive Approaches to Old English Poetry*. Cambridge: D. S. Brewer, 2012.

Hardt, Michael. "Foreword: What Affects Are Good For." In *The Affective Turn*. Ed. Clough and Halley, ix–xiii.
Harvey, Elizabeth D. *Ventriloquized Voices: Feminist Theory and English Renaissance Texts*. London: Routledge, 1995.
Harvey, E. Ruth. *The Inward Wits: Psychological Theory in the Middle Ages and the Renaissance*. London: Warburg Institute, 1975.
Hasler, Antony. "Hoccleve's Unregimented Body." *Paragraph* 13 (1990): 164–83.
Hebron, Malcolm. *The Medieval Siege: Theme and Image in Middle English Romance*. Oxford: Clarendon Press, 1997.
Helmholz, R. H. *The Oxford History of the Laws of England*, Vol. 1: *The Canon Law and Ecclesiastical Jurisdiction from 597 to the 1640s*. New York: Oxford University Press, 2004.
Highmore, Ben. "'Bitter After Taste': Affect, Food and Social Aesthetics." In *The Affect Theory Reader*. Ed. Gregg and Seigworth, 118–37.
Hoffmann, Tobias. "Henry of Ghent's Voluntarist Account of Weakness of Will." In *Weakness of Will from Plato to the Present*. Ed. Hoffmann. Washington, DC: Catholic University of America Press, 2011, 115–37.
Hogan, Patrick Colm. *What Literature Teaches Us about Emotion*. Cambridge: Cambridge University Press, 2011.
Holdsworth, William Searle. *A History of English Law*. Vol. 1. London: Methuen, 1903.
Holsinger, Bruce. *The Premodern Condition: Medievalism and the Making of Theory*. Chicago, IL: University of Chicago Press, 2005.
Homan, Richard L. "Mixed Feelings about Violence in the Corpus Christi Plays." In *Violence in Drama*. Ed. James Redmond. New York: Cambridge University Press, 1991, 93–100.
Horner, Olga. "'Us must make lies': Witness, Evidence, and Proof in the York *Resurrection*." *Medieval English Theatre* 20 (1998): 24–76.
Howe, Nicholas. *The Old English Catalogue Poems*. Copenhagen: Rosenkilde and Bagger, 1985.
Howell, Martha. *The Marriage Exchange: Property, Social Place, and Gender in Cities of the Low Countries, 1300–1550*. Chicago, IL: University of Chicago Press, 2009.
  "The Properties of Marriage in Late Medieval Europe: Commercial Wealth and the Creation of Modern Marriage." In *Love, Marriage, and Family Ties in the Later Middle Ages*. Ed. Isabel Davis, Miriam Muller, and Sarah Rees Jones. Turnhout: Brepols, 2003, 17–61.
Hume, Cathy. *Chaucer and the Cultures of Love and Marriage*. Cambridge: D. S. Brewer, 2012.
Hutson, Lorna. *The Invention of Suspicion: Law and Mimesis in Shakespeare and Renaissance Drama*. Oxford: Oxford University Press, 2007.
Hyams, Paul R. *Rancor and Reconciliation in Medieval England*. Ithaca, NY: Cornell University Press, 2003.
  "What Did Henry III of England Think in Bed and in French about Kingship and Anger?" In *Anger's Past*. Ed. Rosenwein, 92–124.

Jameson, Fredric. *The Antinomies of Realism*. London: Verso, 2013.
Johnson, Eleanor. *Practicing Literary Theory in the Middle Ages: Ethics and the Mixed Form in Chaucer, Gower, Usk, and Hoccleve*. Chicago, IL: University of Chicago Press, 2013.
Johnston, Andrew James, and Margitta Rouse. "Facing the Mirror: Ekphrasis, Vision, and Knowledge in Gavin Douglas's *Palice of Honour*." In *The Art of Vision*. Ed. Johnston, Knapp, and Rouse, 166–83.
Jones, Malcolm. *The Secret Middle Ages: Discovering the Real Medieval World*. Stroud: Sutton, 2002.
Karnes, Michelle. *Imagination, Meditation, and Cognition in the Middle Ages*. Chicago, IL: University of Chicago Press, 2011.
Kiernan, Kevin S. "The Art of the Descending Catalogue, and a Fresh Look at Alisoun." *Chaucer Review* 10,1 (1975): 1–16.
King, Pamela M. "Contemporary Cultural Models for the Trial Plays in the York Cycle." In *Drama and Community: People and Plays in Medieval Europe*. Ed. Alan Hindley. Turnhout: Brepols, 1999, 200–16.
  The York Mystery Cycle and the Worship of the City. Woodbridge, Suffolk and New York: D. S. Brewer, 2006.
King, Peter. "Emotions in Medieval Thought." In *The Oxford Handbook of Philosophy of Emotion*. Ed. Peter Goldie. New York: Oxford University Press, 2010, 167–87.
Kinneavy, Gerald B. "The Poet in *The Palice of Honour*." *Chaucer Review* 3,4 (1969): 280–303.
Knapp, Ethan. *The Bureaucratic Muse: Thomas Hoccleve and the Literature of Late Medieval England*. College Park, PA: Pennsylvania State University Press, 2001.
Knuuttila, Simo. *Emotions in Ancient and Medieval Philosophy*. New York: Oxford University Press, 2004.
Kohanski, Tamarah. "In Search of Malyne." *Chaucer Review* 27,3 (1993): 228–38.
Konstan, David. *Pity Transformed*. London: Duckworth, 2001.
Kratzmann, Gregory. *Anglo-Scottish Literary Relations, 1430–1550*. Cambridge: Cambridge University Press, 1980.
Kruger, Steven. *Dreaming in the Middle Ages*. Cambridge: Cambridge University Press, 1992.
  The Spectral Jew: Conversion and Embodiment in Medieval Europe. Minneapolis, MN: University of Minnesota Press, 2006.
Lacan, Jacques. "Seminar on 'The Purloined Letter.'" Trans. Jeffrey Mehlman. *Yale French Studies* 48 (1972): 39–72.
Lacey, Helen. *The Royal Pardon: Access to Mercy in Fourteenth-Century England*. York: York Medieval Press, 2009.
Lambdin, Laura C., and Robert T. Lambdin. "The Millere Was a Stout Carl for the Nones." In Lambdin and Lambdin, eds. *Chaucer's Pilgrims: An Historical Guide to the Pilgrims in the Canterbury Tales*. Westport, CT: Praeger, 1996, 271–80.
Lampert, Lisa. *Gender and Jewish Difference from Paul to Shakespeare*. Philadelphia, PA: University of Pennsylvania Press, 2004.

Larrington, Carolyne. "The Psychology of Emotion and Study of the Medieval Period." *Early Medieval Europe* 10,2 (2001): 251–6.
Latour, Bruno. *Reassembling the Social: An Introduction to Actor-Network Theory*. Oxford: Oxford University Press, 2005.
Lavezzo, Kathy. "Sobs and Sighs between Women: The Homoerotics of Compassion in *The Book of Margery Kempe*." In *Premodern Sexualities*. Ed. Louise Fradenburg and Carla Freccero. New York: Routledge, 1996, 175–98.
Lawton, Lesley. "The Illustration of Late Medieval Secular Texts, with Special Reference to Lydgate's *Troy Book*." In *Manuscripts and Readers in Fifteenth-Century England: The Literary Implications of Manuscript Study*. Ed. Derek Pearsall. Cambridge: D. S. Brewer, 1983, 41–69.
Lewis, C. S. *English Literature in the Sixteenth Century Excluding Drama*. Oxford: Clarendon Press, 1954.
Lewis, Robert E. et al., eds. *Middle English Dictionary*. Ann Arbor, MI: University of Michigan Press, 2001. Abbreviated to *MED*.
Lipton, Emma. *Affections of the Mind: The Politics of Sacramental Marriage in Late Medieval English Literature*. Notre Dame, IN: University of Notre Dame Press, 2007.
Little, Lester K. "Anger in Monastic Curses." In *Anger's Past*. Ed. Rosenwein, 9–35.
Loomis, Laura Hibbard. "'Sir Thopas': X. The Catalogue Lists, Nos. 88–100." In *Sources and Analogues of Chaucer's "Canterbury Tales"*. Ed. W. F. Bryan and Germaine Dempster. Chicago, IL: University of Chicago Press, 1941, 486–589.
Loughlin, Stephen. "The Complexity and Importance of *timor* in Aquinas's *Summa Theologiae*." In *Fear and Its Representations*. Ed. Scott and Kosso, 1–16.
Love, Heather. *Feeling Backward: Loss and the Politics of Queer History*. Cambridge, MA: Harvard University Press, 2007.
Lynch, Andrew. *Malory's Book of Arms: The Narrative of Combat in "Le Morte Darthur"*. Cambridge: D. S. Brewer, 1997.
  "'Manly Cowardyse': Thomas Hoccleve's Peace Strategy." *Medium Aevum* 73,2 (2004): 306–23.
Macnair, Mike. "Vicinage and the Antecedents of the Jury." *Law and History Review* 17,3 (1999): 537–90.
Malo, Robyn. "Penitential Discourse in Hoccleve's *Series*." *Studies in the Age of Chaucer* 34 (2012): 277–305.
Marks, Richard. *Image and Devotion in Late Medieval England*. Stroud: Sutton, 2004.
Martin, Joanna M. "Responses to the Frame Narrative of John Gower's *Confessio Amantis* in Fifteenth- and Sixteenth-Century Literature." *Review of English Studies* 60,246 (2009): 561–77.
Martin, Loy D. "History and Form in the General Prologue to the Canterbury Tales." *ELH* 45,1 (1978): 1–17.

Massumi, Brian. "The Future Birth of the Affective Fact: The Political Ontology of Threat." In *The Affect Theory Reader*. Ed. Gregg and Seigworth, 52–70.
  Parables for the Virtual: Movement, Affect, Sensation. Durham, NC: Duke University Press, 2002.
McCarthy, Conor. *Marriage in Medieval England: Law, Literature and Practice*. Woodbridge, Suffolk: Boydell Press, 2004.
McDonald, Richard B. "The Reve Was a Sclendre Colerik Man." In *Chaucer's Pilgrims*. Ed. Lambdin and Lambdin, 288–99.
McIntosh, Marjorie K. *Controlling Misbehavior in England, 1370–1600*. Cambridge: Cambridge University Press, 1998.
  "Finding Language for Misconduct: Jurors in Fifteenth-Century Local Courts." In *Bodies and Disciplines: Intersections of Literature and History in Fifteenth-Century England*. Ed. Barbara A. Hanawalt and David Wallace. Minneapolis, MN: University of Minnesota Press, 1996, 88–122.
McLeod, Glenda. *Virtue and Venom: Catalogs of Women from Antiquity to the Renaissance*. Ann Arbor, MI: University of Michigan Press, 1991.
McNamer, Sarah. *Affective Meditation and the Invention of Medieval Compassion*. Philadelphia, PA: University of Pennsylvania Press, 2010.
  "Feeling." In *Middle English: Oxford Twenty-First Century Approaches to Literature*. Ed. Paul Strohm. Oxford: Oxford University Press, 2009 (paperback), 241–57.
  "The Literariness of Literature and the History of Emotion." *PMLA* 130,5 (2015): 1433–42.
McSheffrey, Shannon. "Jurors, Respectable Masculinity, and Christian Morality: A Comment on Marjorie McIntosh's *Controlling Misbehavior*." *Journal of British Studies* 37,3 (1998): 269–78.
  Marriage, Sex, and Civic Culture in Late Medieval London. Philadelphia, PA: University of Pennsylvania Press, 2006.
Mead, Jenna. "Chaucer and the Subject of Bureaucracy." *Exemplaria* 19,1 (2007): 39–66.
Meecham-Jones, Simon. "'He In Salte Teres Dreynte': Understanding Troilus's Tears." In *Emotions and War: Medieval to Romantic Literature*. Ed. Stephanie Downes, Andrew Lynch, and Katrina O'Loughlin. New York: Palgrave Macmillan, 2015, 77–97.
Meyer, Michel. *Le Philosophe et les passions: Esquisse d'une histoire de la nature humaine*. Paris: Hachette, 1991.
Mills, Robert. *Suspended Animation: Pain, Pleasure and Punishment in Medieval Culture*. London: Reaktion Books, 2005.
Miner, Robert. *Thomas Aquinas on the Passions: A Study of "Summa Theologiae" 1a2ae 22–48*. Cambridge: Cambridge University Press, 2009.
Mitnick, John Marshall. "From Neighbor-Witness to Judge of Proofs: The Transformation of the English Civil Juror." *American Journal of Legal History* 32,3 (1988): 201–35.

Moe, Phyllis. "Introduction." In *The ME Prose Translation of Roger d'Argenteuil's Bible en François*. Ed. Moe. Middle English Texts 6. Heidelberg: Carl Winter, 1977.
Morris, Andrew Jeffrey. "Representing the Countryside in Fourteenth-Century England." PhD Diss. University of Minnesota, 2005.
Mueller, Alex. "Corporal Terror: Critiques of Imperialism in *The Siege of Jerusalem*." *Philological Quarterly* 84,3 (Summer 2005): 287–310.
Muir, C. D. "Bride or Bridegroom? Masculine Identity in Mystic Marriages." In *Holiness and Masculinity in the Middle Ages*. Ed. P. H. Cullum and Katherine J. Lewis. Toronto: University of Toronto Press, 2004, 58–78.
Murray, Alexander. *Suicide in the Middle Ages*, Vol. 2: *The Curse on Self-Murder*. New York: Oxford University Press, 2000.
Murray, Jacqueline. "One Flesh, Two Sexes, Three Genders?" In *Gender and Christianity in Medieval Europe: New Perspectives*. Ed. Lisa M. Bitel and Felice Lifshitz. Philadelphia, PA: University of Pennsylvania Press, 2008, 34–51.
Mussetter, Sally. "The York Pilate and the Seven Deadly Sins," *Neuphilologische Mitteilungen* 81 (1980): 57–64.
Newhauser, Richard. "Introduction: Cultural Construction and the Vices." In *The Seven Deadly Sins: From Communities to Individuals*. Ed. Newhauser. Leiden: Brill, 2007, 1–17.
Newton, Esther. *Mother Camp: Female Impersonators in America*. Chicago, IL: University of Chicago Press, 1972.
Ngai, Sianne. *Our Aesthetic Categories: Zany, Cute, Interesting*. Cambridge, MA: Harvard University Press, 2015.
Ugly Feelings. Cambridge, MA: Harvard University Press, 2005.
Nicholson, Roger. "Haunted Itineraries: Reading *The Siege of Jerusalem*." *Exemplaria* 14,2 (2002): 447–84.
"The Trial of Christ the Sorcerer in the York Cycle." *Journal of Medieval and Renaissance Studies* 16,2 (1986): 125–69.
Nisse, Ruth. *Defining Acts: Drama and the Politics of Interpretation in Late Medieval England*. Notre Dame, IN: University of Notre Dame Press, 2005.
"'Oure Fadres Olde and Modres': Gender, Heresy, and Hoccleve's Literary Politics." *Studies in the Age of Chaucer* 21 (1999): 275–99.
Nowlin, Steele. *Chaucer, Gower, and the Affect of Invention*. Columbus, OH: Ohio State University Press, 2016.
"The Legend of Good Women and the Affect of Invention." *Exemplaria* 25,1 (2013): 16–35.
Olson, Paul A. "'The Reeve's Tale': Chaucer's 'Measure for Measure.'" *Studies in Philology* 59,1 (1962): 1–17.
O'Neill, Rosemary. "Counting Sheep in the C Text of *Piers Plowman*." *Yearbook of Langland Studies* 29 (2015): 89–116.
Owst, G. R. *Literature and Pulpit in Medieval England*. Cambridge: Cambridge University Press, 1933.

Parker, R. H. "Accounting in Chaucer's *Canterbury Tales.*" *Accounting, Auditing, & Accountability Journal* 12,1 (1999): 92–112.

Parkinson, David. "The Farce of Modesty in Gavin Douglas's *The Palis of Honoure.*" *Philological Quarterly* 70,1 (1991): 13–26.

  "Introduction." In *Gavin Douglas: The Palis of Honoure.* Ed. Parkinson. Kalamazoo, MI: TEAMS Medieval Institute Publications, 1992, 1–14.

  "Mobbing Scenes in Middle Scots Verse: Holland, Douglas, Dunbar." *Journal of English and Germanic Philology* 85,4 (1986): 494–509.

Pasnau, Robert. *Thomas Aquinas on Human Nature: A Philosophical Study of Summa Theologiae 1a 75–89.* Cambridge: Cambridge University Press, 2002.

Paster, Gail Kern. *The Body Embarrassed: Drama and the Disciplines of Shame in Early Modern England.* Ithaca, NY: Cornell University Press, 1993.

Patterson, Lee. *Negotiating the Past: The Historical Understanding of Medieval Literature.* Madison, WI: University of Wisconsin Press, 1987.

  "'What is Me?': Self and Society in the Poetry of Thomas Hoccleve." *Studies in the Age of Chaucer* 23 (2001): 437–70.

Pearman, Tory Vandeventer. "Disruptive Dames: Disability and the Loathly Lady in the *Tale of Florent*, the *Wife of Bath's Tale*, and the *Weddynge of Sir Gawain and Dame Ragnelle.*" In *The Treatment of Disabled Persons in Medieval Europe: Examining Disability in the Historical, Legal, Literary, Medical, and Religious Discourses.* Ed. Wendy J. Turner and Pearman. Lewiston, NY: Mellen, 2011, 291–312.

Peikola, Matti. "The Catalogue: A Late Middle English Lollard Genre?" In *Discourse Perspectives on English: Medieval to Modern.* Ed. Risto Hiltunen and Janne Skaffari. Amsterdam: John Benjamins, 2003, 105–35.

Pender, Stephen. "Subventing Disease: Anger, Passions, and the Non-Naturals." In *Rhetorics of Bodily Disease and Health in Medieval and Early Modern England.* Ed. Jennifer C. Vaught. Farnham, Surrey: Ashgate, 2010, 193–218.

Perfetti, Lisa, ed. *The Representation of Women's Emotions in Medieval and Early Modern Culture.* Gainesville, FL: University Press of Florida, 2005.

Peters, Edward. "Destruction of the Flesh – Salvation of the Spirit: The Paradoxes of Torture in Medieval Christian Society." In *The Devil, Heresy and Witchcraft in the Middle Ages: Essays in Honor of Jeffrey B. Russell.* Ed. Alberto Ferreiro. Leiden: Brill, 1998, 131–48.

Plamper, Jan. *The History of Emotions: An Introduction.* Trans. Keith Tribe. Oxford: Oxford University Press, 2015.

Plamper, Jan, William Reddy, Barbara Rosenwein, and Peter Stearns. "The History of Emotions: An Interview with William Reddy, Barbara Rosenwein, and Peter Stearns." *History and Theory* 49,2 (May 2010): 237–65.

Ranum, Orest. "The Refuges of Intimacy." *A History of Private Life*, Vol. 3: *Passions of the Renaissance.* Ed. Philippe Ariès and Roger Chartier. Cambridge, MA: Harvard University Press, 1989, 207–63.

Reddy, William M. *The Navigation of Feeling: A Framework for the History of Emotions.* Cambridge: Cambridge University Press, 2001.

Rhodes, William. "Medieval Political Ecology: Labour and Agency on the Half Acre." *Yearbook of Langland Studies* 28 (2014): 105–36.
Rigg, A. G. "Hoccleve's Complaint and Isidore of Seville." *Speculum* 45,4 (1970): 564–74.
Robertson, Elizabeth. "Kissing the Worm: Sex and Gender in the Afterlife and the Poetic Posthuman in the Late Middle English 'A Disputacion betwyx the Body and Wormes.'" In *From Beasts to Souls: Gender and Embodiment in Medieval Europe*. Ed. E. Jane Burns and Peggy McCracken. Notre Dame, IN: University of Notre Dame Press, 2013, 121–54.
Rosenfeld, Jessica. "Compassionate Conversions: Gower's *Confessio Amantis* and the Problem of Envy." *Journal of Medieval and Early Modern Studies* 42,1 (2012): 83–105.
Rosenwein, Barbara H. *Emotional Communities in the Early Middle Ages*. Ithaca, NY: Cornell University Press, 2006.
  Generations of Feeling: A History of Emotions, 600–1700. Cambridge: Cambridge University Press, 2016.
  "Introduction." In *Anger's Past*. Ed. Rosenwein, 1–6.
  "Worrying about Emotions in History." *American Historical Review* 107,3 (June 2002): 821–45.
Rosenwein, Barbara H., ed. *Anger's Past: The Social Uses of an Emotion in the Middle Ages*. Ithaca, NY: Cornell University Press, 1998.
Rozenski, Steven. "'Your Ensaumple and Your Mirour': Hoccleve's Amplification of the Imagery and Intimacy of Henry Suso's *Ars Moriendi*." *Parergon* 25,2 (2008): 1–16.
Salih, Sarah. "Idol Theory." *Preternature* 4,1 (2015): 13–36.
Saunders, Corinne. "Affective Reading: Chaucer, Women, and Romance." *Chaucer Review* 51,1 (2016): 11–30.
  "Mind, Body and Affect in Medieval English Arthurian Romance." In *Emotions in Medieval Arthurian Literature: Body, Mind, Voice*. Ed. Frank Brandsma, Carolyne Larrington, and Corinne Saunders. Cambridge: D. S. Brewer, 2015, 31–46.
Sayers, Edna Edith. "Experience, Authority, and the Mediation of Deafness: Chaucer's Wife of Bath." In *Disability in the Middle Ages: Reconsiderations and Reverberations*. Ed. Joshua R. Eyler. Farnham: Ashgate, 2010, 81–92.
Scheer, Monique. "Are Emotions a Kind of Practice (And Is That What Makes Them Have a History)? A Bourdieuian Approach to Understanding Emotion." *History and Theory* 51,2 (2012): 193–220.
Schleif, Corine. "Men on the Right – Women on the Left: (A)Symmetrical Spaces and Gendered Places." In *Women's Space: Patronage, Place, and Gender in the Medieval Church*. Ed. Virginia Chieffo Raguin and Sarah Stanbury. Albany, NY: State University of New York Press, 2005, 207–49.
Schnell, Rüdiger. "The Discourse on Marriage in the Middle Ages." *Speculum* 73, 3 (1998): 771–86.
Schuurman, Anne. "Pity and Poetics in Chaucer's *Legend of Good Women*." *PMLA* 130,5 (2015): 1302–17.

Scott, Anne, and Cynthia Kosso. "Introduction." In Scott and Kosso, eds. *Fear and Its Representations in the Middle Ages and Renaissance*. Turnhout: Brepols, 2002, xi–xxxvii.

Sedgwick, Eve Kosofsky. "Queer Performativity: Henry James's *The Art of the Novel*." *GLQ* 1,1 (1993): 1–16.

Touching Feeling: Affect, Pedagogy, Performativity. Durham, NC: Duke University Press, 2003.

Sedgwick, Eve Kosofsky, and Adam Frank, eds. *Shame and Its Sisters: A Silvan Tomkins Reader*. Durham, NC: Duke University Press, 1995.

Sheehan, Michael. *Marriage, Family, and Law in Medieval Europe: Collected Studies*. Ed. James K. Farge. Toronto: University of Toronto Press, 1996.

Sheridan, Christian. "Conflicting Economies in the Fabliaux." In *Comic Provocations: Exposing the Corpus of Old French Fabliaux*. Ed. Holly A. Crocker. New York: Palgrave Macmillan, 2006, 97–111.

Simmel, Georg. "The Sociology of Space" ["Sociology des Raumes"]. *Jahrbuch fur Gestzgeburg, Verwaltung and Volkswitschaft* 27 (1903): 27–71.

Smail, Daniel Lord. "Hatred as a Social Institution in Late-Medieval Society." *Speculum* 76 (2001): 90–126.

Smith, D. Vance. "The Application of Thought to Medieval Studies: The Twenty-First Century." *Exemplaria* 22,1 (2010): 85–94.

Smith, Kathryn Ann. *Art, Identity and Devotion in Fourteenth-Century England: Three Women and Their Books of Hours*. Buffalo: University of Toronto Press, 2003.

Smyth, Karen. "Reading Misreadings in Thomas Hoccleve's *Series*." *English Studies* 87,1 (2006): 3–22.

Somerset, Fiona. *Feeling Like Saints: Lollard Writings After Wyclif*. Ithaca, NY: Cornell University Press, 2014.

Southern, Richard W. *The Making of the Middle Ages*. New Haven, CT: Yale University Press, 1953.

Spearing, A. C. *Medieval Autographies: The "I" of the Text*. Notre Dame, IN: University of Notre Dame Press, 2012.

Spufford, Francis, ed. *The Chatto Book of Cabbages and Kings: Lists in Literature*. London: Chatto and Windus, 1989.

Steiner, Emily. *Documentary Culture and the Making of Medieval English Literature*. New York: Cambridge University Press, 2003.

Steiner, Emily, and Candace Barrington, eds. *The Letter of the Law: Legal Practice and Literary Production in Medieval England*. Ithaca, NY: Cornell University Press, 2002.

Stevenson, Jill. *Performance, Cognitive Theory, and Devotional Culture: Sensual Piety in Late Medieval York*. New York: Palgrave Macmillan, 2010.

Stone, David. *Decision-Making in Medieval Agriculture*. Oxford: Oxford University Press, 2005.

Strohm, Paul. *Hochon's Arrow: The Social Imagination of Fourteenth-Century Texts*. Princeton, NJ: Princeton University Press, 1992.

"Sovereignty and Sewage." In *Lydgate Matters: Poetry and Material Culture in the Fifteenth Century*. Ed. Lisa H. Cooper and Andrea Denny-Brown. New York: Palgrave Macmillan, 2008, 57–70.

Taavitsainen, Irma. "Narrative Patterns of Affect in Four Genres of the *Canterbury Tales*." *Chaucer Review* 30,2 (1995): 191–210.

Tambling, Jeremy. "Allegory and the Madness of the Text: Hoccleve's Complaint." *New Medieval Literatures* 6 (2003): 223–48.

Tavormina, M. Teresa. *Kindly Similitude: Marriage and Family in Piers Plowman*. Cambridge: D. S. Brewer, 1995.

Taylor, Jamie K. *Fictions of Evidence: Witnessing, Literature, and Community in the Late Middle Ages*. Columbus, OH: Ohio State University Press, 2013.

Terada, Rei. *Feeling in Theory: Emotion after the "Death of the Subject."* Cambridge, MA: Harvard University Press, 2001.

Thornley, Eva M. "The Middle English Penitential Lyric and Hoccleve's Autobiographical Poetry." *Neuphilologische Mitteilungen* 68 (1967): 295–321.

Tiner, Elza C. "English Law in the York Trial Plays." *Early Drama, Art and Music Review* 18,2 (1996): 103–12. Reprinted in *The Dramatic Tradition of the Middle Ages*. Ed. Clifford Davidson. New York: AMS Press, 2005.

Tolmie, Sarah. "The Professional: Thomas Hoccleve." *Studies in the Age of Chaucer* 29 (2007): 341–73.

Torti, Anna. "Hoccleve's Attitude Towards Women: 'I shoop me do my peyne and diligence / To wynne hir loue by obedience.'" In *A Wyf Ther Was: Essays in Honour of Paule Mertens-Fonck*. Ed. Juliette Dor. Liège: Université de Liège, 1992, 264–74.

Trigg, Stephanie. "Langland's Tears: Poetry, Emotion, and Mouvance." *Yearbook of Langland Studies* 26 (2012): 27–48.

"Introduction: Emotional Histories – Beyond the Personalization of the Past and the Abstractions of Affect Theory." *Exemplaria* (Special issue: *Premodern Emotions*) 26,1 (2014): 3–15.

Truitt, E. R. *Medieval Robots: Mechanism, Magic, Nature, and Art*. Philadelphia, PA: University of Pennsylvania Press, 2015.

Uebel, Michael. *Ecstatic Transformation: On the Uses of Alterity in the Middle Ages*. New York: Palgrave Macmillan, 2005.

Van Court, Elisa Narin. "*The Siege of Jerusalem* and Augustinian Historians: Writing about Jews in Fourteenth-Century England." *Chaucer Review* 29,3 (1995): 227–48.

Van Dijk, Conrad. "Giving Each His Due: Langland, Gower, and the Question of Equity." *Journal of English and Germanic Philology* 108,3 (2009): 310–35.

Von Contzen, Eva. "The Limits of Narration: Lists and Literary History." *Style* (Special issue: *Lists*) 50,3 (2016): 241–60.

Von Nolcken, Christina. "'O, why ne had y lerned for to die?': *Lerne for to Dye* and the Author's Death in Thomas Hoccleve's Series." *Essays in Medieval Studies* 10 (1993): 27–51.

Wack, Mary F. *Lovesickness in the Middle Ages: The "Viaticum" and its Commentaries*. Philadelphia, PA: University of Pennsylvania Press, 1990.

White, Oliver B. "The Ill-Made Knight." *Commonweal* 33,9 (December 20, 1940).
White, Stephen D. "The Politics of Anger." In *Anger's Past*. Ed. Rosenwein, 127–52.
White, T. H. *The Once and Future King*. London: Harper Collins, 1958; 1996.
Whiting, Bartlett Jere, with Helen Wescott Whiting. *Proverbs, Sentences, and Proverbial Phrases from English Writings Mainly before 1500*. Cambridge, MA: Harvard University Press, 1968.
Williams, Miller. *Why God Permits Evil*. Baton Rouge, LA: Louisiana State University Press, 1977.
Windeatt, Barry. "'Love That Oughte Ben Secree' in Chaucer's *Troilus*." *Chaucer Review* 14,2 (1979): 116–31.
  "Postmodernism." In *Chaucer: An Oxford Guide*. Ed. Steve Ellis. Oxford: Oxford University Press, 2005, 400–15.
Winstead, Karen A. "'I am al othir to yow than yee weene': Hoccleve, Women, and the *Series*." *Philological Quarterly* 72,2 (1993): 143–55.
Woods, William F. "The Logic of Deprivation in the 'Reeve's Tale.'" *Chaucer Review* 30,2 (1995): 150–63.

Index

"Absolon" (fictional character), 13–14, 27–43
account, systems patrolled by, 126–7
accounting, women escaping, 130–2, 138
"Accounting for Affect in the *Reeve's Tale*"
    (Bryant), 16–17, 118–32
"Achilles" (fictional character), 147
"Actaeon" (fictional character), 186
Aeneid (Virgil), 201
"Affect Machines" (Salih), 17, 139–55
"Affecting Forms" (Bernau), 18, 181–97
affectiones. *See* affects
affective contract, *The Good Wife's Guide*
    underscoring, 113
affective dissonance, 63
affective economies, 16–17, 127
affective logic, 195
Affective Meditation and the Invention of Medieval
    Compassion (McNamer), 7–8, 158–9, 175
affective piety, 8–9, 160
"Affective Reading" (Saunders), 19
affective turn, 2–4, 5–6
affects (*affectiones*), 2, 135, 198, 200, 203–16
    Altieri on, 197–8
    cognitive processes role of, 199–200
    definition of, 21, 119, 197–8
    of dreamer, 198, 201
    as economic, 127
    engendering of, 15, 70–85
    forms and, 18, 123–32, 181–97
    Gregg on, 20–1
    in-between-ness of, 4, 21
    Jameson on, 23
    as Jewish, 47–62
    as legal, 17–18, 158–74
    machines of, 17, 139–55
    as pre-emotion, 86
    in *Reeve's Tale*, 118–32, 138
    Seigworth on, 20–1
    in the *Series*, 70–85
    Trigg on, 19
    values challenged by, 181–2

"Afterword" (Bale), 13, 203–16
Agamben, Giorgio, 160–1
"Ahithophel" (fictional character), 185–6, 193–4
Ahmed, Sara, 5, 16–17, 79–80, 127, 135, 203
    Lipton drawing on, 17–18, 158–9
    on skin, 101–3, 109
    on social form, 162–3
    on stickiness, 88, 139–40, 148–50, 164–5
"Alcyone" (fictional character), 19
Alexander of Hales, 66
"Aleyn" (fictional character), 123–4, 126, 127–32
"Alison" (fictional character), 27–43
"Alisoun" (fictional character), 91–2, 98–103, 114
Althoff, Gerd, 81–2
Altieri, Charles, 18, 181–2, 197–8, 202–16
amicitia. *See* friendship
anal rape, 37–8
Anderson, Earl, 39–40
anger (*irrous*), 67–8, 69, 138
    as irascible emotion, 57–60, 68–9
    of shepherd, 122–3
anger-as-sin, 68
"Anna" (fictional character). *See also* "Annas,"
    170–2
"Annas" (fictional character). *See also* "Anna"
Anselm of Lucca, 8–9, 54
Antichrist, 192–3
The Antinomies of Realism (Jameson), 70
anti-Semitism, 48–9
apathy (*apatheia*), 57
apostrophe, 201
appeal to emotion (*pathos*), 62
Aquinas, Thomas, 65–6, 68–9, 111–12, 201
archbishop, of Canterbury, 163
Aristotle, 66, 67–8, 134
"Arthur" (fictional character), 13–14, 37–41
assay, 194–5
"Astrophil" (fictional character), 40
Astrophil and Stella (Sidney), 40
attention, 139–55
auditor, 120

239

Index

Auerbach, Eric, 62
Augustine of Hippo, 54–7, 58–9, 65–6, 68, 75
  City of God by, 66, 140–2
authenticity, 209, 213–16
author, 209, 213–16
Avicenna, 68–9

Bailey, Mark, 119
Bale, Anthony, 13, 62–3, 203–16
ballat, 189–91
Barabas, 165–6
Barney, Stephen, 183–4, 196–7
Barnum, Priscilla Heath, 144–6, 180
Barthes, Roland, 214–15, 217
Barton, Richard E., 67–8
Bawcutt, Priscilla, 199–200
"Beadle" (fictional character), 170, 171–2, 174–81
"Beatrice" (fictional character), 34
Becker, Alexis Kellner, 136
Beckwith, Sarah, 174
"Becoming Christian?" (Kruger), 65
"Becoming Flesh, Inhabiting Two Genders" (Burger), 15–16, 90–108
becoming-flesh, 107–8
Beidler, Peter G., 115–16
Belting, Hans, 139–40
"Belus" (fictional character), 140–2
benefit, 162–3
Bennett, J. A. W., 123–4
Bernard of Clairvaux, 63
Bernau, Anke, 13, 18, 181–97, 199–200, 201
"Bertilak" (fictional character), 104
Bible, idolatry denounced by, 144–6
Bible en François (Moe), 68
bibles moralisées. *See* moralized bibles
biblical trial, of Christ, 165–7
Biernoff, Suzannah, 139–40
Biller, Peter, 64–5
"Bishop" (fictional character), 28
"Black Knight" (fictional character), 1–2, 5–6, 9–12, 76. *See also* Chaucer, *Book of the Duchess*
blindness, 201
blocked emotion, 90–108
Boccaccio, Giovanni, 28–9, 41–3
bodies, 69, 90–108, 116, 124–5, 203, 216
Bodies That Matter (Butler), 20
bodily feelings, 9–10, 23
Boethius, 72, 86–7, 88
Boleyn, Anne, 216
  breasts of, 211–16
Bonaventure, 66–7
Book of the Duchess (Chaucer). *See* Chaucer
The Book of Vices and Virtues (D'Orléans), 165–7, 179

Book of Wisdom, 140–2, 147–8
Bourdieu, Pierre, 22, 210–11
Bowers, John, 88
Bracton, Henry, 159–60, 163–7, 171, 174–81
Brandeis, Arthur, 159–60, 166–7
Breen, Katharine, 8–9
Brennan, Teresa, 79, 88, 127
bride, 63
"Bride or Bridegroom?" (Muir), 63
bridegroom, 63
Brown, Matthew Clifton, 86
Brunton (bishop), 159–60
Bryant, Brantley L., 13, 16–17, 21, 118–32, 204, 213–14
The Bureaucratic Muse (Knapp), 133
Burger, Glenn D., 24, 90–108, 110
Burrow, J. A., 72–3, 85
Butler, Judith, 20, 88
Bynum, Caroline Walker, 8–9, 23

"Caiaphas" (fictional character), 14–15, 48–9, 51–2, 56–7, 61–2, 170–1
"Calliope" (fictional character), 182–3, 188–93, 195–6
Cambridge, college in, 123–4
Camelot, 39
Camille, Michael, 151
Campana, Joseph, 200
cannibalism, 49–51
Cannon, Christopher, 29–30, 44
Canterbury, archbishop of, 163
Canterbury Tales (Chaucer). *See* Chaucer
caritas. *See* charity
catalogue, 199
Catherine of Aragon, 211
Catholicism, 151–5
cause, feeling as, 210–11
Caxton, 33
Champagne, Durand de, 110
Chanson de Roland, 35
charity (*caritas*), 32–3, 166
"Charlemagne" (fictional character), 35
"Chastity" (fictional character). *See also* "Diana"
Chastoiement des dames (Robert of Blois). *See The Ladies' Instruction*
Chaucer, Geoffrey, 13–14, 25–43, 109, 115–16, 119–21, 137
  Book of the Duchess by, 1–2, 5–6, 10–12, 19
  General Prologue by, Reeve in, 119–21
  House of Fame by, 200
  Knight's Tale by, 69, 122–3
  Legend of Good Women by, 129, 132, 200
  letter-writing of, 208–11, 216
  Man of Law's Tale by, 75–6
  Merchant's Tale by, 104–6

Index

Miller's Tale by, 43, 126–7, 132, 134
Nun's Priest's Tale by, 30
Parson's Tale by, 166–7
Reeve's Tale, 21, 118–32, 133, 134, 138.
The Riverside Chaucer (Benson), 134
Summoner's Tale by, 131–2
Tale of Melibee by, 44
Troilus and Criseyde, 24, 34–5, 37–8, 122–3, 208–16
Wife of Bath's Prologue and Tale, 15–16, 90–108, 115–16
"Chaucer and Affect Theory," 138
Chaucer's Sexual Poetics (Dinshaw), 109
"Cherubino" (fictional character), 36–7
child, weeping like, 25–43
"Christ Before Annas and Caiaphas," 170–3
"Christ Before Herod," 170
"Christ Before Pilate 2: The Judgement," 170
"Christ Before Pilate 1: The Dream of Pilate's Wife," 168–72
Christ-child, 151
Christianity, 8–9, 59–60, 63, 65, 67, 150–1
Christians, 14–15, 17, 47–62, 66, 139–46, 147–8
 Jews and, 62–3, 65, 67
Christmas, 204–8
Church Fathers, 58–9
City of God (Augustine), 66, 140–2
"Clarice" (fictional character), 64
clarity, 200
classical place (*locus classicus*), 179
clergy, gender of, 63
Clough, Patricia Ticineto, 2–3, 4, 5
cognitive processes, affect's role in, 199–200
Cohen, Jeremy, 67
Colonne, Guido delle, 156
colorings, 188–9, 193
combination, contempt of, 124, 130–2
commodo, 162–3
Complaint (Hoccleve), 70–1
Confessio Amantis (Gower), 60–1, 69
confessional manuals, false witnessing and, 165–7
conscious states, 9–10, 23
consequences, 44, 210–11
Consolatio, 72
constraint, 135
containtment, 135
contempt, of combination, 124, 130–2
contraries, principle of, 68
control, 136
"Cook" (fictional character), 132
Cooper, Lisa H., 119
copy, 195–6
corage, 201
"Counting Sheep" (O'Neill), 133
courtesy (*courtoisie*), 110

courts, 185
covetousness, 166–7
"Criseyde" (fictional character), 28–9, 34–5, 37–8, 40, 208–16
Crocker, Holly A., 24, 70–85
cross-gendered identification, 63
Croxton Play of the Sacrament, 150–1
"Crucifixio Christi," 173–4
Crucifixion, 47–62, 63, 65, 159–60, 173–4, 176
cultural constructivism, 198
Cultural Politics of Emotion (Ahmed), 88
curage, 188, 195–6
"Cutaneous Time in the Late Medieval Literary Imagination" (Davis, I.), 114

Da Ponte, Lorenzo, 36–7
Damascene, John, 67
Dante, 28–9, 34
"David" (fictional character), 69
Davidson, Clifford, 158, 175
Davis, Isabel, 70–1, 114
Davis, Norman, 216
D'Avray, David, 111–12
De doctrina Christiana (Augustine), 75
De fide orthodoxa (Damascene), 67
De legibus et consuetudinibus Angliae (Bracton), 159–60
De natura corporis et animae (William of Saint Thierry), 69
De natura hominis (Nemesius of Emesa), 67, 68–9
Decameron (Boccaccio), 28–9, 41–3
Decretum (Gratian), 161–3, 178
deeth, 120
Deleuze, Gilles, 3, 20–1
delight, distress and, 65–6
Delony, Mikee, 101–3
DeMarco, Patricia, 13, 14–15, 47–62, 214
Derrida, Jacques, 160–2
desire, anger substituted for, 67
devil, 169–70
"Diabolus" (fictional character), 169–70
Dialoge with a Friend (Hoccleve), 15, 71–2, 76–7
"Diana" (fictional character), 186, 187, 188, 193. *See also* "Chastity"
Digby manuscript, 148
Dinshaw, Carolyn, 109
disabling sex difference, 92–6
discipline, 181–2, 190–1, 202
discourse, Foucault on, 22
distinctive realm, of experience, 197–8
distress (*tristitia*), 55–7, 65–6, 124, 127–30
"Dives" (fictional character), 142–4
Dives and Pauper (Barnum), 144–6, 180
Divine Right, 168–9

Donahue, Charles, 161–2, 177
Douglas, Gavin, 18, 181–97, 198, 199–200
dream, of Procula, 169–70
dreamer, 18, 181–203
　affect of, 198, 201
　as toady, 202
　Venus praised by, 189–91, 201
"Dreamer" (fictional character), 1–2, 10–12, 19
dreamy logic, 183–4
Dryden, John, 42

economic affects, 127
"Economics of Justice" (Edwards, E.), 134, 138
Ecstatic Transformation (Uebel), 200
Edmund, St, 147–8
Edwards, Elizabeth, 125–6, 130, 134, 138
ekphrases, relationship of lists with, 201
Elliott, Dyan, 87
emoting, 205–8
emotional communities, 6–9, 22, 205–8
Emotional Communities in the Early Middle Ages (Rosenwein), 6–7, 200
emotional practices, 205–8
emotional scripts, 77–8
emotional utterances. *See* emotives
Emotions in Ancient and Medieval Philosophy (Knuuttila), 66–7
emotions (*passio*), 25–43, 90–108, 198, 203–16
　anger as irascible, 57–60, 68–9
　history of, 1–13, 24
　as performative, 175
　as significant, 217
　sociality of, 162–3
emotives, 6–7, 13–14, 22, 30–2, 116–17
　in letter, 210–11
"Emperor" (fictional character), 75–6
"Empress" (fictional character), 75–85
Empress of Rome, 75–85
enargeia, 200
end (*telos*), 112–13
energeia, 200
engendered assemblage, 15
"Engendering Affect in Hoccleve's *Series*" (Crocker), 15, 70–85
England, 22, 69, 142–6, 150–3, 211–16
　London in, 15, 70–85, 153–5
　in *The Series*, 15, 70–85
English, 5–6, 157, 176. *See also* York trial plays
enjoyment, discipline as mode of, 202
"Enlisting Truth" (Bernau), 201
Enseignment à sa fille Isabelle (Louis IX), 110
Enterline, Lynn, 40
entrainment, 88, 127
envy, neighbors and, 178–9
Etheldreda, St, 153–5

ethics, 136, 161
Eucharist, 174
Europe, 94–6, 148–50
exacting surveillance, 135
excess, 181
experience, distinctive realm of, 197–8
expressive activity, Altieri on, 202–16
extramission theory, 155

fabliaux, 119–23, 126–7, 135
facts, *Good Wife's Guide* obsessed with, 98
the false, 147–8, 165–7, 179, 180
fame, of Venus, 189–91
fantasy, 108
Farrell, William J., 197, 199
Fasciculus Morum (Wenzel), 165–6, 168, 169–70, 178–9
Fastolf, John, 204–8
fear, 182–5, 187–92, 200, 201
Fear and Its Representations in the Middle Ages and Renaissance (Scott and Kosso), 184–5
"Feeling" (McNamer), 7–8, 19
Feeling Backward (Love, H.), 5
Feeling in Theory (Terada), 23
Feeling Like Saints (Somerset), 24
Feeling Persecuted (Bale), 62–3
feelings, 15–16, 19, 90–108, 124–7, 203–16
"Fellicula" (fictional character), 80–5
"Fiammetta" (fictional character), 41–3
fiction, about fiction, 199–200
Fictions of Evidence (Taylor), 175
fictitious sale, 130
figurative language, emotions and, 25–43
fin'amor, 5–7, 10–12, 94–6, 103–4
flesh, as one, 90–108
the folk, 28
forms, 18, 123–32, 181–97
"Fortune" (fictional character), 185
Foster, Frances A., 179
Foucauldian discipline, 134
Foucault, Michel, 22, 179
Fourth Lateran Council, 159, 161–2, 178
Fox, Denton, 183–4, 199
Fox, Robin Lane, 142
Fradenburg, L. O. Aranye, 195–6, 202
France, 22, 64–5, 78–9
Francis, W. Nelson, 165–7, 179
Franciscans, 47–9, 66–7
Frank, Adam, 20
free agents, 126–7
Freud, Sigmund, 3, 20–1, 39–40
The Friars and the Jews (Cohen), 67
friendship (*amicitia*), 162–3, 166–7
Frisch, Andrea, 160–1, 177
"Fyleloly" (fictional character), 38–9

Galen, 67, 68–9
Galloway, Andrew, 63–4
Gaunt, Simon, 123
Gayk, Shannon, 73–4, 87, 140–2
"Gendering Anger" (Barton), 67–8
genders, 63, 87, 90–108, 201–2
General Prologue (Chaucer). *See* Chaucer
Generations of Feeling (Rosenwein), 22
gentiles, idols of the, 141–2
Gesta Romanorum, 71–2, 75–85
"Getting Experience" (Williams), 70
"Ghismonda" (fictional character), 28–9, 41–3
Glanville. *See Tractatus de legibus et consuetudinibus regni Angli qui Glanvilla vocatur*
gods, 75, 92–6, 142, 151, 182–3, 188
    Lancelot influenced by, 28, 38–40
    Marie responding to, 64
    My Compleinte and, 15, 71–2, 73–5
Goethe, Johann Wolfgang von, 217
Goldie, Matthew Boyd, 70–1
Goldin, Simha, 64
"Gombert and the Two Clerks," 126–7. *See also* Chaucer, *Miller's Tale*
The Good Wife's Guide (*Le Ménagier de Paris*), 15–16, 91–2, 95–8, 100–3, 106, 110
    affective contract underscored by, 113
    knight paralleling, 115
    manuscript illustrator of, 113
Gourlay, Kristi, 81–2
Gower, John, 60–1, 69
Grail quest, 37–40
grand narrative, 6–7
Gratiae libri de iudiciorum ordine (Tancred), 161–2
Gratian, 161–3, 178
Gray, Douglas, 181
greed, 163–5
Greeks, 214–15
Green, Richard Firth, 161
Greetham, D. C., 72
Gregg, Melissa, 20–1
Gregory the Great, 59
grief (*tristitia*), 66, 204–8
Grosz, Elizabeth, 20
"Guenevere" (fictional character), 28, 39

habitus. *See* social disposition
Handlyng Synne (Robert of Brunne), 166, 169–70
Hanna, Ralph, 63–4
Hansen, Elaine Tuttle, 109
happy object, 79–80
"Happy Objects" (Ahmed), 203
Hardt, Michael, 3, 20
Harvey, E. Ruth, 73

Harvey, P. D. A., 123–4, 130, 136
hate, 162–5
head appendage, 107–8
heart, private drama of, 158–9
Hebron, Malcolm, 68
"Hector" (fictional character), 17, 146–50, 153–5
Helmholz, Richard, 161–2, 178
Henry (prince), 148–50
Henry of Ghent, 67
Henry V, 78–9
Henry VIII, 216
heresy trials, York trial plays reflecting, 176
"Herod" (fictional character), 170
Higden, Ranulf, 63–4
Hilton, Walter, 75, 133–4
Historia destructionis Troiae (Colonne), 156
historical sources, 214
history, 1–13, 24, 25–43
The History of Emotions (Plamper), 216
Hoccleve, Thomas, 86, 87, 88, 89–108, 133, 205–6
    Boethius debt of, 86–7
    The Series by, 15, 70–85
Hoffmann, Tobias, 67
Holsinger, Bruce, 8–9
Holy Church, 32–3
Homan, Richard L., 63
Homer, 147–8
"Honor" (fictional character), 181–3, 185–9, 191–7
"Horaste" (fictional character), 34–5
Horner, Olga, 180
Horologium Sapientiae (Suso), 77–80
"Hosanna," 171–2
Host, 150–1
House of Fame (Chaucer). *See* Chaucer
Howe, Nicholas, 199
Hsy, Jonathan, 113–14
humoral body, 74–5
The Husbandry, 16–17, 125
Humphrey, Duke of Gloucester, 15, 71–2, 74–5, 76–7, 79–81
Hutson, Lorna, 159, 176
Hyams, Paul R., 81–2, 162–3

idolatry, 17, 140–50
Iliad (Homer), 147–8
The Ill-Made Knight (White, T. H.), 39, 45
"Image" (fictional character), 77–8
images, 139–46
"Imagining Jewish Affect in the *Siege of Jerusalem*" (DeMarco), 14–15, 47–62
"In Search of Malyne" (Kohanski), 135, 138
in-between-ness, of affect, 4, 21
"inconstant warld," 201
inert matter, 138
insecure poet, 201

intensities, 188–9, 195–7
internal rhyme, Parkinson on, 202
intimacy, 214–15
intimate scripts, 8–9, 10–12, 107, 115, 127–30, 209–11
intromission theory, 155
intruder, list as, 196–7
The Invention of Suspicion (Hutson), 176
"An Inventory of Shimmers" (Gregg and Seigworth), 20
irrous. *See* anger
Isaac of Stella, 65–6
Isidore of Seville, 72
Israel, Jerusalem in, 47–62, 151
Italy, Rome in, 151, 211

Jacob's Well (Brandeis), 159–60, 166–7
James, William, 210–11
James IV, 182–3, 202
Jameson, Frederic, 23, 70–1, 213
"Jankyn" (fictional character), 15–16, 91–2, 98–103, 107, 112–14
"January" (fictional character), 106
jape, of malice, 132
Jerome, 66
Jerusalem, Israel, 47–62, 151
Jesus Christ, 14–15, 75–6, 144–6, 150–3, 165–74. *See also* Passion
  swearing crucifying, 176
  in York trial plays, 160
Jewish bodies, Josephus exempted from, 69
Jewish melancholia, 64–5
Jews, 14–15, 47–62, 150–1, 167–9, 176, 179
  Barabas preferred by, 165–6
  Christians and, 62–3, 65, 67
  Kiddush Ha'shem practiced by, 64
"John" (fictional character), 36–7, 69, 123–4, 126, 127–32
John Badby, 88
"John of Gaunt" (fictional character), 5–6
John of Tynemouth, 63–4
Johnson, Eleanor, 86–7, 88
jompre, 209
"Jonathas" (fictional character), 80–5
Jonathas and Fellicula (Hoccleve), 80–5
Jones, Malcolm, 151–3
Josephus, 49–51, 63–4
"Josephus" (fictional character), 59–60, 61, 69
"joyus disciplyne," 181–2, 190–1, 196–7
Judaism, Christianity's relationship with, 63, 65, 67
judgment, Gratian on, 178
jury, Resurrection as like, 180
just exchange, 130

Karnes, Michelle, 9–10
Kempe, Margery, 151
Kiddush Ha'shem, 64
King, Pamela M., 176
King, Peter, 54
Knapp, Ethan, 72–3, 133
knight, 15–16, 44, 103–4, 115–16
Knight's Tale (Chaucer). *See* Chaucer
Knuuttila, Simo, 66–7, 68–9
Kohanski, Tamarah, 135, 138
Kosso, Cynthia, 184–5
Kratzmann, Gregory, 182–3, 199–200
Kruger, Steven, 65, 199–200

Lacan, Jacques, 39, 214–15
The Ladies' Instruction (*Chastoiement des dames*) (Robert de Blois), 110
Lampert, Lisa, 63
"Lancelot" (fictional character), 13–14, 26–43, 45
Langland, William, 28–9, 32–4, 40, 133, 135
The Lanterne of Li3t, 144–6
"Last Judgment" (Towneley), 169–70
Latour, Bruno, 139, 140
"Lavayn" (fictional character), 38–9
Lavezzo, Kathy, 151
Lawton, David, 63–4
legal affect, 17–18, 158–74
Legend of Good Women (Chaucer). *See* Chaucer
Lerne to Die (Hoccleve), 72, 77–80, 83–5
letters, 203–16, 217
Lévi-Strauss, Claude, 210–11
Lewis, C. S., 181
Liber pantegni (Africanus), 64–5
Life of St Edmund (Lydgate), 147–8
life support, 156
Lille, Alan de, 66
Lipton, Emma, 13, 17–18, 23, 158–74, 206–8
lists, 181–97, 199, 200, 201
  disciplinary actions associated with, 202
"The *Litera Troili* and English Letters" (Davis, N.), 216
literariness, 13–14, 31
"The Literariness of Literature" (McNamer), 19
literary texts, 25–6, 214
Little, Lester K., 59, 81–2
Livre du Chevalier de la Tour Landry, 110
loathly hag, transformation of, 107–8, 115–16
locus classicus. *See* classical place
locus of images, 139–40
"The Logic of Deprivation" (Woods), 135, 137
Lollard expressions, of pious feeling, 24
Lombard, Peter, 66
London, England, 15, 70–85, 153–5
Louis IX, 110
love, 208–13, 217

Love, Heather, 5
Love, Nicholas, 62, 158, 173–4, 175
"Love" (fictional character), 40. *See also* "Venus"
lover, 193, 208–13
lower appendage, 107–8
lowly fellow, 164–5
Lucifer, 201
Lydgate, John, 17, 140–2, 146–50, 156, 200
"lynage," 129–30
Lynch, Andrew, 44

maistrie, 90–1, 92–6, 98–103, 108, 112–13
mala fama. *See* reputation
"Malchus" (fictional character), 170, 171–3, 174–81
male mystics, 63
malice, 124, 132
Malo, Robyn, 72–3
Malorian identity, 44
Malory, Thomas, 13–14, 25–43
"Malyne" (fictional character), 125, 127–30
"Man in Black" (fictional character), 19
Man of Law's Tale (Chaucer). *See* Chaucer
Manorial Records (Harvey, P.), 136
"Marie" (fictional character), 49–51, 64
marital affection, 96–8, 102–8, 111–12
marriage, 90–108, 111–12
The Marriage of Figaro, 36–7
Martin, Joanna M., 200
marvel, list's relationship with, 200
Massacre at Mainz, 64
Massumi, Brian, 4, 20–1, 116, 135
Matter of Troy, 148–50
Matthew 66, 81
"mawmettes," 142
"May" (fictional character), 104–6, 182–3
McIntosh, Marjorie, 159
McLeod, Glenda, 183–4, 197
McNamer, Sarah, 7–8, 9, 19, 31, 76, 173–4
 affective dissonance suggested by, 63
 Affective Meditation and the Invention of Medieval Compassion by, 158–9, 175
 emotional scripts linked by, 77–8
 on intimate scripts, 8–9, 10–12, 107–8, 115, 127–30, 210–11
 on performative scripting, 142–4
 on women, 47–9
 on Wycliffite critiques, 144–6
McSheffrey, Shannon, 159
Mead, Jenna, 137
meaning, signifier with, 39
MED. *See Middle English Dictionary*
mediality, distress of, 124, 127–30
Medieval Autographies (Spearing), 85
medieval literature, 25–43

"Medieval Political Ecology" (Rhodes), 133
The Medieval Siege (Hebron), 68
medieval turn, 3
Meditations on the Life of Christ (Love, N.), 158
Meecham-Jones, Simon, 24
melancholia, 64–5
Le Ménagier de Paris. *See The Good Wife's Guide*
"Merchant" (fictional character), 106
Merchant's Tale (Chaucer). *See* Chaucer
Middle Ages, 12–13, 23, 147–8, 183–4, 198, 200
 Bailey on, 119
 "Becoming One Flesh, Inhabiting Two Genders" on, 15–16
 Delony on, 101–3
 marital affection signifying in, 111–12
 marriage reconfigured in, 94–6, 111–12
 McNamer on, 76
 Wack on, 70–1
 "Weeping Like a Beaten Child" on, 25–43
 women in, 39–43
Middle English, 31, 42–3, 134, 144–6. *See also Siege of Jerusalem*
Middle English Dictionary (*MED*), 28, 33–4, 201
"The Miller and the Two Clerks," 126–7. *See also* Chaucer, *Reeve's Tale*
Miller's Tale (Chaucer). *See* Chaucer
Mills, Robert, 63
"Minerva" (fictional character), 194, 197–8. *See also* "Wisdom"
Mirror of the Blessed Life of Jesus Christ (Love, N.), 173–4
misunderstanding, 210
"Mixed Feelings about Violence" (Homan), 63
mobbing scene, 187–8
modern English, 26–7
modernism, 198
Moe, Phyllis, 68
Molendinarius, Robert, 123–4
"A Moral Tale about Two Clerics," 126–7. *See also* Chaucer, *Reeve's Tale*
moral terms, 181–2
Moralia (Gregory the Great), 59
moralized bibles (*bibles moralisées*), 142
morally indifferent animals, 54–7
Morley, Lady, 204–8, 213
Morris, Andrew Jeffrey, 124–5, 133, 134, 136
 "Representing the Countryside" by, 136
Morte d'Arthure (Malory), 13–14, 40–1
motive acts, 68–9
mourning, 204–8
movement (*mouvance*), 32–3
Mozart, Wolfgang Amadeus, 36–7
Murray, Alexander, 67
Murray, Jacqueline, 63

"Muses" (fictional characters), 182–3, 188
My Compleinte (Hoccleve), 15, 71–2, 73–5

Najib, Sadaf, 157
"Nathan" (fictional character), 59, 65
"Nature" (fictional character), 182–3
neighborhood, 174, 180
neighbors, 164–5, 178–9, 206–8
Nemesius of Emesa, 67, 68–9
New Testament, 201
Newton, Esther, 112–13
Ngai, Sianne, 4–5, 15–16, 17–18, 91–2, 158–9, 167
"Nicholas" (fictional character), 29–30, 39–40
Nicholson, Roger, 48–9
"Ninus" (fictional character), 140–2
Nisse, Ruth, 88, 169–70
the non-literary, 204–16
Norfolk, 119–20
Northern Europeans, 148–50
The Northern Passion (Foster), 179
Nowlin, Steele, 122–3, 129, 132, 135, 200
Nun's Priest's Tale (Chaucer). *See* Chaucer
nymph, 191–6, 201–2

objects, 79–80, 155
odio, 162–3
Old Testament, 141–2
Older Scots verse, 202
"On Not Defending Poetry" (Campana), 200
one flesh, 90–108
"One Flesh, Two Sexes, Three Genders?" (Murray, J.), 63
O'Neill, Rosemary, 119, 133, 135, 136, 137
the oneiric, the poetic's parallels with, 199–200
Ordo (Tancred), 161–3, 177
originality, 213
Oschinsky, Dorothea, 121, 136

pagans, Christians finding, 17
Palace of Honor, 182–3, 191–7
The Palis of Honoure, 18, 181–97, 198–9, 200
"Pandarus" (fictional character), 34–5, 208–16
paramours, 37–8
Paris, France, 64–5
Parkinson, David, 183–4, 193–4, 198–9, 200, 201, 202
  on internal rhyme, 202
"Parson" (fictional character), 142
Parson's Tale (Chaucer). *See* Chaucer
The Particulars of Rapture (Altieri), 18, 181–2
Pasnau, Robert, 23
passio. See emotions
Passion, 7–8, 17–18, 47–62, 63, 65, 115
  Jerome on, 66
  York trial plays and, 158, 159–60, 165–6, 173–4

Paster, Gail Kern, 74–5
Paston, John, 204–8
Paston, Margaret, 204–8, 213–16
pathos. *See* appeal to emotion
Patroklos, 147–8
Patterson, Lee, 71–2
"Pauper" (fictional character), 142–4, 180
Pearman, Tory Vandeventer, 115–16
Pecock, Reginald, 144, 148–50, 153–5
penitential literature, 87
performative scripting, 142–4
"Peter" (fictional character), 170, 171–2
Peter the Venerable, 67
Peters, Edward, 55–7
"phisik," 209
physical expression, as emotion, 216
Piers Plowman (Langland), 28–9, 32–4
"Pilate" (fictional character), 167–72, 179
pity, 60–2, 67
Plamper, Jan, 216
"plesance," 201
poet, blindness of, 201
the poetic, the oneiric's parallels with, 199–200
polarity, 156–7
"Polyxena" (fictional character), 147
"Pope" (fictional character), 57–8
potential, 116
Practicing Literary Theory (Johnson, E.), 86
pre-emotions (*propassiones*), 66, 86
presentism, 3
"pretio," 162–3
"Priam" (fictional character), 146
price, 162–3
Pride, 167–9
primal scene, 39–40
princely anger, 68
private drama, of heart, 158–9
"Procula" (fictional character), 167–8, 169–70
"Proof by Witnesses in the Church Courts of Medieval England" (Donahue), 177
propassiones. *See* pre-emotions
property, loss of, 128–30
pro-racial thought, 64–5
Protestantism, 151–5
proverbs, 25–43, 44
Proverbs 13:24, 33–4
psychomachia, 169–70

"questmonger," 166–7

"Rachel" (fictional character), 64
Ranum, Orest, 217
rape, 37–8, 39–40, 114
rapist knight, 15–16, 103–4
the real, virtual as, 108

reason, 18, 62, 66, 75–6, 79, 80, 182
recognition, 29
Redde Rationem (Wimbledon), 136
Reddy, William, 6–7, 13–14, 22, 30–1, 116–17, 175
"Reeve" (fictional character), 16–17, 118–32, 134, 136
Reeve's Tale (Chaucer). *See* Chaucer
Reformation, 153–5
"The Refuges of Intimacy" (Ranum), 217
The Regiment of Princes (Hoccleve), 76, 80–1
regimes, 116–17
"rekenynge," 119–23, 130–2
rents, statute concerning, 177
"Representing the Countryside" (Morris), 133, 134, 136
reputation (*mala fama*), 161
Resurrection, jury as like, 180
A Revelation of Purgatory, 142
Rhetoric (Aristotle), 67–8
Rhodes, William, 119, 133–4, 137
The Riverside Chaucer (Benson), 134
Robert de Blois, 110
Robert of Brunne, 166, 169–70
Robertson, Elizabeth, 87
Rochelle, Jean de la, 65–6, 68–9
"Roland" (fictional character), 35
Romans, 47–62
Romanticism, 198
Rome, Italy, 151, 211
Rosenfeld, Jessica, 166
Rosenwein, Barbara H., 6–8, 22, 81–2, 200, 205–6
on emotional communities, 8–9
Ross, Thomas, 36–7
Round Table, 37–40
Rozenski, Steven, Jr., 72
Rylands, John, 148

"St Cecilia" (fictional character), 141–2
Salih, Sarah, 13, 17, 139–55, 212–14
Samson, Soloman bar, 64
"Sapientia" (fictional character), 77–8
"Saul" (fictional character), 69
Saunders, Corinne, 9–10, 19
Sayers, Dorothy L., 35
The Scale of Perfection (Hilton), 75
Scheer, Monique, 8–9
Scott, Anne, 184–5
Scotus, Duns, 54, 55–7, 66–7, 68–9
Scrope's trial, 176
secularization, 12–13
Sedgwick, Eve Kosofsky, 3, 20–1, 112–13
Seigworth, Gregory J., 20–1
self, 212–13
The Seneschaucy, 124–5, 136
sensitive soul, passions of, 49–57

The Series (Hoccleve), 15, 70–85
seven deadly sins, 175
The Seven Sages of Rome, 100–3
sex difference, as disabling, 92–6
sex/gender system, reorienting of, 95–8
sexual violation, 130–2
Shame and Its Sisters (Sedgwick and Frank), 20
shepherd, anger of, 122–3
Sheridan, Christian, 123
"Sibyl" (fictional character), 201
Sidney, Philip, 40
The Siege of Jerusalem, 14–15, 47–62, 64–5, 66, 68
anger distinguished by, 69
contraries, principle of, influencing, 68
significant emotions, 217
signifier, with meaning, 39
Simmel, Georg, 174
"Simon" (fictional character), 69
"Sinon" (fictional character), 185–6, 193–4
"Sir Aggravayne" (fictional character), 28
"Sir Dinadan" (fictional character), 39
"Sir Ewain" (fictional character), 40–1
"Sir Gawain" (fictional character), 27–8, 40–1, 104
Sir Gawain and the Green Knight, 27–8, 104
"Sir Urry" (fictional character), 13–14, 26–43
skin, 92–3, 95–6, 102–8, 109
Smith, D. Vance, 9–10
Smyth, Karen, 88
social disposition (*habitus*), 8–9, 22, 23, 210–11
social form, 162–3
sociality, of emotion, 162–3
Somerset, Fiona, 3, 24
soul, 69, 87
Southern, Richard W., 8–9
"Sovereignty and Sewage" (Strohm), 156
Spearing, A. C., 85
special dialectic, 214–15
The Spectral Jew (Kruger), 65
Speculum Dominarum (Durand de Champagne), 110
Spinoza, Baruch, 3, 20–1
"spirituall man," 187–8, 189–91, 193
stage, 206–8
statute, on rents, 177
Statute of Glavelet (1316), 161–2
"Stella" (fictional character), 40
"step-dame study," 40
stewardship, 137
stickiness, 79–80, 88, 139–40, 148–50, 164–5, 212–13
of bodies, 203
Stoic, 57–8
Stoicism, 53–4, 65–6, 67
Strohm, Paul, 156

stupor, Aquinas discussing, 201
subject, witnessing as crucial to, 179
"Subject of Bureaucracy" (Mead), 137
suicide, 56–7, 67
Summoner's Tale (Chaucer). *See* Chaucer
surges, 126, 196
surveillance, 124–7, 135
Suso, Henry, 72, 77–80
Suspended Animation (Mills), 63
swearing, Christ crucified by, 176
"Symkyn" (fictional character), 125–6, 127–32
systems, account patrolling, 126–7

Taavitsainen, Irma, 126, 129
Tale of Jereslaus' Wife (Hoccleve), 71–2
Tale of Melibee (Chaucer). *See* Chaucer
Tale of Sir Urry (Malory), 37–40
Tancred, 161–3, 177
"Tancredi" (fictional character), 41–3
Taylor, Jamie K., 175
teleological view, 177
telos. *See* end
Temple of Apollo, 148–50
Temple of Glass (Lydgate), 200
Ten Commandments, 139, 144–6
tenant, 164–5
Terada, Rei, 23
textual community, 22
"Theatricality and Sobriety" (Rosenwein), 22
"Theseus" (fictional character), 76
"Thetis" (fictional character), 147–8
Thomas Hoccleve (Burrow), 85
Thornley, Eva M., 87
"Titus" (fictional character), 47–62, 65, 68, 69
toady, dreamer as, 202
Tolmie, Sarah, 72–3
Tomkins, Silvan, 3, 20–1, 131, 197–8
topos, 9–10
Torti, Anna, 89–108
Touching Feeling (Sedgwick), 112–13
Tournai, Guibert de, 111–12
Towneley plays, 169–70
Tractatus de legibus et consuetudinibus regni Angli qui Glanvilla vocatur, 163
trespassers, 189–91, 195–6
trial plays, 158–74, 175, 176, 177, 206–8
Trigg, Stephanie, 13–14, 19, 23, 25–43, 175, 207–8
tristitia. *See* distress; grief
"Troilus" (fictional character), 28–9, 34–5, 37–8, 208–16
Troilus and Criseyde (Chaucer). *See* Chaucer
Trojans, 148–50, 214–15
Troy, 146–50
Troy Books (Lydgate), 17, 140–2, 146–50, 156
"true" Honor, 195

Uebel, Michael, 200
ugly feelings, 15–16, 90–108
Unconscious, 39
Undoing Gender (Butler), 88
unoriginality, 29
"'Us must make lies'" (Horner), 180

values, affects challenging, 181–2
Vatican, 211
"Venus" (fictional character), 182–3, 186–94, 195, 201. *See also* "Love"
verdict (*veredictum*), 163–4
"Veronica" (fictional character), 47–8, 52–3, 57–8
vices, virtues and, 110
Vinaver, Eugène, 33, 35
Virgil, 201
Virgin Mary, 150–3, 173–4
the virtual, 108, 116
virtues, vices and, 110
visuality, 125–6
La Vita Nuova (Dante), 28–9, 34
voice, 108, 113–14
Volatile Bodies (Grosz), 20
volitions, 54–7
voluntas. *See* will

Wack, Mary F., 70–1, 76–7
Walter of Henley (Oschinsky), 136
Walter of Henley, 16–17, 122–3, 127–30, 136
war, Waspasian declaring, 58–9
"Waspasian" (fictional character), 47–62
Weberian rationality, 134
"Weeping Like a Beaten Child" (Trigg), 13–14, 25–43
Wenzel, Siegfried, 165–6, 168, 169–70, 178–9
Westmoreland, Countess of, 84–5
White, Olive B., 45
White, Stephen D., 81–2
White, T. H., 39, 45
"White" (fictional character), 1–2, 5–6
Whiting, Bartlett Jere, 33–4
"Wife of Bath" (fictional character), 40, 90–108, 109, 112–14
voice of, 108
Wife of Bath's Prologue and Tale (Chaucer). *See* Chaucer
wildness, 73–5
will (*voluntas*), 54–7, 67
"Will" (fictional character), 32–3
William of Middleton, 66
William of Saint Thierry, 69
Williams, Miller, 70
Wimbledon, Thomas, 136
Winchester, 33

Windeatt, Barry A., 199–200, 209–11
Winstead, Karen A., 82–3
wisdom, of proverbs, 29–30, 44
"Wisdom" (fictional character), 185–6, 187. *See also* "Minerva"
witnesses, 177, 178–9, 180, 206–8
witnessing, 158–74, 175, 177, 179
  as false, 179, 180

"Witnessing and Legal Affect in the York Trial Plays" (Lipton), 17–18, 158–74
"wo," in marriage, 92–6, 104–8
women, 39–43, 47–9, 130–2, 138
Woods, William F., 135, 137
writings, 211–16, 217
Wycliffite critiques, 144–6
"wyfis hart," 201

York cycle, 17–18
York trial plays, 158–74, 175, 176, 177, 206–8

CAMBRIDGE STUDIES IN MEDIEVAL LITERATURE

1 Robin Kirkpatrick *Dante's Inferno: Difficulty and Dead Poetry*
2 Jeremy Tambling *Dante and Difference: Writing in the "Commedia"*
3 Simon Gaunt *Troubadours and Irony*
4 Wendy Scase *"Piers Plowman" and the New Anticlericalism*
5 Joseph J. Duggan *The "Cantar de mio Cid": Poetic Creation in its Economic and Social Contexts*
6 Roderick Beaton *The Medieval Greek Romance*
7 Kathryn Kerby-Fulton *Reformist Apocalypticism and "Piers Plowman"*
8 Alison Morgan *Dante and the Medieval Other World*
9 Eckehard Simon (ed.) *The Theatre of Medieval Europe: New Research in Early Drama*
10 Mary Carruthers *The Book of Memory: A Study of Memory in Medieval Culture*
11 Rita Copeland *Rhetoric, Hermeneutics, and Translation in the Middle Ages: Academic Traditions and Vernacular Texts*
12 Donald Maddox *The Arthurian Romances of Chrétien de Troyes: Once and Future Fictions*
13 Nicholas Watson *Richard Rolle and the Invention of Authority*
14 Steven F. Kruger *Dreaming in the Middle Ages*
15 Barbara Nolan *Chaucer and the Tradition of the "Roman Antique"*
16 Sylvia Huot *The "Romance of the Rose" and its Medieval Readers: Interpretation, Reception, Manuscript Transmission*
17 Carol M. Meale (ed.) *Women and Literature in Britain, 1150–1500*
18 Henry Ansgar Kelly *Ideas and Forms of Tragedy from Aristotle to the Middle Ages*
19 Martin Irvine *The Making of Textual Culture: 'Grammatica' and Literary Theory, 350–1100*
20 Larry Scanlon *Narrative, Authority, and Power: The Medieval Exemplum and the Chaucerian Tradition*
21 Erik Kooper (ed.) *Medieval Dutch Literature in its European Context*
22 Steven Botterill *Dante and the Mystical Tradition: Bernard of Clairvaux in the "Commedia"*
23 Peter Biller and Anne Hudson (eds) *Heresy and Literacy, 1000–1530*
24 Christopher Baswell *Virgil in Medieval England: Figuring the "Aeneid" from the Twelfth Century to Chaucer*
25 James Simpson *Sciences and the Self in Medieval Poetry: Alan of Lille's 'Anticlaudianus' and John Gower's 'Confessio Amantis'*
26 Joyce Coleman *Public Reading and the Reading Public in Late Medieval England and France*
27 Suzanne Reynolds *Medieval Reading: Grammar, Rhetoric and the Classical Text*

28 Charlotte Brewer *Editing 'Piers Plowman': The Evolution of the Text*
29 Walter Haug *Vernacular Literary Theory in the Middle Ages: The German Tradition, 800–1300, in its European Context*
30 Sarah Spence *Texts and the Self in the Twelfth Century*
31 Edwin D. Craun *Lies, Slander and Obscenity in Medieval English Literature: Pastoral Rhetoric and the Deviant Speaker*
32 Patricia E. Grieve *"Floire and Blancheflor" and the European Romance*
33 Huw Pryce (ed.) *Literacy in Medieval Celtic Societies*
34 Mary Carruthers *The Craft of Thought: Meditation, Rhetoric, and the Making of Images, 400–1200*
35 Beate Schmolke-Hasselmann *The Evolution of Arthurian Romance: The Verse Tradition from Chrétien to Froissart*
36 Siân Echard *Arthurian Narrative in the Latin Tradition*
37 Fiona Somerset *Clerical Discourse and Lay Audience in Late Medieval England*
38 Florence Percival *Chaucer's Legendary Good Women*
39 Christopher Cannon *The Making of Chaucer's English: A Study of Words*
40 Rosalind Brown-Grant *Christine de Pizan and the Moral Defence of Women: Reading Beyond Gender*
41 Richard Newhauser *The Early History of Greed: The Sin of Avarice in Early Medieval Thought and Literature*
42 Margaret Clunies Ross (ed.) *Old Icelandic Literature and Society*
43 Donald Maddox *Fictions of Identity in Medieval France*
44 Rita Copeland *Pedagogy, Intellectuals, and Dissent in the Later Middle Ages: Lollardy and Ideas of Learning*
45 Kantik Ghosh *The Wycliffite Heresy: Authority and the Interpretation of Texts*
46 Mary C. Erler *Women, Reading, and Piety in Late Medieval England*
47 D. H. Green *The Beginnings of Medieval Romance: Fact and Fiction, 1150–1220*
48 J. A. Burrow *Gestures and Looks in Medieval Narrative*
49 Ardis Butterfield *Poetry and Music in Medieval France: From Jean Renart to Guillaume de Machaut*
50 Emily Steiner *Documentary Culture and the Making of Medieval English Literature*
51 William E. Burgwinkle *Sodomy, Masculinity, and Law in Medieval Literature: France and England, 1050–1230*
52 Nick Havely *Dante and the Franciscans: Poverty and the Papacy in the "Commedia"*
53 Siegfried Wenzel *Latin Sermon Collections from Later Medieval England: Orthodox Preaching in the Age of Wyclif*
54 Ananya Jahanara Kabir and Deanne Williams (eds.) *Postcolonial Approaches to the European Middle Ages: Translating Cultures*
55 Mark Miller *Philosophical Chaucer: Love, Sex, and Agency in the "Canterbury Tales"*
56 Simon A. Gilson *Dante and Renaissance Florence*
57 Ralph Hanna *London Literature, 1300–1380*

58 Maura Nolan *John Lydgate and the Making of Public Culture*
59 Nicolette Zeeman *'Piers Plowman' and the Medieval Discourse of Desire*
60 Anthony Bale *The Jew in the Medieval Book: English Antisemitisms, 1350–1500*
61 Robert J. Meyer-Lee *Poets and Power from Chaucer to Wyatt*
62 Isabel Davis *Writing Masculinity in the Later Middle Ages*
63 John M. Fyler *Language and the Declining World in Chaucer, Dante, and Jean de Meun*
64 Matthew Giancarlo *Parliament and Literature in Late Medieval England*
65 D. H. Green *Women Readers in the Middle Ages*
66 Mary Dove *The First English Bible: The Text and Context of the Wycliffite Versions*
67 Jenni Nuttall *The Creation of Lancastrian Kingship: Literature, Language and Politics in Late Medieval England*
68 Laura Ashe *Fiction and History in England, 1066–1200*
69 J. A. Burrow *The Poetry of Praise*
70 Mary Carruthers *The Book of Memory: A Study of Memory in Medieval Culture (Second Edition)*
71 Andrew Cole *Literature and Heresy in the Age of Chaucer*
72 Suzanne M. Yeager *Jerusalem in Medieval Narrative*
73 Nicole R. Rice *Lay Piety and Religious Discipline in Middle English Literature*
74 D. H. Green *Women and Marriage in German Medieval Romance*
75 Peter Godman *Paradoxes of Conscience in the High Middle Ages: Abelard, Heloise, and the Archpoet*
76 Edwin D. Craun *Ethics and Power in Medieval English Reformist Writing*
77 David Matthews *Writing to the King: Nation, Kingship, and Literature in England, 1250–1350*
78 Mary Carruthers (ed.) *Rhetoric Beyond Words: Delight and Persuasion in the Arts of the Middle Ages*
79 Katharine Breen *Imagining an English Reading Public, 1150–1400*
80 Antony J. Hasler *Court Poetry in Late Medieval England and Scotland: Allegories of Authority*
81 Shannon Gayk *Image, Text, and Religious Reform in Fifteenth-Century England*
82 Lisa H. Cooper *Artisans and Narrative Craft in Late Medieval England*
83 Alison Cornish *Vernacular Translation in Dante's Italy: Illiterate Literature*
84 Jane Gilbert *Living Death in Medieval French and English Literature*
85 Jessica Rosenfeld *Ethics and Enjoyment in Late Medieval Poetry: Love after Aristotle*
86 Michael Van Dussen *From England to Bohemia: Heresy and Communication in the Later Middle Ages*
87 Martin Eisner *Boccaccio and the Invention of Italian Literature: Dante, Petrarch, Cavalcanti, and the Authority of the Vernacular*
88 Emily V. Thornbury *Becoming a Poet in Anglo-Saxon England*
89 Lawrence Warner *The Myth of "Piers Plowman": Constructing a Medieval Literary Archive*

90 Lee Manion *Narrating the Crusades: Loss and Recovery in Medieval and Early Modern English Literature*
91 Daniel Wakelin *Scribal Correction and Literary Craft: English Manuscripts 1375–1510*
92 Jon Whitman (ed.) *Romance and History: Imagining Time from the Medieval to the Early Modern Period*
93 Virginie Greene *Logical Fictions in Medieval Literature and Philosophy*
94 Michael Johnston and Michael Van Dussen (eds.) *The Medieval Manuscript Book: Cultural Approaches*
95 Tim William Machan (ed.) *Imagining Medieval English: Language Structures and Theories, 500–1500*
96 Eric Weiskott *English Alliterative Verse: Poetic Tradition and Literary History*
97 Sarah Elliott Novacich *Shaping the Archive in Late Medieval England: History, Poetry, and Performance*
98 Geoffrey Russom *The Evolution of Verse Structure in Old and Middle English Poetry: From the Earliest Alliterative Poems to Iambic Pentameter*
99 Ian Cornelius *Reconstructing Alliterative Verse: The Pursuit of a Medieval Meter*
100 Sara Harris *The Linguistic Past in Twelfth-Century Britain*
101 Eric Kwakkel and Rodney Thomson (eds.) *The European Book in the Twelfth Century*
102 Irina Dumitrescu *The Experience of Education in Anglo-Saxon Literature*
103 Jonas Wellendorf *Gods and Humans in Medieval Scandinavia: Retying the Bonds*
104 Thomas A. Prendergast and Jessica Rosenfeld (eds.) *Chaucer and the Subversion of Form*
105 Katie L. Walter *Middle English Mouths*
106 Lawrence Warner *Chaucer's Scribes*
107 Glenn D. Burger and Holly A. Crocker (eds.) *Medieval Affect, Feeling, and Emotion*

For EU product safety concerns, contact us at Calle de José Abascal, 56–1°,
28003 Madrid, Spain or eugpsr@cambridge.org.

www.ingramcontent.com/pod-product-compliance
Lightning Source LLC
LaVergne TN
LVHW021806060526
838201LV00058B/3250